GETTING YOURS

Matthew Lesko is the founder of Washington Researchers and Information U.S.A., Inc., an information service based in Washington, D.C., which through consulting, seminars, and publications helps business clients draw on the vast informational resources of the federal government and elsewhere for their own needs. He lectures widely to business groups, has done regular features on National Public Radio and WOR Radio on finding free help from the government in many different areas, and writes a monthly column for *Good Housekeeping* on money and personal finance. His articles have appeared in *Inc.*, *Boardroom Reports*, *Industry Week*, and other publications. Penguin Books also publishes Mr. Lesko's book *Information U.S.A.*, a guide to government offices, departments, and agencies.

D0615894

GETTING YOURS

THE COMPLETE GUIDE TO GOVERNMENT MONEY

THIRD EDITION

BY MATTHEW LESKO

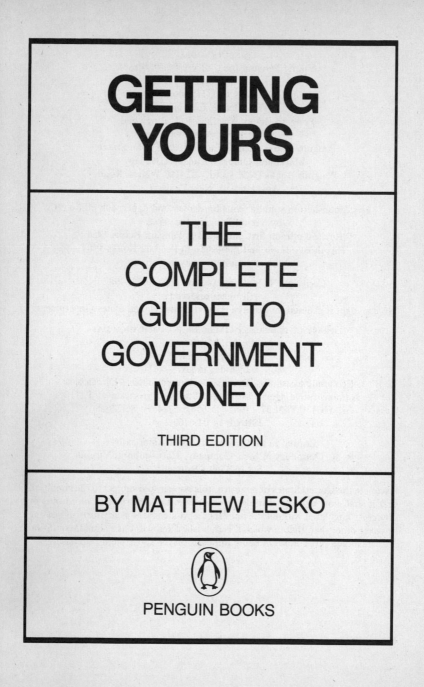

PENGUIN BOOKS

PENGUIN BOOKS
Viking Penguin Inc., 40 West 23rd Street,
New York, New York 10010, U.S.A.
Penguin Books Ltd, Harmondsworth,
Middlesex, England
Penguin Books Australia Ltd, Ringwood,
Victoria, Australia
Penguin Books Canada Limited, 2801 John Street,
Markham, Ontario, Canada L3R 1B4
Penguin Books (N.Z.) Ltd, 182–190 Wairau Road,
Auckland 10, New Zealand

First published in simultaneous hardcover and paperback editions
by Viking Penguin Inc. 1982
Revised edition first published in Penguin Books 1984
This third edition first published in Penguin Books 1987
Published simultaneously in Canada

LIBRARY OF CONGRESS CATALOGING IN PUBLICATION DATA
Lesko, Matthew.
Getting yours.
Includes index.
1. Economic assistance, Domestic—United States—Directories.
2. Administrative agencies—United States—Directories.   I. Title.
HC110.P63L37   1987   658.1'5224   86-22688
ISBN 0 14 04.6760 2

Printed in the United States of America by
R. R. Donnelley & Sons Company, Harrisonburg, Virginia
Set in Times Roman

CONTENTS

Introduction   vii

PART 1
HOW TO USE THE BOOK

Definitions   3
The Numbering System   4
Finding a Program   5
Getting the Money   6
Eleven Lessons for Applicants   7
Guidelines for Writing a Grant Proposal   10
Further Sources of Information   13
State Sources of Money and
    Help to Start or Expand a Business   15
Examples   101

PART 2
PROGRAMS

US Department of Agriculture   131
US Department of Commerce   151
US Department of Defense   159
US Department of Health and Human Services   160
US Department of Housing and Urban Development   203
US Department of the Interior   218
US Department of Justice   225
US Department of Labor   230
US Department of State   234
US Department of Transportation   235
US Department of Treasury   242
Appalachian Regional Commission   243
Equal Employment Opportunity Commission   247

Federal Mediation and Conciliation Service 248
General Services Administration 249
Government Printing Office 251
National Credit Union Administration 252
National Foundation on the Arts and the Humanities 253
National Science Foundation 266
Railroad Retirement Board 270
Small Business Administration 271
Smithsonian Institution 275
Tennessee Valley Authority 277
Veterans Administration 278
Environmental Protection Agency 284
National Gallery of Art 291
Overseas Private Investment Corporation 292
ACTION 293
Nuclear Regulatory Commission 296
US Department of Energy 297
United States Information Agency 303
Federal Emergency Management Agency 304
US Department of Education 309
Harry S Truman Scholarship Foundation 335
Pension Benefit Guaranty Corporation 336

Index 337

INTRODUCTION

If you want to build a house or chicken coop, get a job, start a business, get a college degree, improve your neighborhood, pursue an idea for an invention, or even build a tennis court or golf course, it is likely you can do it with funds from the federal government. Many people have done so. If you haven't and want to, this book is for you.

For generations the federal government has provided money to its citizens in order to accomplish a number of social and economic objectives, such as alleviating human miseries, improving the environment, bolstering business and creating jobs, smoothing over dislocations in the economy, funding the ambitious and scholarly, as well as scientific, research and enhancing the quality of life through support of the arts and humanities. Thousands of programs have come and gone as the needs of the country have changed, and as administrations have won and lost elections. There are currently some 1,000 programs that annually give taxpayers over $700 billion in grants, loans, loan guarantees and direct payments. That works out to an average of $4,800 for *every* adult living in the United States. One other important thing to remember is that individuals are eligible for over half of these programs.

EFFECTS OF REAGANOMICS: STILL AS MANY OPPORTUNITIES

Traditionally the problem with taking advantage of these government giveaways is that Uncle Sam does not advertise to let the public know of their availability. Or, if you happen to hear about a program, it normally takes a Herculean effort to find the right office to get the proper information. Now the Reagan Administration and budget cuts have compounded the problem. Although the news headlines over the past few years have emphasized budget cuts, Gramm-Rudman, and Reaganomics, the perception and the reality of this problem have become two different animals. The perception nationwide is that there have been massive cutbacks in the federal government and that people should no longer look to the government for help. Sure, a few programs have been eliminated, and some have been reduced, but the truth is that the total budget continues to increase every year. Here are some facts:

- *The bureaucracy and budget keep growing.* Each year the federal budget continues to get bigger. That is why the deficit is so mammoth. Since 1981 the number of bureaucrats on the federal payroll has actually increased by 150,000. What is more important is that even the amount of money made available in the 82 federal programs described in this book increased in 1985 by over $1.2 billion dollars.
- *More cutbacks have occurred in telling the public about programs than in the amount of money actually available from the program.* For example, last year the amount of money given to college students increased over 30 percent, but all funds were cut out for the US Department of Education's toll-free "800" number to let people know about the programs.
- *Programs that have decreased in one area have increased in another.* For example, the Small Business Administration cut back on its direct-loan program by 5 percent, which represented about $55 million. However, at the same time the SBA increased its loan guarantee program by $140 million, almost three times the amount of reduction in the direct-loan program.
- *New organizations are starting programs where others are cutting back.* Now that the federal government is cutting back on direct loans, state governments have set up dozens of loans, grants and other incentive programs to help new businesses.
- *Headlines about budget cuts are causing fewer applications.* With the public believing in all the news stories about budget cuts, fewer people are actually applying for a record amount of money. Some programs had applications drop by 300 percent when the funding level remained exactly the same as the previous year.

In my view, Reaganomics has actually *increased the chances* for entrepreneurs to take advantage of government opportunities.

JUMPING OVER BUREAUCRATIC HURDLES

You may think that getting government money requires something magical like taking a Congressman to dinner or knowing the right people to influence. Perhaps you are convinced that it is not you but others who are eligible. The fact is, with so many programs covering so many different areas, it is hard to be ineligible for all of them, and the only magic involved is finding the right program and persevering until you get the funds.

Perseverance is the key factor that usually separates those who succeed in getting government money from those who do not. Remember, it is not going to require just one telephone call to convince some bureaucrat to send you a check in the mail. If it was that easy, our deficit would be ten times as big as it is now. What normally happens is that little bureaucratic hurdles will be put in your way, and how you handle them will determine the success or failure of your getting a financial boost. An example of the ultimate in conquering bureaucratic hurdles is shown in the case of Steven Stern of Boston, Massachusetts.

> About three years ago, Steven Stern saw me one night on the David Letterman show when I talked about a government program that gave loans to teenage entrepreneurs. The next morning, Steven called my office and asked for more details about the program. He explained how he was 16 years old and wanted to start a lawn-mowing service in Boston. I told him that I really didn't know much about the details of the program, but I did give him the name and address of the office that runs the program (the same one listed in this book).
>
> Steven called me back about two days later and said that the Washington office referred him to the regional office in Boston. When he called the Boston office, he was told that he could not apply for that program because the money was set aside for teenagers in rural areas, which Boston was not. He asked me what he could do now, and I suggested he call Washington back and get a copy of the law that authorizes the program. I told him that the law would give him the facts to work with.
>
> When Steven got a copy of the law, he was surprised to find that it stated that the money was indeed intended for teenagers in rural areas, but it also said that it can be used to fund lawn-mower service businesses. What a match! So he took a copy of the law to the government office in Boston

and rubbed their noses in the facts. The local office then conceded that he should apply for the money, and gave him an application.

But at this point Steven was stopped again. Just as they handed him the application they asked if he belonged to a 4-H club. This was another requirement for the money. Well, Steven went to a city high school where students didn't know one end of a cow from another, let alone belong to a 4-H club. But this did not stop Steven. The next day he rounded up four of his buddies and started what is probably the first and only inner-city 4-H club.

After meeting all the eligibility requirements, Steven sent in his application and three months later received a $3,000 loan to start his business. Within two years, Steven was making $10,000 a year from his business and able to support himself through Babson College.

Not all cases are going to be as difficult as Steven's, but they can be, and you have to have the stamina to overcome any hurdle the government puts in your path. Remember that someone is going to get the money every year, and it might as well be you.

PART 1
HOW TO USE
THE BOOK

DEFINITIONS

The following are terms used frequently throughout the book:

Loans: money lent by a federal agency for a specific period of time and with a reasonable expectation of repayment. Loans may or may not require payment of interest.

Guaranteed/insured loans: programs in which federal agencies agree to pay back part or all of a loan to a private lender if the borrower defaults.

Grants: money given by federal agencies for a fixed period of time. Grants include money dispersed to states according to a prescribed formula (formula grants), fellowships, scholarships, research grants, evaluation grants, planning grants, technical assistance grants, survey grants, construction grants and unsolicited contracts.

Direct payments: funds provided by federal agencies to individuals, private firms, and institutions. The use of direct payments may be "specified" to perform a particular service or "unrestricted," e.g., retirement and pension payments.

Insurance: coverage under specific programs to assure reimbursement for losses sustained. Insurance may be provided directly by federal agencies or through insurance companies and may or may not require the payment of premiums.

THE NUMBERING SYSTEM

Each of the government programs described in this book is identified by a unique five-digit federal program number. The programs are listed in numerical order and referred to by these numbers throughout the book and the index.

FINDING A PROGRAM

The following steps will help identify the program for you.

Step 1 Read the examples: These stories will stir your curiosity, expand your mind and give you insights into using government funds in ways you never dreamed of. They will also lead you to sources of money for similar aims. An agency that supports one endeavor is likely to help another in a related area.

Step 2 Refer to the subject index: Start with a broad subject area such as crime or health, and then look for the specific program within that category. If you cannot find it at first, don't despair. It does not mean that there is no such program. In fact, most likely there *is* one. It only means that you and the government use different terms to describe the same program.

Step 3 Find the relevant agency: If you are unsuccessful with the Index, use the Contents to find the agency or office interested in your subject. For example, if you are interested in trade, look under the US Department of Commerce; for starting a small business, see Small Business Administration. Then review all the programs included with it, since the arrangement of the book groups them together.

Step 4 Contact a program in a related area: If you still cannot find the program that meets your particular requirements, find one that covers a related subject. For example, look under the US Department of Commerce for fishing. Then contact that department or agency for further guidance.

GETTING THE MONEY

Once you have identified the program or programs that can help you, your work has just begun. Now you have to get the money. Volumes and volumes have been written and consultants have been paid thousands of dollars to counsel individuals and organizations on the ways and means of obtaining government financing. There is no mystery in the method. You do not need a Ph.D. or a Washington office. All you need is patience, determination and hard work, if you are eligible.

ELEVEN LESSONS FOR APPLICANTS

The following tips are meant to offer advice and encouragement to both the novice and the "old pro" government money seeker.

1. **When you find one program, assume that there are more.** When you identify a program that comes close to meeting your needs, ask the program director about similar programs in other departments. Find out whether new programs are in the offing. The alternatives may present opportunities more suited to your needs, or they may be combined with the existing program for a package funding.

2. **The money may not be where you think it is.** As the examples in the following sections will show, much of the money comes from unexpected sources. For example, the Department of Agriculture supports teenage entrepreneurs, and the Department of Labor will finance doctoral dissertations.

3. **Don't be discouraged if you think you are not eligible.** You may discover a program that meets your needs only to find that the funding is not available to individuals. Don't be discouraged. Examples in the following sections describe how people have formed nonprofit organizations or worked with local governments in order to receive the available money. Moreover, many of the programs for state and local governments make individuals their ultimate beneficiaries. Contact the program director to identify the local office administering the funds.

4. **Examine a successful application.** You have the right, in most cases, to see copies of successful applications. If you encounter any difficulty, write the federal office in charge of the program, and request a copy under the Freedom of Information Act.

5. **Talk to those who give the money.** Before you actually fill out any applications, it is well worth your time to review your forms with the program officials, either in person if at all pos-

sible, or over the telephone. Many of the funding agencies have offices throughout the country to assist you. Such contact should help tailor your answers to the government's expectations. It will give them what they want to see.

6. **Obtain copies of appropriation committee hearings.** Each government agency has to justify to the Congress, annually, its request for money. Public hearings are held by both the House and the Senate for government officials to present their cases. Often the program of your interest may be discussed in these hearings, and these transcripts are available to add insight into their objectives and future. If you need extra background information on your subject, contact your Congressman's office for information on how to obtain copies of these published hearings.

7. **Personalize your approach.** Remember that the program officers are there to help you if you give them half a chance. Be friendly, open and courteous. Establish yourself as an individual so that you are more to them than just a faceless number. Even getting money from the federal government can be a people business, and it is up to you to encourage it.

8. **Give them what they want.** When you prepare your application, give the government exactly what it asks for, even though it may not make much sense to you. Don't fight it. You will need all your energy to get your money. It is unlikely that you will have any to spare for changing the government's ways, even if you are right.

9. **Start small.** Even if you need a large amount of money, start small. It may be wiser and easier. Initially, ask for enough money to complete a small portion of your project. The next year, ask for the rest. In this way the program officer can get to know you before he gives you a large amount of money.

10. **Try again.** If your proposal is rejected, learn what you did wrong and try again next year, or try with a different program. Many proposals are rejected because of bad timing or a rela-

tively minor hitch. Don't worry. Your failure will not be held against you.

11. When the bureaucracy is stuck, use your Congressman. Try to use your Congressman's office only for those times when the bureaucracy comes to a halt on your paperwork. Sometimes this is the only way to get it moving again.

GUIDELINES FOR WRITING A GRANT PROPOSAL

Some of the programs identified in the following pages are referred to as grants. Grants are like direct payments or loan guarantees in that you do not have to pay the money back. However, grants usually require considerably more documentation than other programs. Whether you are looking for a grant to make a movie or to construct a playground in your neighborhood, here are some starting points. Also heed suggestions in the section Eleven Lessons for Applicants.

1 Contact the agency in charge of the program you want. After you select a program or programs that meet your needs, phone or write the federal agency contact person to learn more about the grant. Be sure to request the program guidelines which many government agencies prepare for the purpose of helping applicants.

2 Prepare a preliminary proposal. Once you have a basic idea for a proposal, write a one- to two-page rough draft of your proposal which outlines proposed goals, rationale, estimates of cost and expected achievements.

Here are two centers that can help you get information on how to write a grant proposal:

Grantsmanship Center
1030 S. Grand Avenue
Los Angeles, CA 90015
213-749-4721
800-421-9512 (information about
  grantsmanship workshops)

Offers instruction on where to obtain funding and how to prepare proposals. Maintains a 4,000-volume reference library and conducts seminars on proposal writing in most major US cities.

Foundation Center
888 Seventh Avenue
New York, NY 10019
212-975-1120
202-331-1400 (Washington, DC)
216-861-1933 (Cleveland, Ohio)
415-397-0902 (San Francisco, CA)
800-424-9836 (information on 100
    cooperating collections with books
    on grants writing)

Acquires and gives out information about foundations and the grants they award. Maintains three branch offices, each with an extensive research library. A toll-free number is available to get information about the nearest library where books on the subject are available.

3. Look for support. Make copies of the preliminary draft proposal and distribute them to those who have an interest in the topic. Ask them to review the proposal and make comments. Since letters of endorsement are often requested as part of the application process, look for individuals or groups that may be willing to support the proposal in writing.

4. Request a grant application kit. If possible, make a trip to the agency's regional office or headquarters and get to know some of the agency personnel. It might be helpful to attend a grantsmanship workshop (see above) which teaches specific grant-writing techniques. You might also want to review a few of the more popular books and brochures that have been written on the subject of competing for grant money. Check your local library for the following titles: *Developing Skills in Proposal Writing* by Mary Hall (Continuing Education Publications, Portland, Oregon); *Foundation Fundamentals* by Carol Kurzig (Foundation Center, New York, New York); and *Program Planning and Proposal Writing* by Norman J. Kiritz (Grantsmanship Center, Los Angeles, California).

5. Accumulate all necessary information. Research the subject thoroughly and become an expert on the topic. Keep a notebook handy to jot down ideas and review these notes from time to time.

Now you actually are ready to begin polishing your proposal for submission. Here are some suggestions on what should be included in your final product.

6. State the problem. One of the most important elements of a proposal is a clear, concise and well-supported statement of the problem to be addressed in the proposal; it is advantageous to include concrete evidence, perhaps essential.

7. State the outcome. Once you have defined the problem, talk about the outcome you hope for, discuss your objectives, and justify your strategy in writing. Describe your course of action and highlight the innovative features of the proposal. State how this problem can be remedied, and show what plans you have for quantifiable results.

8. Prepare a budget. An essential part of any proposal is the budget. Try to be as realistic and economical as possible, and certainly don't ask for too much money. Identify the facilities, transportation, or support services needed, and justify all these projected expenses. It is a good idea to consult someone in the grant agency about the financial aspects of the program.

9. Get the final proposal reviewed. At some point seek out a neutral party to review the proposal for continuity, clarity and reasoning. Ask for constructive criticism.

10. Be Neat!! You may very well prepare a top-notch proposal, but it won't look good if your paperwork is sloppy. Proposals should be typed, copied and packaged correctly and neatly. A cover letter should always accompany the proposal.

11. Always ask for advice. Don't be afraid to ask for help. A federal civil servant responsible for the program of interest to you will always be accessible for advice on how to proceed. The hardest part of the whole process is actually finding a program that meets your needs, but once you have that, try your best. Don't get frustrated, and if you don't get the grant, try again and again after that if necessary.

FURTHER SOURCES OF INFORMATION

If you are looking for further information on government programs, you may find one or more of the following sources helpful.

1. **Catalog of Federal Domestic Assistance.** This 1,000-page document is the most complete source of information on government programs. It is published by the Office of Management and Budget once a year with updates. Subscriptions are available for $32.00 from:

> Superintendent of Documents
> US Government Printing Office
> Washington, DC 20402
> 202-783-3238

2. **Federal Assistance Programs Retrieval System (FAPRS).** This is a computerized information system containing much of the same information in the *Catalog of Federal Domestic Assistance.* It is designed to identify quickly specific federal assistance programs for which applicants are eligible. It can be accessed through computer terminals in many government regional offices and in university libraries. The price of a search varies with the request. For an access point near you contact:

> Federal Program Information Branch
> Budget Review Division
> Office of Management and Budget
> 17th and Pennsylvania Avenues, N.W.
> Washington, DC 20503
> 202-395-6182

3. **Federal Information Centers.** There are thirty-eight such centers throughout the country, and their job is to personally assist the public in finding information in the federal government. For a center near you, check the white pages of your telephone book under "US Government."

4. Your Congressman's Office. This is a good place to turn to when all else fails. Remember, your congressman works for you in Washington. He can be reached by contacting his local district office or:

c/o US Capitol
Washington, DC 20515
202-224-3121

STATE SOURCES OF MONEY AND HELP TO START OR EXPAND A BUSINESS

Although there are approximately 100 federal money programs to help the business community, state governments are more and more becoming very active in providing their own assistance, both financial and technical, to would-be and existing entrepreneurs. State governments realize that the economic prosperity of their state depends on their ability to offer lucrative business opportunities. Here are some examples of the kinds of services offered by state governments:

1) $50,000 to open a computer store
2) Free marketing studies
3) Free consulting to locate venture capital
4) $10 million for a leverage buyout or to build a new plant
5) Free directory of 260 venture capital sources
6) Computer printouts of available land or office space
7) Free newsletter identifying contracting opportunities
8) Special help for women entrepreneurs
9) $20 million loan at one-half the prime rate
10) Money to train your employees
11) One-stop hotlines for locating state permits
12) Free marketing help for selling to federal, state and local government
13) Free help in preparing a business plan
14) $1 million for 20 years at 4.5 percent to start a business
15) Free marketing help and low-cost loans for selling abroad

Many states also operate incubator programs which give new entrepreneurs a lot more than money to start their business. A 61-year-old woman in Minneapolis named Gilda Brouthers wanted to start a business making chocolate candy. After the bank turned her down, she took advantage of a local incubator program which not only lent her the money she needed but also gave her office space to use, secretarial help, copying services, word processing equipment and management consulting services, all to make her look like a big-time operator.

Within two years her business was grossing a quarter of a million dollars.

State sources are becoming excellent places for new businesses because not only do they have money programs to help you start a business, they can help identify federal and private sources of money. Look for your state below and contact the offices listed to see how they can help you. If you cannot get the help you need, shop around for a more willing state—it may be worth a move to fulfill your dreams. The big companies do it, so you can too.

TYPES OF MONEY AND HELP AVAILABLE

The types of money programs and assistance available depends upon the state. One important thing to remember is that state assistance programs continue to grow, and if a given state doesn't have a certain type of program this year, one may be coming.

Described below are the major types of programs which are offered by the states. Not all of the states have all of the programs, but most of the states have most of the programs.

FREE MONEY
Usually in the form of grants, it works the same as free money from the federal government. You do *not* have to pay it back.

LOANS
Like the federal government, the states will lend money directly to entrepreneurs. Also, like the feds, loans are usually at interest rates that are below the rates charged at commercial institutions and are also set aside for those companies that have trouble getting loans elsewhere. This makes it an ideal source for more risky types of ventures.

LOAN GUARANTEES
This too works just like the federal program described earlier. For this program the state government will go to the bank with you and cosign your loan. This too is ideal for high-risk ventures that normally could not get a loan.

INTEREST SUBSIDIES ON LOANS
This is a unique program that is not used by the federal government. Here the state will subsidize the interest rate you are charged by a bank. In other words, if the bank gives you a loan for $50,000 at 10 percent per year interest, your interest payments would be $5,000 per year, and the state would pay, say, $2,500 and you pay $2,500. This is like getting the loan at 5 percent instead of 10 percent.

VENTURE-CAPITAL FINANCING
Many states are now launching their own venture-capital firms to invest in high-risk companies. This is like having a rich uncle invest in your company. Venture capital is money you do not have to pay back, but in return you usually have to give up some equity in your company. This could be in the form of stock, or loans that can turn into stock, or some sort of royalty arrangement.

LOW-INTEREST LOANS SOLD TO THE PUBLIC
This form of financing is called either Industrial Revenue Bonds or General Obligation Bonds. They can be used only to purchase fixed assets, like a factory or equipment. In the case of Industrial Revenue Bonds, the state will raise money from the general public to buy your equipment. It's like having the public lend you long-term money directly but with a catch, you get it cheaper. Because the state acts as the middle man, the people who lend you the money do not have to pay federal taxes on the interest they charge you. As a result, you get the money cheaper because they get a tax break. If you cannot pay back the money, the public holding the bonds are stuck, and not the state. If the state issues General Obligation Bonds to buy your equipment, this means that it will be the same as an Industrial Revenue Bond except that the state guarantees that you will pay back the money. So they will pay the public when the money comes due, if you can't.

MANAGEMENT TRAINING
Whether it is in the form of week-long workshops or one-on-one counseling, many states offer free- or low-cost training in subjects ranging from bookkeeping to energy conservation.

BUSINESS CONSULTING
Free- and low-cost management expertise is made available on most any subject you can think of. States know that most small- and medium-size businesses have the greatest proportion of their costs dedicated to management. In addition, lack of management expertise and capital are the two most common deficiencies that lead to business failure.

MARKET STUDIES
Most every state will provide you with free or inexpensive marketing information for marketing within or out of the state. All states have state data centers that not only collect demographic and other information about markets within the state, but also have access to federal data that can pinpoint national markets. Many states also provide the services of graduate business students at local universities to do the leg work and analysis for you.

BUSINESS SITE SELECTION
Every state has specialists who will work with you to identify the best place for you to locate your business. The amount of personal assistance you get will depend upon the size of the business you plan to start. Businesses that require more employees have to be careful where they locate in order to ensure an adequate supply of labor.

LICENSING, REGULATION AND PERMITTING
If you want to know what forms or documents you need to do business in a given state, most states now have one-stop information centers; many have toll-free "800" numbers that can help you through the red tape for anything you require.

MONEY TO TRAIN YOUR EMPLOYEES
Many states have programs that use federal money to help train your employees. For example, if it takes six months for you to train someone on the job, the state may pay 50 percent of that person's salary for him to learn your business. The state gets a skilled worker and you get your training costs cut in half. Other states have programs that will send your employee to school for a few months to learn what he has to do in your business.

RESEARCH AND DEVELOPMENT

All states provide research and development assistance to entrepreneurs. It is an area of assistance which is growing rapidly as more and more states try to attract high-technology-related companies. Through such programs, a little computer-software company can use the computer expertise of the faculty of state universities, or marketing problems can be solved with the help of marketing professors. Many states are even setting up clearing houses so that small businesses can have one place to turn to to find expertise through a statewide university system.

SELLING TO THE GOVERNMENT

If your business is interested in selling to the government, whether it be federal, state or local government, special state offices have been established to help you identify who in the government buys your product and what you have to do to get them to purchase it.

SELLING OVERSEAS

Whether you are selling advertising or manufacturing yo-yo's, you are not going to grow in the long run if you don't investigate overseas markets. Most states realize this and have established special offices to help you identify and sell to overseas markets. Many states have even opened up offices in foreign countries to act as your representative on-the-spot.

OFFICE SPACE, COMPUTERS, TELEPHONE SERVICE AND MORE

Hundreds of such programs are now operating in most every state of the union. These are programs where instead of just giving you free money and kicking you out the door to sink or swim, they give you much more than just money. They give you free- or low-cost services and equipment such as office space, management consulting, computer equipment, telephone services, financial planning, etc. They keep you in this incubatorlike environment until your company is strong enough to make it by itself. And that is when they kick you out the door to sink or swim in the real world.

HELP IN APPLYING FOR FEDERAL MONEY

Most every state has established special offices where trained management consultants will help you identify free-money and loan programs that are available from the federal government. More importantly than helping you find the money, they will also help you apply for the money. It's nice to have that kind of assistance when you are dealing with the federal bureaucracy.

SPECIAL HELP FOR MINORITIES AND WOMEN

If you are a minority or a woman entrepreneur, most all the states now have special free services to help your business get started or grow.

LOCATING RICH INVESTORS

Many states are now helping new entrepreneurs find rich investors to support new businesses. And some states, including New Hampshire and Arizona, have established databases of rich people who are looking for small business investment opportunities. The demand is so great that the rich people have to pay to be included in the database.

ALABAMA

SMALL BUSINESS DEVELOPMENT CENTERS

Offer free information and counseling to individuals who wish to start or expand their own business. Also offer workshops and seminars. Topics include: financial planning and managerial assistance. For the location of the SBDC serving your area, contact: Small Business Development Center, Alabama State University, 915 South Jackson Street, Montgomery, AL 36195, 205-269-1102.

ALABAMA DEVELOPMENT OFFICE

Maintains the latest factual information on industrial sites and buildings; details involving labor, utilities, taxes and tax exemptions, financing and financial incentives, transportation, training, laws and regulations; information on natural resources, geography, climate, education and research and the quality of life in Alabama; and specific data on municipalities. ADO has a staff of 50, including seven highly qualified industrial development project managers. A project manager is specifically assigned to work with you, from start to finish of your project. These services are cost-free, and your inquiry will be held in strict confidence. Contact: Alabama Development Office, State Capitol, Montgomery, AL 36130, 205-263-0048.

DATA RESEARCH CENTER
Prepares cost and feasibility studies for clients of the Alabama Development Office. Staff prepares studies and reports containing information on natural resources, quality of life, demographics, economics, training and other subjects to meet your specific needs. Contact: Alabama Development Office, Data Research Center, State Capitol, Montgomery, AL 36130, 205-263-0048.

ONE-STOP PERMITTING
All permitting for air, water and land can be accomplished at this one location. Contact: Alabama Development Office, Department of Environmental Management, State Capitol, Montgomery, AL 36130, 205-263-0048.

AID TRAINING
Conducts start-up, upgrade and management training programs for companies in Alabama. Previous clients include: General Electric, Shell Chemical, Union Carbide, Weyerhaeuser and Wyle Laboratories. Contact: Alabama Industrial Development Training, 4505 Executive Park Drive, Montgomery, AL 36116, 205-261-4158.

ONE-STOP FINANCING
Industrial Finance Division of the Alabama Development Office is a one-stop source for funding, assistance and information in the area of industrial finance. Qualified individuals assist you in finding the most economical and efficient method of financing industrial locations or expansions. Contact: Alabama Development Office, Industrial Finance Division, State Capitol, Montgomery, AL 36130, 205-263-0048.

INDUSTRIAL DEVELOPMENT BOND ISSUES
Used for purchase of land, buildings, machinery and equipment for new industry and new additions for existing industry. Projects financed by IDB are 100 percent exempt from all property taxes for the entire bond amortization period, which is normally 20 years. Interest rate is 70–85 percent of prime and the term is normally 10–20 years. Can finance up to 100 percent of the project costs. Contact: Alabama Development Office, Industrial Finance Division, State Capitol, Montgomery, AL 36130, 205-263-0048.

URBAN DEVELOPMENT ACTION GRANT
Subordinated loan for gap financing, which can be used for the purchase of land, buildings, machinery, equipment and new expansions. Interest rates, which are generally below market rates, are set by the federal government. Term is 10–20 years. Grant is available only in eligible communities and cannot exceed ¼ of the project cost. There is no limit on the total amount of the project. Contact: Alabama Development Office, Industrial Finance Division, State Capitol, Montgomery, AL 36130, 205-263-0048.

STATE ECONOMIC DEVELOPMENT LOAN PROGRAM
Can be used for the purchase of land, buildings, machinery, equipment and new expansion. There is a $250,000 limit per project, the interest rate is normally two points below prime, terms are generally 5–15 years, and it can finance up to 40 percent of the project costs. Contact: Alabama Development Office, Industrial Finance Division, State Capitol, Montgomery, AL 36130, 205-263-0048.

SMALL BUSINESS ADMINISTRATION (SBA) 503 LOAN
Can be used for purchase of land, buildings, machinery, equipment and new expansion. With this combination type of loan package, the small business can get a better financial program than is otherwise available on the market. The bank loans 50 percent of the project cost; the SBA loans 40 percent of the project cost at below market rates (usually this is equivalent to the 20-year treasury note rate). The SBA portion will have a maturity of 15, 20 or 25 years, depending on the project. Con-

tact: Alabama Development Office, Industrial Finance Division, State Capitol, Montgomery, AL 36130, 205-263-0048.

STATE INDUSTRIAL SITE PREPARATION GRANTS

Help new and expanding manufacturing industries pay for industrial site preparation. May be used for conducting land and labor surveys and for grading, draining and providing access to specific sites. Amount of the grant depends upon the amount of expenses for construction and equipment. To qualify, the new or existing expanding industry must fall in SIC classification 20–39. Contact: Alabama Development Office, Industrial Finance Division, State Capitol, Montgomery, AL 36130, 205-263-0048.

SPECULATIVE BUILDING REVOLVING LOAN FUND

Industrial development boards may borrow up to 25 percent of the cost of constructing a speculative building for industrial development purposes with no interest on the money borrowed from the fund. Contact: Alabama Development Office, Industrial Finance Division, State Capitol, Montgomery, AL 36130, 205-263-0048.

ALASKA

SMALL BUSINESS ASSISTANCE CENTER

Provides assistance to qualified businesses including preparation of: business plans, marketing and feasibility studies and loan packages. Minority construction businesses are assisted with: obtaining bonding, estimating, job specification review and bidding and project management. Contact: Small Business Assistance Center, Courthouse Square, 250 Cushman Street, Suite 4-A, Fairbanks, AK 99701, 907-451-8466.

AIDA REVENUE BOND FINANCING PROGRAM

Eligible projects include most types of commercial and industrial activity involving the construction of new plant and equipment, as well as acquisition. Borrower must locate a purchaser or purchasers who agree to buy 100 percent of the revenue bonds issued by AIDA for this project. The interest rate on the loan and any other charges are determined jointly by the borrower and the lender. Current AIDA charges include a $100 preliminary application fee and a financing fee of 1 percent for the first $1 million of bonds, declining to ½ percent for the next $4 million and ¼ percent for the next $10 million of bonds, then ¹/₁₀ percent for bonds above $10 million. Contact: Alaska Industrial Development Authority, 1577 C Street, Suite 304, Anchorage, AK 99501-5177, 907-274-1651.

AIDA FEDERALLY GUARANTEED LOAN PROGRAM

Loan program to finance accounts receivable, inventory, working capital, equipment and some refinancing of existing debt. The Authority will provide up to $500,000 per borrower by purchasing from the lender a participation in a loan that is guaranteed by the United States or an agency or instrumentality of the United States. AIDA assesses no fees on these loans. The composite rate of interest to the borrower on a guaranteed loan which is purchased by the Authority may not exceed the rate charged by the Authority by more than 1.5 percent for loans of $100,000 or less, or by 1 percent for loans in excess of $100,000. Presently the Authority's rate is equal to the Moody's Aa Corporate Bond Index and is fixed for the entire term of the loan. Contact: Alaska Industrial Development Authority, 1577 C Street, Suite 304, Anchorage, AK 99501-5177, 907-274-1651.

AIDA UMBRELLA BOND FINANCING PROGRAM

Loan program to finance accounts receivable, inventory, working capital, equipment and some refinancing of existing debt. The borrower must locate a qualified financial institution that will be the lender/originator. Currently, there is the $100 preliminary application fee and the 1 percent commitment fee to the Authority. The bond sale costs vary but are usually about 3 percent of the loan amount. Interest rates are determined by the marketplace and hence vary. As a guide, the AIDA portion of a long-term loan will generally carry an interest rate approximately equal to the Weekly Bond Buyer's Revenue Bond Index plus ½ to 1 percent. Contact: Alaska Industrial Development Authority, 1577 C Street, Suite 304, Anchorage, AK 99501-5177, 907-274-1651.

ARIZONA

ARIZONA ENTERPRISE DEVELOPMENT CORPORATION
Provides loans to small expanding businesses through the US Small Business Administration 503 Program. Can be used for purchase of land, buildings, machinery and equipment, construction, renovation/leasehold improvements and related professional fees. Working capital, debt refinancings and consolidations are not eligible uses. Eligible recipients are for-profit businesses generating an average net profit of less than $2 million for the preceding two years with a net worth of less than $6 million, and located in Arizona but outside Phoenix and Tucson, which have similar programs. AEDC issues an SBA guaranteed debenture. Proceeds are loaned to small businesses for 15- to 25-year terms. Interest rates are ¾ percent above US Treasury Bonds of the same maturity. Maximum AEDC debenture amount is $500,000. Second mortgage position on all financed assets. Small business equity is 10 percent of project costs. Contact: AEDC, Development Finance Program, Arizona Department of Commerce, 1700 West Washington, Fifth Floor, Phoenix, AZ 85007, 602-255-1782 or 602-255-5705.

REVOLVING LOAN PROGRAMS
Provide loans for economic development projects. Can be used for site/facility acquisition and improvements, construction, machinery and equipment, building rehabilitation and leasehold improvements. Under certain circumstances a limited amount of loan proceeds may be used for working capital. Eligible recipients are small for-profit businesses located throughout Arizona except Maricopa and Pima counties. Below-market interest rates with negotiable terms (up to 25 years). Small business equity is generally 10 percent of project costs. Contact: Arizona Department of Commerce, Development Finance Unit, 1700 West Washington, Phoenix, AZ 85007, 602-255-5705.

URBAN DEVELOPMENT ACTION GRANTS
Used by eligible cities and towns and all Indian reservations to provide subordinated loans to new and expanding businesses, usually for 10 percent to 25 percent of a project. Eligible uses include site improvements for and/or construction of commer-

cial, industrial and mixed-use developments; industrial and commercial rehabilitation, water mains and sewers; and machinery and equipment with useful lives over five years. Working capital and debt refinancing and consolidation are not eligible uses. Favorable rates and terms are negotiated to ensure that good projects will proceed. Applicants must demonstrate that a project would not go forward without UDAG funds. Contact: Arizona Department of Commerce, 1700 West Washington, Fourth Floor, Phoenix, AZ 85007, 602-255-5705.

ARKANSAS

SMALL BUSINESS DEVELOPMENT CENTERS
Provide management assistance to the Arkansas small business community. Professional consultants work with entrepreneurs just getting started, as well as established business owners on an individual basis. Assistance is offered in such areas as financial analysis and proposal, financial projections, accounting and record keeping, business plans, general management and international trade. Seminars are also offered. For the location of the SBDC serving your area contact: Small Business Development Center, University of Arkansas at Little Rock, Central Office, Library, Fifth Floor, Room 512, 33rd and University, Little Rock, AR 72204, 501-371- 5381 (toll-free number in Arkansas: 1-800-482-5850 x5381).

MINORITY BUSINESS DEVELOPMENT DEPARTMENT
Offers technical assistance and access to financial resources including a $1 million Minority Economic Development Fund. Assists minority businesses in selling to government agencies. Sponsors workshops/seminars and industry training programs. Contact: Minority Business Development Department, 1 Capitol Mall, Room 4C-300, Little Rock, AR 72201, 501-371-1060.

JOB TRAINING PARTNERSHIP ACT
Offers several training options to fit specific business needs. Training is customized, and the company may be reimbursed up to 50 percent of the wages paid to eligible trainees. Contact: Arkansas Employment Security Division, Office of JTPA Services, PO Box 2981, Little Rock, AR 72203, 501-371-JTPA.

ARKANSAS INDUSTRIAL DEVELOPMENT COMMISSION

Provides financial assistance for both start-up and existing businesses. Offers a maximum of $500,000 fixed asset financing to businesses with a three-year operating history. Contact: Arkansas Industrial Development Commission, 1 State Capitol Mall, Little Rock, AR 72201, 501-371-7786.

CALIFORNIA

OFFICE OF LOCAL DEVELOPMENT

Provides case studies, handbooks, slide presentations, on-site training workshops and seminars on a wide range of topics, including: downtown revitalization, industrial development, streamlining the local permit process and financing. Contact: Office of Local Development, California Department of Commerce, 1121 L Street, Suite 600, Sacramento, CA 95814, 916-322-1398.

OFFICE OF BUSINESS DEVELOPMENT

Identifies available locations for business development in California and provides site-specific information on regional economic trends, labor supply, wage rates, real estate prices, infrastructure needs, transportation costs, regulations, taxes, tax-exempt bond financing and government-sponsored job training. The Office also assists businesses dealing with regulatory and licensing agencies. Contact: Office of Business Development, California Department of Commerce, 1121 L Street, Suite 600, Sacramento, CA 95814, 916-322-5665.

OFFICE OF SMALL BUSINESS

Offers workshops, seminars, individual counseling and publications. The staff works with local community organizations, professional associations and seven regional corporations throughout the state to provide sources of financing, consultation and business education assistance. Directs entrepreneurs to specific resources in finance, management, marketing and law. Referrals can be made to consultants who operate on both a fee and no-fee basis. Helps entrepreneurs locate organizations that will develop workable business plans that address identifying business markets, competition, sales strategy, management controls and more. Contact: Office of Small Business, 1121 L Street, Suite 600, Sacramento, CA 95814, 916-445-6545.

SMALL BUSINESS DEVELOPMENT CENTERS
Located throughout the state, these centers provide management and technical assistance, business information and statistical data, entrepreneurial skills training, and access to existing sources of federal, state and local assistance for all small businesses located in the designated service areas. For the location of the Small Business Development Center serving your area, contact: Small Business Development Center, 1121 L Street, Suite 600, California Department of Commerce, Sacramento, CA 95814, 916-324-8102.

OFFICE OF SMALL AND MINORITY BUSINESS
Offers assistance to businesses interested in participating in the State of California's purchasing/contracting system. An analyst in each subject area is available as your liaison to the State. Contact: Office of Small and Minority Business, Department of General Services, 1808 14th Street, Suite 100, Sacramento, CA 95814, 916-322-5060.

CALIFORNIA STATE CONTRACTS REGISTER
Published twice monthly, the Register announces available state service and construction opportunities as well as valuable commodity information. $60 for a one-year subscription. Contact: California State Contracts Register, Department of General Services, Office of Fiscal Services, PO Box 151, Sacramento, CA 95801, 916-322-5060.

CALIFORNIA EMPLOYMENT
DEVELOPMENT DEPARTMENT
Maintains Job Services offices in communities around the state which: list hard-to-fill positions on an interstate clearance network and screen applicants at no charge to employers; and help employers qualify for federal and state tax credits for the hiring of individuals from certain targeted groups. Services include referrals to eligible applicants and certifications for credit claims.

Contact: California Employment Development Department, 800 Capitol Mall, Sacramento, CA 95814, 916-445-8008.

JOB TRAINING PARTNERSHIP ACT
Allocates federal funds at the local level to train people for private sector employment. Activities eligible under JTPA include job search assistance, retraining, relocation assistance, support services (limited to 15 percent), job development and related training activities. Contact: Job Training Partnership Office, 800 Capitol Mall, Sacramento, CA 95814, 916-445-4546.

OFFICE OF PERMIT ASSISTANCE
"One-stop" agency for the state which will review an applicant's project and provide blank application forms for all required state permits. A Permit Handbook, available upon request, describes in detail over 40 major permits issued by state agencies for projects affecting the environment. Will also organize consolidated public hearings for projects involving several agencies to reduce the time of separate agency hearings. Contact: Office of Permit Assistance, 1400 10th Street, Sacramento, CA 95814, 916-322-4245.

CALIFORNIA COMMISSION FOR ECONOMIC DEVELOPMENT
Publishes "Doing Business in California: A Guide for Establishing a Business." Provides the businessperson with an introduction, under one cover, to California's requirements, regulations, forms, fees and offices related to establishing a business in the state. Contact: California Commission for Economic Development, Office of the Lieutenant Governor, State Capitol, Room 1028, Sacramento, CA 95814, 916-445-8994.

EMPLOYMENT TRAINING PANEL
Provides funds to train the skilled work-force that a new or expanding business may need. Trainees are selected by business from a large pool of experienced workers and trained to business standards on a business timetable. The Panel can contract directly with a business which can provide its own training or subcontract the training to a public or private school. Training can be in a classroom, laboratory, on the job or any combi-

nation. Contact: Central Valley Office, Employment Training Panel, 800 Capitol Mall, MIC 64, Sacramento, CA 95814, 916-324-3615.

OFFICE OF LOCAL DEVELOPMENT

The California Department of Commerce administers a variety of state and federal loan and grant programs through this office. A "Funding Resource Guide," available from this office, lists 260 funding sources. These include funding sources for: renovation of abandoned industrial businesses, training and technical assistance and central business district revitalization. Contact: Office of Local Development, California Department of Commerce, 1121 L Street, Suite 600, Sacramento, CA 95814, 916-322-1398.

CALIFORNIA INNOVATION DEVELOPMENT LOANS

Provide direct loans to assist innovators in the development of new technologies. Companies, nonprofit organizations and political subdivisions planning projects in areas experiencing long-term economic deterioration are eligible to apply for these loans. Funds must be used for the financing of fixed assets or working capital. Loans range from $100,000 to $500,000. Contact: Office of Business Development, California Department of Commerce, 1121 L Street, Suite 600, Sacramento, CA 95814, 916-322-5665.

SMALL BUSINESS LOAN GUARANTEES

Loan guarantees to firms unable to secure conventional financing are available through seven regional development corporations established by the state. Guarantees have been issued on short-term and long-term loans and revolving lines of credit, as well as seasonal inventory accounts-receivable loans. The guaranteed portion of a loan is generally limited to 90 percent of the required total financing, with the maximum guarantee not exceeding $350,000. Loan terms vary from one to seven years, with interest rates usually one to two points above bank prime. Contact: Office of Business Development, California Department of Commerce, 1121 L Street, Suite 600, Sacramento, CA 95814, 916-322-5665.

INDUSTRIAL DEVELOPMENT BONDS

Provide low-interest financing to businesses wanting to locate or expand their operations through the use of tax-exempt industrial development bonds. Can be used to finance land acquisition, building construction, equipment purchases, architectural and engineering fees and other incidental costs associated with the project. In addition, 10 percent of the net proceeds of the bond sale can be set aside for working capital. The State of California maintains an interest rate limit on all revenue bonds and general obligation bonds issued in the state. The present limit that applies for industrial development bonds is 12 percent with a 5 percent discount. Contact: Office of Business and Industrial Development, California Department of Economic and Business Development, 1121 L Street, Suite 600, Sacramento, CA 95814, 916-322-5665.

COLORADO

BUSINESS INFORMATION CENTER

Provides business a start-up kit including information on taxes, regulations, licensing and permits and health and safety regulations. Contact: Business Information Center, Department of Regulatory Agencies, Office of Regulatory Reform, Room 110, 1525 Sherman Street, Denver, CO 80203, 303-866-3933.

SMALL BUSINESS ASSISTANCE CENTERS

Provide information and assistance on: management organization analyses, business plans, financial counseling, feasibility studies, market research and loan packaging. For the location of the center serving your area, contact: Small Business Assistance Center, Colorado Division of Commerce and Development, Department of Local Affairs, 1313 Sherman Street, Room 523, Denver, CO 80203, 303-866-2205 (toll-free number in Colorado: 1-800-521-1243).

ONE-STOP LICENSE AND PERMIT ASSISTANCE

Provides information and assistance for new businesses wishing to obtain the necessary licenses and permits. Contact: Office of Regulatory Reform, Department of Regulatory Agencies, 1525 Sherman Street, #110, Denver, CO 80203, 303-866-3933.

STATE CONTRACT ASSISTANCE

Assists small businesses by helping them understand the state's purchasing process and making sure they can compete for contracts with state agencies. Contact: Division of Purchasing, Department of Administration, 1525 Sherman Street, 7th Floor, Denver, CO 80203, 303-866-2361.

MINORITY BUSINESS DEVELOPMENT CENTER

Offers the following services: business consulting and counseling; market opportunities; assistance with the state government purchasing process; identification of financial assistance and bonding services, business ownership opportunities, training, library of business references and in-house computer networks. Modest fees are charged for participation. Contact: Minority Business Development Center, 428 East 11th Avenue, Denver, CO 80203, 303-832-2228.

COLORADO HOUSING FINANCE AUTHORITY

This office offers three basic financing programs: 1) Index: for businesses between $200,000 and $10 million in sales for equipment and building expansion; 2) Quality Investment Capital Program: loans for working capital or refinancing; and 3) Guarantee financing for exporting businesses. Local authorities also provide development loans which can be used to finance 20 percent to 40 percent of a project. Contact: Colorado Business Development, Division of Commerce and Development, 1313 Sherman Street, Room 523, Denver, CO 80203, 303-866-2205.

FARMERS HOME ADMINISTRATION

Guarantees business and industrial loans in nonmetropolitan areas of Colorado. Guarantees up to 90 percent of a loan from a bank or other lender to any kind of business that benefits a rural community. Contact: Farmers Home Administration, 2490 West 26th Avenue, Denver, CO 80211, 303-964-0151.

COLORADO STATEWIDE
DEVELOPMENT CORPORATION

Assists in financing small businesses which will create jobs for low- and moderate-income people. Maximum loan amount is

$100,000. Substantial leveraging of outside funds and participation by a financial institution are required. Businesses must be located in communities of less than 50,000 population. Contact: Division of Commerce and Development, 1313 Sherman Street, Room 523, Denver, CO 80203, 303-866-2205.

CONNECTICUT

CONNECTICUT SMALL BUSINESS DEVELOPMENT CENTERS
Geared to assist prospective businesspersons in establishing a new firm. Provide a variety of services. For the location of the SBDC serving your area, contact: Connecticut Small Business Development Center, University of Connecticut, 39 Woodland Street, Hartford, CT 06105, 203-241-4982.

SMALL BUSINESS OFFICE
Provides personalized managerial assistance for small businesses of any kind, in any stage of planning, start-up or maturity. Help is available in developing business plans, on managerial methods, on sales and market planning, on business expansion strategies and on operating efficiencies. Assistance is provided in the preparation of applications for various private and public financing programs. Contact: Small Business Office, Connecticut Department of Economic Development, 210 Washington Street, Hartford, CT 06106, 203-566-4051.

CONNECTICUT TECHNOLOGY ASSISTANCE CENTER (CONNTAC)
One-stop clearinghouse of information on all the public and private-sector services, programs and resources available to help high-technology companies and entrepreneurs planning to establish or expand operations in Connecticut. Contact: Connecticut Technology Assistance Center, Connecticut Department of Economic Development, 210 Washington Street, Hartford, CT 06106, 203-566-4051.

LOCAL BUSINESS DEVELOPMENT ORGANIZATIONS
Provide the minority businessperson with assistance in a range of management services: feasibility studies, profit and loss state-

ments, organization charts, operating procedures, etc. Also offers specialized help in such fields as marketing, accounting, and inventory control, or they arrange for assistance through other local organizations. For the location of the office serving your area, contact: Local Business Development Organizations, Office of Small Business Affairs, Connecticut Department of Economic Development, 210 Washington Street, Hartford, CT 06106, 203-566-4051.

BUSINESS RESOURCE CENTERS

BRCs are a link between Local Business Development Organizations and the private sector, helping new businesses locate capital sources, promote markets for goods and services and develop new business opportunities, etc. For the location of the BRC serving your area, contact: Business Resource Centers, Office of Small Business Affairs, Connecticut Department of Economic Development, 210 Washington Street, Hartford, CT 06106, 203-566-4051.

INDUSTRIAL REVENUE BONDS

Provide long-term industrial revenue bond financing to cover the purchase and development of land; construction, purchase or remodeling of buildings; purchase of machinery and equipment; and purchase and installation of pollution abatement equipment. Project types include manufacturing, processing, assembling, research facilities, offices, warehousing and certain recreational facilities. Contact: Connecticut Development Authority, 217 Washington Street, Hartford, CT 06106, 203-522-3730.

CONNECTICUT PRODUCT
DEVELOPMENT CORPORATION

Assists the development of new products, procedures and techniques by Connecticut firms when private financing is not available. Makes funds available for joint ventures with Connecticut industrial firms. Contact: Connecticut Product Development Corporation, 78 Oak Street, Hartford, CT 06106, 203-566-2920.

CONNECTICUT DEVELOPMENT CREDIT CORPORATION

Makes long-term loans to small- and medium-sized businesses. Funding is usually applied toward working capital, equipment and plant construction and renovation. CDCC loans are made only in those cases where financing is not available from banks or other normal credit sources. Almost all CDCC loans are secured by mortgages on real estate and/or chattels. Contact: Connecticut Development Credit Corporation, PO Box 714, Meriden, CT 06450, 203-235-3327.

DELAWARE

DELAWARE SMALL BUSINESS DEVELOPMENT CENTERS
Offer counseling, management and technical assistance and training. Counseling services are provided at no cost to small business owners and prospective owners who cannot afford commercial assistance. For the location of the SBDC serving your area, contact: Delaware Small Business Development Center, Bureau of Economics and Business Research, 005 Purnell Hall, Newark, DE 19716, 302-451-2747 (toll-free hotline for Kent and Sussex counties: 1-800-222-2279).

ENVIRONMENTAL PERMITTING
Single source which helps coordinate the preliminary review process leading to the issuance of multiple environmental permits. Applicants meet with state and local government representatives to be advised about permits and other requirements that may be applicable to their individual project. After the meeting the applicants receive a letter outlining the necessary requirements. Contact: Department of Natural Resources and Environmental Control, Development Advisory Service, 89 Kings Highway, PO Box 1401, Dover, DE 19903, 302-736-5409.

DELAWARE ENERGY OFFICE
Conducts free on-site energy audits. Workshops and seminars are offered on controlling energy costs and energy conservation measures for small businesses. Contact: Delaware Energy Office, Small Business Program, Margaret M. O'Neill Building, Dover, DE 19901, 302-736-5644 (toll-free Energy Hotline in Delaware: 1-800-282-8616).

DELAWARE STATE CHAMBER OF COMMERCE

Sponsors a series of special programs on small business financing which include segments on dealing with your banker. Offers "Small Business Financing Traveling Road Shows." Contact: Delaware State Chamber of Commerce, One Commerce Center, Suite 200, Wilmington, DE 19801, 302-655-7221 (toll-free number for Kent and Sussex counties: 1-800-292-9507).

INDUSTRIAL REVENUE BONDS

Used to finance fixed assets within the following categories: industrial, commercial, agricultural and pollution control. Long-term, low-interest-rate financing may be obtained; generally 75 percent of prime. Financing is limited to a maximum of $10 million for each project with the exception of pollution control projects, which have no maximum. Contact: Delaware Development Office, 99 Kings Highway, PO Box 1401, Dover, DE 19903, 302-736-4271.

DISTRICT OF COLUMBIA

SMALL BUSINESS DEVELOPMENT CENTER

Offers numerous free services including: technical assistance; management counseling; management training; research, publications and information services; special projects and financial facilitation. Contact: Howard University Small Business Development Center, School of Business and Public Administration, Georgia Avenue and Fairmont Street, NW, Howard University, Washington, DC 20059, 202-636-5150.

MINORITY BUSINESS OPPORTUNITY COMMISSION

Provides assistance with district government procurement opportunities, seminars on district government resources, and information on private sector contracting, and joint ventures, mergers and acquisitions. Contact: Minority Business Opportunity Commission, 613 G Street, NW, Room 926, Washington, DC 20001, 202-727-3818.

"ONE-STOP" BUSINESS AND PERMIT CENTER

Provides information and processing of business licenses and permits. Contact: District of Columbia Department of Consumer and Regulatory Affairs, 614 H Street, NW, Washington, DC 20001, 202-727-7100.

NATIONAL DEVELOPMENT COUNCIL

Coordinates and implements the Small Business Revitalization Program, a federally sponsored plan for mobilizing private sector capital for growing smaller business and industry. Contact: National Development Council, 1025 Connecticut Avenue, NW, Washington, DC 20036, 202-466-3906.

REVOLVING LOAN FUND

Directs loans to be used in conjunction with private funds, ranging from 30 days to 2 years. Relatively short-term gap-financing. Contact: District of Columbia Office of Business and Economic Development, 1350 Pennsylvania Avenue, NW, Room 208, Washington, DC 20004, 202-727-6600.

FLORIDA

SMALL BUSINESS DEVELOPMENT CENTERS

Provide training programs and free one-on-one counseling on such aspects of business as: financial and accounting analysis, commercial loan packages, market analysis, steps to starting a business, personnel management, international trade, business plans, feasibility studies and inventor and innovation assistance. For the location of the SBDC serving your area, contact: Small Business Development Center, Tallahassee Small Business Regional Center, 1605 East Plaza Drive, Tallahassee, FL 32308, 904-644-6524.

FLORIDA DEPARTMENT OF COMMERCE

Provides assistance, directly or by referral, in the areas of: labor force, marketing/production, plant expansion and start-up, legislative updates, statistical and informational data; and community development. Contact: Florida Department of Commerce, Bureau of Business Assistance, 107 West Gaines Street, Suite G-26, Collins Building, Tallahassee, FL 32301, 904-488-9357 (toll-free number in Florida: 1-800-342-0771).

FLORIDA FIRST CAPITAL FINANCE CORPORATION, INC.
Financing is available for land acquisition, building construction, purchase of building, renovation and modernization, and machinery and equipment. FFCFC is authorized to sell debentures with SBA guarantees for up to 40 percent of eligible project cost, with a $500,000 maximum. The bank portion of the loan will be at the current market rate of interest. Interest rate on the Small Business Administration portion of the loan will be ¾ of 1 percent above the long-term treasury bond rate of comparable term at time of closing. Minimum term of 10 years required from the private lender. Maturities of 15, 20 and 25 years are available on FFCFC (SBA) portion, depending on useful life of assets and terms of private lender. Contact: Florida First Capital Finance Corporation, Inc., PO Box 5826, Tallahassee, FL 32301, 904-487-0466.

GEORGIA

SMALL BUSINESS DEVELOPMENT CENTERS
Offer free counseling to small businesses. Provide information on: financial planning, sales techniques, display and advertising, marketing evaluation, risk management, organization structure, inventory control, refinancing, exporting, and starting a business. For the location of the SBDC serving your area, contact: Small Business Development Center, Georgia State University, Suite 1055, 1 Park Place South, Atlanta, GA 30303, 404-658-3550.

COMMUNITY DEVELOPMENT BLOCK GRANTS
Individual communities apply for available funding. Selected businesses receive funding for development from the community. Also provides referrals to other sources of funding for businesses. Contact: Georgia Department of Community Af-

fairs, Community and Economic Development Division, 40 Marietta Street NW, Suite 800, Atlanta, GA 30303, 404-656-3839.

HAWAII

SMALL BUSINESS INFORMATION SERVICE

Free information and referral service which provides up-to-date information to anyone interested in starting a business or expanding a present business by increasing sales, improving profitability and expanding employment in Hawaii. Provides businesses with information on: permits and licensing, market data, business plan writing services, consulting services, government procurement, alternative financing, and business classes. Contact: Small Business Information Service, Hawaii Department of Planning and Economic Development, 250 South King Street, Room 724, Honolulu, HI 96813, 808-548-7645 or 808-548-7887 (toll-free number for out-of-state: Sprint-access seven-digit number + 617-5553).

HAWAII ENTREPRENEUR TRAINING AND DEVELOPMENT INSTITUTE

Conducts entrepreneurship training and provides management and technical assistance to small businesses and potential entrepreneurs in Hawaii and other countries. Specialty services available to businesses are business plan writing, marketing studies, feasibility analysis and complete loan proposal preparation. Contact: Hawaii Entrepreneur Training and Development Institute, 1750 Kalakaua Avenue, Suite 1409, Honolulu, HI 96826, 808-955-8655 (cable: "HETADI").

HAWAII ISLAND ECONOMIC DEVELOPMENT BOARD

Supports both start-up and established businesses in locating operations on the island of Hawaii. Assists businesses in developing plans; coordinates fixed-asset financing with local financial institutions and the Small Business Administration; provides information on permitting, zoning and other governmental rules and regulations; and provides site selection information. Contact: Hawaii Island Economic Development Board, First Federal Building, 75-5737 Kuakini Highway, #206, Kailua-Kona, HI 96740, 808-329-4713.

KAUAI ECONOMIC DEVELOPMENT BOARD

Acts as a resource center of information and assists sole proprietorships as well as corporations. Local and other entrepreneurs can receive assistance from KEDB in the following areas: securing financing, site selection and state and county permits and regulations for business. Statistics, studies and other business information can also be obtained with the assistance of KEDB. Contact: Kauai Economic Development Board, 4370 Kukui Grove Street, Suite 211-C, Lihue, HI 96766, 808-245-6692.

SMALL BUSINESS CENTER

Sponsored by the Hawaii Chamber of Commerce, the SBC provides a wide range of services to small businesses. Major products of the SBC include entrepreneur training, business consulting, financial assistance and loan packaging and information and referral services. The SBC regularly conducts special entrepreneur training programs for selected applicants who show the best potential for creating their own viable businesses. Contact: Small Business Center, Hawaii Chamber of Commerce, 735 Bishop Street, Honolulu, HI 96813, 808-531-4111.

PACIFIC BUSINESS CENTER PROGRAM

Makes the diverse resources of the University of Hawaii more accessible to small businesses in Hawaii and the American Flag Pacific Islands. Supports and encourages the transfer of innovation and technology developed through University research to private industry. Links the knowledge and expertise in the University and small businesses that lack the financial and technical capacity to monitor, and adapt to, technological change and improved management techniques. PBCP maintains a catalog of faculty consultants who can provide small businesses with advice and assistance ranging from financial planning and business communication skills to operations research and engineering. Counseling and referral services are free to program clients, and faculty consultants are available at reasonable rates. Contact: Pacific Business Center Program, University of Hawaii at Manoa, BUSAD D-202, 2404 Maile Way, Honolulu, HI 96822, 808-948-6286.

HAWAII EMPLOYERS COUNCIL

Assists businesses in personnel administration, supervisory training, industrial relations, contract negotiation and counter-organizing. Contact: Hawaii Employers Council, 2682 Waiwai Loop, Honolulu, HI 96819, 808-836-1511.

ALU LIKE, INC.

Provides technical and/or consultant support to existing native Hawaiian-owned businesses, prospective Hawaiian entrepreneurs, and community economic enterprise developments. The state office works with the Island centers mainly in community economic enterprise initiatives, while the five Multi-Service Centers focus on business start-ups and expansion. Contact: ALU LIKE-Oahu, 1316 Kaumualii Street, Honolulu, HI 96817, 808-848-1486.

MAUI ECONOMIC DEVELOPMENT BOARD, INC.

Develops programs to enhance Maui's economic diversification and vitality. Currently engaged in developing a Research and Technology Park for new and innovative small businesses. MEDB has also established several Continuing Action Panels in which entrepreneurs in new agricultural, electronics, aquaculture and R & D ventures can share experiences and obtain information. Conducts conferences on topics of interest to small businesses and offers informational services to prospective new businesses. Contact: Maui Economic Development Board, Inc., PO Box 187, Kahului, HI 96732, 808-877-3839.

HONOLULU JOB TRAINING PROGRAM

Has funds available for industry-based training specifically designed for a company or group of similar companies and can reduce training and labor costs through tax credits and incentives. Allows a company to train individuals in its own way for its own jobs. Contact: Honolulu Job Training Program, 715 South King Street, Fifth Floor, Honolulu, HI 96813, 808-523-4221.

SMALL BUSINESS HAWAII

SBH has a three-prong program: education for the community and the membership; advisory and counseling service for its members; and nonpartisan political action. Publishes monthly newsletter, "Small Business News." Sponsors bimonthly "Share and Tell Business Forums" and an Annual Small Business Conference in January. Contact: Small Business Hawaii, 811-A Cooke Street, Honolulu, HI 96813, 808-533-2183.

ECONOMIC DEVELOPMENT CORPORATION OF HONOLULU
Encourages business investments in Honolulu through promotional activities and efforts to remove or modify disincentives to business investments (e.g., taxes and government regulations). Entrepreneurs wishing to start new businesses are welcome to contact EDCH for advice and assistance. Contact: Economic Development Corporation of Honolulu, 1001 Bishop Street, Pacific Tower, Suite 874, Honolulu, HI 96813, 808-545-4533.

HAWAII BUSINESS LEAGUE
Activities are divided into three broad categories: legislative action, information services and membership programs. Provides information on matters of current interest and on IRS rules and regulations as they affect small businesses. Conducts seminars on a broad range of subjects affecting small businesses in Hawaii. Contact: Hawaii Business League, 1177 Kapiolani Boulevard, Suite 201, Honolulu, HI 96814, 808-533-6819.

STATE PERMIT INFORMATION COUNTER
Focuses on state land and water-use permits required by law or regulation. Identifies the requirements of agencies such as the State Land Use Commission, Department of Land and Natural Resources, Department of Health and Department of Transportation. Offers general guidance and information on federal and county permit requirements. Provides basic information about state permits, tax maps, flood hazard maps, historic site maps, land-use-boundary maps, Special Management Area maps and aerial photographs. Maintains a computerized inventory of potential environmental hazards and constraints. Various agency permit application forms are available. The Information Counter also has a computer terminal of the Hawaii Planning Activities Support System (H-PASS). Given the location and a brief description of a proposed activity, H-PASS can produce a list of

government permits likely to be required, with agency names, locations and helpful staff contacts. Contact: State Permit Information Counter, Hawaii Department of Planning and Economic Development, Room 610, Sixth Floor, Kamamalu Building, 250 South King Street, Honolulu, HI 96813, 808-548-8467.

INDUSTRY AND PRODUCT PROMOTION PROGRAM

Offers state sponsorship and financial assistance for local manufacturers in providing exposure for Hawaii products. Contact: Small Business Information Service, Hawaii Department of Planning and Economic Development, 250 South King Street, Room 724, Honolulu, HI 96813, 808-548-7645 or 808-548-7887 (toll-free number for out-of-state: local Sprint-access seven-digit number + 617-5553).

HAWAII CAPITAL LOAN PROGRAM

Provides loans for small businesses for the financing of plant construction, conversion or expansion; land acquisition for expansion; and acquisition of equipment, machinery, supplies or materials; or for working capital. Applicants must be unable to obtain financing from private lending institutions. Maximum loan amount is $250,000. Maximum loan period varies from 6 to 20 years. Current interest rate is 7½ percent per annum. Contact: Small Business Information Service, Hawaii Department of Planning and Economic Development, 250 South King Street, Room 724, Honolulu, HI 96813, 808-548-7645 or 808-548-7887 (toll-free number for out-of-state: local Sprint-access seven-digit number + 617-5553).

IDAHO

IDAHO BUSINESS DEVELOPMENT CENTERS

Individuals and businesses can obtain help with existing operations, expansion or starting a new business. Provides a wide range of services including: counseling and technical assistance, skills training and technical research. These services are available to all prospective and existing businesses in Idaho. Some services and publications require a minimal charge. For the location of the center serving your area, contact: Boise State

University, Idaho Business Development Center, 1910 University Drive, Boise, ID 83725, 208-385-1640.

CERTIFIED DEVELOPMENT COMPANY LOANS

Provide long-term, fixed-rate second mortgage financing for the expansion of small- and medium-size businesses. There are eight Certified Development Companies operating in the district that promote, package and service these loans. The objective of the program is economic development and increased employment. These loans are for fixed asset financing only, with maturity up to 25 years. For the location of the CDCs, contact: US Small Business Administration, 1020 Main Street, Suite 290, Boise, ID 83702, 208-334-1780.

ILLINOIS

SMALL BUSINESS DEVELOPMENT CENTERS

Offer small business management counseling and training and technical assistance. Assistance is provided in such specific areas as: procuring federal contracts; capital formation; business skills; international trade; economic and business analyses and minority- and women-owned business concerns. Locally based SBDCs also broker the services of private trade and business groups, chambers of commerce and the Service Corps of Retired Executives (SCORE) and help to coordinate the many business assistance programs offered throughout the Illinois Department of Commerce and Community Affairs. For the location of the SBDC serving your area, contact: Statewide Program Administrator, Business Assistance Office, 620 East Adams, Springfield, IL 62701, 217-785-6174 (toll-free number in Illinois: 800-252-2923).

TELTAPES

The Department of Commerce and Community Affairs provides a telephone Teltape system whereby callers in Illinois dial toll-free 800-835-3222 (800-TEL-DCCA) and receive taped information on a wide variety of business-related topics. To obtain a listing of Teltape topics and their code numbers, call the Department at 800-252-2923 and request the informational bulletin on Teltapes. This hotline accepts instate calls only. Contact: Department of Commerce and Community Affairs, 620 East Adams, Springfield, IL 62701, 217-785-6162.

ONE-STOP PERMIT CENTER

Provides information to new and existing businesses for all state government forms and applications. Also provides guidance in preparing forms and acts as a referral service to direct you to other avenues of assistance. Distributes a business start-up packet. Contact: One-Stop Permit Center, Illinois Department of Commerce and Community Affairs, Business Assistance Office, 620 East Adams Street, Third Floor, Springfield, IL 62701, 217-785-6162 (toll-free number in Illinois: 800-252-2923).

FRIENDS OF SMALL BUSINESS

Informal networking group designed to provide people in the small business community with the opportunity to meet and exchange ideas. Contact: Friends of Small Business, 225 West Randolph, HQ 30C, Chicago, IL 60606, 312-727-3225.

ILLINOIS VENTURE FUND

Provides equity capital for start-up and early stage companies located in Illinois. Money can be used for research and development expenses, working capital needs and fixed assets. Investments will take the form of common stock or securities which convert to common stock. The Fund is long-term and capital-gains-oriented; investments are expected to remain for four to seven but no more than ten years. The amount of an investment will range from less than $300,000 to $1 million or more. Contact: Marketing Staff, Illinois Department of Commerce and Community Affairs, 620 East Adams Street, Springfield, IL 62701, 217-782-1460.

BUILD ILLINOIS INCUBATOR ASSISTANCE PROGRAM

Offers financial assistance to communities to operate business incubators for young, start-up businesses. A small business incubator is a facility that provides lower-than-market-rate rents, a number of shared office services and a range of management support assistance. The Department of Commerce and Community Affairs will competitively award $1 million in financing support in the form of no-interest loans for small business incubators. Funds are available for up to 50 percent of the costs but not to exceed $650,000 per project. Contact: Marketing Staff, Illinois Department of Commerce and Community Affairs, 620 East Adams Street, Springfield, IL 62701, 217-782-1460.

ILLINOIS DEVELOPMENT FINANCE AUTHORITY DIRECT LOAN FUND

Provides subordinated, fixed-interest loans for 20 to 30 percent of the cost of fixed asset projects. Assists credit-worthy small or medium-sized industrial or manufacturing firms that cannot meet all their financial requirements from conventional sources, and is intended to create jobs in areas of high unemployment. Money can be used for purchase of land or buildings, building construction and renovation, and machinery and equipment. The average amount of an IDFA loan is $150,000. Interest is based on US Treasury Bond rates and is set at a fixed rate. Loan approval requires 60 to 90 days. Loan maturity ranges from 7 to 25 years, matching the life of assets. Contact: Marketing Staff, Illinois Department of Commerce and Community Affairs, 620 East Adams Street, Springfield, IL 62701, 217-782-1460.

BUILD ILLINOIS SMALL BUSINESS DEVELOPMENT PROGRAM

Provides direct financing to small businesses for expansion and subsequent job creation or retention. Money can be used for land and buildings; machinery and equipment; working capital; and construction or renovation. Provides loans which will not exceed 25 percent of the total cost of a project. The maximum amount which may be invested in any one project is $750,000. Loans are long-term, fixed-rate and low-interest. Contact: Marketing Staff, Illinois Department of Commerce and Community Affairs, 620 East Adams Street, Springfield, IL 62701, 217-782-1460.

INDIANA

INDIANA INSTITUTE FOR
NEW BUSINESS VENTURES, INC.

Builds networks of management, educational, technical and financial resources which can provide the professional expertise required to start and operate a small business. The Institute has implemented a number of programs which provide one-on-one services to individuals in the emerging business sector: The Indiana Emerging Business Forum; Enterprise Advisory Service; Indiana Seed Capital Network; Capital Formation Matching Grants; and Small Business Counselors. Introduces businesses to appropriate funding sources: commercial banks; state loan guarantee programs; Certified Development Corporation; Small Business Investment Corporations; venture capitalists; seed capital funds; individual investors; and others. Contact: Indiana Institute for New Business Ventures, Inc., One North Capitol, Suite 501, Indianapolis, IN 46204, 317-634-8418.

MINORITY BUSINESS DEVELOPMENT

Assists minority businesses in bidding on procurement awards from the State of Indiana. Contact: Indiana Department of Administration, Minority Business Development, 100 North Senate Avenue, Room 502, Indianapolis, IN 46204, 317-232-3061.

IOWA

SMALL BUSINESS ADVISORY
COUNCIL/SMALL BUSINESS DIVISION

Provides advocacy, assistance and guidance to create, nurture and develop small businesses. Offers: information, sources of financial assistance, referrals, technical assistance and training in marketing products or services to the government, information on educational programs, and a forum for receiving and reviewing complaints from individual small businesses that relate to rules or decisions by state agencies and referring questions to the proper agency when appropriate. Contact: Small Business Division, Iowa Development Commission, 600 East Court Avenue, Des Moines, IA 50309, 515-281-8310 or 515-281-8324 (toll-free number in Iowa: 1-800-532-1216).

CALL ONE
Toll-free number for small business information. Responds to immediate questions and concerns of small businesses. Also channels specific requests to more specialized programs and resources. Contact: Toll-free number in Iowa is 1-800-532-1216. Outside Iowa, call 515-281-8310. Staff members will give you an immediate answer or find the information you need within five working days. Contact: Iowa Development Commission, 600 East Court Avenue, Des Moines, IA 50309.

VENTURE CAPITAL
Available in certain situations to provide capital infusion to companies which a conventional lender may view as high-risk. Venture capital is not viewed as a loan; instead the investor may take an equity position in the company. Contact: Iowa Development Commission, 600 East Court Avenue, Suite A, Des Moines, IA 50309, 515-281-3925 (toll-free number in Iowa: 1-800-532-1216).

IOWA PRODUCT DEVELOPMENT CORPORATION
Provides risk capital to stimulate new product development for innovative products, processes or techniques in situations where financial aid would not be reasonably available from commercial sources. Priority is given to applicants whose business is agriculture-related, or whose business is located in an area which the Board determines has been severely affected by depressed agricultural prices and whose proposed product or invention is to be used to convert all or a portion of the business to nonagriculture-related industrial or commercial activity. Contact: Iowa Product Development Corporation, 600 East Court Avenue, Suite A, Des Moines, IA 50309, 515-281-3925.

IOWA BUSINESS DEVELOPMENT CREDIT CORPORATION
Provides loans to firms that lack sufficient collateral or financial backing for conventional loans. Loans may be for up to $500,000 plus the amount of bank participation and may be amortized on a schedule up to 15 years. Interest rates will be set commensurate with the "going rate" for this type of credit. Proceeds may be used for fixed assets or working capital. Contact:

Iowa Business Development Credit Corporation, 901 Insurance Exchange Building, Fifth and Grand, Des Moines, IA 50309, 515-282-2164.

SMALL BUSINESS ADMINISTRATION GUARANTEED LOANS

Can be used for fixed asset and operating capital. Loans made by private lenders, usually banks, can be guaranteed by SBA. Guaranty may reach $500,000 or 90 percent, which ever is less. Interest rates, loan conditions and terms are negotiable between the lender and the borrower. Contact: US Small Business Administration Loan Officer, 749 Federal Building, Des Moines, IA 50309, 515-284-4422.

IOWA SMALL BUSINESS LOAN PROGRAM

Assists the development and expansion of small business in Iowa through the sale, by Iowa Finance Authority, of bonds and notes which are exempt from federal income tax, and through the use of the proceeds to provide limited types of financing for new or existing small businesses. Small business is defined as having 20 or fewer employees or less than $3 million in sales. The loan may be used for purchasing land, construction, building improvements or equipment. Funds cannot be used for working capital, inventory or operating purposes. Maximum loan is $10 million. Rates will vary with the level of risk. Contact: Iowa Finance Authority, 550 Liberty Building, 418 Sixth Avenue, Des Moines, IA 50309, 515-281-4058.

KANSAS

"ONE-STOP" CLEARINGHOUSE

Centralizes all information needed to establish or operate a business in Kansas. Provides all necessary state applications and forms required by agencies which license, regulate or tax business, and answer questions about starting or expanding business in Kansas. Contact: One-Stop Permitting, Development Division, Kansas Department of Economic Development, 503 Kansas Avenue, Sixth Floor, Topeka, KS 66603, 913-296-3483.

SMALL BUSINESS INSTITUTE
University and college business majors, under the guidance of
a professor, meet regularly with the small business owner. Written reports stating the problems, alternatives and suggested solutions are then submitted. Contact: College of Business
Administration, Kansas State University, Calvin Hall, Manhattan, KS 66506, 913-532-5529.

CENTER FOR ENTREPRENEURSHIP
AND SMALL BUSINESS MANAGEMENT
Develops and conducts seminars for special-interest groups and
practicing entrepreneurs and small business managers. An information bank, library and publications are available for practitioners, academicians and students. Contact: Center for
Entrepreneurship, College of Business Administration, Wichita
State University, 130 Clinton Hall, Box 48, Wichita, KS 67208,
316-689-3000.

SMALL BUSINESS DEVELOPMENT CENTERS
Perform extensive basic business management services such as
disseminating business management information and helping
entrepreneurs. Also perform such services as management
audits, market studies, financial analysis, feasibility studies and
business planning. For the location of the SBDC serving
your area, contact: College of Business Administration, Wichita
State University, Clinton Hall, Box 88, Wichita, KS 67208,
316-689-3367.

SMALL BUSINESS EDUCATION
Offers basic educational programs for small business groups.
Workshops and seminars are offered to help small business
managers to increase sales, motivate employees, study trade
areas, improve record keeping and analysis and deal with inadequate financing, cash flow and accounts receivable problems.
Contact: Community Economic Development, Division of Cooperative Extension Service, Kansas State University, Umber-
ger Hall, Room 115, Manhattan, KS 66506, 913-532-5840.

BUSINESS AND ENGINEERING TECHNICAL APPLICATIONS PROGRAM (BETA)

Assists business and industry on technical (science and engineering) and administrative problems by providing specific technical information relevant to a company's business. Contact: BETA, Space Technology Center, University of Kansas, 2291 Irving Hill Drive, Campus West, Lawrence, KS 66045, 913-864-4775.

MINORITY BUSINESS PROGRAM

Technical assistance is provided to minorities and women seeking to start, improve or expand a business. Contact: Minority Business Division, Kansas Department of Economic Development, 503 Kansas Avenue, Sixth Floor, Topeka, KS 66603, 913-296-3805.

BUSINESS DEVELOPMENT ASSISTANCE

Provides financial assistance in the form of direct loans, purchase of evidences of indebtedness, loan guarantees of rental repayments of leases to help solve the job and income problems in areas of high unemployment or low family income. Business development assistance is limited to operations in designated areas or development districts. Contact: Business Development Division, Economic Development Administration, Rocky Mountain Regional Office, 333 West Colfax Avenue, Station 300, Denver, CO 80202, 303-837-4474.

MINORITY ENTERPRISES SMALL BUSINESS INVESTMENT COMPANY

Provides debt/equity capital to qualifying minority entrepreneurs. Funds can be used for such needs as working capital, purchase of equipment, debt restructuring, business expansion and acquisition of shareholder or partnership interest. Contact: Central Systems Equity Corporation, 1743 North Hillside, Wichita, KS 67214, 316-683-9004.

KANSAS VENTURE CAPITAL, INC.

Provides debt/equity capital to small businesses. May loan up to $200,000 to any company that meets SBA requirements of a small business. Funds can be used for such needs as working capital, purchase of equipment, debt restructuring, business expansion and acquisition of shareholder or partner interest. Contact: Kansas Development Credit Corporation, Inc., First National Bank Towers, Suite 1030, Topeka, KS 66603, 913-235-3437.

KANSAS DEVELOPMENT CREDIT CORPORATION
KDCC operates by borrowing money from more than 400 member Kansas banks. Loans from these funds may range up to $250,000 and can be made to companies which could not secure financial assistance from conventional lenders. Contact: Kansas Development Credit Corporation, Inc., First National Bank Towers, Suite 1030, Topeka, KS 66603, 913-235-3437.

KENTUCKY

BUSINESS INFORMATION CLEARINGHOUSE
One-stop center for permit/license applications and business information. Acts as a referral service for government financial and management assistance programs and serves as a regulatory reform advocate for business. Assistance is available to all new and existing businesses without regard to business size, type or location. Contact: Business Information Clearinghouse, Kentucky Department of Economic Development, Commerce Cabinet, 22nd Floor, Capital Plaza Tower, Frankfort, KY 40601, 502-564-4252 (toll-free number in Kentucky: 1-800-626-2250).

SMALL BUSINESS DIVISION
Serves as both an advocate and an information/referral service for prospective and established small business owners/managers. Assists the small business community and all prospective small business entrepreneurs in developing, promoting and retaining small enterprises. Prepares applications for the Commonwealth Small Business Development Corporation 503 Financial Assistance Loan Program and the Kentucky Development Finance Authority Financial Assistance Loan Program. Provides management and technical assistance through counseling and entrepreneurial training and follow-up. Participates

in a statewide small business assistance service delivery system and directs prospective and established entrepreneurs to local sources of assistance. Promotes support of small business by encouraging communities to develop strategies for small business growth and development. Provides information on new creative development methods. Identifies and fosters support of new programs and services to assist small businesses. Serves as a small business data resource center. One-on-one assistance is not available. Contact: Small Business Division, Kentucky Department of Economic Development, Commerce Cabinet, Capital Plaza Tower, 22nd Floor, Frankfort, KY 40601, 502-564-4252.

INDUSTRIAL DEVELOPMENT PROGRAM
Provides confidential, professional and technical expertise to new and expanding industries in Kentucky including such information as plant location assistance, etc. Contact: Industrial Development and Marketing Division, Kentucky Department of Economic Development, 2300 Capital Plaza Tower, Frankfort, KY 40601, 502-564-7140.

BLUE GRASS STATE SKILLS CORPORATION
Provides custom training of industrial workers to skill levels specified by industrial employers, at little or no cost to the employers. Contact: Blue Grass State Skills Corporation, Room 2135, Capital Plaza Tower, Frankfort, KY 40601, 502-564-3472.

MINORITY BUSINESS DIVISION
Coordinates minority enterprise activities throughout the state's administrative structure; and acts as an advocacy agency for the furtherance and expansion of minority businesses through the utilization of resources available through the state or under the purview of the state. Includes public sector purchasing assistance, education and training and advocacy for minority business enterprise. Contact: Minority Business Division, Kentucky Department of Economic Development, Commerce Cabinet, 2222 Capital Plaza Tower, Frankfort, KY 40601, 502-564-2064.

SBA 503 LOAN PROGRAM

Provides funds for up to 40 percent of the total cost of an expansion project for a term of up to 25 years at a fixed rate of interest. Maximum of $500,000 participation per project. This program is generally for healthy, established small businesses. Project size is generally $100,000 to $5 million. (Projects under $100,000 will be considered.) The interest rate is fixed at the long-term US Treasury Bond Rate for periods up to 25 years plus ¾ percent. Contact: Kentucky Development Finance Authority, 24th Floor, Capital Plaza Tower, Frankfort, KY 40601, 502-564-4554.

KDFA DIRECT LOAN PROGRAM

Offers a mortgage loan program to work in conjunction with private financing. The program is designed to allow businesses to obtain the long-term financing needed to encourage growth. Projects financed must be agribusiness, tourism or industrial ventures. KDFA may participate up to 25 percent of a project, but will make a loan for no more than $5000 per job, with a maximum loan amount of $250,000. The minimum KDFA loan amount is $25,000. Projects must create new jobs or have a significant impact on the economic growth of a community. The interest rate is tied to the term of the loan (i.e., a 10-year loan would have an interest rate of 5.067 percent; a 15-year loan a rate of 6.421 percent; and a 20-year loan a rate of 7.066 percent). Contact: Kentucky Development Finance Authority, 24th Floor, Capital Plaza Tower, Frankfort, KY 40601, 502-564-4554.

INDUSTRIAL REVENUE BOND ISSUE PROGRAM

This program allows companies with sufficient financial strength to take advantage of tax-exempt rates of interest. Bonds may be issued for any eligible project which does not require the approval of the Industrial Revenue Bond Oversight Committee. The local government must request that KDFA issue the bond. An issuing fee of .1 percent of the amount of the issue is charged, with a maximum of $10,000, and an application fee of $350 is credited toward the issuing fee to cover KDFA's expenses. Contact: Kentucky Development Finance Authority, 24th Floor, Capital Plaza Tower, Frankfort, KY 40601, 502-564-4554.

LOUISIANA

SMALL BUSINESS DEVELOPMENT CENTER

Provides management assistance, counseling, continuing education and an informational resource center for the 12 northeast Louisiana parishes. The management and technical assistance services are provided at no charge. A small fee may be charged for workshops or seminars. Contact: NLU Small Business Development Center, College of Business Administration, Northeast Louisiana University, Monroe, LA 71209, 318-342-2129.

COST-FREE TRAINING

The Office of Commerce and Industry conducts labor availability studies in the plant site area, recruits trainees, designs the training schedule and produces manuals and training films in consultation with company production officials. It also provides materials and equipment and hires instructors. Trainees attend classes on their own time without pay and without assurance of guaranteed employment. The company for whom the training program is conducted has absolute control over hiring. There is no cost to the company for the start-up training program. Contact: Louisiana Department of Commerce, PO Box 94185, Baton Rouge, LA 70804, 504-342-5361.

INDUSTRIAL REVENUE BONDS

Allow local authorities, development boards and public trusts to issue up to $10 million in tax-exempt revenue bonds to finance the construction and equipping of new industrial facilities and/or expansions. The facilities and equipment are then leased to the participating company at a rent sufficient to retire the bonds. At the end of the lease period the company has the option to purchase the facility at a nominal figure or to continue to lease at a low rate. Contact: Louisiana Department of Commerce, PO Box 94185, Baton Rouge, LA 70804, 504-342-5361.

LOUISIANA MINORITY BUSINESS DEVELOPMENT AUTHORITY

Promotes business opportunities by granting loans to minority businesses. Contact: Louisiana Minority Business Development Authority, PO Box 44185, Baton Rouge, LA 70804, 504-342-5359.

MAINE

NEW ENTERPRISE INSTITUTE
A business development and research project in the Center for Research and Advanced Study, University of Southern Maine. Offers businesspersons the following services: administration and information, management assistance, marketing and technology, education and a Small Business Development Center. Contact: New Enterprise Institute, Center for Research and Advanced Study, University of Southern Maine, 246 Deering Avenue, Portland, ME 04102, 207-780-4420.

MAINE DEVELOPMENT FOUNDATION
Legislatively established, nonprofit corporation through which business, government and education leaders pool resources to stimulate business development in Maine. The Foundation provides high-level, professional assistance in such areas as: industrial and commercial real estate development; location and financing of industrial and commercial facilities; business financing; export market development; joint public/private development projects; legislation development and securing public assistance and approvals. Most of the Foundation's services are available at no charge. As requested, the Foundation works on a strictly confidential basis. Contact: Maine Development Foundation, One Memorial Circle, Augusta, ME 04330, 207-622-6345.

MAINE STATE DEVELOPMENT OFFICE
Promotes and attracts new industry to the state and encourages and assists the expansion of existing business activity. The professional staff provides assistance in the following areas: technical, site location, financial packaging, training, business, export and the Community Industrial Building Fund. Contact: Maine State Development Office, 193 State Street, Augusta, ME 04333, 207-289-2656.

UMBRELLA BOND PROGRAM
Loans available for individuals and small businesses with plans for establishing new or expanding existing industrial, manufacturing, agricultural, fishing or recreational ventures within Maine.

The maximum amount of a loan is $1 million. Interest rates will be determined upon the sale of the Umbrella Bonds. Maturity is not to exceed 25 years on industrial, agricultural and recreational real estate mortgages or 10 years for industrial and agricultural machinery and equipment. Contact: Finance Authority of Maine, State House, Augusta, ME 04333, 207-289-3095.

MARYLAND

SMALL BUSINESS DEVELOPMENT CENTER
Free services include: management and technical assistance; counseling; training; research, publications and information; and financial facilitation. Contact: Small Business Development Center, College of Business and Management, University of Maryland, College Park, MD 20742, 301-454-5072.

MARYLAND BUSINESS ASSISTANCE CENTER
The state offers an extensive array of programs and services to assist businesses in expanding their operations. The state's toll-free hotline is an instant link to these various programs and services including: confidential location assistance, flexible public financing, state-funded employee training, selling to the government, enterprise zones, foreign trade zones and the licensing and permit process. Contact: Maryland Business Assistance Center, 45 Calvert Street, Annapolis, MD 21401, 301-269-2945 (toll-free number in Maryland: 1-800-OK-GREEN).

DEPARTMENT OF ECONOMIC AND COMMUNITY DEVELOPMENT
Provides businesses with a comprehensive array of financing alternatives including insurance for working capital loans and for long-term financing of fixed assets. Insured financing can mean greater leverage and lower financing costs for expanding Maryland companies. In addition, Maryland's "umbrella" bond program offers mid-sized firms access to the tax-exempt financing market. A financial specialist will work confidentially with a company to help clarify its needs and identify available resources. Loans and guarantees vary from $35,000 to $10 million. Interest rates may be conventional, floating, fixed rate or tax-

exempt. Maturity may be up to 30 years. Contact: Department of Economic and Community Development, Maryland Business Assistance Center, 45 Calvert Street, Annapolis, MD 21401, 301-269-2945 (toll-free number in Maryland: 1-800-OK-GREEN).

DEVELOPMENT CREDIT FUND, INC.
Provides below-market financing to minority-owned companies doing business in Maryland. Contact: Development Credit Fund, Inc., 1925 Eutaw Place, Baltimore, MD 21217, 301-523-6400.

MASSACHUSETTS

"CALL ONE" BUSINESS SERVICE CENTER
Toll-free, direct hotline which offers information and assistance on a variety of business topics including: licensing and permits, regulations, demographics, hourly wages and taxes. Contact: Massachusetts Department of Commerce and Development, 100 Cambridge Street, Boston, MA 02202, 617-727-4005 (toll-free number in Massachusetts: 1-800-632-8181).

SMALL BUSINESS ASSISTANCE DIVISION
Provides one-stop, comprehensive assistance for the small business. Services include technical, management and financial assistance to those wishing to start a business as well as to those already in business. Contact: Small Business Assistance Division, 100 Cambridge Street, Boston, MA 02202, 617-727-4005.

MASSACHUSETTS SMALL BUSINESS DEVELOPMENT CENTERS
Free counseling is offered on a one-to-one basis with individualized services tailored to the specialized needs of the client. Conduct seminars, workshops, courses and conferences addressing a wide range of business concerns. A nominal fee is charged for training. In addition, three Specialty Centers offer unique services: Capital Formation Service, Technology, Productivity and Innovation Center and Minority Business Training and Resource Center. For the location of the SBDC serving your area, contact: Massachusetts Department of Commerce,

100 Cambridge Street, Boston, MA 02202, 617-727-4005 (toll-free number in Massachusetts: 1-800-632-8181).

SITE INVENTORY TRACKING EXCHANGE (SITE)

Maintains a computerized listing of available industrial land and building space throughout Massachusetts with a comprehensive printout of site attributes. In-state and out-of-state firms seeking to start up, locate or expand in Massachusetts may request this free service at any time. Contact: SITE Program, Massachusetts Department of Commerce, 100 Cambridge Street, Boston, MA 02202, 617-727-3215.

MASSACHUSETTS SMALL BUSINESS PURCHASING PROGRAM

Assists businesses in participating in state purchasing. A weekly publication, "The Goods and Services Bulletin," contains information for businesses interested in bidding on state contracts. Contact: Small Business Assistance Division, Massachusetts Department of Commerce, 100 Cambridge Street, Boston, MA 02202, 617-727-4005.

STATE OFFICE OF MINORITY BUSINESS ASSISTANCE

Increases access to public construction work for minority and women-owned business enterprise, and for other related activities, including information and referral, education and training, and advocacy. Contact: SOMBA, 100 Cambridge Street, 13th Floor, Boston, MA 02202, 617-727-8692.

MASSACHUSETTS INDUSTRIAL FINANCE AGENCY

Promotes employment growth through industrial revenue bonds, loan guarantees and pollution control bonds. MIFA financing is available for commercial real estate if these projects are located in locally identified Commercial Area Revitalization Districts (CARD). CARDs are situated primarily in older downtown areas. Contact: Massachusetts Industrial Finance Agency, 125 Pearl Street, Boston, MA 02110, 617-451-2477.

MASSACHUSETTS TECHNOLOGY DEVELOPMENT CORPORATION

Provides capital to new and expanding high technology companies which have the capacity to generate significant employment growth in Massachusetts as well as other public benefits. MTDC makes both debt and equity investments, usually in the form of a direct purchase of common or preferred stock accompanied by a loan on very favorable terms. MTDC will invest a minimum of $100,000 and a maximum of $250,000 in first-round institutional financing. Generally, the private sector investors who are MTDC's partners will invest two to four times the amount of capital which MTDC provides. Contact: MTDC, 84 State Street, Suite 500, Boston, MA 02109, 617-723-4920.

COMMUNITY DEVELOPMENT FINANCE CORPORATION

Provides flexible financing for working capital needs and real estate development projects when there is some clear public benefit. Offers three investment programs for economic development projects: Venture Capital Investment Program, Community Development Investment Program and Small Loan Guarantee Program. Contact: Massachusetts Community Development Finance Corporation, 131 State Street, Suite 600, Boston, MA 02109, 617-742-0366.

MASSACHUSETTS BUSINESS DEVELOPMENT CORPORATION

Provides loans for businesses which cannot obtain all their financial requirements from conventional sources. Types of loans: working capital, leveraged buy-outs, second mortgages, government guaranteed loans, SBA 503 loans and long-term loans for new equipment or energy conversion. MBDC can provide up to 100 percent financing. Loans are medium- to long-term. Contact: Massachusetts Business Development Corporation, One Boston Place, Boston, MA 02108, 617-723-7515.

MASSACHUSETTS CAPITAL RESOURCE COMPANY

Invests in both traditional and technology-based industries, high-risk start-up companies, expanding businesses, management buy-outs, and turnaround situations. Virtually any Massachusetts-based company can qualify. MCRC will invest from $100,000 to $5 million. Contact: Massachusetts Capital Resource Company, 545 Boylston Street, Boston, MA 02116, 617-536-3900.

MASSACHUSETTS GOVERNMENT LAND BANK

Offers below-market mortgage financing to qualifying public-purpose development projects lacking sufficient public/private investment. Project investments generally range from $200,000 to $3 million. Contact: Massachusetts Government Land Bank, 6 Beacon Street, Suite 900, Boston, MA 02108, 617-727-8257.

MICHIGAN

MICHIGAN BUSINESS OMBUDSMAN

Helps clear the channels of communication, simplifying contacts with state government. Services include: an ability to unwind government red tape, a one-stop source for permits and licensing assistance, and information on starting a business in Michigan. Contact: Michigan Department of Commerce, Office of the Michigan Business Ombudsman, PO Box 30107, Lansing, MI 48909, 517-373-6241 (toll-free number in Michigan: 1-800-232-2727).

SMALL BUSINESS CENTERS

Provide personal assistance and counseling in the following areas: business procurement and export development, financial packaging, capital acquisition, license and permit information, plus additional state and local resources available to business owners in Michigan. For the location of the SBC serving your area, contact: Michigan Department of Commerce, Local Development Services Bureau, PO Box 30225, Lansing, MI 48909, 517-373-3530.

DIVISION OF MINORITY BUSINESS ENTERPRISE

Provides assistance with education and training, management and financial packaging. Contact: Michigan Department of Commerce, Division of Minority Business Enterprise, PO Box 30225, Lansing MI 48909, 517-373-8430.

OFFICE OF WOMEN BUSINESS OWNERS

Provides assistance with education and training, management and financial packaging. Contact: Michigan Department of Commerce, Office of Women Business Owners, PO Box 30225, Lansing, MI 48909, 517-373-6224.

LABOR TRAINING

Numerous programs are offered to train or help finance training for a company's workers. Details on labor training programs and assistance in developing a training package for qualifying businesses and industries are available upon request. Contact: Office of Business and Community Development, Michigan Department of Commerce, PO Box 30225, Lansing, MI 48909, 517-373-3550.

MICHIGAN STRATEGIC FUND

Consolidates and streamlines state economic development efforts that provide financing to businesses. It also increases cooperation between public and private investors. Provides a range of financial services to businesses that meet carefully defined criteria. Services include: working capital, tax-exempt revenue bonds, loan guarantees, small business loans, product development grants, tax-exempt bond issues, and export financing. Contact: Michigan Department of Commerce, Office of Development Finance, PO Box 30004, Lansing, MI 48909, 517-373-7550.

MANUFACTURING SERVICES BUREAU

Offers information and counseling on developing a financial assistance package. Company representatives, MSB experts, local government officials and private lenders together assemble components of the package, drawing on available state, federal and local resources. Contact: Manufacturing Services Bureau, Michigan Department of Commerce, PO Box 30225, Lansing, MI 48909, 517-373-8495.

MINNESOTA

SMALL BUSINESS DEVELOPMENT CENTERS

Resource centers where information, counseling and assistance are coordinated and disseminated to persons who plan to start a small business or are presently operating a small business. The SBDC provides the entrepreneur with education and training opportunities which cover a wide range of business topics. For the location of the SBDC serving your area, contact: University of Minnesota, Agricultural Extension Service, Small

Business Development Center, Department of Agriculture and Applied Economics, 248 Classroom Office Building, St. Paul, MN 55108, 612-376-3433.

SMALL BUSINESS INSTITUTES
Provide counseling services to small businesses using students under faculty supervision. The SBI technical assistance program is available upon request and provided at no cost to the applicant. Assistance can be provided for a variety of business problems. For the location of the SBI serving your area, contact: Bethel College, Small Business Institute, PO Box 77, 3900 Bethel Drive, St. Paul, MN 55112, 612-638-6318.

SMALL BUSINESS ASSISTANCE OFFICES
Provide training and other direct assistance in the development, financing and operation of qualified small businesses. For the location of the office serving your area, contact: Small Business Assistance Office, Minnesota Department of Energy and Economic Development, 900 American Center Building, 150 East Kellogg Boulevard, St. Paul, MN 55101, 612-296-3871.

MINNESOTA TRADE OFFICE
Assists small and medium-sized companies in developing international trade and export possibilities. Contact: Minnesota Trade Office, 90 West Plato Boulevard, St. Paul, MN 55107, 612-297-4222 (Telex: 853610 MTOAG).

OFFICE OF PROJECT MANAGEMENT
Assists businesses with financial packages utilizing a variety of resources. Contact: Office of Project Management, Minnesota Department of Energy and Economic Development, 900 American Center Building, 150 Kellogg Boulevard, St. Paul, MN 55101, 612-296-5021.

MINNESOTA SMALL BUSINESS DEVELOPMENT LOANS
Assists small businesses in their start-up or expansion in Minnesota. Fixed interest rates below the rate paid by the federal government on its loans and long-term commitments—up to 20 years are available. Loans range between $250,000 and $1 million. Contact: Minnesota Department of Energy and Economic

Development, 900 American Center, 150 East Kellogg Boulevard, St. Paul, MN 55101, 612-296-6424.

THE MINNESOTA FUND

Provides direct loans, at fixed interest, on fixed assets for new and existing businesses. The maximum loan amount is $250,000 and cannot exceed 20 percent of the total project cost. Interest rates are negotiated and terms are 15 years for land and buildings and 7 years for machinery. Contact: Minnesota Department of Energy and Economic Development, 900 American Center, 150 East Kellogg Boulevard, St. Paul, MN 55101, 612-296-6424.

MISSISSIPPI

MISSISSIPPI RESEARCH AND DEVELOPMENT CENTERS

Provide free information and assistance for businesspersons who wish to start a business or expand their existing business. Also offers workshops and seminars. For the location of the MRDC serving your area, contact: Mississippi Research and Development Center, 3825 Ridgewood Road, Jackson, MS 39211, 601-982-6684.

START-UP TRAINING PROGRAM FOR INDUSTRY

Designs training plan for your company, recruits and pays competent instructors to conduct training, conducts pre-employment assessment/screening, and coordinates pre-employment and on-the-job skill development. Contact: Coordinator of Industry Services, Vocational-Technical Division, Mississippi State Department of Education, PO Box 771, Jackson, MS 39205, 601-359-3074.

MISSISSIPPI DEPARTMENT OF
ECONOMIC DEVELOPMENT

Offers loan guarantees to a maximum of $200,000; Industrial Revenue Bonds up to $10 million; and the Small Business Administration (503) Loan Program with a maximum participation of $500,000 per project. Contact: Mississippi Department of Economic Development, PO Box 849, Jackson, MS 39205, 601-359-3437.

MISSOURI

GREATER KANSAS CITY CHAMBER OF COMMERCE
Provides business, demographic and statistical data. Offers counseling and other services. Contact: Greater Kansas City Chamber of Commerce, Ten Main Center, Sixth Floor, 920 Main Street, Kansas City, MO 64106, 816-221-2424.

ONE-STOP SHOP
Provides businesses with a single contact point where they can get complete and accurate information on all requirements for doing business in Missouri. To help new business owners, they have published a booklet entitled "Starting a New Business in Missouri." Contact: Missouri Division of Community and Economic Development, PO Box 118, Jefferson City, MO 65102, 314-751-4982.

BUSINESS AND INDUSTRY EXTENSION OFFICES
Provide free counseling to present and potential business owners. Contact: Business and Industry Extension Office, 1601 East 18th Street, Suite 200, Kansas City, MO 64108, 816-472-0227.

BUSINESS RESOURCE CENTER
Provides business assistance to minority business owners. Contact: Business Resource Center, 1139 Olive, Room 500, St. Louis, MO 63101, 314-621-7410.

BLACK ECONOMIC UNION
Provides an information referral/counseling service for minority businesses. Contact: Black Economic Union, 1710 Paseo, Kansas City, MO 64127, 816-474-1080.

EMPLOYEE TRAINING FUNDS
Provide employers with state and federal funds to train their employees specifically for their business. With the aid of the employer, a training program is "customized" to meet the pre-

cise needs of any business. During on-the-job training, 50 percent of the employees' wages are reimbursed to offset the employer's costs for the time spent training the employee and any reduced productivity during the predetermined period of on-the-job training. Additional funds are available to train disadvantaged workers. Contact: Missouri Customized Training Program, 221 Metro Drive, Jefferson City, MO 65101, 314-751-4750.

MISSOURI TIME DEPOSITS FOR INDUSTRIAL DEVELOPMENT
The State Treasurer of Missouri is making available $10 million to $15 million annually which will be placed on deposit with Missouri banks that make loans to manufacturers locating new operations or expanding existing facilities in the state. Manufacturers may use the loans for working capital, interim construction, financing, equipment, inventory or site development. Contact: Office of the State Treasurer, PO Box 210, Jefferson City, MO 65105, 314-751-2372.

MONTANA

BUSINESS ASSISTANCE DIVISION
Provides a variety of services including: technical assistance, marketing, international trade, financial planning, procurement, etc. Contact: Business Assistance Division, Montana Department of Commerce, 1424 Ninth Avenue, Helena, MT 59620, 406-444-3923.

UNIVERSITY CENTER FOR BUSINESS AND MANAGEMENT DEVELOPMENT
Provides business training, research and technical assistance to small businesses. For the location of the center serving your area, contact: University Center for Business and Management Development, 445 Reid Hall, Montana State University, Bozeman, MT 59717, 406-994-2057.

BUSINESS DEVELOPMENT ASSISTANCE
Provides technical assistance and information to small businesses. This assistance could cover such subjects as financial

packaging, marketing, product testing and development and quality control. Contact: Business, Assistance Division, Montana Department of Commerce, 1424 Ninth Avenue, Helena, MT 59620, 406-444-4325.

US GOVERNMENT PROCUREMENT ASSISTANCE
Provides technical assistance on a one-to-one basis to those small businesses having problems in expanding, contracting with the government and the private sector and other areas. Contact: Business Assistance Division, Montana Department of Commerce, 1424 Ninth Avenue, Helena, MT 59620, 406-444-4325.

DEVELOPMENT FINANCE TECHNICAL ASSISTANCE
Technical assistance is available to businesses in the areas of financial analysis, financial planning, loan packaging, industrial revenue bonding, state and private capital sources and business tax incentives. Contact: Business Assistance Division, Montana Department of Commerce, 1424 Ninth Avenue, Helena, MT 59620, 406-444-4323.

DEVELOPMENT FINANCE PROGRAMS
Offer a series of programs designed to help small businesses obtain attractive capital financing. The focus of these programs is to increase the availability of long-term, fixed-rate financing to Montana small businesses. All programs operate through existing commercial lending institutions. Contact: Montana Economic Development Board, 1424 Ninth Avenue, Helena, MT 59620, 406-444-2090.

MONTANA CAPITAL COMPANIES
Designed to make private venture or equity capital an available resource within the state. Through the program, the state offers a 25 percent tax credit incentive (up to $25,000) to investors in qualified Montana capital companies, which in turn must invest these funds in small, basic Montana firms. Contact: Montana Economic Development Board, 1424 Ninth Avenue, Helena, MT 59620, 406-444-2090.

NEBRASKA

NEBRASKA DEPARTMENT OF ECONOMIC DEVELOPMENT

Small Business Division works with higher education business development centers in providing entrepreneurial identification; development of business plans; market planning; and management assistance. Also offers direct technical assistance in finance packaging, export promotion, job training, procurement assistance and opportunity identification. Contact: Nebraska Department of Economic Development, Small Business Division, Box 94666, 301 Centennial Mall South, Lincoln, NE 68509-4666, 402-471-3111.

NEBRASKA BUSINESS DEVELOPMENT CENTERS

Offer a variety of programs including: individual management consultations; workshops and seminars; business and financial analysis; market research assistance; feasibility studies; monthly business reports; Nebraska rural communities program; special studies; new business counseling; and capital formation. For the location of the BDC serving your area, contact: Nebraska Business Development Center, College of Business Administration, University of Nebraska at Omaha, Omaha, NE 68182, 402-554-2521.

US SMALL BUSINESS ADMINISTRATION

Provides information on obtaining contracts with the federal government. The Procurement Automated Source System (PASS) is a computerized registry of businesses having capabilities fitting the needs of the government or contractors. Contact: US Small Business Administration, Management Assistance, Empire State Building, Nineteenth and Farnam Streets, Omaha, NE 68102, 402-221-3604.

NEBRASKA TECHNICAL ASSISTANCE CENTERS

Provide consultants for short-term diagnostic assistance, including periodic visits by staff engineering professionals to Nebraska manufacturers. Coordinate educational activities such as workshops, seminars and conferences. Provide information on available sources of management, and marketing and financial assistance. For the location of the center serving your area, contact: Nebraska Technical Assistance Center, W191 Nebraska Hall, University of Nebraska–Lincoln, Lincoln, NE 68588-0535, 402-472-5600 (toll-free number in Nebraska: 800-742-8800).

SMALL BUSINESS REVITALIZATION PROGRAM

The SBRP does not have funds to loan; however, they have the knowledge to assist, at no charge, in putting together a financial package. Contact: Nebraska Investment Finance Authority, Gold's Galleria, Suite 304, 1033 O Street, Lincoln, NE 68508, 402-477-4406.

SMALL BUSINESS ADMINISTRATION 503 LOAN

Through SBA 503 lenders can provide small business customers with long-term, low-interest, fixed asset financing. The SBA 503 loan package consists of three sources—the private lending institution, the Small Business Administration and the small business concern. The private lending institution provides up to 50 percent of the total project cost at conventional interest rates. SBA provides up to 40 percent of the project cost not to exceed $500,000 at an interest rate approximately ¾ percent above long-term US Treasury Bond rates. The remaining project cost is the equity injection provided by the small business concern. Contact: Business Development Corporation of Nebraska, 1044 Stuart Building, Lincoln, NE 68508, 402-474-3855.

BUSINESS DEVELOPMENT CORPORATION OF NEBRASKA

The BDCN is designed for the pooling of loan funds for participating in long-term capital loans to deserving businesses in situations where regular bank credit is not available. Loans may be up to $250,000 for 5- to 15-year terms for plant construction, equipment and materials and working capital. Contact: Business Development Corporation of Nebraska, 1044 Stuart Building, Lincoln, NE 68508, 402-474-3855.

NEBRASKA INVESTMENT FINANCE AUTHORITY

Provides lower-cost financing for industrial, agricultural, commercial, health care and residential development. The Business Development Loan Program furnishes low-cost funds for the purchase of all types of equipment for businesses in Nebraska. NIFA will participate with local banks throughout the state to provide funds to eligible borrowers at below-market, fixed interest rates. NIFA participation in the loans will be a maximum of $850,000 and a minimum of $40,000. Loan terms are subject to the equipment depreciation schedule under federal tax code with the maximum loan being seven years. Contact: Nebraska Investment Finance Authority, Gold's Galleria, Suite 304, 1033 O Street, Lincoln, NE 68508, 402-477-4406.

COMMUNITY DEVELOPMENT BLOCK GRANT

CDBG funds are intended to supplement other financial resources to address local economic development issues. CDBG-funded projects must address job creation activities for low and moderate-income residents. Contact: Division of Community Affairs, Nebraska Department of Economic Development, PO Box 94666, 301 Centennial Mall South, Lincoln, NE 68509, 402-471-3111.

INDUSTRIAL DEVELOPMENT REVENUE BONDS

Lower-cost financing for eligible projects through tax-exempt bond issues which can be authorized by counties and municipalities. Eligible projects must be of an industrial nature. May be used for projects with capital expenditures up to a maximum of $10 million including all capital expenditures for a project of three years prior to and three years after the issue. Interest rates on the bonds are based on the company's credit but are lower than those of conventional loans because the interest is tax-exempt. Contact: Nebraska Department of Economic Development, PO Box 94666, 301 Centennial Mall South, Lincoln, NE 68509, 402-471-3111.

NEVADA

BUSINESS DEVELOPMENT COUNCIL

Offers planning and counseling services to those small firms that provide the majority of goods and services for the area. Also provides demographic information through its Marketing Guide and acts as a referral service to prospective developers. Contact:

Business Development Council, Greater Reno-Sparks Chamber of Commerce, 133 North Sierra Street, Reno, NV 89501, 702-786-3030.

NEVADA SMALL BUSINESS DEVELOPMENT CENTERS
Offer a management assistance program free of charge to small businesses in Nevada (usually less than 100 employees). Services include: one-on-one counseling, market research assistance, business skills assessment, capital formation assistance, business plan analysis, feasibility studies, marketing strategies and business workshops and seminars. For the location of the SBDC serving your area, contact: Nevada Small Business Development Center, College of Business Administration, University of Nevada–Reno, Business Building, Room 411, Reno, NV 89557-0016, 702-784-1717.

NEVADA COMMISSION ON ECONOMIC DEVELOPMENT
Provides information on: availability of financing; economic development districts; industrial parks; land availability; feasibility studies; educational/training programs; and labor market information. Contact: Nevada Commission on Economic Development, Capitol Complex, Carson City, NV 89710, 702-885-4325.

RENO-SPARKS CHAMBER OF COMMERCE
Provides small business counseling, publishes business source guides, monthly newsletter and calendar. Opportunity to meet business owners at monthly mixers and events. Annual dues. Mixers open to the public. Contact: Reno-Sparks Chamber of Commerce, 133 North Sierra Street, Reno, NV 89501, 702-786-3030.

NORTHERN NEVADA JOB TRAINING PROGRAM
On-the-Job Training (OJT) is a program designed to assist employers in reducing the cost of training new employees. The applicants are hired on a permanent basis and if their probationary period of training is satisfactory, it is expected that they will be retained by the employer. The employer will be reimbursed up to 50 percent for the first three months of the training costs for each trainee they hire. The purpose of the reimbursement is to compensate the employer for bringing the trainee up

to full production. The employer decides who will work for their company. Applicants are pre-screened and tested. The employer makes the final hiring decision. Relatives and former employees are exempted from this program. Contact: Northern Nevada Job Training Program, 120 South Wells, Reno, NV 89502, 702-885-8353 (toll-free number in Nevada: 1-800-648-0599).

TRAINING AND CONSULTATION SECTION (TACS)

Program to help employers protect their workers from work-related injury and illness and to build safeguards against safety and health hazards. Employers may request either conferences or on-site consultations. Employees and employee groups may also participate. Training and Consultation Section personnel do not conduct compliance inspections and do not cite employers for violations of state safety and health standards they may observe during their visits, nor do they assess penalties. Contact: Division of Occupational Safety and Health, 1370 South Curry Street, Carson City, NV 89710, 702-885-5240.

NEVADA REVOLVING LOAN PROGRAM

Designed for small business expansion which creates jobs for low- to moderate-income persons. Can lend up to 40 percent, or $100,000, whichever is the lesser of the total project cost. Remainder is financed through bank loan (60 percent) and owner cash (10 percent). The loan rate is one percent fixed interest for each year not to exceed 7 percent or seven years. (Working capital loans restricted to five-year maturity rate.) Typical collateral for loan is a second deed of trust on the project property. Contact: Nevada Small Business Revitalization Program, 1100 East Williams Street, Suite 117, Carson City, NV 89710, 702-885-4420.

NEVADA SMALL BUSINESS
REVITALIZATION PROGRAM

Provides financial assistance to small businesses and economic development planning through SBA and HUD Block Grant monies. Contact: Nevada Small Business Revitalization Program, Community Services Office, 1100 East Williams, Suite 117, Carson City, NV 89710, 702-885-4420.

INDUSTRIAL DEVELOPMENT REVENUE BONDS

Provide for up to 100 percent financing for land, building, improvements and capital equipment for firms that incur from $1 to $10 million in development costs and meet applicable state statutes and federal tax codes. Contact: Nevada Department of Commerce, 201 South Fall Street, Carson City, NV 89710, 702-885-4340.

NEW HAMPSHIRE

SMALL BUSINESS DEVELOPMENT CENTER

Program of management counseling, education and information referral. Services provided to entrepreneurs and existing firms include individual consulting in areas such as marketing, financial analysis, loan packaging, production control and general management as well as numerous training programs focused on specific business needs. All consulting and information referral services are offered without charge. Nominal fees are charged for most training programs. Contact: Small Business Development Center, New Hampshire Small Business Program, 110 McConnell Hall, Durham, NH 03824, 603-862-3556 (toll-free number in New Hampshire: 800-322-0390).

SBIR DATA MATCH

Assists technology-based companies and individuals to make the most of R & D opportunities presented by the Small Business Innovation Research Program by matching interests and skills with federal agency needs and by helping develop sound proposals for funding. Contact: New Hampshire Small Business Program, 110 McConnell Hall, Durham, NH 03824, 603-862-3556.

THE UNIVERSITY OF NEW HAMPSHIRE CONSULTING CENTER

Services offered by the Center include: product development, process development, long-range research and planning, modeling, software development, technical trouble shooting, feasibility studies, development of laboratory testing procedures, market analysis, risk analysis and planning and educational programs. Contact: Consulting Center, Research Office, Horton Social Science Center, University of New Hampshire, Durham, NH 03824, 603-862-3750.

BUSINESS ASSISTANCE FOR NORTHERN NEW HAMPSHIRE

Provides direct technical and managerial assistance to new and growing companies as well as acting as a one-stop referral source for linking private business with public and private organizations that offer support services for business. In addition, the program administers a unique loan program, the New Hampshire Job Start Program, which provides funding to new and existing firms and acts to help leverage additional financing from the banking community. Contact: New Hampshire Small Business Program, 110 McConnell Hall, Durham, NH 03824, 603-862-3556.

TECHNICAL ASSISTANCE PROGRAM

Provides marketing and technical assistance services to firms and communities in selected areas of New Hampshire. Contact: New Hampshire Small Business Program, 110 McConnell Hall, Durham, NH 03824, 603-862-3556.

VENTURE CAPITAL NETWORK

A formal "market" where entrepreneurs and other growing concerns needing financing can be linked with individuals of means and other sources of venture capital. Contact: New Hampshire Small Business Program, 110 McConnell Hall, Durham, NH 03824, 603-862-3556.

NORTHERN COMMUNITY INVESTMENT CORPORATION

Provides direct loans, loan guarantees and technical and financial development of industrial, commercial and residential property. Its market area is limited to the northern three counties of New Hampshire (Carroll, Coos and Grafton). NCIC financing is available for working capital, equipment purchase, leasehold improvements or major expansion. Contact: Northern Community Investment Corporation, PO Box 188, Littleton, NH 03561, 603-298-5546.

NEW HAMPSHIRE BUSINESS DEVELOPMENT CORPORATION

Provides additional financing to all types of promising new and existing businesses establishing a medium of credit not otherwise available to them. $25,000 to $150,000 net NHBDC investment. The term is set at that amount of time, by mutual agreement, required to successfully amortize the investment. Interest rates are determined by mutual negotiation. Contact: New Hampshire Business Development Corporation, 10 Fort Eddy Road, Concord, NH 03301, 603-224-1432.

GRANITE STATE CAPITAL, INCORPORATED

Provides equity capital and constructive counsel to assist talented and capable entrepreneurs to build substantial businesses. Contact: Granite State Capital, Inc., 10 Fort Eddy Road, Concord, NH 03301, 603-228-9090.

NEW HAMPSHIRE INDUSTRIAL DEVELOPMENT REVENUE BOND FINANCING

Offers tax-exempt revenue bond financing to credit-worthy companies meeting certain standards. The interest rate is generally 20 percent to 30 percent lower than in conventional financing. Contact: Industrial Development Authority, Four Park Street, Room 302, Concord, NH 03301, 603-271-2391.

NEW JERSEY

OFFICE OF SMALL BUSINESS ASSISTANCE

Provides information and counseling on starting a business in New Jersey. Contact: Office of Small Business Assistance, New Jersey Department of Commerce and Economic Development, 1 West State Street, CN 823, Trenton, NJ 08625, 609-984-4442.

OFFICE OF MINORITY BUSINESS ENTERPRISE

Provides information and assistance to minority-owned firms in bidding on state procurement contracts. Contact: Office of Minority Business Enterprise, New Jersey Department of Commerce and Economic Development, Division of Administration, CN 822, Trenton, NJ 08625, 609-292-0500.

NEW JERSEY ECONOMIC DEVELOPMENT AUTHORITY

Arranges low-interest, long-term financing and other forms of assistance for businesses locating or expanding in New Jersey. Programs include: Tax-exempt Industrial Development Bond Financing; Loan Guarantees and Direct Loans; SBA 503 Loan Program; and Local Development Financing Fund Loans. Contact: New Jersey Economic Development Authority, Capital Place One, CN 990, Trenton, NJ 08625, 609-292-1800.

CORPORATION FOR BUSINESS ASSISTANCE IN NEW JERSEY

Provides small businesses with fixed asset financing up to 25 years for the acquisition of land and building, machinery and equipment, construction, renovation and restoration. Maximum CBA participation is $500,000 per project. Interest rate is near long-term US Treasury Bond rates for CBA portion. Contact: Corporation for Business Assistance in New Jersey, 200 South Warren Street, Suite 600, Trenton, NJ 08608, 609-633-7737.

NEW MEXICO

DEVELOPMENT TRAINING PROGRAMS

New and expanding industries may obtain state-sponsored funds to train a New Mexico work force. The state provides one-half of the wage to be paid to an employee, and the employer pays the other half during the training period. Contact: New Mexico Economic Development and Tourism Department, Bataan Memorial Building, Room 201 EDB, Santa Fe, NM 87503, 505-827-6200 (TWX 910-985-0512).

INDUSTRIAL SITE LOCATION ASSISTANCE

Any firm engaged in site location will receive assistance from professional economic and/or industrial developers. A professional developer is assigned to each client. The full range of expertise of the office, i.e., research, public and private sector agency support, is available to meet the needs of each client.

Contact: New Mexico Economic Development and Tourism Department, Bataan Memorial Building, Room 201 EDB, Santa Fe, NM 87503, 505-827-6200 (TWX 910-985-0512).

NEW MEXICO ECONOMIC DEVELOPMENT AND TOURISM DEPARTMENT

Provides information and assistance in obtaining loans. Available sources of financing include: Economic Incentive Loan Program; Industrial and Agricultural Finance Authority; SBA 503 Guaranteed Loan: Business Development Corporation; Community Development Block Grant; Community Development Assistance Fund; and Industrial Revenue Bonds. Low interest and long-term loans are available. Contact: New Mexico Economic Development and Tourism Department, Bataan Memorial Building, Room 201 EDB, Santa Fe, NM 87503, 505-827-6200 (TWX 910-985-0512).

NEW YORK

SMALL BUSINESS DIVISION ASSISTANCE PROGRAM

Provides a variety of programs to assist small businesses in getting started or expanding their operations. These programs include: Small Business Advocacy; NYS Small Business Advisory Board; Interagency Small Business Task Force; Business Services Ombudsman; Procurement Assistance; Training and Technical Assistance; Small Business Counseling; and State Training and Manpower Program (STAMP). Contact: New York Department of Commerce, Division for Small Business, 230 Park Avenue, New York, NY 10169, 212-309-0400.

OFFICE OF BUSINESS PERMITS

Provides information and assistance in obtaining the necessary licenses and permits for doing business in New York. Contact: Office of Business Permits, Alfred E. Smith State Office Building, Albany, NY 12225, 518-474-8275 (toll-tree number in New York: 1-800-342-3464).

MINORITY AND WOMEN'S BUSINESS DIVISION

Offers assistance in business planning and financial packaging. Staff conducts regularly scheduled meetings with minority and women-owned firms and organizations throughout each region of New York State. Staff is bilingual and has expertise in all aspects of business. Contact: Minority and Women's Business Division, 230 Park Avenue, Suite 1825, New York, NY 10169, 212-309-0440.

NEW YORK JOB DEVELOPMENT AUTHORITY
Functions as a bank, making business and industrial loans for real estate, machinery and equipment. Contact: New York Job Development Authority, One Commerce Plaza, Albany, NY 12210, 518-474-7580.

NEW YORK BUSINESS DEVELOPMENT CORPORATION
Makes loans to small, undercapitalized firms when funding is not available from usual lending sources. Contact: New York Business Development Corporation, 41 State Street, Albany, NY 12207, 518-463-2268.

URBAN DEVELOPMENT CORPORATION
Provides financing for small, minority and women-owned businesses through a variety of programs. Contact: Urban Development Corporation, 1515 Broadway, New York, NY 10036, 212-930-9000.

NORTH CAROLINA

SMALL BUSINESS RESOURCE CENTERS
Local points of contact for information about small businesses. Management, counseling, training and other Small Business Administration services. For the location of the SBRC serving your area, contact: Greater Charlotte Chamber of Commerce, 129 West Trade Street, PO Box 32785, Charlotte, NC 28232, 704-377-6911.

SMALL BUSINESS INSTITUTE
Provides long-term small business counseling through the use of graduate/senior student and faculty advisory teams. Service

available at no cost. Contact: Small Business Institute, Department of Business Administration, UNCC, Charlotte, NC 28223, 704-597-4424.

NORTH CAROLINA SMALL BUSINESS AND TECHNOLOGY DEVELOPMENT CENTER

Provides advanced small business counseling and training through use of university research facilities, private sector consultants, faculty, graduate students and volunteer counselors. Service is free. Contact: North Carolina SBTDC, 820 Clay Street, Raleigh, NC 27605, 919-733-4643.

MINORITY BUSINESS ASSISTANCE

Provides a range of business-related services to small businesses owned by economically/socially disadvantaged individuals and/ or women. Contact: North Carolina State MBDA, North Carolina Department of Commerce, 430 North Salisbury Street, Raleigh, NC 27611, 919-733-2712.

NORTH CAROLINA DEPARTMENT OF COMMERCE BUSINESS ASSISTANCE DIVISION

Although the State of North Carolina has no loans available for small businesses, this office will assist small business owners and direct them to Small Business Administration Programs. Provides information and guidance in economic development within the state. Sponsors training activities that encourage small business growth. Contact: Business Assistance Division, North Carolina Department of Commerce, 430 North Salisbury Street, Raleigh, NC 27611, 919-733-7980.

NORTH DAKOTA

SMALL BUSINESS INSTITUTE

Teams of undergraduate or graduate level students, under faculty supervision, provide management counseling to small businesses. Contact: Small Business Institute, Business Administration and Economics, North Dakota State University, Putnam Hall, Fargo, ND 58105, 701-237-7690.

CENTER FOR INNOVATION
AND BUSINESS DEVELOPMENT

Provides numerous services including: invention evaluation, technology transfer, technical development and business development. Contact: Center for Innovation and Business Development, Box 8103, University Station, Grand Forks, ND 58202, 701-777-3132.

NORTH DAKOTA ECONOMIC
DEVELOPMENT COMMISSION

Works closely with new or expanding businesses in advising or arranging the financial aspects of their venture. Staff members work with all major funding sources and will serve as a liaison between the business and the financier when appropriate. The EDC also administers the North Dakota Industrial Revenue Bond Guarantee Program. Contact: North Dakota Economic Development Commission, Liberty Memorial Building, Bismarck, ND 58501, 701-224-2810 (toll-free number in North Dakota: 1-800-472-2100; out-of-state: 1-800-437-2077).

OHIO

SMALL BUSINESS ENTERPRISE CENTERS

Offer free advice and assistance for small businesses in the areas of: management and technical assistance; legal assistance; technical resources; educational programs; funding sources; and procurement assistance. For the location of the center serving your area, contact: Small Business Enterprise Center Office, Ohio Department of Development, PO Box 1001, Columbus, OH 43266-0101, 614-466-5700.

WOMEN'S BUSINESS RESOURCE PROGRAM

Helps companies locate financing methods and loan packaging, purchasing and procurement opportunities with government agencies and private industry. Additional services include: a business reference library; statistics for women's business enterprises; listings of women's business and professional organizations; and a calendar of seminars and workshops of special interest to women entrepreneurs. Contact: Women's Business

Resource Program, Small and Developing Business Division, Ohio Department of Development, PO Box 1001, Columbus, OH 43266-0101, 614-466-4945.

BUSINESS DEVELOPMENT SERVICES
Provide businesses with relocation and site selection services. Contact: Business Development Division, Ohio Department of Development, PO Box 1001, Columbus, OH 43266-0101, 614-466-2317 (toll-free number in Ohio: 1-800-282-1085; out-of-state: 1-800-848-1300).

TECHNOLOGY INFORMATION EXCHANGE-INNOVATION NETWORK (TIE-IN)
Database of business opportunities, technical resources and programs providing assistance to start-up and developing businesses. For the location of the TIE-IN access site nearest you, contact: Division of Technological Innovation, Department of Development, 30 East Broad Street, PO Box 1001, Columbus, OH 43266-0101, 614-466-2115.

ONE-STOP BUSINESS PERMIT CENTER
Provides start-up business kit as well as assistance in obtaining all necessary permits. Contact: One-Stop Business Permit Center, 30 East Broad Street, Columbus, OH 43216, 614-462-8748 (toll-free number in Ohio: 1-800-248-4040).

ECONOMIC DEVELOPMENT FINANCING DIVISION
Offers direct loans, loan guarantees, and industrial and hospital revenue bonds. Contact: Economic Development Financing Division, Ohio Department of Development, PO Box 1001, Columbus, OH 43266-0101, 614-466-5420.

OKLAHOMA

SMALL BUSINESS DEVELOPMENT CENTERS
Provide free information and assistance to small businesspersons wishing to start or expand their business. One-on-one counseling is available. For the location of the SBDC serving your area,

contact: Small Business Development Center, East Central University, 1036 East 10th Street, Ada, OK 74820, 405-436-3190.

VENTURE CAPITAL EXCHANGE

Introduces entrepreneurs to active, informal investors commonly referred to as venture capitalists or angels. There is a $100 fee for each entrepreneur opportunity application. This payment covers the cost of VCE's services for one year. Investors may register for one year of VCE activity for $100. VCE receives no fees or commissions related to the eventual outcome of the information it exchanges. Contact: Venture Capital Exchange, Enterprise Development Center, The University of Tulsa, 600 South College Avenue, Tulsa, OK 74104, 918-592-6000, extension 3152 or 2684.

OKLAHOMA INDUSTRIAL FINANCE AUTHORITY

Provides supplemental funding in loan packages involving manufacturing industries. May loan up to 25 percent of the project's total cost of land, buildings and stationary manufacturing equipment. Interest rate is currently 10 percent. Contact: Oklahoma Industrial Finance Authority, 4024 Lincoln Boulevard, Oklahoma City, OK 73105, 405-521-2182.

OREGON

SMALL BUSINESS DEVELOPMENT CENTERS

Provide services and resources to the small business community. The network offers business counseling, business training, current information and resources and a referral information service. All services are offered at little or no cost. For the location of the SBDC serving your area, contact: OSBDCN State Offices, Lane Community College, 1059 Willamette Street, Eugene, OR 97401, 503-726-2250.

BUSINESS DEVELOPMENT DIVISION

Offers a variety of management services to existing Oregon businesses. Contact: Business Development Division, 595 Cottage Street, NE, Salem, OR 97310, 503-373-1225.

"ONE-STOP" PERMIT INFORMATION OFFICE

Answers questions and solves problems related to regulations and obtaining permits. Contact: "One-Stop" Permit Information Office, 595 Cottage Street, NE, Salem, OR 97310, 503-373-1234.

ECONOMIC DEVELOPMENT DEPARTMENT

Offers assistance in obtaining a wide variety of federal and state loans and grants including: Industrial Development Revenue Bonds; Umbrella Revenue Bond; Oregon Business Development Fund; Port Revolving Loan Fund; Oregon Resource and Technology Development Corporation; Small Business Administration 503 Loan Program; Small Business Administration Loan Guarantee Program; and Urban Development Action Grant. Contact: Economic Development Department, 595 Cottage Street, NE, Salem, OR 97310, 503-373-1200.

PENNSYLVANIA

SMALL BUSINESS ACTION CENTER

Offers assistance in dealing with business questions, complaints and problems. With one confidential phone call, the Center can help you cut through the red tape of bureaucratic delay and regulatory runaround. With a single phone call you can: 1) identify those government regulations and taxes affecting your company; 2) receive all the state forms and applications you need from one source (they maintain an inventory of these forms, so there is no need to contact several different government agencies and departments); 3) learn about available federal, state, local and private funding sources. (They are not set up to provide financing, but they can supply you with the information and guidance you need to apply for financial assistance); 4) get answers to business-related problems and complaints with state agencies; 5) receive information on technical and managerial training and counseling services (such as accounting, marketing and production); 6) obtain helpful information on exports. They also publish a Small Business Newsletter which provides business management tips, a calendar of state and federal filing dates, and information on upcoming seminars, current legislation, regulations and services. (Reprints of inter-

est from business publications are also offered.) Contact: Small
Business Action Center, PO Box 8100, Harrisburg, PA 17105,
717-783-5700.

SMALL BUSINESS DEVELOPMENT CENTERS
Located at colleges and universities throughout the state, these
centers offer management assistance and counseling services to
small businesses. The SBDC services include assistance with
accounting, record keeping, business planning, market research
and financial analysis. Although most of its services are free,
there are fees for short courses or workshops, or for some of
the services described above. For the location of the SBDC
serving your area, contact: State Director's Office, Wharton
School, Small Business Development Center, 343 Vance Hall/
CS, Philadelphia, PA 19104, 215-898-1219.

PENNSYLVANIA TECHNICAL
ASSISTANCE PROGRAM (PENNTAP)
Helps small businesses and industries which have technical problems to "link up" with technical resources that provide solutions
and answers. Full-time technical specialists work on a one-to-
one basis with the client on such areas as production, computerized systems, product development, new process, energy sources
and related questions. Sponsored by the Pennsylvania Department of Commerce and Pennsylvania State University, PENN-
TAP does not charge for any of its services. For the location
serving your area, contact: Pennsylvania State University, Capitol Campus, Small Business Development Center, Crags Building, Route 230, Middletown, PA 17057, 717-948-6031.

OFFICE OF MINORITY BUSINESS ENTERPRISE
Serves as a liaison between state government procurement officials and minority businesses. The office encourages state government to award contracts to minority firms, while working to
increase private sector awareness of the goods and services provided by these businesses. The bureau also develops and coordinates training seminars for the minority businessperson and
serves as a general information source for the minority business
community. Contact: Office of Minority Business Enterprise,

Pennsylvania Department of Commerce, Room 487, Forum Building, Harrisburg, PA 17120, 717-783-1301.

PENNSYLVANIA INDUSTRIAL
DEVELOPMENT AUTHORITY (PIDA)

Administers long-term, low-interest business loans to stimulate economic activity in areas of high unemployment. Funds may be used for land and building acquisitions, new construction and/or expansion of existing buildings. PIDA can provide up to 70 percent of the financing for eligible projects. The loan ceiling at the present time is as follows: $500,000 for areas with less than 10 percent unemployment; $1 million for areas with 10 percent or more unemployment. Interest rate varies from $4\frac{1}{2}$ percent to $10\frac{1}{2}$ percent, depending on the unemployment rate in your county. Contact: Pennsylvania Department of Commerce, Bureau of Economic Assistance, PIDA, 405 Forum Building, Harrisburg, PA 17120, 717-787-6245.

PENNSYLVANIA CAPITAL LOAN FUND PROGRAM

Makes low-interest loans to businesses for capital development projects which will result in long-term net new employment opportunities. Loans may be used for the purchase of buildings and associated land, building renovation, the purchase of machinery and equipment and for working capital. Loans for working capital must be secured by inventory and accounts receivable. Loans of up to $50,000 or 20 percent of the total project cost, whichever is less, may be made to eligible businesses. Contact: Pennsylvania Department of Commerce, Bureau of Economic Assistance, 405 Forum Building, Harrisburg, PA 17120, 717-783-1768.

EMPLOYEE OWNERSHIP ASSISTANCE PROGRAM

Provides low-interest loans to employee groups considering ownership of a firm for feasibility studies and technical assistance and can also provide funds for purchase of the firm's assets, for rehabilitation and improvement of the plant and equipment, and for working capital. Funds for feasibility studies and professional services is available up to $100,000 or 50 percent of total project costs, whichever is less. Feasibility studies must be completed within one year from the loan's date of approval by the Department. Professional services must be completed within 18 months of the loan's approval. Loans for acquiring a firm's assets are available up to $1.5 million or 25 percent of the total project cost, whichever is less. The interest rate for financial assistance loans is 5 percent statewide. Terms of the loan cannot exceed 20 years. Contact: Pennsylvania Department of Commerce, 405 Forum Building, Harrisburg, PA 17120, 717-783-6890.

INDUSTRIAL REVENUE BONDS
Provide tax-exempt financing for land, buildings and equipment to businesses engaged in industrial and commercial activities. Projects are certified through local Industrial Development Authorities. Maturities for bonds can range between 10 and 35 years. Loans made under the program range from 10 to 20 years. The interest rate varies from 65 percent to 85 percent of the floating prime rate. Refinancing of existing facilities is not permitted with loan proceeds. Commercial businesses must have a minimum project cost of $200,000 and create or preserve 20 jobs, while a manufacturing project should have a minimum cost of $100,000 and create or preserve five jobs. Contact: Revenue Bond & Mortgage Program, Pennsylvania Department of Commerce, Bureau of Economic Assistance, 405 Forum Building, Harrisburg, PA 17120, 717-783-1108.

PENNSYLVANIA MINORITY BUSINESS DEVELOPMENT AUTHORITY
Provides long-term, low-interest loans and guarantees for the establishment and expansion of minority businesses. Economically disadvantaged businesses who are unable to obtain financing from traditional sources are eligible to obtain financing in medium amounts, with terms up to 20 years at an interest rate that is one-half of the prime rate. PMBDA provides, through independent firms located throughout the state, technical assistance to all loan recipients during the initial phases of their business development. Assistance is available in management skills, accounting and financial planning systems, marketing strategy and similar areas. Contact: Headquarters/Central Region, 406 South Office Building, Harrisburg, PA 17120, 717-783-1127.

RHODE ISLAND

RHODE ISLAND DEPARTMENT OF ECONOMIC DEVELOPMENT

Responds to business inquiries concerning state and local problems or information needs. Provides counseling, export assistance, federal procurement assistance, research and marketing and site selection assistance. Contact: Rhode Island Department of Economic Development, 7 Jackson Walkway, Providence, RI 02903, 401-277-2601.

RHODE ISLAND SMALL BUSINESS DEVELOPMENT CENTERS

Provide one-on-one consultation services to existing and start-up small businesses. Run seminars and training programs. Maintain a pool of professional consultants in a variety of financial management and marketing specialties. For the location of the SBDC serving your area, contact: Rhode Island Small Business Development Center, Bryant College, Smithfield, RI 02917, 401-232-6111.

BROWN VENTURE FORUM

Brings together entrepreneurs, venture capitalists, experienced business executives and others who share the goal of starting and expanding businesses. Free open meetings are held each month. The Forum also sponsors start-up clinics and workshops. Contact: Brown Venture Forum, Box 1949, Providence, RI 02912, 401-863-3528.

RHODE ISLAND DEPARTMENT OF ECONOMIC DEVELOPMENT

Provides information on the many financial assistance programs available to help new and expanding businesses. Programs include: Industrial Revenue Bonds; Insured Mortgage Financing; Revolving Loan Funds; Business Investment Funds, etc. Contact: Rhode Island Department of Economic Development, 7 Jackson Walkway, Providence, RI 02903, 401-277-2601.

SOUTH CAROLINA

SMALL BUSINESS DEVELOPMENT CENTERS
Provide free information and assistance to small businesspersons who wish to start or expand their business. One-on-one counseling is available. For the location of the SBDC serving your area, contact: Small Business Development Center, College of Business Administration, University of South Carolina, Columbia, SC 29208, 803-777-5118.

CUSTOMIZED INDUSTRIAL TRAINING
Provides tailored job training, both preemployment and on the job, to meet the specific needs of new and expanding manufacturers. Training is normally conducted prior to employment. Trainees are not paid for the time spent in training. Contact: Division of Industrial and Economic Development, South Carolina State Board for Technical and Comprehensive Education, 111 Executive Center Drive, Columbia, SC 29210, 803-758-6926.

SOUTH CAROLINA STATE DEVELOPMENT BOARD
Makes Industrial Revenues Bonds available to enterprises engaged in any of the following: with products of agriculture, mining or industry; manufacturing or growing; processing or assembling; storing, warehousing, distributing or selling; and research in connection with any of the preceding. The maximum term of individual bond issues is 40 years, but in practice terms range from 10 to 25 years depending on the money market. There is no limit on interest rates, which are negotiated between the bond purchaser and the company using the facility. Contact: South Carolina State Development Board, PO Box 927, Columbia, SC 29202, 803-758-3046.

SOUTH CAROLINA JOBS-ECONOMIC DEVELOPMENT AUTHORITY POOLED INVESTMENT PROGRAM
Obtains low-cost variable and/or fixed rate funds for small businesses through the sale of tax-exempt industrial revenue bonds. The maximum loan available to a single enterprise is $10 million and the minimum loan is considered $100,000. The term of the bonds issued is determined by the local bank which issues the credit. Contact: Jobs-Economic Development Authority, Num-

ber One Main Building, 1203 Gervais Street, Columbia, SC 29201, 803-758-2094.

JOBS-ECONOMIC DEVELOPMENT AUTHORITY

Direct state loans are available to assist private for-profit enterprises and are confined to manufacturing, industrial or service businesses. Funds may be used for land, facility construction, acquisition or renovation, equipment, raw materials and, in some locations, working capital. Loan rates vary from 85 percent of prime to prime plus 1 percent, depending upon terms, of the average local prime rate of major lending institutions, but not less than 8.5 percent. The rate is fixed. The loan amount cannot exceed $10,000 per new job created; the maximum loan amount is $250,000. The term of a JEDA loan cannot exceed 15 years. Contact: Jobs-Economic Development Authority, 1203 Gervais Street, Columbia, SC 29201, 803-758-2094.

BUSINESS DEVELOPMENT CORPORATION
OF SOUTH CAROLINA

Provides financing to businesses unable to secure loans from conventional lending sources. BDCSC makes direct loans to businesses for new and expanding operations. The maximum loan term is 10 years. The corporation borrows money from member institutions at .5 percent above the prime rate and in turn charges a slightly higher rate on loans to businesses. The rate may be fixed or variable. Loan proceeds can be used for most business purposes, including fixed asset financing and working capital, as long as the expenditure is related to creating or maintaining jobs. Contact: Business Development Corporation of South Carolina, Suite 225, Enoree Building, 111 Executive Center Drive, Columbia, SC 29210, 803-798-4064.

SOUTH DAKOTA

SMALL BUSINESS DEVELOPMENT CENTERS

Provide free information and assistance to small businesspersons who wish to start or expand their business. One-on-one counseling is available. For the location of the SBDC serving your area, contact: Small Business Development Center, South Dakota Chamber of Commerce, PO Box 747, Rapid City, SD 57709, 605-343-1744.

STATE DEVELOPMENT OFFICE

Although the state does not have any direct loan or grant money available, this office will help new and expanding businesses prepare packages to obtain private financing, industrial revenue bonds, SBA loans and even block grants. Contact: South Dakota Department of State Development, Capitol Link Plaza, Box 6000, Pierre, SD 57501, 1-800-843-8000 (in South Dakota 800-952-3625).

TENNESSEE

SMALL BUSINESS DEVELOPMENT CENTERS

Provide managerial and technical help, research studies and other types of specialized assistance of value to small businesses. These university-based centers provide individual counseling and practical training for small business owners. For the location of the SBDC serving your area, contact: The Fogelman College of Business and Economics, Memphis State University, Memphis, TN 38152, 901-454-2431.

SMALL BUSINESS INSTITUTES

Senior and graduate students at schools of business administration, and their faculty advisors, provide on-site management counseling. For the location of the SBI serving your area, contact: Memphis State University, College of Business Administration, SBI Director, Memphis, TN 38152, 901-454-2500.

OFFICE OF MINORITY BUSINESS ENTERPRISE

Provides minority businesses with greater access to local economic planning data and resources of local governments, provides minority entrepreneurs with greater access to data concerning existing and emerging business trends and market conditions in Tennessee, provides assistance with loan packaging and preparation of business plans, and publishes a business newsletter for minority businesses in the state. Contact: Tennessee Department of Economic and Community Development, Office of Minority Business Enterprise, Room 1027, Andrew Jackson Building, Nashville, TN 37219, 615-741-2546 (toll-free number in Tennessee: 1-800-342-8470).

OFFICE OF SMALL BUSINESS
Serves as an information center for new small businesses and a one-stop center for business people in need of information on licenses, permits and taxes. Also assists small businesses in identifying procurement opportunities. Contact: Tennessee Department of Economic and Community Development, Office of Small Business, Room 1025, Andrew Jackson Building, Nashville, TN 37219, 615-741-5020 (toll-free number in Tennessee: 1-800-342-8470).

DEPARTMENT OF ECONOMIC
AND COMMUNITY DEVELOPMENT
Provides information on obtaining a wide variety of loans and grants for use as start-up financing, working capital or funds for expansion. Contact: Tennessee Department of Economic and Community Development, Program Management Section, James K. Polk Building, Nashville, TN 37219, 615-741-6201 (toll-free number in Tennessee: 1-800-342-8470).

TEXAS

REGIONAL BUSINESS DEVELOPMENT CENTER
Specialists work with local chambers of commerce, businessmen and industrial developers to help each part of the state maintain an active, diversified economy. Programs that can assist small businesses include: financial assistance, market development, business location services and information services. Contact: Texas Economic Development Commission, 410 East Fifth Street, PO Box 12728, Capitol Station, Austin, TX 78711, 512-472-5059.

INDUSTRIAL START-UP TRAINING
Program specifically designed to help meet the immediate manpower needs of industries considering plant location in Texas. Contact: Texas Economic Development Commission, Industrial

Locations and Services Department, PO Box 12728, Capitol Station, Austin, TX 78711, 512-472-5059.

BUSINESS REGULATIONS ASSISTANCE CENTER
Information is available for new business start-ups on how to: incorporate, acquire permits and licenses, comply with state requirements and locate assistance and expertise through various state agencies. Contact: Business Regulations Assistance Center, Texas Economic Development Commission, PO Box 12728, Capitol Station, Austin, TX 78711, 512-472-5059.

TEXAS ECONOMIC DEVELOPMENT COMMISSION
The Finance Department administers several financial assistance programs including Industrial Revenue Bonds, Small Business Revitalization, Rural Loan Fund and the Texas Small Business Industrial Development Corporation. Contact: Texas Economic Development Commission, 410 East 5th Street, PO Box 12728, Capitol Station, Austin, TX 78711, 512-472-5059.

ONE-STOP TAX INFORMATION HOTLINE
Provides information on all taxes. Contact: Comptroller of Public Accounts, 111 East 17th Street, Austin, TX 78774, 512-475-1931 (toll-free number in Texas: 1-800-252-5555).

UTAH

SMALL BUSINESS DEVELOPMENT CENTERS
Provide free information and assistance for small businesspersons who wish to start or expand their business. One-on-one counseling is available. For the location of the SBDC serving your area, contact: Small Business Development Center, 660 South-200 East, Room 418, Salt Lake City, UT 84111, 801-581-7905.

CERTIFIED DEVELOPMENT COMPANIES
Provide small businesses with long-term financing for land/building acquisition, and building construction, expansion, renovation and modernization, and machinery and equipment. Maximum CDC Loan amount is 40 percent up to $500,000. Terms are 15,

20 or 25 years. Interest rates are near long-term US Treasury Bond rates. Contact: Utah Division of Economic and Industrial Development, 6150 State Office Building, Salt Lake City, UT 84114, 801-533-5325.

DAVIS COUNTY ECONOMIC DEVELOPMENT DEPARTMENT

Loans can be used for land and building acquisition, building construction and renovation, machinery and equipment and working capital. The maximum participation is 35 percent up to $100,000. Term for capital assets is 5–20 years, for working capital, 3–7 years. Interest rates are negotiable. Contact: Davis County Economic Development Department, PO Box 305, Farmington, UT 84025, 801-451-3264.

VERMONT

SMALL BUSINESS DEVELOPMENT CENTERS

Offer, at little or no cost, the following services: small business workshops, in-depth counseling, business planning, comprehensive resource and information library and a referral system linking other small business assistance organizations. For the location of the SBDC serving your area, contact: Small Business Development Center, University of Vermont Extension Service, Morrill Hall, Burlington, VT 05405, 802-656-4459.

VERMONT INDUSTRIAL DEVELOPMENT AUTHORITY

Makes low-interest (at present 4 percent) loans available to businesses for the purchase or construction of land or buildings, and machinery and equipment for use in an "industrial facility." VIDA may make loans for up to 30 percent of a project, with a local development corporation generally providing 10 percent of the project costs and the balance being loaned by an independent lending institution or government agency. Contact: Vermont Industrial Development Authority, 58 East Street, Montpelier, VT 05602, 802-223-7226.

SMALL BUSINESS REVITALIZATION PROGRAM

Provides long-term debt financing at reasonable rates through the utilization of a combination of federal, state and private

sources of capital. Staff is available to look at borrower's needs
and sort through the variety of public programs to recommend
the best combination financing package to meet those needs.
Contact: The Vermont Agency of Development and Community Affairs, 109 State Street, Montpelier, VT 05602, 802-828-
3221 (toll-free number in Vermont: 1-800-622-4553; out-of-state:
1-800-341-2211).

VIRGINIA

OFFICE OF SMALL BUSINESS
AND FINANCIAL SERVICES
Provides information on sources of technical, management and
financial assistance programs operating throughout Virginia. The
Office has a One-Stop Shop and Clearinghouse for prospective
and established business owners which provides information on
the various state agencies as well as business information. Contact: Office of Small Business and Financial Services, Virginia
Department of Economic Development, 1000 Washington
Building, Richmond, VA 23219, 804-786-3791.

SMALL BUSINESS DEVELOPMENT CENTER
Free services include: management counseling; technical assistance; management training; research, publications, and information; special projects and financial facilitation. Contact: George
Mason University Small Business Development Center, School
of Business Administration, George Mason University, 4400
University Drive, Fairfax, VA 22030, 703-323-2568.

VIRGINIA BUSINESS OPPORTUNITIES
A weekly publication of current business opportunities with the
Commonwealth of Virginia. Cost is $60 per year. Contact: Vir-
ginia Business Opportunities, Virginia Department of General
Services, Division of Purchases and Supply, PO Box 1199, Rich-
mond, VA 23209, 804-786-5494.

SMALL BUSINESS FINANCING AUTHORITY
The Umbrella Industrial Development Bond Program provides
long-term financing of fixed assets through a mechanism gen-

erally available only to larger businesses. Contact: Small Business Financing Authority, 1000 Washington Building, Richmond, VA 23219, 804-786-3791.

INDUSTRIAL REVENUE BONDS
Financing covers the cost of land, buildings, machinery and equipment. Bonds provide up to 100 percent financing, and they permit an interest-cost saving over conventional financing owing to the tax-free interest received by investors who buy the bonds. Contact: Division of Industrial Development, Community Development Division, 1010 State Office Building, Richmond, VA 23219, 804-786-4486.

LOCAL DEVELOPMENT CORPORATIONS
Some LDCs make direct loans to small businesses in their localities. Other services may include site selection and assistance in applying for industrial revenue bonding and Small Business Administration Loans. For the names and addresses of Local Development Corporations in Virginia, contact: Virginia Department of Economic Development, Office of Small Business and Financial Services, 1000 Washington Building, Richmond, VA 23219, 804-786-3791.

SMALL BUSINESS INVESTMENT COMPANIES
Provide equity capital and long-term loans to small firms. Often, a SBIC also provides management assistance to the companies it finances. A SBIC may invest up to 20 percent of its capital in a single small business. All financings must be for at least 5 years, except that a borrower may elect to have a prepayment clause included in the financing agreement. For the names and addresses of SBICs in Virginia, contact: Virginia Department of Economic Development, Office of Small Business and Financial Services, 1000 Washington Building, Richmond, VA 23219, 804-786-3791.

WASHINGTON

OFFICE OF SMALL BUSINESS
Provides information of importance to small businesses through seminars, publications and general counseling. Assists firms

wishing to provide goods and services to state agencies. Refers clients needing in-depth management and technical assistance to appropriate organizations for help. Contact: Office of Small Business, Washington Department of Trade and Economic Development, General Administration Building, Olympia, WA 98504, 206-753-5614.

SMALL BUSINESS DEVELOPMENT CENTERS
Provide assistance with: new business formation, manufacturing counseling, market research, financial counseling, new products evaluation and testing, feasibility studies and organization analyses. For the location of the SBDC serving your area, contact: Small Business Development Center, College of Business and Economics, Washington State University, Pullman, WA 99164, 509-335-1576.

INDUSTRIAL REVENUE BONDS
Eligible projects include only those industrial facilities intended for one of the following purposes: manufacturing, processing, production, assembly, warehousing, transportation, pollution control, solid waste disposal or energy production. Contact: Industrial Development Division, Washington State Department of Commerce and Economic Development, 101 General Administration Building, AX-13, Olympia, WA 98504, 206-753-3065.

COMMUNITY DEVELOPMENT CORPORATIONS
Certified firms under the Small Business Administration 503 Program can lend up to 40 percent of a project's cost up to a maximum of $500,000 for a term of up to 25 years for less than market-rate interest. Contact: Washington Community Development Corporation, 400 108th Street, NE, Suite 300, Bellevue, WA 98004, 206-454-4188.

WEST VIRGINIA

WEST VIRGINIA DIVISION OF SMALL BUSINESS
Offers a one-stop resource center to supply and assist with the filing of state and federal forms. Programs include: managerial and technical assistance, financial resources/loan packaging, ed-

ucation and training, procurement, advocacy, legislation and Minority Business Enterprise/Women-owned Business Enterprise Program. Contact: Small Business Division, State Capitol Complex, Charleston, WV 25305, 304-348-2960 (toll-free number in West Virginia: 1-800-Call WVA).

WEST VIRGINIA DEVELOPMENT AUTHORITY DIRECT LOANS

Offers a direct loan to your company at low interest with flexible terms for up to 50 percent of the project. General ceiling on any loan has been $500,000. Contact: Small Business Division, State Capitol Complex, Charleston, WV 25305, 304-348-2960 (toll-free number in West Virginia: 1-800-CALL WVA).

WEST VIRGINIA CERTIFIED DEVELOPMENT CORPORATION

Provides long-term fixed-rate loans for small- and medium-sized firms. Interest rates will be tied to rates on US Treasury Bills at the time the loan is made. The maximum amount for which a loan can be made under this program is $500,000. Contact: Small Business Division, State Capitol Complex, Charleston, WV 25303, 304-348-2960 (toll-free number in West Virginia: 1-800-CALL WVA).

WISCONSIN

SMALL BUSINESS DEVELOPMENT CENTERS

Provide free information and assistance for small businesspersons who wish to start or expand their business. One-on-one counseling is available. For the location of the SBDC serving your area, contact: Small Business Development Center, 602 State Street, Madison, WI 53703-1099, 608-263-7766.

CUSTOMIZED LABOR-TRAINING FUNDS

Trains or retrains Wisconsin workers in order to provide the skilled labor required for business development and employment. Businesses must submit an application to qualify. Contact: Wisconsin Department of Development, 123 West Washington Avenue, Madison, WI 53702, 608-266-1018.

PERMIT INFORMATION CENTER

Provides information on obtaining all permits necessary to do business in Wisconsin. Contact: Wisconsin Department of Development, Permit Information Center, 123 West Washington Avenue, PO Box 7970, Madison, WI 53707, 608-266-1018 (toll-free number in Wisconsin: 1-800-HELP BUS).

WISCONSIN DEPARTMENT OF DEVELOPMENT

Provides a booklet which contains a complete listing and brief description of the many federal, state and local financing programs available to businesses. Financing may be used for long-term capital, working capital, unforeseen damages, export financing, research grants, labor training, etc., depending upon the program. Contact: Wisconsin Department of Development, 123 West Washington Avenue, PO Box 7970, Madison, WI 53707, 608-266-1018.

SMALL ENTERPRISE ECONOMIC DEVELOPMENT (SEED) PROGRAM

Offers long-term, fixed-rate financing to small- and medium-sized businesses at less than prime rate. An eligible borrower is a business or an individual affiliated with a business which has current gross annual sales of $35 million or less, a satisfactory credit history and an ability to support debt service. SEED money can be used for the purchase, expansion and improvement of land, plant and equipment and for depreciable research and development expenditures, so long as such projects result in the creation and maintenance of jobs. Contact: Wisconsin Housing and Economic Development Authority, James Wilson Plaza, Suite 300, 131 West Wilson Street, Madison, WI 53701-1728, 608-266-7884.

WISCONSIN BUSINESS DEVELOPMENT FINANCE CORPORATION

Participates with financial institutions to provide small businesses with financing for up to 25 years. This can be used to purchase land and buildings and machinery and equipment and for construction and modernization of facilities. Financing can vary from $100,000 to $500,000. Interest rates are always less than conventional financing. Contact: Wisconsin Business Development Finance Corporation, PO Box 2717, Madison, WI 53701-2717, 608-258-8830.

WYOMING

SMALL BUSINESS INSTITUTE
Twice a year, the Small Business Institute coordinates semester-long (3–4 months) projects throughout the state matching small businesses with upper level business students and faculty in the University of Wyoming's College of Commerce and Industry. Normally, two students and one faculty member, with expertise in the project's area, work as a team in whatever type of business consultation is required by the small business. This service is provided by the Wyoming business community at no charge to the client business. Contact: Institute of Business and Management Services, College of Commerce and Industry, PO Box 3275, University Station, University of Wyoming, Laramie, WY 82071, 307-766-2363.

WYOMING BUSINESS DEVELOPMENT CENTERS
Provide free counseling services to small businesses. Also offer seminars and small business management classes. For the location of the BDC serving your area, contact: Wyoming Business Development Center, 944 East Second Street, Casper, WY 82601, 307-235-4825.

JOB TRAINING PARTNERSHIP ACT
Provides funds to support worker training and retraining. Can provide direct subsidies up to 50 percent of wages during on-the-job training as well as for support services. Contact: Division of Manpower Planning, Barrett Building, Cheyenne, WY 82002, 307-777-7671.

WYOMING DEPARTMENT OF ECONOMIC PLANNING AND DEVELOPMENT
Provides a comprehensive package of available financing. Programs include: Block Grants, Industrial Revenue Bonds, Small Business Administration 503 Loan Program and others. Contact: Wyoming Department of Economic Planning and De-

velopment, Herschler Building, Cheyenne, WY 82002, 307-777-7285 (toll-free number: 1-800-262-3425).

CAPITAL CORPORATION OF WYOMING, INC.
Financing available for new facilities, plant expansion, shops and warehouses, professional offices and equipment inventory or venture capital. Provides equity financing to expanding businesses and new business start-ups. Contact: Capital Corporation of Wyoming, Inc., Box 612, Casper, WY 82602, 307-235-5438.

LOCAL DEVELOPMENT COMPANIES
Provide financial assistance and information on sites, buildings or other capital goods available for firms in their area. They work with private funds raised through the sale of stock, subscriptions or contributions, or by notes of indebtedness. For the names and addresses of the approximately 28 local development companies in Wyoming, contact: Wyoming Department of Economic Planning and Development, Herschler Building, Cheyenne, WY 82002, 307-777-7285 (toll-free number: 1-800-262-3425).

EXAMPLES

The examples that follow are grouped into nine topical categories. Each shows how specific individuals and organizations have used a government program to improve themselves or their environment.

PURSUING THE ARTS

Artists and scholars can obtain government funds to help them through their struggling periods as well as their prosperous ones. The following stories show how some of the famous and not-so-famous have used government funds to help their careers.

Students Take a Walk for the Humanities. Nine students at Oberlin College walked 412 miles in January 1980, financed by a $10,000 youth grant from the National Endowment for the Humanities (program #45.115). The students were following the exact route taken by hundreds of escaping slaves on the Underground Railway during the mid-nineteenth century. At stops along the way, the students gave a slide presentation on the Underground Railway, generating great interest in the historical significance of the region.

Texas Choreographer Receives $7,500. Deborah Hay, a choreographer in Austin, Texas, received $7,500 worth of grants (program #45.002), which enabled her to rent rehearsal space, pay dancers and choreograph.

Young Filmmaker Preserves Harlem's Cotton Club. The historical and musical importance of the Cotton Club, Harlem's most famous nightclub and the showcase of some of the best-known black performers, including Duke Ellington and Billie Holiday, is being preserved on film thanks to a youth grant (program #45.115) from the National Endowment for the Humanities. A twenty-five-year-old filmmaker (youth grants are made to individuals under the age of thirty) received a $10,000 grant in 1979 to make his film on the Cotton Club. The money was used to offset the cost of collecting old film clips and still photos and to film interviews with people associated with the club in its heyday.

Gloria Steinem Among Distinguished Fellows. The Smithsonian Institution's Woodrow Wilson International Center for Scholars offers year-long fellowships (program #60.020) for scholars and other distinguished individuals from nonacademic professions. Here are a few examples from recent years:

- Robert Donovan, author and journalist, did research for a book on "National Security Policy in President Harry S Truman's Second Term in Office."
- Polish scholar Bronislaw Geremek, director of medieval studies at the Academy of Sciences in Warsaw, worked on "Social Marginality in the Pre-Industrial Age."
- Journalist Gloria Steinem investigated "Feminism and Its Impact on the Premises and Goals of Current Political Theory."

All Kinds of Music. The National Endowment for the Arts funds a variety of musicians and composers under its music programs (#45.005 and #45.014). Here is a sampling:

- The Amarillo Symphony in Amarillo, Texas, received an $8,000 grant in 1980 to support the continuation of concerts in the schools in the region and to help pay traveling expenses of guest artists.
- Joseph Schwantner wrote "Aftertones of Infinity" while he was receiving a $7,500 Arts Endowment music grant in 1979. His orchestral composition went on to win the 1979 Pulitzer prize for music.
- Jazz saxophonist Jimmy Giuffre of West Stockbridge, Massachusetts, was the recipient of a $10,000 grant which helped support him while he composed and performed.
- Music lovers in West Virginia will continue to hear performances by the Charleston Symphony Orchestra in their hometowns as a result of a $15,000 grant given to defray the costs of the orchestra's extensive touring program throughout the state.

Support for Rural Theater in Iowa. The Old Creamery Theater in Garrison, Iowa, provides live theater to folks who normally wouldn't see it: farmers in the rural areas of Iowa. Because it plays on tour and gives workshops in acting and other phases of the theater, the Old Creamery has received more than $50,000 from the National Endowment for the Arts (program #45.010). In addition, it has received $1,500 in 1980 and $5,000 in 1981 (program #45.008) to subsidize its resident theater program.

Grants Help Filmmakers Win Academy Awards. In 1975 a filmmaker named Barbara Kopple received a grant (program #45.006) of $27,980 to make a movie about coal miners. The film, *Harlan County, U.S.A.*, went on to win an Academy Award for feature documentaries in 1976. The same program gave Ira Wohl $25,000 in 1978 to help him with the costs of a movie he was making about a retarded member of his family. The film, *Best Boy*, won the feature documentary Academy Award in 1979.

Getting Seen in the Visual Arts. Two examples of artists who received money from the Arts Endowment's Visual Arts Program (#45.009) follow:

- Ed Ruscha, a Los Angeles painter and printmaker, received $5,000 in 1967 to work on his art. Since then, he has become well known and widely admired in art circles.
- In 1972, Robert Arneston obtained a $7,500 grant to work on ceramics. Arneston's pieces are now featured in major exhibitions and are in the collections of many major American museums.

Researchers Can Work with Smithsonian Specialists. Each year scholars performing pre- and postdoctoral research are selected to receive an average stipend of $14,000 to work for one year with Smithsonian specialists (program #60.001). Recent projects included "The 1940s in New York—Radical Politics and Avant Garde Art"; "A History of Music in the White House"; "Research in Experimental Radio Astronomy" and "Socioecology of Venezuelan Red Howler Monkeys."

Funding for Writers. The following are writers who received grants ranging from $5,000 to $6,000 from the National Endowment for the Arts Literature Program (#45.004) in the early to mid-1970s: Alice Adams, author of *Families and Survivors* and *Listening to Billie;* Erica Jong, author of *Fear of Flying* and *Fanny;* William Gaddis, author of *JR*, which won a National Book Award, and John Milton, author of *Notes to a Bald Buffalo*. Poets who have benefited from the program include Lucille Clifton, Daniel Mark Epstein, Linda Pastan, and Charles Wright.

BUSINESS

There are close to two hundred programs available to entrepreneurs and corporations. These programs range from providing a few thousand dollars of seed money for a part-time venture to the well-publicized $500 million loan guarantee for the Chrysler Corporation. For complete coverage of financial assistance available to the business community, review the programs available within the following organizations:

US Department of Agriculture
US Department of Commerce
US Department of Defense
US Department of Health and Human Services
US Department of Housing and Urban Development
US Department of the Interior
US Department of Labor
US Department of State
US Department of Transportation
US Department of the Treasury
Equal Employment Opportunity Commission
Federal Trade Commission
General Services Administration
Community Services Administration
Small Business Administration
Overseas Private Investment Corporation
Department of Energy
Federal Emergency Management Agency

The stories presented below show how various individuals and corporations have used government programs to start or help their businesses. In each case a federal program was used to help fulfill the dreams of a small businessman or woman, as well as to provide employment and economic opportunity to members of the local community.

Posh Health Spa Saved. The Golden Door, one of the country's most glamorous health spas, was once threatened with a major setback when it was notified that its facility stood in the path of a proposed freeway. Undaunted, owner Deborah Magganti applied for and received $1.75 million worth of technical and financial assistance from the Small Business Administration (program #59.009) to build a new fitness farm that now counts famous Hollywood personalities among its regular customers.

Loans for Lucille's Auto Shop. A $25,000 Small Business Administration loan (program #59.012) provided the working capital for the first woman-owned automobile transmission repair shop in the United States. "Transmissions by Lucille" in Pittsburgh opened its doors in 1975 and has grown into a half-million-dollar business, employing eighteen people, most of whom are men.

Insurance for U.S. Plants Abroad. In order to protect its investment in the troubled Middle East, Baldwin Piano Company received $162,000 worth of Foreign Investment Insurance (program #70.003) for its plant in Israel. This insurance, offered by the Overseas Private Investment Corporation, protects Baldwin against the threat of war, revolution and expropriation.

Jimmy Carter and Miss Lillian. In 1962 Jimmy Carter and his mother, Miss Lillian, received a $175,000 Small Business Administration loan (program #59.012) to construct a cotton gin building, a cotton warehouse and an office building. They also used the money to buy and install machinery and equipment. The loan was fully paid off on schedule.

From Family Business to Fortune 500. When Rose and Jim Totino decided to expand the market for the pizzas that were so popular at their restaurant in Minneapolis, a $50,000 Small Business Administration loan (program #59.012) enabled them to open a pizza manufacturing plant. Totino's Finer Foods grew from 25 pies a week to 200,000 daily. The business was then purchased by the Pillsbury Company and Mrs. Totino was named a corporate vice president, the first woman to hold the position in the firm's history.

Dairy Man Parlays Excess Cream into Ice Cream Parlor. The owner of a dairy in Wilkes-Barre, Pennsylvania, decided that the best way to dispose of his dairy's excess cream was to start his own ice cream parlor and restaurant. After local banks refused to lend him the $550,000 needed to open the restaurant, the Department of Agriculture agreed to guarantee the loan through their Business and Industry Loan Program (#10.422). The restaurant now provides an outlet for the dairy's excess cream as well as jobs for some eighty-five area residents.

Cure for Nursing Home. A small nursing home failed to meet state requirements and was faced with a shutdown. The facilities required a costly new fire sprinkler system along with a number of new beds. Because the owner was a woman and lived in a rural section of Ohio, the Department of Agriculture provided her with a $90,000 insured loan (program #10.422) to purchase the needed equipment.

Money to Meet OSHA Standards. The Maywood Packing Company, an olive-packing business in Corning, California, was about to go out of business because its aging plant failed to meet many of the requirements of the Occupational Safety and Health Act (OSHA). Maywood was the community's largest employer, and if it closed, 250 people would be left jobless. A $696,700 loan from the Small Business Administration (program #59.012) saved the day. Most of the money was used to reconstruct the facility in order to meet OSHA standards. The remaining $50,000 was earmarked for working capital in order to carry the business during the eight-month construction period.

Millions for Small Business. A $24 million loan guarantee from the Department of Commerce (program #20.802) enabled a small Philadelphia-based shipping concern to purchase a $30 million oil tanker. In another case, the Department of Commerce guaranteed a $5 million loan (program #20.802) that enabled a Chicago-area shipper to purchase three new barges for the transportation of petroleum products on the Great Lakes.

Big Catch for Small Fisherman. A shrimp boat operator in Louisiana made his living on an old but reliable boat. When the boat finally broke down, the fisherman faced paying $400,000 for a new boat or going out of business. Luckily he was able to qualify for a Department of Commerce fishing vessel loan (program #11.415) which provided him with the needed money at a lower interest rate and longer payment schedule than standard commercial financing.

Condemned Sausage Company Salvaged. In 1972 Discovery Foods, a successful sausage and meat processing factory in Los Angeles, was facing a forced shutdown because it had failed to meet consumer health standards. A $1,250,000 loan from the Small Business Administration (program #59.012) provided the money to construct a new processing plant. The facility contained costly cooking and refrigeration machinery that enabled it to comply with health standards.

Baseball Star Hits Home Run with SBA. Lou Brock, a former major league baseball star who holds the all-time record for stolen bases, received a $100,000 loan guarantee from the Small Business Administration (program #59.012) to buy a Dodge dealership in East St. Louis, Illinois.

Franchising Made Easy. Three businessmen in a suburb of Detroit decided to pool their resources and buy a Dunkin' Donuts franchise. Because none of them had any experience running a restaurant, the local banks refused to provide them with additional financing. So they applied to the Small Business Administration and received a 90 percent guarantee on a $265,000 loan (program #59.012). In 1980, when they started their Dunkin' Donuts, they expected sales to reach $5,000 a week eventually. To their surprise, they earned more than that the first week they were open.

Black Entrepreneur Breaks into New Market. In 1976 Teddy Jackson and a friend turned to the Philadelphia Minority Business Development Center to help start their own fuel oil company. The Center financed the acquisition of an inland oil terminal facility worth $60,000 (program #11.800). This help made Jackson one of the few minority entrepreneurs in this country to own a bulk-fuel terminal. In a seven-year span, Jackson's firm grew from $60,000 in sales to more than $15 million, and at age 29 Jackson became one of the youngest black entrepreneurs in the fuel oil business. His major clients now include the city of Philadelphia, the Commonwealth of Pennsylvania, the federal government, Philadelphia Electric and Amtrak.

Hawaiian Dairy Business Saved. Dairy cows in Hawaii are fed leaves from pineapple plants that have been sprayed with a pesticide called hepticlore. However, before the leaves are edible they must be set aside until the pesticide decays. In 1982, on the island of Oahu, the leaves were not set aside long enough, and the pesticide contaminated the milk of many of the cows. At the request of the dairy farmers, more than $7 million was provided through the Dairy Indemnity Payments program (#10.053) to cover the losses faced by the dairy farmers, allowing them to keep the cows' milk off the market until the problem cleared up.

Cuban Is No Chicken. Frank Hernandez, a Cuban living in Florida, took out a Direct Investment Loan (program #70.005) for $1 million in order to set up a poultry farm in the Dominican Republic. No sooner had he set up the business than a bad storm hit the island and ruined his farm. He took out yet another loan (#70.005) to set up the farm again. His enterprise is doing so well that he is now thinking of setting up another farm in Morocco.

New Factory Supported by SBA. Louis F. Ruiz of Tulare, California, started a business in 1967 selling Mexican foods. Initially he sold 14,000 shares of stock to local residents to raise start-up capital. The business was an instant success, as sales grew from $40,000 to $500,000 in just one year. However, Mr. Ruiz soon faced financial difficulties. California meat inspectors found that his plant did not meet federal standards, and he faced a choice of either building/buying a new plant or going out of business. He decided to build and turned to the Minority Business Development Agency for assistance in obtaining a $500,000 loan from the Small Business Administration (program #11.800) to build the new plant. Ruiz now has a new factory, and the business keeps growing.

For additional business examples see the section on Rural Living (page 127). A handy compilation of the various money and nonmoney programs available to business is presented in *Handbook for Small Business: A Survey of Small Business Programs of the Federal Government* ($6.50). Copies are available from:

Superintendent of Documents
US Government Printing Office
Washington, DC 20402
202-783-3238

EDUCATION

Individuals can advance their education with federal funds through a wide range of programs that offer money either directly or indirectly through financial institutions, schools, social service organizations and nonprofit groups. Although most of the money is from the Department of Education, there are a number of educational opportunities scattered throughout the government. The stories below describe many of the major programs.

Upward Bound Pulls Up Neglected Iowan. A young cerebral palsy victim in Iowa was neglected by his parents. He was forced to sleep alone in an unheated bedroom and sent to public schools while his brothers and sisters attended private schools. No one seemed to care about him until he joined Upward Bound (program #84.047). The program provided him with extensive counseling and tutoring in reading, writing and speech. His grades improved, and he was accepted at a local college. He is now a counselor at a school in Minnesota working with mentally and physically impaired students and adults.

Bilingual Program Trains Machine Operator. In 1975 a Spanish-speaking machine operator in New York City lost his job of fifteen years when a local textile factory closed down. Through the Department of Education's Bilingual Vocational Training Program (#84.077), he took courses in basic maintenance and was hired as a maintenance man at a large New York housing project. He continued to take advanced courses through the program and today he supervises a crew of fifteen maintenance men.

Work-Study Helps Pay for Student's Studies. The Department of Education's College Work-Study Program (#84.033) provides money to colleges and universities for up to 80 percent of the salaries of part-time jobs held by students in financial need. For example, a student in Massachusetts was able to support his day-to-day expenses and pay part of his tuition by working about fifteen hours a week clearing tables and serving meals in the school dining hall. Other typical positions funded under the program include work in libraries, athletic facilities and departmental offices.

From Maine Marines to Nuclear Navy. State marine schools, which receive support from the federal government (program #20.806), offer a low-cost education for future engineers and shipbuilders. For example, a student from Maine entered the Maine Maritime Academy in 1964. Upon graduation he fulfilled a three-year commitment to the school by working as an engineer on an oil tanker in the US Merchant Marine. After completing his stint at sea, he took a job at a steam turbine manufacturing company and a year and a half later joined a shipbuilding firm, where he helped design a power plant for a nuclear-powered submarine.

German Studies Lead to Book, Articles, Course and Award. Wayne Thompson, a professor at Lynchburg College, a school of 2,200 students in Lynchburg, Virginia, received a $15,000 stipend in 1977 from the National Endowment for the Humanities (program #45.143). Thompson used the fellowship to attend the University of California at Santa Barbara, where he researched the topic "German Social Democracy in the 20th Century." Out of his fellowship work came a book, *In the Eye of the Storm: Kurt Riezler and the Crisis of Modern Germany,* and five articles published in scholarly journals. In addition, Thompson initiated a new course at Lynchburg College, "German Political Thought," and was given a faculty award for distinguished scholarship by his colleagues.

Supplemental Funds Make Ends Meet. A Department of Education Supplemental Educational Opportunity Grants program (#84.007) gives money to colleges that use it to subsidize the tuition of poverty-stricken students. For example, Tri-County Technical College in Pendleton, South Carolina, received $43,000 worth of supplemental grant money in 1980. This money in turn was parceled out to extremely needy students, allowing them to complete their college education.

Counselor Cuts College Costs. A young woman hoped to attend a college that charges $3,600 a year, but her parents were afraid that the cost would be too much for them to bear. After consulting her high school counselor, she discovered that she was eligible for a $1,300-a-year educational opportunity grant from the Department of Education (program #84.063).

Famous Fulbrights. Fulbright Scholarships (program #82.001) enable talented students to spend a year studying abroad. Here are some of the more well-known Fulbright scholars: Harrison Schmitt, the Republican senator from New Mexico and a former astronaut, received a Fulbright in 1957 to study geology at the University of Oslo. One of his Senate colleagues, Senator Daniel Patrick Moynihan, Democrat from New York, studied at the London School of Economics under a Fulbright Scholarship in 1950. Opera star Anna Moffo went to Italy in 1954. Dancer Yuriko Kimura received a scholarship in 1966 to study modern dance with Martha Graham.

Education Loans for RNs. Prospective nurses can receive government money to help pay for nursing school. Under the Department of Health and Human Services Nursing Student Loans program (#13.364), Arizona State University in Tempe, Arizona, received $33,000 in nursing loan funds to help defray tuition costs for full- or part-time students in the nursing baccalaureate program.

Cure for Medical School Bill. Dr. David B. Flannery made it through his last two years of medical school with the help of a National Health Service Corps Scholarship (program #13.288). After he completed his three years of residency in 1979, Dr. Flannery, a pediatrician, repaid his scholarship by serving two years as head of the Louisa Health Center for Young People in Louisa, Virginia (population 2,000).

Loan Helps Student to Attend College of His Choice. The college education of a New Jersey student was made possible by a Department of Education guaranteed student loan (program #84.032). The student's mother, a widow, could afford to send her son to a local school, but he wanted to attend a more costly out-of-state college. A guaranteed loan made by a local bank— $5,500 at 7 percent interest paid out over four years—helped cover the additional expense. The student is now paying off the loan in monthly installments spread over ten years.

Heritage Helps Man Get Financial Aid for College. A young married man, one of whose parents was a full-blooded Sioux Indian, wanted to become a doctor but did not have the funds to support his family while he went back to school. He applied for an Indian Education Grant (program #15.114) in order to go to the University of North Dakota, and received an $8,000 grant. The money enabled him to major in medicine with a minor in biology, and he eventually graduated with a degree in medicine.

For a free booklet describing six federal financial aid programs for college students, "Student Consumer's Guide," contact:

> US Department of Education
> P.O. Box 84
> Washington, DC 20033
> 800-638-6700
> (in Maryland, 800-492-6602)

ENERGY

Although the actual number of energy-related programs is small, their growth is something to watch. It appears that a new program is created every week. In no time at all, the number of energy programs may outnumber those for agriculture. The following stories identify the major programs available.

Conservation Grants to Schools. Chadron State College in Nebraska received an $18,000 grant from the Department of Energy (program #81.052) to insulate a classroom building and install thermostats that automatically lower classroom temperatures at night. Energy savings amounted to more than $6,000 a year.

Energy Audits Reduce Consumption. Money from the Department of Energy's State Energy Conservation program (#81.041) is being put to use in Rhode Island to cut heating bills. Since 1978 the Rhode Island state energy office has channeled $75,000 to a nonprofit corporation named RISE (Rhode Island Is Saving Energy), which provides free energy audits and also suggests ways to reduce energy consumption. In one particularly successful example of RISE's work, the consumption of heating oil at a large older home in Providence dropped from

23 gallons per day to 12 gallons after the owners received their free energy audit and decided to insulate their home.

Thermal Window Blinds. Alan Ross of Brattleboro, Vermont, received an $8,000 grant from the Energy Department's Appropriate Technology program (#81.051) to design and produce thermal insulating window blinds made from paper boxboard, jute, pine and reflective foil.

Photoelectric Cells Get Boost. Two loans from the Small Business Energy Loan Program (#59.030) worth $350,000 provided working capital to SOLEC International, Inc., and enabled the Los Angeles firm to buy sophisticated machinery to manufacture photoelectric cells that transform the sun's rays into electric energy. SOLEC's products have had many successful applications and have been used in devices to activate attic fans and to recharge batteries of boats at sea.

Weatherization Lowers Fuel Bills. From 1976 through 1979 low-income residents of Pennsylvania saved more than $5 million on their fuel bills. They participated in a Department of Energy grant program (#81.042) that gives money to low-income citizens to insulate and otherwise weatherize their homes. The money is sent to states and distributed to individuals through local nonprofit community action agencies. During the first four years of the program more than 50,000 homes received weatherization treatment, including storm windows, insulation and weather stripping.

Dallas Goes Big for Conservation. The Texas state energy office is using the Department of Energy's Energy Extension Service program (#81.050) to help individuals and small businesses resolve energy problems. The $800,000 received in 1980 was distributed throughout the state to perform energy audits on homes and small businesses and to give workshops for businessmen on how to save energy in their offices and stores. In Dallas alone, more than 200 energy audits were performed in the first half of 1980.

Stove Business Gets Hot. A nonprofit community action group in Vermont began making wood-burning stoves with the help of a $45,000 grant from the New England Regional Commission.

The plant, which began in 1975, was manned by local residents whose wages were paid by funds from the CETA program (#17.232). The stoves were originally given away or sold at reduced prices to low-income people in the area, but as word of the new stove spread, demand increased and the operation started to show a profit. Its success almost stopped federal funding until new regulations were promulgated that allowed the community action agency to own 51 percent of the stovemaking company as long as all profits were ear-marked for economic development projects. To set the new, profit-making firm on its feet, the Community Services Administration awarded it an Emergency Energy Conservation Services Program grant for $172,500.

First Grant for Electric Vehicle Manufacturers. Electric Vehicle Associates, Inc., in Cleveland, Ohio, is the first firm in the nation to receive a loan guarantee under the Energy Department's loan program (#81.036). The company received $2.5 million in 1980 to produce electric-powered cars. The money was used for working capital, equipment, expenses and other costs associated with transforming Ford Fairmonts into electric cars.

Success in Hot Water. An inventor in New Orleans, Harry E. Wood, received a $72,000 grant from the Department of Energy (program #81.036) to perfect his design of a high-efficiency water heater. The grant enabled Wood to construct and install a large water heater in an apartment building. The experimental unit worked so well that Wood subsequently received orders for eight more of the heaters.

Resort No Longer Suffers from Gas Shortage. Business at La Cortina, a year-round recreational facility in Killington, Vermont, suffered badly during the gasoline shortage in the summer of 1974. The future of the lodge seemed uncertain until the Small Business Administration granted it a $40,000 emergency loan (program #59.012). The loan saved the day, allowing La Cortina's owners to gear up for the winter season.

Inventors of Energy Products Succeed Thanks to Uncle Sam. The Department of Energy looks for energy-saving inventions (program #81.036) and provides grants averaging $70,000 to help inventors launch their business. Here are two recent examples:

A 27-year-old inventor from upstate New York invented a rubber extrusion solar collector that could be unrolled and cut off to whatever size necessary. He tried to market the product, but in the beginning he didn't have the necessary credibility to obtain the needed financial backing. He applied to the Department of Energy, Energy-Related Inventions Program (#81.036), and received a grant to launch his business. In a few short years, his company, called Solar Roll, began selling the product all over the world and it has made the young inventor a millionaire.

Dan Benshmul, an inventor from New York, designed a unique method of recovering heat from chimneys and furnaces. With a grant from the Department of Energy (program #81.036) he was able to start a business and began selling his invention to industries. He now runs a thriving business selling to furnace installers and looks forward to entering the consumer market. A home version of his product is now included in the Sears Roebuck catalog.

Energy Projects from Solar to Wind Funded. The Department of Energy also offers grants ranging from $350 to $50,000 to encourage the development of new forms of energy-related technology (program #81.051). Here are four recent examples:

A group of private citizens in Arizona received the necessary funding to design an integrated, renewable energy farm system, which includes a solar box oven, a greenhouse and a food dryer. Eventually it will also include refrigeration.

The citizens of Calienta, Nevada, a remote low-income community, received funding to devise a geothermal system, which has resulted in significant energy savings for the community.

The Paiute Indian tribe in Nevada received the financing to install a solar energy system for their fish hatchery, where the fish must be raised in such an even temperature that both heating and cooling are necessary.

A Guam resident was able to finance the construction of a lighted navigation buoy system powered by wind generators. The buoys, which help guide fishing and recreational boats, enable fishermen to work after sunset.

BUYING AND IMPROVING A HOME

The examples in this section will refer only to single-family dwellings. There are a large number of programs covering multifamily dwellings, and most of these can be found within the Departments of Agriculture and Housing and Urban Development.

Hill House Gets HUD Help. Terry Savage of Lolo, Montana, built his home into the side of a hill in order to retain the earth's heat. As an experimental home, it qualified for the Department of Housing and Urban Development's mortgage insurance for unusual domiciles (program #14.152). Tapping another source of money, Savage obtained a grant from the state of Montana to build a small-scale hydroelectric dam in a nearby stream to generate his own electricity.

Condos and Co-ops. The Department of Housing and Urban Development provides mortgage insurance to help individuals buy condominiums (program #14.133) and cooperative apartments (program #14.163). In Washington, D.C., for example, long-time residents of areas undergoing rehabilitation were being forced out of their apartments as their buildings were converted into condominiums. With the help of HUD mortgage insurance, they were able to buy their own apartments and remain in their neighborhoods.

Advantages to Older Areas. Rundown areas of St. Petersburg, Florida, are being revitalized as a result of a mortgage insurance program administered by the Department of Housing and Urban Development (program #14.123). Young people settling in St. Petersburg can use the money not only to buy their homes but also to repair and reconstruct them.

Solar Outhouse. A man in Jamestown, Missouri, received a $1,200 grant from the Department of Energy (program #81.051) in 1979 to design and build a solar-heated outhouse. The "Above Ground Aerobic and Solar-Assisted Composting Toilet" uses solar heat to warm the structure and to aid the decomposition of waste material.

Solar Fence Keeps in Pigs. The Department of Energy awarded a $1,120 grant (program #81.051) to Dr. David A. Sleep, Department of Agriculture, American Samoa Government in Pago Pago, to build a solar-powered electric fence. The fence was built to enclose wild pigs that had been overrunning a part of the island not served by electrical power.

Couple's First House. A young married couple living outside Cleveland were eager to buy a house before their first child was born. But because they were young and had yet to establish a credit rating, private banks refused to give them a mortgage. Luckily they qualified for mortgage insurance issued by the Department of Housing and Urban Development (program #14.117). They got their house, and thanks to the HUD insurance, their down payment and interest rates were lower than on conventional mortgages.

Rehabilitation Loan Reduces Monthly Payments. In the late 1970s a young couple in Bradford, Pennsylvania, bought a large old home that was in dire need of repair. Almost immediately they began to have trouble meeting their monthly mortgage payments. They discovered, however, they were eligible for a Section 312 Rehabilitation Loan from the Department of Housing and Urban Development (program #14.220), which enabled them to refinance their mortgage and drastically reduce their monthly payments.

Veteran Keeps Moving Up. The Veterans Administration's Direct Loans program enabled a young Vietnam veteran to buy a house even though his financial resources were scarce. In 1975 the veteran and his wife were living in a small apartment in Pennsylvania. They wanted to buy a house but had never been able to save enough money. The veteran sought advice from his local Veterans Administration office and discovered that he was eligible to receive a $30,000 direct loan (program #64.118) to finance the house they wanted. A few years later their fortunes improved and they decided to move to a bigger house. This time they took advantage of the VA's guaranteed loan program (#64.114) and were able to buy the new house without spending a fortune on the down payment.

First Home Is on Wheels. A young man in Oklahoma was able to buy his first house—a mobile home—with some help from the Department of Housing and Urban Development. Too young to have established a credit rating, the potential homeowner was turned down by local lenders when he applied for a mortgage. With HUD mortgage insurance (program #14.110), however, he secured a loan with a lower down payment than nonguaranteed financing and a reduced rate of interest.

House for $1.00. A divorced mother of two bought a rundown house in 1979 in Columbus, Ohio, for $1.00 through a program funded by the Department of Housing and Urban Development (program #14.222). Before the purchase, the woman, a machinist at a factory, was paying $250 a month to rent an apartment. Working with officials of the state housing agency, she developed a rehabilitation plan for her $1.00 house. After the plan was approved, she received a long-term $10,500 loan to finance the improvements, 20 percent of which she completed herself. Now this urban homesteader owns her home and pays only $140 a month on her improvement loan.

Country Living. Lloyd P. Klabunde, a wheat farmer in Emmet, North Dakota, began his farm career in 1946 on 320 acres of land he rented from a neighbor. As he prospered, he added to his leased land and in 1964 he took out a $48,000 farm ownership loan (program #10.407) from the Department of Agriculture to buy 800 acres of farmland, including the original parcel of 320 acres that constituted his first farm. Klabunde now operates an 1,800-acre farm (he rents the additional 1,000 acres) and is one of the most successful farmers in the region.

For additional examples see the section on Rural Living (page 127).

GETTING A JOB

In addition to direct employment, the government offers a wide range of programs with employment opportunities. Here are a few examples.

Job Corps Student Gets Top Job. James Daniels was out of school and out of work when he joined the Job Corps (program

#17.232) in 1966. He was hired as a security officer at a Job Corps Center in Kentucky and resumed school part-time. In 1977 Daniels received his bachelor's degree in sociology from Indiana State University and was named manager of residential living at the Job Corps Center in Crystal Springs, Mississippi. The following year he was made director of the Crystal Springs Center. He is the first person helped by the Job Corps to head a Job Corps Center.

Help for Those Hurt by Imports. It looked as if a laid-off assembly line worker near Jackson, Mississippi, would have to put his house on the market to make ends meet. He lost his job when the electronics company he worked for cut back production owing to competition from low-cost imports. His savings were almost gone when he took advantage of the Department of Labor's weekly trade readjustment allowance (program #17.245) to supplement his unemployment income. The extra money meant that the family home was saved.

Welfare Mother Wins Job. A mother of five in Lowell, Massachusetts, had been collecting welfare for five years when she joined the Department of Labor's Work Incentive program (#13.646). A high school graduate, she received counseling and training at the local Work Incentive (WIN) program office and was accepted into a technical institute, where she received training in computer sciences. WIN paid her tuition. Upon graduation, she took a job as a computer technician earning over $5 per hour. She was so pleased with the position, she urged her sister to enroll in WIN. Her sister is now a wage earner as well.

IMPROVING YOUR NEIGHBORHOOD

There are hundreds of federal programs available that can assist communities in improving their neighborhoods. Although most of the money is earmarked for local governments and nonprofit organizations, individuals can play an instrumental role in obtaining federal funds by identifying a relevant program and helping local government officials prepare the necessary paperwork. Once funds are received, local residents are often hired to become paid directors of the project. Citizens can also band together and form a nonprofit organization to receive federal funds. Here are a few success stories.

Eyesore Transformed into Gym and Playground. Owing to efforts of the local Boys' Club, an abandoned coal bunker in Jersey City, New Jersey, is now the centerpiece of a new park and recreational facility. With a $227,500 grant from the Department of the Interior's Urban Park and Recreation Recovery Program (#15.919), and with additional money from foundations, the local United Way, a local bank, community groups and the Colgate-Palmolive Company, the Boys' Club built a solar-heated swimming pool, a 12,000-square-foot rooftop playground, community and craft rooms and a gymnasium.

Government Subsidizes Home Improvement. Dismayed by the unsightly appearance of homes in a low-income area in Indianapolis, a community group worked through the city government to receive an Urban Development Action Grant (program #14.221) in order to subsidize expensive home improvements. The poor residents received grant money directly to spruce up their homes; higher-income homeowners in the area received partial rebates for their repairs.

Rats on the Run. With the help of a $1.2 million grant from the Department of Health and Human Services (program #13.994), the District of Columbia mounted one of the most successful rat eradication programs in the country. In sections of the city where rats infested as many as 70 percent of the households, the rate was reduced to less than 4 percent.

New Lease on Life for Nursery School. When two women who ran a successful nursery school were informed that they were going to lose their lease, they applied for a $45,000 Department of Agriculture insured loan (program #10.422). The money was used to buy property and put up a new building, thus ensuring the school's survival.

Ski Town Transformed to Resort Area. The famous ski town of Steamboat Springs, Colorado, the home and training ground of more Olympic skiers than any other American ski area, began to develop in the late 1960s thanks to over $5 million worth of loans provided by the Small Business Administration (program

#59.013) in cooperation with a local bank. The money was channeled through a local development company to aid hotels, motels, restaurants, lodges, ranches, campgrounds, an auto dealership, a gas station, a supermarket and ski facilities. As a result, the number of full-time jobs available in Steamboat Springs has more than doubled.

Local Food Bank Flourishes. Two men who ran a dining room in Arizona for the needy in the mid-1960s discovered they could get discarded but edible food free from markets and food processing plants. They soon found that they could obtain so much food that they organized a food bank and began distributing it to other charitable organizations. The Department of Labor (program #17.232) provided them with funds to hire nine staff members, and the Community Services Administration provided them with $160,000 to hold workshops and seminars in communities around the country to spread information about establishing food banks.

Day Care Centers Fortified with Breakfast Program. In 1977 MANNA, a local anti-hunger group in Nashville, Tennessee, generated enough support among teachers, parents and students to force the local school board to adopt a Department of Agriculture free breakfast program (#10.553) in one Nashville school. As the program grew to include other schools so did MANNA. The group now has a staff of 40 and has also received money from a Community Food and Nutrition program as well as the Child Care Food Program (#10.558). The funds are used to feed lower-income preschoolers in local day care centers.

Neighborhood Arts Center Off and Running. The Neighborhood Arts Center in Atlanta, Georgia, got its start in 1975 when a group of community activists blocked the demolition of an old school building and persuaded city officials to rent it for $100 a year. The arts center, which emphasizes black culture, is financed in part by three federal agencies. The National Endowment for the Arts gave it a $22,000 grant (program #45.010) to continue providing cultural outlets to the predominantly black population in the neighborhood. The Department of Agriculture provides funds to serve free lunches to children attending classes during the summer (program #10.559). And salaries of the center's twenty-six-member staff are paid from funds provided by the Department of Labor's Comprehensive Employment and Training Programs (#17.232).

Marine Museum Remains Afloat. The Penobscot Marine Museum continues to serve the community around Searsport, Maine, thanks in part to help from the Department of Education's Institute of Museum Services (program #45.301). The museum's collection features paintings and ship models and is housed in several buildings, including the old town hall and three former homes of sea captains. The $10,000 grant it received in 1980 went to pay for heating, electricity and staff salaries.

Historic Mill Reopens. The historic Valley Falls Mill complex in Central Falls, Rhode Island, is once again operating thanks to help from the Department of the Interior. Built in 1849, the mill was operated until the 1930s when it fell into disrepair. In 1977 the state historic preservation commission conducted a survey of the mill, aided by a $14,000 grant from the Department of the Interior (program #15.904), and placed it on the National Register of Historic Places. A corporation was then founded to rehabilitate the mill, the largest building in the town, to make housing units for senior citizens. In addition to being eligible for the Small Business Administration's section 8(a) funds to finance the rehabilitation, the officers of the for-profit corporation also received a special challenge grant of $240,000 from the Department of the Interior to reactivate the electrical generating capacity of the mill. Now the mill provides the electricity and heat for the entire housing project. The special grant that enabled the corporation to reactivate the mill is similar to another Department of the Interior program (#15.904); this one, however, offered the corporation more money.

Money Channeled for Youngsters. In 1973 the Department of Health and Human Services gave a three-year seed-money grant worth $300,000 to Al Duca, a painter and sculptor in Gloucester, Massachusetts, to refine further his program that kept teenagers drug-free and out of trouble. Seventy percent of the money was used to pay stipends to youngsters involved in useful community projects. The rest financed administrative costs and the development of training programs and materials to spread word of the project. Out of that experiment grew Channel One, an organization primarily supported by local businesses and community agencies, as well as the state and federal governments. In Gloucester, youngsters from all walks of life worked on several projects, including construction of an education center and the restoration of a historic graveyard. Other Channel One programs have sprung up in hundreds of communities across the country, all based on the Gloucester model. And now, in addition to his painting and sculpture, Al Duca works as the Channel One program director for the Gloucester Community Development Corporation.

For additional examples see sections on Rural Living, and on Buying or Improving a House. The 400-page publication, *People Power: What Communities Are Doing to Counter Inflation,* provides countless stories showing how individuals have improved their communities by using federal programs. Copies are free from Consumer Information Center, Department 682-H, Pueblo, CO 81009.

SURPLUS PROPERTY

Not all government programs simply provide money. A number of programs offer surplus property as well as goods and services at no cost, or at prices that would be substantially higher elsewhere. The following list identifies the more popular nonmoney programs:

- Nonprofit organizations can receive free surplus food (program #10.550).
- More than 140 varieties of grasses, legumes, shrubs and trees are free for conservation purposes (program #10.905).
- Tools, machinery and other surplus equipment are free to educational institutions through the Tools for Schools Program of the Department of Defense (program #12.001).
- The Department of Defense offers free ships, cannons, works of art, manuscripts, books and other military property (program #12.700).
- Free pigs, goats and other wild animals are available to nonprofit organizations (program #15.900).

- Federal surplus land can be purchased at substantial savings if used for low- or moderate-income housing (program #14.211).
- Individuals can receive houses for next to nothing in urban areas (program #15.603).
- Surplus automobiles, airplanes, office supplies and other items are free to some and for sale to others (programs #39.002, #39.003, and #39.007).

Also look at the following programs: #13.676, #15.214, #15.217, #15.218, #40.002, #60.013, #68.001, #81.004, #81.022 and #84.145.

RURAL LIVING

Most of us are aware that the Department of Agriculture offers hundreds of programs to help farmers produce, store and market their products. However, what is not so well known is that you can also qualify for Department of Agriculture money if:

- you are not in the agriculture business but are simply living in a small town;
- you are in the winery, beekeeping or aquaculture business;
- you wish to build a tennis court or golf course;
- you are twelve years old and want to start a business.

For a majority of the programs available to farmers and those people living in small towns, review the list described under the Department of Agriculture (page 133). Keep in mind also that small communities can benefit from programs in some of the other government departments, such as the Department of Housing and Urban Development and the Department of Commerce.

The following stories demonstrate how individuals have used Department of Agriculture money and other agencies to resolve other-than-typical farming problems.

Mortgage Money for Young Teachers. A young couple fresh out of college moved to a small Oklahoma town to take teaching jobs. They found a house they wanted to buy for $50,000 but could not meet the local bank's demand for a 20 percent down payment ($10,000). They solved their problem by applying for and receiving an Above-Moderate-Income Housing Loan (program #10.429) which required only a $2,000 down payment.

Barn and Farm Transformed into Golf Course and Clubhouse. A farmer in Alabama received a $22,000 Recreation Facility Loan (program #10.413) to convert part of his land into a nine-hole golf course with a clubhouse. Another Alabama farmer used a $13,000 loan (program #10.413) to help build a 20-acre sport fishing lake complete with cottages and concession stands.

Nearly Half a Million for Catfish. A $400,000 loan (program #10.407) enabled an Arkansas man to start a catfish farm in the southeastern section of the state, where the confluence of several rivers and the ready availability of moisture-holding clay make conditions ideal for aquaculture. The loan was used to construct dams to form breeding and storage pools, build an irrigation and drainage system between the pools, and to buy the land and fish food. The fish are sold cleaned and ready to cook to fishmongers in Arkansas, Tennessee, Kentucky, Illinois and Indiana, and alive to farmers in Indiana and Illinois to stock their sport-fishing ponds.

Loan for Tot Lot and Tennis Courts. The people living in Kinnen, Alabama, lacked local recreational facilities until the town received a $50,000 insured loan from the Department of Agriculture (program #10.423) to build a park, complete with tennis courts, a baseball diamond, a picnic area and a playground for toddlers called a "Tot Lot."

Money for Loss of Honey. In 1971 beekeeper Ken Moore of southwestern Ohio received $6,000 from the Department of Agriculture (program #10.060) when the honey produced from his field bee colony dropped from 40 to 80 pounds per hive to 10 or 12 pounds. Because Mr. Moore's bees were being affected by the insecticide used by local farmers to kill the alfalfa weevil, he was eligible for Beekeeper Indemnity Payments.

Employee Turns Employer. A man in Oil City, Louisiana, was making a good living as a heavy equipment operator for a company that prepared and cleaned up oil well sites, when his employer suddenly died. Because he is a member of a minority group, he was able to obtain a $225,000 insured loan (program #10.422) from the Department of Agriculture to buy the business from the employer's heirs. It is now a true family business. The owner manages the firm's field operations, his son is employed as a heavy equipment operator, and his wife and daughter run the office.

Bouquet from USDA for Winery. After heavy rain wiped out most of the year's crop of raisins, a vineyard owner near Fresno, California, turned to the Department of Agriculture for help. He received a $16,000 operating expenses loan (program #10.406) to hire workers, repair machinery and buildings and buy fertilizer and insurance. In addition, he received a $22,400 equipment loan to buy posts and wire to stake his grape vines properly.

Seed Money for Teenage Entrepreneurs. A group of youngsters in Erie County, Pennsylvania, received a $500 loan from the Department of Agriculture (program #10.406) to buy a young steer. They raised the steer, fattened it up and sold it at the county fair for a profit. A teenager in Pennsylvania received a $500 loan (program #10.406) to start a summer landscaping business on a small scale. The money was used to purchase a lawnmower, grass clippers, saws, pruning shears and other equipment. The initial loan money enabled him to operate his small business for three consecutive summers.

Aid for Small-Town Airlines. Big Sky Transportation Company was started in 1978 to provide commuter air service to small cities and towns in Montana, Idaho and Wyoming. Almost immediately the airline began to run into trouble owing to the harsh Montana winters, which played havoc with the airplanes. Faced with mounting financial woes, the officers of the company looked to federal agencies for help and received a Federal Aviation Administration loan guarantee (program #20.105) worth $500,000 to buy two Cessna airplanes, which were better suited to winter flying conditions than the planes they had. Moreover, another airline, Frontier Airways, decided in 1979 to cancel service to eight small cities in Montana and North Dakota. The Civil Aeronautics Board determined that flights to and from these cities constituted "essential" air service and awarded Big Sky Transportation Company a $15 million one-year subsidy (program #26.003) to take over the route in July 1980. Both sources of federal assistance helped Big Sky turn the corner and develop into a financially healthy enterprise.

PART 2
PROGRAMS

US DEPARTMENT OF AGRICULTURE

AGRICULTURE RESEARCH SERVICE

10.001 AGRICULTURAL RESEARCH— BASIC AND APPLIED RESEARCH

Type of Assistance: Dissemination of technical information and grants from $15,000 to $120,000.

Applicant Eligibility: Individuals, nonprofit organizations, state and local governments.

Objective: To make agricultural research discoveries, evaluate alternative ways of attaining goals and provide scientific and technical information.

Contact: Deputy Director for Agricultural Research Service, Department of Agriculture, Washington, DC 20250, 202-447-3656.

ANIMAL AND PLANT HEALTH INSPECTION SERVICE

10.051 COMMODITY LOANS AND PURCHASES (PRICE SUPPORTS)

Type of Assistance: Direct payments and loans ranging from $50 to $50,000.

Applicant Eligibility: Individuals.

Objective: To improve and stabilize farm income, to assist in bringing about a better balance between supply and demand of the commodities, and to assist farmers in the orderly marketing of their crops.

Contact: Agricultural Stabilization and Conservation Service, Department of Agriculture, PO Box 2415, Washington, DC 20013, Cotton, Grain and Rice Support Division, 202-447-7641; Commodity Operations Division, 202-447-5074.

10.052 COTTON PRODUCTION STABILIZATION (COTTON DIRECT PAYMENTS)

Type of Assistance: Direct payments ranging from $3 to $50,000.

Applicant Eligibility: Individuals.

Objective: To assure adequate cotton production that is needed to meet domestic and foreign demand for fiber, to protect income for farmers and to assure adequate supplies at fair and reasonable prices.

Contact: Commodity Analysis Division, Agricultural Stabilization and Conservation Service, Department of Agriculture, PO Box 2415, Washington, DC 20013, 202-447-6696.

10.053 DAIRY INDEMNITY PROGRAM

Type of Assistance: Direct payments ranging from $849 to $1,119,462.
Applicant Eligibility: Individuals.
Objective: To indemnify dairy farmers and manufacturers of dairy products who are directed to remove their milk, milk cows or dairy products from commercial markets because of contamination with residues of pesticides resulting from no misaction on the part of the dairy farmer or the manufacturer of the dairy product. Fair market value for the milk is paid.
Contact: Emergency Operations and Livestock Division, Agricultural Stabilization and Conservation Service, Department of Agriculture, PO Box 2415, Washington, DC 20013, 202-447-7673.

10.054 EMERGENCY CONSERVATION PROGRAM

Type of Assistance: Direct payments ranging from $3 to $64,000.
Applicant Eligibility: Individuals.
Objective: To enable farmers to perform emergency conservation measures to control wind erosion on farmlands, or to rehabilitate farmlands damaged by wind erosion, floods, hurricanes or other natural disasters; and to carry out emergency water conservation or water-enhancing measures during periods of severe drought.
Contact: Conservation and Environmental Protection Division, Agricultural Stabilization and Conservation Service, Department of Agriculture, PO Box 2415, Washington, DC 20013, 202-447-6221.

10.055 FEED GRAIN PRODUCTION STABILIZATION (FEED GRAIN DIRECT PAYMENTS)

Type of Assistance: Direct payments ranging from $3 to 50,000.
Applicant Eligibility: Individuals.
Objective: To assure adequate production needed to meet domestic and foreign demand, to protect income for farmers and to ensure adequate supplies at fair and reasonable prices.
Contact: Commodity Analysis Division, Agricultural Stabilization and Conservation Service, Department of Agriculture, PO Box 2415, Washington, DC 20013, 202-447-4417.

10.056 STORAGE FACILITIES AND EQUIPMENT LOANS (FARM FACILITY LOANS)

Type of Assistance: Direct loans.
Applicant Eligibility: Individuals.
Objective: To complement the commodity loan and grain reserve programs by providing adequate financing for needed on-farm storage facilities, drying equipment and operating equipment, thereby affording farmers the opportunity for orderly marketing of their crops. Loans are used to finance the purchase of storage structures and to remodel existing facilities.
Contact: Cotton, Grain and Rice Price Support Division, Agricultural Stabilization and Conservation Service, Department of Agriculture, PO Box 2415, Washington, DC 20013, 202-447-5094.

10.058   WHEAT PRODUCTION STABILIZATION (WHEAT DIRECT PAYMENTS)
Type of Assistance: Direct payments ranging from $3 to $50,000.
Applicant Eligibility: Individuals.
Objective: To ensure adequate production that is needed to meet domestic and foreign demand for food, to protect income for farmers and ensure adequate supplies at fair and reasonable prices.
Contact: Commodity Analysis Division, Agricultural Stabilization and Conservation Service, Department of Agriculture, PO Box 2415, Washington, DC 20013, 202-447-4146.

10.059   NATIONAL WOOL ACT PAYMENTS (WOOL AND MOHAIR INCENTIVE PAYMENTS)
Type of Assistance: Direct payments ranging from $5 to $359,373.
Applicant Eligibility: Individuals.
Objective: To encourage increased domestic production of wool at prices fair both to producers and to consumers in a way that has the least adverse effect on domestic and foreign trade and to encourage producers to improve the quality and marketing of their wool and mohair.
Contact: Commodity Analysis Division, Department of Agriculture, PO Box 2415, Washington, DC 20013, 202-447-7674.

10.062   WATER BANK PROGRAM
Type of Assistance: Direct payments ranging from $8 to $65 per acre.
Applicant Eligibility: Individuals.
Objective: To conserve surface waters, preserve and improve the nation's wetlands, increase migratory waterfowl habitats in nesting, feeding and breeding areas in the US and secure other environmental benefits. Agreements are for 10 years with eligible landowners to help preserve important breeding and nesting areas of migratory waterfowl. During the agreement, the participants agree in return for annual payments not to drain, burn, fill or otherwise destroy the wetland character of such areas and not to use areas for agricultural purposes.
Contact: Conservation and Environmental Protection Division, Agricultural Stabilization and Conservation Service, Department of Agriculture, PO Box 2415, Washington, DC 20013, 202-447-6221.

10.063   AGRICULTURAL CONSERVATION PROGRAM
Type of Assistance: Direct payments ranging from $3 to $3,500.
Applicant Eligibility: Individuals.
Objective: Control of erosion and sedimentation, voluntary compliance with federal and state requirements to solve point and nonpoint source pollution, improve water quality and ensure a continued supply of necessary food and fiber. The program is directed toward the solution of critical soil, water, woodland and pollution abatement problems on farms and ranches. The conservation practices are to be used on agricultural land and must be performed satisfactorily and in accordance with applicable specifications.
Contact: Conservation and Environmental Protection Division, Ag-

ricultural Stabilization and Conservation Service, Department of Agriculture, PO Box 2415, Washington, DC 20013, 202-447-6221.

10.064 FORESTRY INCENTIVES PROGRAM

Type of Assistance: Direct payments ranging from $3 to $10,000 per year.

Applicant Eligibility: Individuals, groups, Indian tribes, corporations or legal entities.

Objective: To bring private non-industrial forest land under intensified management, to increase timber production, to ensure adequate supplies of timber and to enhance other forest resources through a combination of public and private investment on the most productive sites on eligible individual or consolidated ownerships of efficient size and operation.

Contact: Conservation and Environmental Protection Division, Agricultural Stabilization and Conservation Service, Department of Agriculture, PO Box 2415, Washington, DC 20013, 202-447-6221.

10.065 RICE PRODUCTION STABILIZATION (RICE DIRECT PAYMENTS)

Type of Assistance: Direct payments ranging from $3 to $50,000.

Applicant Eligibility: Individuals.

Objective: To provide the production needed to meet domestic and foreign demand, to protect income for farmers and to ensure adequate supplies at fair and reasonable prices.

Contact: Commodity Analysis Division, Agricultural Stabilization and Conservation Service, Department of Agriculture, PO Box 2415, Washington, DC 20013, 202-447-5954.

10.067 GRAIN RESERVE PROGRAM (FARMER-HELD AND -OWNED GRAIN RESERVE)

Type of Assistance: Direct payments ranging from $25 to $79,500.

Applicant Eligibility: Individuals.

Objective: To insulate sufficient quantities of grain from the market to increase price to farmers. To improve and stabilize farm income and assist farmers in the orderly marketing of their crops.

Contact: Cotton, Grain and Rice Price Support Division, Agricultural Stabilization and Conservation Service, Department of Agriculture, PO Box 2415, Washington, DC 20013, 202-382-9886.

10.068 RURAL CLEAN WATER PROGRAM

Type of Assistance: Direct payments up to $50,000.

Applicant Eligibility: Individuals.

Objective: To improve water quality in approved project areas in the most cost effective manner, to assist agricultural landowners in the reduction of agricultural nonpoint source water pollutants, and to develop and test programs, policies and procedures for controlling agricultural nonpoint source pollution.

Contact: Conservation and Environmental Protection Division, Agricultural Stabilization and Conservation Service, Department of Agriculture, PO Box 2415, Washington, DC 20013, 202-447-6221.

AGRICULTURAL MARKETING SERVICE

10.156 FEDERAL-STATE MARKETING IMPROVEMENT PROGRAM

Type of Assistance: Grants ranging from $1,000 to $75,000.
Applicant Eligibility: State governments.
Objective: To solve marketing problems at the state and local level through pilot marketing service projects conducted by the states. Projects may deal in such areas as providing marketing services for improving the marketability of agricultural products, expanding export markets, improving economic and physical efficiency of marketing, and assembling and disseminating marketing information.
Contact: Director, Federal-State Marketing Improvement Program, Agricultural Marketing Service, Department of Agriculture, Washington, DC 20250, 202-447-2704.

COOPERATIVE STATE RESEARCH SERVICE

10.200 GRANTS FOR AGRICULTURAL RESEARCH, SPECIAL RESEARCH GRANTS

Type of Assistance: Grants ranging from $41,675 to $150,000.
Applicant Eligibility: Nonprofit organizations and state governments.
Objective: To carry out research to facilitate or expand promising breakthroughs in areas of the food and agricultural sciences of importance to the nation and to facilitate or expand ongoing state-federal food and agricultural research programs. Areas of research are generally limited to high priority problems of a regional or national scope. Areas currently considered are animal health and aquaculture research.
Contact: Administrator, Cooperative State Research Service, Department of Agriculture, Washington, DC 20250, 202-447-4423.

10.202 COOPERATIVE FORESTRY RESEARCH

Type of Assistance: Grants ranging from $33,831 to $443,715.
Applicant Eligibility: State governments.
Objective: To encourage and assist the states in carrying on a program of forestry research at forestry schools, and to develop a trained pool of forest scientists capable of conducting needed forestry research.
Contact: Administrator, Cooperative State Research Service, Department of Agriculture, Washington, DC 20250, 202-447-4423.

10.203 PAYMENTS TO AGRICULTURAL EXPERIMENT STATIONS UNDER HATCH ACT

Type of Assistance: Grants ranging from $579,722 to $5,553,777.
Applicant Eligibility: State governments.
Objective: To support agricultural research at state agricultural ex-

periment stations. Its purpose is to promote efficient production, marketing, distribution and utilization of products of the farm as essential to the health and welfare of people and to promote a sound prosperous agriculture and rural life. Funds may be used for meeting expenses for research and investigations for printing and disseminating the results of such research, retirement of employees, administrative planning and direction, and for the purchase and rental of land and the construction, acquisition, alteration or repair of buildings necessary for conducting research.

Contact: Administrator, Cooperative State Research Service, Department of Agriculture, Washington, DC 20250, 202-447-4423.

10.205   PAYMENTS TO 1890 LAND-GRANT COLLEGES AND TUSKEGEE INSTITUTE

Type of Assistance: Grants ranging from $459,971 to $2,113,723.
Applicant Eligibility: 1890 Land-Grant colleges and Tuskegee Institute.
Objective: To support continuing agricultural research at eligible colleges, including Tuskegee Institute. Its purpose is to promote efficient production, marketing, distribution and utilization of products of the farm as essential to the health and welfare of people and to promote a sound, prosperous agriculture and rural life. Funds can be used for expenses of conducting agricultural research, contributing to the retirement of employees, administrative planning and direction, the purchase and rental of land and the construction, acquisition, alteration or repair of buildings necessary for conducting agricultural research.

Contact: Administrator, Cooperative State Research Service, Department of Agriculture, Washington, DC 20250, 202-447-4423.

10.206   GRANTS FOR AGRICULTURAL RESEARCH— COMPETITIVE RESEARCH GRANTS

Type of Assistance: Grants ranging from $3,000 to $180,000.
Applicant Eligibility: Individuals, nonprofit organizations, state governments.
Objective: To promote research in food, agriculture and related areas to further the programs of USDA through the award of research grants on a competitive basis. The initially selected areas for research are biological nitrogen fixation, biological stress on plants, photosynthesis, genetic mechanisms of crop improvement, and human nutritional requirements. Funds may be used for costs necessary to conduct the research.

Contact: Director, Competitive Research Grants Office, Department of Agriculture, West Auditors Building, Room 112, 15th and Independence Avenue, SW, Washington, DC 20251, 202-475-5022.

10.207   ANIMAL HEALTH AND DISEASE RESEARCH

Type of Assistance: Grants ranging from $7,943 to $346,564.
Applicant Eligibility: Public nonprofit institutions.
Objective: To support animal health and disease research at eligible schools of veterinary medicine, and state agricultural experiment sta-

tions whose purpose is to improve the health and productivity of food animals and horses through effective prevention, control or treatment of disease, reduction of losses from transportation and other hazards, and protect human health through control of animal diseases transmissible to people.

Contact: Administrator, Cooperative State Research Service, Department of Agriculture, Washington, DC 20250, 202-447-4423.

10.209   1890 RESEARCH FACILITIES

Type of Assistance: Grants ranging from $232,520 to $1,400,000.

Applicant Eligibility: Land-Grant colleges and Tuskegee Institute.

Objective: To assist in the acquisition and improvement of research facilities and equipment. Available in the states of Alabama, Arkansas, Delaware, Florida, Georgia, Kentucky, Louisiana, Maryland, Mississippi, Missouri, North Carolina, Oklahoma, South Carolina, Tennessee, Texas, and Virginia.

Contact: Administrator, Cooperative State Research Service, Department of Agriculture, Washington, DC 20250, 202-447-4423.

10.210   FOOD AND AGRICULTURAL SCIENCES NATIONAL NEEDS GRADUATE FELLOWSHIP GRANTS

Type of Assistance: Project grants ranging from $10,440 to $154,500.

Applicant Eligibility: Colleges and universities offering masters or doctoral degrees in food and agricultural sciences.

Objective: To award grants to colleges and universities to encourage students to complete a graduate degree in food and agricultural sciences.

Contact: Higher Education Programs, Agricultural Research Service, Department of Agriculture, Administration Building, Room 350-A, 14th and Independence Avenue, SW, Washington, DC 20250, 202-447-7854.

10.211   HIGHER EDUCATION STRENGTHENING GRANTS

Type of Assistance: Project Grants up to $107,777.

Applicant Eligibility: 1890 Land-Grant Institutions, Tuskegee Institute, and the University of the District of Columbia.

Objective: In the areas of food and agricultural sciences, strengthen institutional capacities to respond to state, regional or international educational needs.

Contact: Administrator, Cooperative State Research Service, US Department of Agriculture, Washington, DC 20250, 202-447-4423.

FARMERS HOME ADMINISTRATION

10.404   EMERGENCY LOANS

Type of Assistance: Guaranteed/insured loans ranging from $500 to $6 million.

Applicant Eligibility: Individuals.

Objective: To assist farmers, ranchers and aquaculture operators with loans to cover losses resulting from a major and/or natural disaster, for annual farm operating expenses and for other needs necessary to return the disaster victims' farming operations(s) to a financially sound basis in order that they will be able to return to local sources of credit as soon as possible. Loans may be used to repair, restore or replace damaged or destroyed farm property and supplies which were lost or damaged as a direct result of a natural disaster; provide annual operating expenses for up to six full crop-years following the disaster; under certain conditions to refinance debts made necessary by the disaster; and finance adjustments in the farming, ranching or aquaculture operation(s) determined necessary to restore or maintain applicants on a sound financial basis.
Contact: Administrator, Farmers Home Administration, Department of Agriculture, Washington, DC 20250, 202-382-1632.

10.405 FARM LABOR HOUSING LOANS AND GRANTS (LABOR HOUSING)

Type of Assistance: Grants and guaranteed/insured loans ranging from $20,000 to $2,300,000.
Applicant Eligibility: Individuals, nonprofit organizations, state and local governments.
Objective: To provide decent, safe and sanitary low-rent housing and related facilities for domestic farm laborers. Funds may be used for construction, repair or purchase of housing; acquiring the necessary land and making improvements on the land for the housing; and developing related facilities including recreation areas, central cooking and dining facilities, small infirmaries, laundry facilities and other essential equipment and facilities.
Contact: Multiple Family Housing Processing Division, Farmers Home Administration, Department of Agriculture, Washington, DC 20250, 202-382-1604.

10.406 FARM OPERATING LOANS

Type of Assistance: Guaranteed/insured loans up to $200,000.
Applicant Eligibility: Individuals.
Objective: To enable operators of not larger than family farms (primarily limited resource operators, new operators, and low-income operators) to make efficient use of their land, labor and other resources. Youth loans enable rural youths to establish and operate modest income-producing farm or nonfarm projects that are educational and practical and provide an opportunity to learn basic economic and credit principles. Funds may be used for a wide range of necessary agricultural expenses.
Contact: Director, Farm Real Estate & Production Division, Farmers Home Administration, Department of Agriculture, Washington, DC 20250, 202-447-4572.

10.407   FARM OWNERSHIP LOANS
Type of Assistance: Guaranteed/insured loans ranging from $200,000 to $300,000.
Applicant Eligibility: Individuals.
Objective: To assist eligible farmers and ranchers, including farming cooperatives, partnerships and corporations to become owner-operators of not larger than family farms; to make efficient use of the land, labor and other resources; to carry on sound and successful operations on the farm, and to afford the family, cooperative, partnership or corporation an opportunity to have a reasonable standard of living. Loans may be used for a wide range of necessary agricultural expenses.
Contact: Administrator, Farmers Home Administration, Department of Agriculture, Washington, DC 20250, 202-447-7967.

10.410   LOW-INCOME HOUSING LOANS
Type of Assistance: Guaranteed/insured loans ranging from $1,000 to $60,000.
Applicant Eligibility: Individuals.
Objective: To assist rural low-income families to obtain decent, safe and sanitary dwellings and related facilities. Loans may be used for construction, repair or purchase of housing; to provide necessary and adequate sewage disposal facilities; for water supply for the applicant and his family; for weatherization; to purchase or install essential equipment which upon installation becomes part of the real estate; and to buy a site on which to place a dwelling for applicant's own use.
Contact: Administrator, Farmers Home Administration, Department of Agriculture, Washington, DC 20250, 202-447-7967.

10.411   RURAL HOUSING SITE LOANS
Type of Assistance: Guaranteed/insured loans ranging from $45,200 to $571,000.
Applicant Eligibility: Nonprofit organizations.
Objective: To assist public or private nonprofit organizations interested in providing sites for housing, to acquire and develop land in rural areas to be subdivided as adequate building sites and sold on a nonprofit basis to families eligible for low- and moderate-income loans; and to also aid cooperatives and broadly based nonprofit rural rental housing applicants. Funds may be used for the purchase and development of adequate sites, including necessary equipment which becomes a permanent part of the development; water and sewer facilities if not available; payment of necessary engineering, legal fees and closing costs; and needed landscaping and other necessary building-related facilities.
Contact: Administrator, Farmers Home Administration, Department of Agriculture, Washington, DC 20250, 202-382-1474.

10.414   RESOURCE CONSERVATION AND DEVELOPMENT LOANS

Type of Assistance: Guaranteed/insured loans ranging from $30,000 to $500,000.

Applicant Eligibility: Nonprofit organizations and public agencies.

Objective: To provide loan assistance to local sponsoring agencies in authorized areas where acceleration of program of resource conservation, development and utilization will increase economic opportunities for local people. Loan funds may be used for rural community public outdoor-oriented water-based recreational facilities; soil and water development, conservation, control and use facilities; shift-in-land use facilities; community water storage facilities and special purpose equipment to carry out the above purposes.

Contact: Director, Community Facilities Division, Farmers Home Administration, Department of Agriculture, Washington, DC 20250, 202-382-1490.

10.415   RURAL RENTAL HOUSING LOANS

Type of Assistance: Guaranteed/insured loans ranging from $60,000 to $2 million.

Applicant Eligibility: Individuals, nonprofit organizations, cooperatives.

Objective: To provide economically designed and constructed rental and cooperative housing and related facilities suited for independent living for rural residents. Loans can be used to construct, purchase, improve or repair rental or cooperative housing.

Contact: Administrator, Farmers Home Administration, Department of Agriculture, Washington, DC 20250, 202-382-1604.

10.416   SOIL AND WATER LOANS

Type of Assistance: Guaranteed/insured loans ranging from $3,300 to $100,000.

Applicant Eligibility: Individuals.

Objective: To facilitate improvement, protection and proper use of farmland by providing adequate financing and supervisory assistance for soil conservation; water development, conservation and use; forestation; drainage of farmland; the establishment and improvement of permanent pasture; the development of pollution abatement and control facilities on farms; and related measures. Loans may be used for a wide range of soil and water conservation methods.

Contact: Administrator, Farmers Home Administration, Department of Agriculture, Washington, DC 20250, 202-447-7967.

10.417   VERY LOW-INCOME HOUSING REPAIR LOANS AND GRANTS

Type of Assistance: Direct loans and grants ranging from $200 to $7,500.

Applicant Eligibility: Individuals.

Objective: To give very low-income rural homeowners an opportunity to make essential repairs to their homes to make them safe and to remove health hazards to the family or the community. This includes repairs to the foundation, roof or basic structure as well as water and waste disposal systems, and weatherization.
Contact: Administrator, Farmers Home Administration, Department of Agriculture, Washington, DC 20250, 202-477-7697.

10.418 WATER AND WASTE DISPOSAL SYSTEMS FOR RURAL COMMUNITIES

Type of Assistance: Grants and direct loans ranging from $2,900 to $2,600,000.
Applicant Eligibility: Nonprofit organizations and local governments.
Objective: To provide human amenities, alleviate health hazards and promote the orderly growth of the rural areas of the nation by meeting the need for new and improved rural water and waste disposal facilities. Funds may be used for the installation, repair, improvement or expansion of a rural water facility including distribution lines, well-pumping facilities and costs related thereto, and the installation, repair, improvement or expansion of a rural waste disposal facility including the collection and treatment of sanitary, storm and solid wastes.
Contact: Administrator, Farmers Home Administration, Department of Agriculture, Washington, DC 20250, 202-447-7967.

10.419 WATERSHED PROTECTION AND FLOOD PREVENTION LOANS

Type of Assistance: Guaranteed/insured loans ranging from $4,000 to $7,500,000.
Applicant Eligibility: Nonprofit organizations, state and local governments.
Objective: To provide loan assistance to sponsoring local organizations in authorized watershed areas for share of cost for works of improvement. Loan funds may be used to help local sponsors provide the local share of the cost of watershed works of improvement for flood prevention, irrigation, drainage, water quality management, sedimentation control, fish and wildlife development, public water-based recreation, and water storage and related costs.
Contact: Director, Community Facilities Division, Farmers Home Administration, Department of Agriculture, Washington, DC 20250, 202-382-1490.

10.420 RURAL SELF-HELP HOUSING TECHNICAL ASSISTANCE

Type of Assistance: Grants ranging from $26,000 to $1,520,400.
Applicant Eligibility: Nonprofit organizations, state and local governments.
Objective: To provide financial support for the promotion of a program of technical and supervisory assistance which will aid needy individuals

and their families in carrying out mutual self-help efforts in rural areas. Organizations may use funds to hire the personnel to carry out a program of technical assistance for self-help housing in rural areas; to pay necessary and reasonable office and administrative expenses; to make essential equipment such as power tools available to families participating in self-help housing construction; and to pay fees for training self-help group members in construction techniques or for other professional services needed.
Contact: Administrator, Farmers Home Administration, Department of Agriculture, Washington, DC 20250, 202-382-1474.

10.421 INDIAN TRIBES & TRIBAL CORPORATION LOANS
Type of Assistance: Guaranteed/insured loans ranging from $750,000 to $3 million.
Applicant Eligibility: Native Americans only.
Objective: To enable tribes and tribal corporations to mortgage lands as security for loans from the Farmers Home Administration to buy additional land within the reservation. Loan funds may be used to acquire land for lease to tribal members, to lease to cooperative grazing units, or for use for recreational and commercial purposes, rounding out grazing units or elimination of fractional heirships.
Contact: Office of Indian Affairs, Farmers Home Administration, Department of Agriculture, Washington, DC 20250, 202-447-7967.

10.422 BUSINESS AND INDUSTRIAL LOANS
Type of Assistance: Guaranteed/insured loans ranging from $11,000 to $50 million.
Applicant Eligibility: Individuals, nonprofit organizations, local governments.
Objective: To assist public, private or cooperative organizations (profit or nonprofit), Indian tribes or individuals in rural areas to obtain quality loans for the purpose of improving, developing or financing business, industry and employment; improving the economic and environmental climate in rural communities including pollution abatement and control.
Contact: Administrator, Farmers Home Administration, Department of Agriculture, Washington, DC 20250, 202-447-7967.

10.423 COMMUNITY FACILITIES LOAN
Type of Assistance: Guaranteed/insured loans ranging from $6,000 to $5,178,000.
Applicant Eligibility: Nonprofit organizations, state and local governments.
Objective: To construct, enlarge, extend or otherwise improve community facilities providing essential services to rural residents. Funds may be for projects supporting overall community development such as fire and rescue services; transportation; traffic control; community social, cultural, health and recreational benefits; industrial park sites; access ways; and utility extensions.

Contact: Director, Community Facilities Division, Farmers Home Administration, Department of Agriculture, Washington, DC 20250, 202-382-1490.

10.427   RURAL RENTAL ASSISTANCE PAYMENTS

Type of Assistance: Direct payments (dollar amount not available.)

Applicant Eligibility: Individuals, nonprofit organizations, state and local governments.

Objective: To reduce the rents paid by low-income families occupying eligible Rural Rental Housing (RRH), Rural Cooperative Housing (RCH) and Farm Labor Housing (FLH) projects financed by the Farmers Home Administration. Rental assistance may be used to reduce the rents paid by low-income senior citizens or families and domestic farm laborers and families whose rents exceed 25 percent of an adjusted annual income which does not exceed the limit established for the state.

Contact: Administrator, Farmers Home Administration, Department of Agriculture, Washington, DC 20250, 202-382-1604.

FEDERAL CROP INSURANCE CORPORATION

10.450   CROP INSURANCE

Type of Assistance: Insurance ranging from $1 to $250,000.

Applicant Eligibility: Individuals.

Objective: To improve agricultural stability through a sound system of crop insurance by providing all-risk insurance for individual farmers to assure a basic income against droughts, freezes, insects and other natural causes of disastrous crop losses. Insurance is available on crops in more than 3,000 agricultural counties in 49 states.

Contact: Manager, Federal Crop Insurance Corporation, Department of Agriculture, Washington, DC 20250, 202-447-6795.

EXTENSION SERVICE

10.500   COOPERATIVE EXTENSION SERVICE

Type of Assistance: Grants ranging from $738,053 to $18,082,177.

Applicant Eligibility: Land-grant institutions.

Objective: To provide educational programs based upon local needs in the broad fields of agricultural production and marketing, rural development, home economics and youth development. Funds are available to land-grant institutions which, through state and county extension service personnel, provide educational and technical assistance to farmers, producers and marketing firms on how to apply new technical developments in agricultural research; community organizations to develop natural, economic and human resources; homemakers and youth in the areas of food and nutrition, home management, family economics, child development and parent education; and 4-H youth in

the area of leadership development and career guidance through work projects, demonstration projects, camping and achievement programs.
Contact: Extension Service, Department of Agriculture, Washington, DC 20250, 202-447-3377.

FOOD AND NUTRITION SERVICE

10.550 FOOD DISTRIBUTION (FOOD DONATION PROGRAM)
Type of Assistance: Donation of goods.
Applicant Eligibility: State governments.
Objective: To improve the diets of school children and needy persons in households, on Indian reservations and in charitable institutions; the elderly; and other individuals in need of food assistance and to increase the market for domestically produced foods acquired under surplus removal or price support operations.
Contact: Food Distribution Division, Food and Nutrition Service, Department of Agriculture, Alexandria, VA 22302, 703-756-3680.

10.551 FOOD STAMPS
Type of Assistance: Direct payments averaging approximately $42.77 per month per person.
Applicant Eligibility: State governments.
Objective: To improve diets of low-income households by supplementing their food-purchasing ability by providing households with a free coupon allotment which varies according to household size. The coupons may be used in participating retail stores to buy food for human consumption and garden seeds and plants to produce food for personal consumption by eligible households.
Contact: Deputy Administrator, Family Nutrition Programs, Food and Nutrition Service, Department of Agriculture, Alexandria, VA 22302, 703-756-3026.

10.553 SCHOOL BREAKFAST PROGRAM
Type of Assistance: Donation of goods and grants of approximately $.73 per meal.
Applicant Eligibility: Nonprofit organizations and state governments.
Objective: To assist states in providing nutritious breakfasts for school children through cash grants and food donations. Funds are available to reimburse participating public and nonprofit private schools of high school grade or under for breakfasts meeting the nutritional requirements prescribed by the Secretary of Agriculture and served to eligible children.
Contact: Director, Child Nutrition Division, Food and Nutrition Service, Department of Agriculture, Alexandria, VA 22302, 703-756-3590.

10.555 NATIONAL SCHOOL LUNCH PROGRAM
Type of Assistance: Grants.
Applicant Eligibility: Nonprofit organizations and state governments.

Objective: To assist states, through cash grants and food donations, in making the school lunch program available to all school children, thereby promoting their health and well-being. Funds are available to reimburse participating public and nonprofit private schools of high school grade or under, including residential child care institutions, for lunches meeting the nutritional requirements prescribed by the Secretary of Agriculture and served to eligible children.

Contact: Director, Child Nutrition Division, Food and Nutrition Service, Department of Agriculture, Alexandria, VA 22302, 703-767-3590.

10.556 SPECIAL MILK PROGRAM FOR CHILDREN

Type of Assistance: Grants.

Applicant Eligibility: Nonprofit organizations and state governments.

Objective: To encourage the consumption of fluid milk by children of high school grade and under through reimbursement to eligible schools and institutions.

Contact: Director, Child Nutrition Division, Food and Nutrition Service, Department of Agriculture, Alexandria, VA 22302, 703-756-3590.

10.557 SPECIAL SUPPLEMENTAL FOOD PROGRAM FOR WOMEN, INFANTS AND CHILDREN

Type of Assistance: Grants (dollar amount not available).

Applicant Eligibility: State governments.

Objective: To supply supplemental nutritious foods and nutrition education to low-income participants identified to be at nutritional risk with respect to their physical and mental health. This includes making foods available to pregnant, postpartum and breastfeeding women, and infants and children up to five years of age, through local public or nonprofit private health or welfare agencies.

Contact: Special Supplemental Food Programs Division, Food and Nutrition Service, Department of Agriculture, Alexandria, VA 22302, 703-756-3746.

10.558 CHILD CARE FOOD PROGRAM

Type of Assistance: Grants; and sale, exchange or donation of property and goods.

Applicant Eligibility: Nonprofit organizations and state governments.

Objective: To assist states, through grants-in-aid and other means, to initiate, maintain or expand food service programs for children in public and private nonprofit, nonresidential child care institutions. Funds are made available to, but not limited to, day care centers, settlement houses and recreational centers, family and group day care programs, Head Start Centers and institutions providing day care services for handicapped children.

Contact: Director, Child Nutrition Division, Food and Nutrition Service, Department of Agriculture, Alexandria, VA 22302, 703-756-3590.

10.559 SUMMER FOOD SERVICE PROGRAM FOR CHILDREN

Type of Assistance: Grants.

Applicant Eligibility: Nonprofit organizations and state governments.

Objective: To assist states, through grants-in-aid and other means, to initiate, maintain and expand food service programs for children in public and nonprofit service institutions and summer camps when school is not in session. Funds are made available to eligible service institutions which conduct a regularly scheduled program for children from areas in which poor economic conditions exist, for any period during the months of May through September.
Contact: Director, Child Nutrition Division, Food and Nutrition Service, Department of Agriculture, Alexandria, VA 22302 703-756-3590.

10.560   STATE ADMINISTRATIVE EXPENSES FOR CHILD NUTRITION
Type of Assistance: Grants ranging from $173,000 to $3,832,000.
Applicant Eligibility: State governments.
Objective: To provide each state educational agency with funds for use for its administrative expenses in supervising and giving technical assistance to the local school districts and institutions in their conduct of child nutrition programs.
Contact: Director, Child Nutrition Division, Food and Nutrition Service, Department of Agriculture, Alexandria, VA 22302, 703-756-3590.

10.561   STATE ADMINISTRATIVE MATCHING GRANTS FOR FOOD STAMP PROGRAM
Type of Assistance: Grants ranging from $532,000 to $103,869,000.
Applicant Eligibility: State governments.
Objective: To provide federal financial aid to state agencies for costs incurred to operate the Food Stamp program.
Contact: Deputy Administrator, Family Nutrition Programs, Food and Nutrition Service, Department of Agriculture, Alexandria, VA 22302, 703-756-3026.

10.564   NUTRITION EDUCATION AND TRAINING PROGRAM
Type of Assistance: Grants ranging from $50,000 to $417,181.
Applicant Eligibility: State governments.
Objective: Grants are made to state education agencies to provide for the nutritional training of educational and food service personnel, the food service management training of school food service personnel and the conduct of nutrition education activities in schools and child care institutions.
Contact: Nutrition and Technical Services Division, Food and Nutrition Service, Department of Agriculture, Alexandria, VA 22302, 703-756-3880.

10.565   COMMODITY SUPPLEMENTAL FOOD PROGRAM
Type of Assistance: Grants; sale, exchange or donation of property and goods.
Applicant Eligibility: Individuals.
Objective: To improve the health and nutritional status of infants, children up to the age of six, pregnant, post-partum and breast-feeding

women through the donation of supplemental foods, provision of nutrition education and referral for health services.
Contact: Deputy Administrator, Family Nutrition Programs, Food and Nutrition Service, Department of Agriculture, Alexandria, VA 22302, 703-756-3026.

10.567 NEEDY FAMILY PROGRAM
Type of Assistance: Grants; sale, exchange or donation of property and goods.
Applicant Eligibility: State agencies.
Objective: To improve the diets of needy persons in households on or near Indian reservations and to increase the market for domestically produced foods acquired under surplus removal or price support operations.
Contact: Food Distribution Division, Food and Nutrition Service, Department of Agriculture, Alexandria, VA 22302, 703-756-3660.

FOREST SERVICE

10.600 FOREIGN AGRICULTURAL MARKET DEVELOPMENT AND PROMOTION
Type of Assistance: Direct payments.
Applicant Eligibility: Individuals and nonprofit organizations.
Objective: To create, expand and maintain markets abroad for US agricultural commodities.
Contact: Assistant Administrator, Commodity and Marketing Programs, Foreign Agricultural Service, Department of Agriculture, Washington, DC 20250, 202-447-4761.

10.652 FORESTRY RESEARCH
Type of Assistance: Grants ranging from $2,000 to $100,000.
Applicant Eligibility: Nonprofit organizations, state and local governments.
Objective: To provide funds for research in the fields of timber management, watershed management, forest range management, wildlife habitat management, forest recreation, forest fire protection, forest insect and disease protection and control, forest products utilization, forest engineering, forest production economics, forest products marketing and forest survey.
Contact: Deputy Chief for Research, Forest Service, Department of Agriculture, PO Box 2417, Washington, DC 20013, 202-447-7075.

10.664 COOPERATIVE FORESTRY ASSISTANCE
Type of Assistance: Grants ranging from $40,000 to $5 million.
Applicant Eligibility: State goverments.
Objective: To assist in the advancement of forest resources management; the encouragement of the production of timber; the prevention and control of insects and diseases affecting trees and forests; the

prevention and control of rural fires; the efficient utilization of wood and wood residues, including the recycling of wood fiber; the improvement and maintenance of fish and wildlife habitat; and the planning and conduct of urban forestry programs. Funds are made available to assist the State Forester or equivalent agencies in programs on private, state, local and other nonfederal forest lands.

Contact: Deputy Chief, State and Private Forestry, Forest Service, Department of Agriculture, PO Box 2417, Washington, DC 20013, 202-382-9036.

10.665   SCHOOLS AND ROADS—GRANTS TO STATES

Type of Assistance: Grants ranging from $73 to $69,212,545.
Applicant Eligibility: State governments or US territories.
Objective: To share receipts from the National Forests with the states in which the National Forests are situated.
Contact: Director of Fiscal and Accounting Management, Forest Service, Department of Agriculture, Room 701 RPE, PO Box 2417, Washington, DC 20013, 703-235-8159.

10.666   SCHOOLS AND ROADS—GRANTS TO COUNTIES

Type of Assistance: Grants ranging from $3 to $4,230,741.
Applicant Eligibility: Counties.
Objective: To share receipts from National Grasslands and Land Utilization Projects with the counties in which these are situated.
Contact: Director of Fiscal and Accounting Management, Forest Service, Department of Agriculture, Room 701 RPE, PO Box 2417, Washington, DC 20013, 703-235-8159.

10.668   ADDITIONAL LANDS—GRANTS TO MINNESOTA

Type of Assistance: Grants averaging $711,904.
Applicant Eligibility: State of Minnesota.
Objective: To share National Forest receipts with the state of Minnesota in connection with lands situated in the counties of Cook, Lake and St. Louis which are withdrawn from entry and appropriation under the public laws of the United States.
Contact: Director of Fiscal and Accounting Management, Forest Service, Department of Agriculture, Room 701 RPE, PO Box 2417, Washington, DC 20013, 703-235-8159.

RURAL ELECTRIFICATION ADMINISTRATION

10.850   RURAL ELECTRIFICATION LOANS
AND LOAN GUARANTEES

Type of Assistance: Guaranteed/insured loans ranging from $250,000 to $1,180,000.
Applicant Eligibility: Nonprofit organizations, state and local governments.
Objective: To assure that people in eligible rural areas have access to

electric services comparable in reliability and quality to the rest of the nation. Funds are used to supply central station electric services on a continuing basis in rural areas.
Contact: Administrator, Rural Electrification Administration, Department of Agriculture, Washington, DC 20250, 202-382-9540.

10.851 RURAL TELEPHONE LOANS AND LOAN GUARANTEES
Type of Assistance: Guaranteed/insured loans ranging from $200,000 to $30 million.
Applicant Eligibility: Nonprofit organizations, state and local governments.
Objective: To ensure that people in eligible rural areas have access to telephone service comparable in reliability and quality to the rest of the nation.
Contact: Administrator, Rural Electrification Administration, Department of Agriculture, Washington, DC 20250, 202-382-9540.

10.852 RURAL TELEPHONE BANK LOANS
Type of Assistance: Direct loans ranging from $250,000 to $15 million.
Applicant Eligibility: Nonprofit organizations, state and local governments.
Objective: To provide supplemental financing to extend and improve telephone service in rural areas.
Contact: Governor, Rural Telephone Bank, Department of Agriculture, Washington, DC 20250, 202-382-9540.

SOIL CONSERVATION SERVICE

10.900 GREAT PLAINS CONSERVATION
Type of Assistance: Direct payments up to $35,000.
Applicant Eligibility: Individuals.
Objective: To conserve and develop the Great Plains soil and water resources by providing technical and financial assistance to farmers, ranchers and others in planning and implementing conservation practices. Funds are available only for soil and water conservation measures determined to be needed to protect and stabilize a farm or ranch unit against climatic and erosion hazards.
Contact: Deputy Chief for Programs, Soil Conservation Service, Department of Agriculture, PO Box 2890, Washington, DC 20013, 202-447-4527.

10.901 RESOURCE CONSERVATION AND DEVELOPMENT
Type of Assistance: Grants ranging from $10,000 to $500,000.
Applicant Eligibility: Nonprofit organizations, state and local governments.
Objective: To assist local people in initiating and carrying out long-range programs of resource conservation and development for the

purposes of achieving a dynamic rural community with a satisfactory level of income and a pleasing environment, and creating a favorable investment climate attractive to private capital.

Contact: Deputy Chief for Programs, Soil Conservation Service, Department of Agriculture, PO Box 2890, Washington, DC 20013, 202-447-4527.

10.904 WATERSHED PROTECTION AND FLOOD PREVENTION

Type of Assistance: Advisory services, and grants ranging from $300 to $13 million.

Applicant Eligibility: Nonprofit organizations, state and local governments.

Objective: To provide technical and financial assistance in planning and carrying out works of improvement to protect, develop and utilize the land and water resources in small watersheds. Assistance is provided in planning, designing and installing watershed works of improvement; sharing costs of flood prevention, irrigation, drainage, sedimentation control and public water-based fish and wildlife and recreation; and extending long-term credit to help local interests with their share of the costs.

Contact: Deputy Chief for Programs, Soil Conservation Service, Department of Agriculture, PO Box 2890, Washington, DC 20013, 202-447-4527.

10.905 PLANT MATERIALS FOR CONSERVATION

Type of Assistance: Donation of property and goods.

Applicant Eligibility: Individuals, nonprofit organizations, state and local governments.

Objective: To assemble, evaluate, select, release and introduce into commerce new and improved plant materials for soil, water and wildlife conservation, and environmental improvement.

Contact: Deputy Chief for Technology, Soil Conservation Service, Department of Agriculture, PO Box 2890, Washington, DC 20013, 202-447-4630.

10.910 RURAL ABANDONED MINE PROGRAM

Type of Assistance: Direct payments from $750 to $992,400.

Applicant Eligibility: Individuals, nonprofit organizations, state and local governments.

Objective: To protect people and the environment from the adverse effects of past coal mining practices and to promote the development of soil and water resources of unreclaimed mined lands. Funds are available only for conservation practices determined to be needed for the reclamation, conservation and development of up to 320 acres per owner of rural abandoned coal mine land or lands and waters affected by coal mining activities.

Contact: Deputy Chief for Programs, Soil Conservation Service, Department of Agriculture, PO Box 2890, Washington, DC 20013, 202-447-4527.

US DEPARTMENT OF COMMERCE

INTERNATIONAL TRADE ADMINISTRATION

11.108 EXPORT PROMOTION SERVICES
Type of Assistance: Grants.
Applicant Eligibility: Individuals, organizations.
Objective: To encourage local business firms to enter into and expand their marketing efforts in export trade and to inform U.S. business firms of export methods, benefits, and opportunities, and assist them to identify and assess potential overseas trade, contacts and opportunities.
Contact: Office of the Managing Director, Room 3012, Export Promotion Services, Department of Commerce, Washington, DC 20230, 202-377-8220.

11.109 TRADE ADJUSTMENT ASSISTANCE
Type of Assistance: Direct and guaranteed/insured loans up to $3 million.
Applicant Eligibility: Firms.
Objective: To provide trade adjustment assistance to firms and industries adversely affected by increased imports.
Contact: Office of Trade Adjustment Assistance, International Trade Administration, Department of Commerce, 14th and E Streets, NW, Washington, DC 20230, 202-377-5005.

ECONOMIC DEVELOPMENT ADMINISTRATION

11.300 ECONOMIC DEVELOPMENT—GRANTS FOR PUBLIC WORKS AND DEVELOPMENT FACILITIES
Type of Assistance: Grants ranging from $50,000 to $5,600,000.
Applicant Eligibility: Nonprofit organizations, state and local governments.
Objective: To assist in the construction of public facilities needed to initiate and encourage long-term economic growth in designated geographic areas where economic growth is lagging behind the rest of the nation. Funds may be used for such public facilities as water and sewer systems, access roads to industrial parks or areas, port facilities, railroad sidings and spurs, public tourism facilities, vocational schools and site improvements for industrial parks.
Contact: Deputy Assistant Secretary for Operations, Economic De-

velopment Administration, Department of Commerce, Washington, DC 20230, 202-377-3081.

11.301 ECONOMIC DEVELOPMENT—
BUSINESS DEVELOPMENT ASSISTANCE

Type of Assistance: Guaranteed/insured loans ranging from $260,000 to $111 million.

Applicant Eligibility: Individuals, private or public corporations or Indian tribes.

Objective: To sustain industrial and commercial viability in designated areas by providing financial assistance to businesses that create or retain permanent jobs or expand or establish plants in redevelopment areas for projects where financial assistance is not available from other sources, on terms and conditions that would permit accomplishment of the project and further economic development in the area.

Contact: Deputy Assistant Secretary for Finance, Finance Directorate, Economic Development Administration, Department of Commerce, Room H7844, Herbert Hoover Building, Washington, DC 20230, 202-377-5067.

11.302 ECONOMIC DEVELOPMENT—
SUPPORT FOR PLANNING ORGANIZATIONS

Type of Assistance: Grants ranging from $25,000 to $120,000.

Applicant Eligibility: Areas designated as redevelopment areas.

Objective: To foster multi-county district (and redevelopment area) economic development planning and implementaton capability and thereby promote effective utilization of resources in the creation of full-time permanent jobs for the unemployed and the underemployed in redevelopment areas.

Contact: Office of Planning, Technical Assistance, Research and Evaluation, Economic Development Administration, Department of Commerce, Room H7864, Herbert Hoover Building, Washington, DC 20230, 202-377-5111.

11.303 ECONOMIC DEVELOPMENT—
TECHNICAL ASSISTANCE

Type of Assistance: Grants ranging from $7,500 to $500,000.

Applicant Eligibility: Nonprofit organizations, state and local governments.

Objective: To solve problems of economic growth in Economic Development Administration-designated geographic areas and other areas of substantial need through administrative and demonstration project grants, feasibility studies, management and operational assistance and other studies.

Contact: Director, Office of Planning, Technical Assistance, Research and Evaluation, Economic Development Administration, Room H7864, Herbert Hoover Building, Department of Commerce, Washington, DC 20230, 202-377-5111.

**11.304   ECONOMIC DEVELOPMENT—
PUBLIC WORKS IMPACT PROJECTS**
Type of Assistance: Grants for projects of $600,000 or less.
Applicant Eligibility: Public and private nonprofit organizations; states and cities.
Objective: To provide immediate useful work to unemployed and underemployed persons in designated projects areas through the construction of public facilities.
Contact: Director, Office of Public Works, Economic Development Administration, Department of Commerce, Room H7824, Herbert Hoover Building, Washington, DC 20230, 202-377-3081.

**11.305   ECONOMIC DEVELOPMENT—STATE AND LOCAL
ECONOMIC DEVELOPMENT PLANNING**
Type of Assistance: Grants ranging from $20,000 to $88,000.
Applicant Eligibility: State and local governments.
Objective: To develop the capability of state and local governments to undertake an economic development planning process that is comprehensive in scope, coordinated with that of other levels of governmental planning activities, and leading to the formulation of development goals and specific strategies to achieve them, with particular emphasis on reducing unemployment and increasing incomes.
Contact: Director, Office of Planning, Technical Assistance, Research and Evaluation, Economic Development Administration, Department of Commerce, Room H7864, Herbert Hoover Building, Washington, DC 20230, 202-377-5111.

**11.306   ECONOMIC DEVELOPMENT—
DISTRICT OPERATIONAL ASSISTANCE**
Type of Assistance: Grants up to $25,000.
Applicant Eligibility: Chief officers of governing bodies of Economic Development Districts.
Objective: To assist Economic Development Districts in providing professional services to their local governments.
Contact: Director, Office of Planning, Technical Assistance, Research and Evaluation, Economic Development Administration, Department of Commerce, Room H7864, Herbert Hoover Building, Washington, DC 20230, 202-377-5111.

**11.307   SPECIAL ECONOMIC DEVELOPMENT AND
ADJUSTMENT ASSISTANCE PROGRAM—
SUDDEN AND SEVERE OR LONG-TERM
ECONOMIC DETERIORATION**
Type of Assistance: Grants.
Applicant Eligibility: Public or private nonprofit organizations.
Objective: To assist state and local areas in the development and implementation of strategies designed to arrest and reverse the problems associated with long-term, economic deterioration.
Contact: Deputy Assistant Secretary for Operations, Economic De-

velopment Administration, Room H7824, Herbert Hoover Building, Department of Commerce, Washington, DC 20230, 202-377-3081.

NATIONAL OCEANIC AND ATMOSPHERIC ADMINISTRATION

11.405   ANADROMOUS AND GREAT LAKES FISHERIES CONSERVATION

Type of Assistance: Grants ranging from $2,000 to $533,100.
Applicant Eligibility: Individuals.
Objective: To cooperate with the states and other nonfederal interests in the conservation, development and enhancement of the nation's anadromous fish (fish that go upriver to spawn), and the fish in the Great Lakes and Lake Champlain that ascend streams to spawn, and for the control of sea lamprey. Funds may be used for spawning area improvement, installment of fishways, construction of fish protection devices and hatcheries and research to improve management and increase anadromous fish resources.
Contact: Fishery Management Office, National Marine Fisheries Service, Page Building 2, 3300 Whitehaven St., NW, Washington, DC 20235, 202-634-7449.

11.407   COMMERCIAL FISHERIES RESEARCH AND DEVELOPMENT

Type of Assistance: Grants ranging from $2,000 to $340,000.
Applicant Eligibility: State governments.
Objective: To promote state commercial fishery research and development in the 50 states, Puerto Rico, the Virgin Islands, Guam, American Samoa and trust territory of the Pacific Islands. Funds may be used for research and development of commercial fishery resources, including construction of facilities.
Contact: Director, Office of Fisheries Management, National Marine Fisheries Service, 3300 Whitehaven Street, NW, Washington, DC, 20235, 202-634-7449.

11.408   FISHERMEN'S CONTINGENCY FUND

Type of Assistance: Direct payments ranging from $500 to $25,000.
Applicant Eligibility: Individuals.
Objective: To compensate US commercial fishermen for damage to or loss of fishing gear and resulting economic loss due to oil- and gas-related activities in any area of the Outer Continental Shelf.
Contact: Chief, Financial Services Division, National Marine Fisheries Service, 3300 Whitehaven Street, NW, Washington, DC 20235, 202-634-4688.

11.409   FISHING VESSEL AND GEAR DAMAGE COMPENSATION FUND

Type of Assistance: Direct payments ranging from $600 to $150,000.
Applicant Eligibility: Individuals.

Objective: To compensate US fishermen for the loss, damage or destruction of their vessels by foreign fishing vessels and their gear by any vessel.
Contact: Chief, Financial Services Division, National Marine Fisheries Service, Department of Commerce, 3300 Whitehaven Street, NW, Washington, DC 20235, 202-634-7496.

11.410 FISHERMEN'S GUARANTY FUND
Type of Assistance: Insurance ranging from $1,000 to $3 million.
Applicant Eligibility: Individuals.
Objective: To provide for reimbursement of losses incurred as a result of the seizure of a US commercial fishing vessel by a foreign country on the basis of rights or claims in territorial waters or on the high seas which are not recognized by the US.
Contact: Financial Services Division, National Marine Fisheries Service, 3300 Whitehaven St., NW, Washington DC 20235, 202-634-4688.

11.415 FISHING VESSEL OBLIGATION GUARANTEES
Type of Assistance: Guaranteed/insured loans ranging from $15,000 to $10 million.
Applicant Eligibility: Individuals.
Objective: To provide government guarantees of private loans to upgrade the US fishing fleet. Guarantees are made on mortgages for up to 87.5 percent of actual vessel costs, for lenders providing funds for construction, reconstruction or reconditioning of fishing vessels.
Contact: Chief, Financial Services Division, National Marine Fisheries Service, Department of Commerce, 3300 Whitehaven Street, NW, Washington, DC 20235, 202-634-7496.

11.417 SEA GRANT SUPPORT
Type of Assistance: Grants ranging from $60,000 to $2,280,900.
Applicant Eligibility: Individuals and state governments.
Objective: To support establishment of major university centers for marine research, education, training and advisory services, and also individual efforts in these same areas. Funds may be used for research and development, education and training and advisory services.
Contact: Director, National Sea Grant College Program, National Oceanic and Atmospheric Administration, 6010 Executive Boulevard, Rockville, MD 20852, 301-443-8926.

11.419 COASTAL ZONE MANAGEMENT
PROGRAM ADMINISTRATION
Type of Assistance: Grants ranging from $125,000 to $1,750,000.
Applicant Eligibility: State governments.
Objective: To assist states in implementing and administering coastal zone management programs that have been approved by the Secretary of Commerce.
Contact: Chief, Coastal Programs Division, Office of Ocean & Coastal Resource Management, National Oceanic and Atmospheric Admin-

istration, Department of Commerce, 3300 Whitehaven Street, NW, Washington, DC 20235, 202-634-1672.

11.420 COASTAL ZONE MANAGEMENT— ESTUARINE SANCTUARIES

Type of Assistance: Grants ranging from $10,000 to $1,620,000.
Applicant Eligibility: Coastal states.
Objective: To assist states in the acquisition, development and operation of estuarine sanctuaries for the purpose of creating natural field laboratories to gather data and make studies of the natural and human processes occurring within the estuaries of the coastal zone.
Contact: Director, Sanctuary Programs Division, Office of Ocean & Coastal Resource Management, National Oceanic and Atmospheric Administration, Department of Commerce, 3300 Whitehaven Street, NW, Washington, DC 20235, 202-634-4236.

11.421 COASTAL ENERGY IMPACT PROGRAM— FORMULA GRANTS

Type of Assistance: Grants ranging from $75,000 to $1 million.
Applicant Eligibility: State governments.
Objective: To provide financial assistance to coastal states to plan and construct public facilities and services and for the amelioration of environmental and recreational loss attributable to Outer Continental Shelf (OCS) energy development activities. Funds are available only to those states which have or have had adjacent OCS oil and gas leasing and development activities.
Contact: Chief, Coastal Programs Division, Office of Ocean & Coastal Resource Management, National Oceanic and Atmospheric Administration, Department of Commerce, 3300 Whitehaven Street, NW, Washington, DC 20235, 202-634-1672.

11.422 COASTAL ENERGY IMPACT PROGRAM— PLANNING GRANTS

Type of Assistance: Grants ranging from $75,000 to $192,000.
Applicant Eligibility: State governments.
Objective: To assist the states and units of local government to study and plan for the social, economic and environmental consequences on the coastal zone of new or expanded energy facilities, and to encourage rational and timely planning and management of energy facility siting and energy resource development.
Contact: Chief, Coastal Programs Division, Office of Ocean & Coastal Resource Management, National Oceanic and Atmospheric Administration, Department of Commerce, 3300 Whitehaven Street, NW, Washington, DC 20235, 202-634-1672.

11.426 FINANCIAL ASSISTANCE FOR MARINE POLLUTION RESEARCH

Type of Assistance: Grants ranging from $15,000 to $180,000.
Applicant Eligibility: Individuals, nonprofit organizations, state and local

governments, universities, colleges, technical schools and laboratories.
Objective: To determine the ecological consequences of dumping industrial, municipal and dredged waste materials into the ocean.
Contact: National Ocean Service, Office of Oceanography and Marine Services, NOAA, N/OMS3 Ocean Assessments Division, Rockville, MD 20852, 301-443-8734.

11.427 FISHERIES DEVELOPMENT AND UTILIZATION RESEARCH AND DEVELOPMENT GRANTS AND COOPERATIVE AGREEMENTS PROGRAM

Type of Assistance: Grants ranging from $5,000 to $2,500,000.
Applicant Eligibility: Individuals, nonprofit organizations, state and local governments.
Objective: To foster the development and strengthening of the fishing industry of the United States and increase the supply of wholesome, nutritious fish and fish products available to consumers.
Contact: Office of Industry Studies, National Marine Fisheries Service, National Oceanic and Atmospheric Administration, Department of Commerce, Washington, DC 20235, 202-634-7451.

11.428 INTERGOVERNMENTAL CLIMATE-DEMONSTRATION PROJECT

Type of Assistance: Grants ranging from $15,000 to $105,000.
Applicant Eligibility: State and local governments, profit and nonprofit organizations, and individuals.
Objective: To aid states in the initiation of regional climate centers which will supply guidance, information and climate data to users in the private and public sectors.
Contact: National Climate Program Office, National Oceanic and Atmospheric Administration, Department of Commerce, 11400 Rockville Pike, Rockville, MD 20852, 301-443-8981.

NATIONAL TELECOMMUNICATIONS AND INFORMATION ADMINISTRATION

11.550 PUBLIC TELECOMMUNICATIONS FACILITIES

Type of Assistance: Grants ranging from $3,500 to $705,500.
Applicant Eligibility: Nonprofit organizations, state and local governments.
Objective: To assist, through matching grants, in the planning and construction of public telecommunications facilities in order to extend delivery of public telecommunications services to as many citizens of the U.S. and territories as possible by the most efficient and economical means, including the use of broadcast and nonbroadcast technologies; increase public telecommunications services and facilities available to, operated by, and owned by minorities and women; and strengthen the capability of existing public television and radio stations to provide public telecommunications services to the public.

Contact: Director, Public Telecommunications Facilities Division/NTIA, Room 4625, Department of Commerce, 14th Street and Constitution Avenue, NW, Washington, DC 20230, 202-377-5802.

NATIONAL BUREAU OF STANDARDS

11.609 MEASUREMENT AND ENGINEERING RESEARCH AND STANDARDS

Type of Assistance: Grants.

Applicant Eligibility: Universities, nonprofit organizations and state and local governments.

Objective: To provide scientific research for measurement and engineering research and standards. Grant money may be used to further scientific research in areas of fire research, precision measurement, building research, automated manufacturing, weights and measures and other areas of specific research.

Contact: National Bureau of Standards, Gaithersburg, MD 20899.

OFFICE OF MINORITY BUSINESS ENTERPRISE

11.800 MINORITY BUSINESS DEVELOPMENT— MANAGEMENT AND TECHNICAL ASSISTANCE

Type of Assistance: Grants ranging from $10,000 to $2,145,000.

Applicant Eligibility: Individuals, nonprofit organizations, state and local governments.

Objective: To provide free financial, management and technical assistance to economically and socially disadvantaged individuals who need help in starting and/or operating a business. Primary objectives of the assistance are to increase the gross receipts and decrease the failure rates of the client firms.

Contact: Director, Office of Field Operations, Room 6725, Minority Business Development Agency, Department of Commerce, 14th and Constitution Avenue, NW, Washington, DC 20230, 202-377-8015.

US DEPARTMENT OF DEFENSE

DEFENSE LOGISTICS AGENCY

12.001   INDUSTRIAL EQUIPMENT LOANS TO EDUCATIONAL INSTITUTIONS (TOOLS FOR SCHOOLS)

Type of Assistance: Use of property, facilities and equipment.
Applicant Eligibility: Nonprofit educational institutions.
Objective: In order to develop skilled manpower as an individual preparedness measure, qualified educational institutions and training schools may be loaned idle equipment from the Defense Industrial Reserve.
Contact: Directorate of Supply Operations, Defense Logistics Agency, Cameron Station, Alexandria, VA 22304-1600, 202-274-6269.

OFFICE OF THE ASSISTANT SECRETARY (MANPOWER, RESERVE AFFAIRS AND LOGISTICS)

12.609   SELECTED RESERVE EDUCATIONAL ASSISTANCE PROGRAM (NEW GI BILL)

Type of Assistance: Direct payments for specified use.
Applicant Eligibility: Individuals enlisted, Selected Reserve Service.
Objective: To encourage and sustain membership in the National Guard and Reserve components. Provides for educational assistance for pursuit of an undergraduate degree and noncollege degree programs at institutions of higher learning.
Contact: Assistant Secretary of Defense (Reserve Affairs), Pentagon, Room 3E25, Washington, DC 20301-1500, 202-695-7459/7429.

SECRETARIES OF MILITARY DEPARTMENTS

12.700   DONATIONS/LOANS OF OBSOLETE DOD PROPERTY

Type of Assistance: Use of property, facilities and equipment.
Applicant Eligibility: Nonprofit organizations, state and local governments.
Objective: To donate or lend obsolete combat material, surplus to the needs of DOD, to veterans' organizations, soldiers' monument associations, state museums, incorporated museums and incorporated municipalities.
Contact: Appropriate Military Department, Pentagon, Washington, DC 20301.

US DEPARTMENT OF HEALTH AND HUMAN SERVICES

Key to acronyms used in addresses in 13.000 section:

ADAMHA	Alcohol, Drug Abuse, and Mental Health Administration	NINCDS	National Institute of Neurological and Communicative Disorders and Strokes
BHM	Bureau of Health Manpower	OAMS	Office of Administrative Management Services
BHPR	Bureau of Health Professions		
BMS	Bureau of Medical Services	OMCH	Office of Maternal and Child Health
DHHS	Department of Health and Human Services	PHS	Public Health Service
HRA	Health Resources Administration		

PUBLIC HEALTH SERVICE—1

13.103   FOOD AND DRUG ADMINISTRATION—RESEARCH
Type of Assistance: Grants ranging from $6,000 to $360,000.
Applicant Eligibility: Nonprofit organizations, state and local governments.
Objective: To assist public and other nonprofit institutions to establish, expand and improve research activities concerned with foods, food additives, shellfish sanitation, poison control, drug and cosmetic hazards, human and veterinary drugs, medical devices and diagnostic products, biologics, and radiation-emitting devices and materials.
Contact: Chief, State Contracts and Assistance Agreements Branch, HFA-520, Room 15A17, 5600 Fishers Lane, Rockville, MD 20857, 301-443-6170.

13.108   HEALTH EDUCATION ASSISTANCE LOANS
Type of Assistance: Guaranteed/insured loans not to exceed $80,000.
Applicant Eligibility: Individuals.
Objective: To authorize loans for educational expenses available from eligible lenders such as banks, credit unions, savings and loan associ-

ations, pension funds, insurance companies and eligible educational institutions. Loans are made to graduate students enrolled at eligible health professions institutions. The loans are insured by the federal government.
Contact: Division of Student Assistance, Health Resources Services Administration, DHHS, Parklawn Building, Room 8-38, 5600 Fishers Lane, Rockville, MD 20857, 301-443-1173.

13.110   MATERNAL AND CHILD HEALTH FEDERAL CONSOLIDATED PROGRAMS
Type of Assistance: Grants ranging from $50,000 to $1 million.
Applicant Eligibility: Public or nonprofit private institutions of higher learning.
Objective: To carry out special projects of regional and national significance, training and research; genetic disease testing, counseling and information development and dissemination programs and comprehensive hemophilia diagnostic and treatment centers.
Contact: Division of Maternal and Child Health, Department of Health and Human Services, Parklawn Building, Room 6-05, 5600 Fishers Lane, Rockville, MD 20857, 301-443-2170.

13.111   ADOLESCENT FAMILY LIFE RESEARCH GRANTS
Type of Assistance: Grants ranging from $15,000 to $150,000.
Applicant Eligibility: State and local governments; public or private organizations.
Objective: To encourage and support research projects and demonstration projects concerning the societal causes and consequences of adolescent premarital sexual relations, contraceptive use, pregnancy and childbearing.
Contact: Office of Adolescent Pregnancy Programs, Office of the Assistant Secretary for Health, DHHS, Room 1351 HHS-N, 330 Independence Ave., SW, Washington, DC 20201, 202-245-0146.

13.112   CHARACTERIZATION OF ENVIRONMENTAL HEALTH HAZARDS
Type of Assistance: Grants ranging from $23,000 to $1,214,000.
Applicant Eligibility: Universities, colleges, hospitals, state or local governments.
Objective: This program seeks to identify and measure the biological, chemical and physical factors that are hazardous, which is an essential first step to establishing the relationship between different levels of exposure to these factors and probable injuries. Researchers examine how environmental elements affect the liver, lungs, intestines and the nervous systems. They also investigate possible carcinogenic, genetic and reproductive effects.
Contact: Research Grants, Research Career Development Awards, National Institute of Environmental Health Sciences, PO Box 12233, Research Triangle Park, NC 27709, 919-541-7723.

13.113 BIOLOGICAL RESPONSE TO ENVIRONMENTAL HEALTH HAZARDS

Type of Assistance: Grants ranging from $4,000 to $985,000.

Applicant Eligibility: Universities, colleges or hospitals, state or local governments, nonprofit research institutions.

Objective: To focus on understanding how chemical and physical agents cause pathological changes in molecules, cells, tissues and organs and become manifested as respiratory disease; neurological, behavioral and developmental abnormalities and cancer and other disorders.

Contact: Research Grants, National Institute of Environmental Health Sciences, PO Box 12233, Research Triangle Park, NC 27709, 919-541-7723.

13.114 APPLIED TOXICOLOGICAL RESEARCH AND TESTING

Type of Assistance: Grants ranging from $43,000 to $723,000.

Applicant Eligibility: Universities, colleges or hospitals, state or local governments, nonprofit research institutions.

Objective: This program develops scientific information on potentially toxic and hazardous chemicals by concentrating on toxicological research, testing and test development and validation efforts. Specific goals of the program include the determination of the toxicological profiles of chemicals and development and validation of existing and emerging methodologies which can be successfully employed for prediction of the human response to toxic agents.

Contact: Research Grants, National Institute of Environmental Health Sciences, PO Box 12233, Research Triangle Park, NC 27709, 919-541-7723.

13.115 BIOMETRY AND RISK ESTIMATION

Type of Assistance: Grants ranging from $31,000 to $1,345,000.

Applicant Eligibility: Universities, colleges or hospitals, state or local governments, nonprofit research institutions.

Objective: Estimating the probable risks such as cancer, reproductive effects, and other adverse effects from various environmental hazards. The major emphases are on refining existing methods for estimating human risk from data derived from studying laboratory animals and on examining the quantitative issues involved in designing short-term tests and interpreting data obtained from these tests.

Contact: Research Grants, National Institute of Environmental Health Sciences, PO Box 12233, Research Triangle Park, NC 27709, 919-541-7723.

13.116 PROJECT GRANTS AND COOPERATIVE AGREEMENTS FOR TUBERCULOSIS CONTROL PROGRAMS

Type of Assistance: Grants ranging from $30,000 to $500,000.

Applicant Eligibility: Public health agencies of state and local governments.

Objective: To assist state and local health agencies in carrying out tuberculosis control activities designed to prevent transmission of infection and disease.
Contact: Chief, Grants Mangement Branch, Centers for Disease Control, PHS, DHHS, 1600 Clifton Road, NE, Atlanta, GA 30333, 404-262-6575.

13.117 GRANTS FOR PREVENTIVE MEDICINE RESIDENCY PROGRAM

Type of Assistance: Grants ranging from $36,909 to $123,578.
Applicant Eligibility: Any accredited public or private school of medicine, osteopathy or public health.
Objective: To promote post-graduate education of physicians in preventive medicine to advance the cause of health promotion and disease prevention.
Contact: Division of Medicine, Bureau of Health Professions, Health Resources and Services Administration, Parklawn Building, 5600 Fishers Lane, Rockville, MD 20857, 301-436-6190.

13.124 NURSE ANESTHETIST TRAINEESHIPS

Type of Assistance: Project grants ranging from $951 to $17,010.
Applicant Eligibility: Public and private nonprofit organizations.
Objective: To support full-time study for registered nurses who have completed twelve months of study in nurse anesthetist training programs.
Contact: Division of Nursing, Department of Health and Human Services, Parklawn Building, Room 5C-26, 5600 Fishers Lane, Rockville, MD 20857, 301-443-6333.

13.125 MENTAL HEALTH PLANNING AND DEMONSTRATION PROJECTS

Type of Assistance: Project grants ranging from $80,000 to $250,000.
Applicant Eligibility: States.
Objective: To promote the development of support systems for the long-term mentally ill, and to assist states in the delivery of mental health services.
Contact: Director, Office of State and Community Liaison, NIMH, Parklawn Building, Room 110-26, 5600 Fishers Lane, Rockville, MD 20857, 301-443-3606.

13.126 SMALL BUSINESS INNOVATION RESEARCH

Type of Assistance: Project grants ranging from $37,000 to $500,000.
Applicant Eligibility: Individuals.
Objective: To use small business to stimulate technological innovation to meet alcohol, drug and mental health research and development needs.
Contact: Parklawn Building, 5600 Fishers Lane, Rockville, MD 20857, 301-443-4223, 301-443-5280 or 301-443-3107.

13.127 EMERGENCY MEDICAL SERVICE FOR CHILDREN (EMS for children)

Type of Assistance: Project grants.
Applicant Eligibility: Nonprofit organizations, state and local governments.
Objective: To support expansion and improvement of emergency medical services for children who need treatment for trauma and critical care.
Contact: Division of Maternal and Child Health, Bureau of Health Care Delivery and Assistance, Health Resources and Services Administration, Parklawn Building, Room 6-05, 5600 Fishers Lane, Rockville, MD 20857, 301-443-2170.

13.128 REFUGEE ASSISTANCE–MENTAL HEALTH

Type of Assistance: Project grants, $200,000 to $500,000.
Applicant Eligibility: State mental health departments.
Objective: To ensure the availability of essential mental health services for refugees in states with large numbers of refugees.
Contact: Acting Director, Cuban/Haitian Mental Health Unit, National Institute of Mental Health, Parklawn Building, Room 18A-33, 5600 Fishers Lane, Rockville, MD 20857, 301-443-2130.

13.129 TECHNICAL AND NONFINANCIAL ASSISTANCE TO COMMUNITY HEALTH CENTERS

Type of Assistance: Project grants up to $100,000.
Applicant Eligibility: States.
Objective: To provide assistance to community health centers.
Contact: Director, Division of Primary Care Services, Bureau of Health Care Delivery and Assistance, Parklawn Building, Room 7A-55, 5600 Fishers Lane, Rockville, MD 20857, 301-443-2270.

13.130 PRIMARY CARE SERVICES—PLANNING AND DEVELOPMENT COOPERATIVE AGREEMENTS

Type of Assistance: Project grants up to $100,000.
Applicant Eligibility: States.
Objective: To coordinate local, state and federal planning in primary care service delivery to establish community health centers and the assignment of National Health Service Corps physicians.
Contact: Director, Division of Primary Care Services, BHCDA, Parklawn Building, Room 7A-55, 5600 Fishers Lane, Rockville, MD 20857, 301-443-2270.

13.131 SHARED RESEARCH FACILITIES FOR HEART, LUNG AND BLOOD DISEASES

Type of Assistance: Project grants.
Applicant Eligibility: Nonprofit organizations.
Objective: To expand or create physical resources for the application of technology to fundamental research in heart, lung and blood diseases. Awards may be used to modernize and improve existing physical facilities.

Contact: Director, Division of Extramural Affairs, National Heart, Lung and Blood Institute, Bethesda, MD 20892, 301-496-7416.

13.217 FAMILY PLANNING SERVICES
Type of Assistance: Grants ranging from $20,000 to $1 million.
Applicant Eligibility: Nonprofit organizations, state and local governments.
Objective: To provide educational counseling, comprehensive medical and social services necessary to enable individuals to freely determine the number and spacing of their children, and by so doing helping to reduce maternal and infant mortality thereby promoting the health of mothers and children. Funds may be used for contraceptive services, infertility services, and special services to adolescents.
Contact: Asst. Secretary for Population Affairs, Department of Health & Human Services, Room 1351, 330 Independence Avenue, SW, Washington, DC 20201, 202-245-0151.

13.224 COMMUNITY HEALTH CENTERS
Type of Assistance: Grants ranging from $25,000 to $4 million.
Applicant Eligibility: Nonprofit organizations, state and local governments.
Objective: To support the development and operation of community health centers which provide primary health services, supplemental health services, and environmental health services to medically underserved populations. Priorities focus on capacity building in medically underserved areas and maintenance of existing centers, expansion of population and service coverage in existing centers, monitoring and assessment of project performance, development and implementation of mechanisms for improving quality of care, and maximizing third party reimbursement levels through improved project administration and management.
Contact: Director, Division Primary Care Services, Bureau of Health Care Delivery and Assistance, Parklawn Building, Room 7A-55, 5600 Fishers Lane, Rockville, MD 20857, 301-443-2260.

13.226 HEALTH SERVICES RESEARCH
AND DEVELOPMENT GRANTS
Type of Assistance: Grants ranging from $7,000 to $290,000.
Applicant Eligibility: Individuals, nonprofit organizations, state and local governments.
Objective: To support research, development, demonstration, and evaluation activities aimed toward developing new options for health services delivery and health policy; to test the assumptions on which current policies and delivery practices are based; and to develop the means for monitoring the performance of the health care system. Also to support research for the development of useful information to communities that are implementing Emergency Medical Services Systems (EMS). The program supports research studies in many categories of

concerns, including cost containment, health insurance, planning and regulation, technology and computer science applications.
Contact: National Center for Health Services Research and Health Care Technology Assessment, Department of Health and Human Services, Parklawn Building, 5600 Fishers Lane, Rockville, MD 20857, 301-443-4033.

13.228 INDIAN HEALTH SERVICES— HEALTH MANAGEMENT DEVELOPMENT PROGRAM
Type of Assistance: Grants ranging from $15,000 to $3 million.
Applicant Eligibility: Native Americans.
Objective: To raise to the highest possible level the health of American Indians and Alaskan Natives by providing a full range of curative, preventive and rehabilitative health services that include public health nursing, maternal and child health care, dental and nutrition services, psychiatric care and health education. Also to increase the Indian communities' capacity to man and manage their health programs and to build the capability of the American Indian to manage their health programs.
Contact: Contracts and Grants, Indian Health Services, 5600 Fishers Lane, Rockville, MD 20857, 301-443-5204.

13.242 MENTAL HEALTH RESEARCH GRANTS
Type of Assistance: Grants ranging from $15,000 to $590,000.
Applicant Eligibility: Individuals, nonprofit organizations, state and local governments.
Objective: To develop new knowledge of and approaches to the causes, diagnoses, treatment, control and prevention of mental diseases through basic, clinical and applied research; to develop and test new models and systems for mental health services delivery; and to otherwise develop and improve knowledge relevant to the provision of mental health services through organized systems and networks of services.
Contact: Director, Division of Extramural Research Programs (Behavioral Sciences, Clinical Treatment, Neurosciences, Pharmacologic and Somatic Treatments and Applied Therapeutics, Research and Small Grants), National Institute of Mental Health, 5600 Fishers Lane, Rockville, MD 20857 301-443-3563.

13.244 MENTAL HEALTH CLINICAL OR SERVICE-RELATED TRAINING GRANTS
Type of Assistance: Grants ranging from $25,000 to $200,000.
Applicant Eligibility: Nonprofit organizations, state and local governments.
Objective: To encourage mental health specialists to work in areas where shortages exist, to increase the number of minority mental health professionals and to assure that the skills and knowledge are appropriate to the needs of those served.
Contact: Director, Division of Human Resources, National Institute

of Mental Health, 5600 Fishers Lane, Rockville, MD 20857, 301-443-4257.

13.246 MIGRANT HEALTH CENTERS GRANTS
Type of Assistance: Grants ranging from $30,000 to $1,250,000.
Applicant Eligibility: Nonprofit organizations.
Objective: To support the development and operation of migrant health centers and projects which provide primary, ambulatory, and inpatient health services, supplemental health services, and environmental health services which are accessible to migrant and seasonal farm workers and their families.
Contact: Director, Migrant Health Program, Bureau of Health Care Delivery and Assistance, Parklawn Building, Room 7A-55, 5600 Fishers Lane, Rockville, MD 20857, 301-443-1153.

13.258 NATIONAL HEALTH SERVICE CORPS
Type of Assistance: Direct loans ranging from $10,000 to $50,000.
Applicant Eligibility: Any public and nonprofit private health or health-related organization.
Objective: To improve the delivery of health care services to residents in areas critically short of health personnel.
Contact: National Health Service Corps, Health Resources and Services Administration, Parklawn Building, 5600 Fishers Lane, Rockville, MD 20857, 301-443-2900.

13.260 FAMILY PLANNING SERVICES
Type of Assistance: Grants ranging from $90,000 to $275,000.
Applicant Eligibility: Nonprofit organizations, state and local governments.
Objective: To provide job-specific training for personnel to improve the delivery of family planning services.
Contact: Office of Population Affairs, DHHS, Room 1351, 330 Independence Avenue, SW, Washington, DC 20201, 301-472-0151.

13.262 OCCUPATIONAL SAFETY AND HEALTH RESEARCH GRANTS
Type of Assistance: Grants ranging from $5,000 to $250,000.
Applicant Eligibility: Individuals, nonprofit organizations, state and local governments.
Objective: To understand the underlying characteristics of occupational safety and health problems; to discover effective solutions in dealing with them; to eliminate or control factors in the work environment which are harmful to the health and safety of workers; and to demonstrate technical feasibility or application of new or improved occupational safety and health procedures, methods, techniques or systems.
Contact: Procurement and Grants Office, Centers for Disease Control, PHS/DHHS, 1600 Clifton Road, NE, Atlanta, GA 30333, 404-262-6575.

13.263   OCCUPATIONAL SAFETY AND HEALTH—TRAINING GRANTS

Type of Assistance: Grants ranging from $300,000 to $700,000.
Applicant Eligibility: Nonprofit organizations, state and local governments.
Objective: To develop specialized professional personnel in occupational safety and health problems with training in occupational medicine, nursing and industrial hygiene and safety.
Contact: Procurement and Grants Office, Centers for Disease Control, PHS/DHHS, 1600 Clifton Road, NE, Atlanta, GA 30333, 404-262-6575.

13.268   CHILDHOOD IMMUNIZATION GRANTS

Type of Assistance: Grants ranging from $10,000 to $2,384,964.
Applicant Eligibility: Nonprofit organizations, state and local governments.
Objective: To assist states and communities in establishing and maintaining immunization programs for the control of vaccine-preventable diseases of childhood (including measles, rubella, poliomyelitis, diphtheria, pertussis, tetanus and mumps).
Contact: Director, Centers for Disease Control, PHS/DHHS, 1600 Clifton Road, NE, Atlanta, GA 30333, 404-329-3291.

13.271   ALCOHOL RESEARCH SCIENTIST DEVELOPMENT AND RESEARCH SCIENTIST AWARDS

Type of Assistance: Grants ranging from $33,000 to $50,200.
Applicant Eligibility: Individuals.
Objective: To provide support for research relating to the problems of alcohol abuse and alcoholism prevention, treatment and rehabilitation, and to raise the level of competence and to increase the number of individuals engaged in such research.
Contact: Division of Extramural Research, Director, National Institute on Alcohol Abuse and Alcoholism, PHS/DHHS, 5600 Fishers Lane, Rockville, MD 20857, 301-443-2530.

13.272   ALCOHOL NATIONAL RESEARCH SERVICE AWARDS FOR RESEARCH TRAINING

Type of Assistance: Grants ranging from $9,000 to $131,000.
Applicant Eligibility: Individuals.
Objective: To provide support to individuals for predoctoral and postdoctoral research training in specific alcohol abuse-related areas via an individual National Research Service Award. An institutional National Research Service grant provides support to enable nonprofit institutions to develop research training opportunities for individuals interested in careers in particular specified alcohol abuse-related fields.
Contact: Division of Extramural Research, Director, National Institute on Alcohol Abuse and Alcoholism, PHS/DHHS, 5600 Fishers Lane, Rockville, MD 20857, 301-443-2530.

13.273   ALCOHOL RESEARCH PROGRAMS

Type of Assistance: Grants ranging from $10,000 to $366,000.

Applicant Eligibility: Individuals, nonprofit organizations, state and local governments.

Objective: To develop new knowledge and approaches to the causes, diagnosis, treatment, control and prevention of alcohol abuse and alcoholism through basic, clinical, and applied research, investigations, experiments and studies.

Contact: Director, Division of Extramural Research, National Institute on Alcohol Abuse and Alcoholism, PHS/DHHS, 5600 Fishers Lane, Rockville, MD 20857, 301-443-2530.

13.277   DRUG ABUSE RESEARCH SCIENTIST DEVELOPMENT AND RESEARCH SCIENTIST AWARDS

Type of Assistance: Grants ranging from $25,000 to $45,000.

Applicant Eligibility: Individuals.

Objective: To provide support for research relating to the problems of narcotic addiction and drug abuse and to raise the level of competence and to increase the number of individuals engaged in such research via special levels of NIDA support.

Contact: Division of Research, National Institute on Drug Abuse, ADAMHA, PHS/DHHS, Parklawn Building, Room 9-36, 5600 Fishers Lane, Rockville, MD 20857, 301-443-1887.

13.278   DRUG ABUSE NATIONAL RESEARCH SERVICE AWARDS FOR RESEARCH TRAINING

Type of Assistance: Grants from $6,552 to $30,000.

Applicant Eligibility: Individuals, nonprofit organizations.

Objective: An Individual National Research Service award provides support to individuals for predoctoral and postdoctoral research training in specified drug-related areas; an institutional National Research Service grant provides support to enable nonprofit institutions to develop research training opportunities for individuals interested in careers in particular specified drug abuse–related fields.

Contact: Division of Training, National Institute on Drug Abuse, ADAMHA, PHS/DHHS, Parklawn Building, 5600 Fishers Lane, Rockville, MD 20857, 301-443-1887.

13.279   DRUG ABUSE RESEARCH PROGRAMS

Type of Assistance: Grants ranging from $12,000 to $243,000.

Applicant Eligibility: Individuals, nonprofit organizations, state and local governments.

Objective: To develop new knowledge and approaches to the epidemiology, etiology, diagnosis, treatment, control and prevention of narcotic addiction and drug abuse through basic, clinical and applied research, investigations, experiments and studies.

Contact: Division of Research, National Institute on Drug Abuse, ADAMHA, PHS/DHHS, Parklawn Building, Room 9-36, 5600 Fishers Lane, Rockville, MD 20857, 301-443-1887.

13.281 MENTAL HEALTH RESEARCH SCIENTIST DEVELOPMENT AND RESEARCH SCIENTIST AWARDS

Type of Assistance: Grants ranging from $15,000 to $45,000.
Applicant Eligibility: Individuals, nonprofit organizations, state and local governments.
Objective: Objective: To provide support for research relating to the problems of mental illness and mental health and to raise the level of competence and increase the number of individuals engaged in such research via special levels of National Institute of Mental Health support.
Contact: Chief, Research Scientist Development Program, National Institute of Mental Health, Room 10104, 5600 Fishers Lane, Rockville, MD 20857, 301-443-4347.

13.282 MENTAL HEALTH NATIONAL RESEARCH SERVICE AWARDS FOR RESEARCH TRAINING

Type of Assistance: Grants averaging $6,552.
Applicant Eligibility: Individuals, nonprofit organizations.
Objective: An individual National Research Service award provides support to individuals for predoctoral and postdoctoral research training in specified mental health–related areas; an institutional National Research Service grant provides support and enables nonprofit institutions to develop research training opportunities for individuals interested in careers in a particular specified mental health-related field. The Minority Access to Research Careers programs (MARC) are intended to assist institutions with substantial minority enrollment in the training of greater numbers of scientists and teachers in fields related to mental health, alcoholism and drug abuse.
Contact: Director, Division of Extramural Research Programs, Room 10105, National Institute of Mental Health, 5600 Fishers Lane, Rockville, MD 20857, 301-443-3563.

13.288 NATIONAL HEALTH SERVICE CORPS SCHOLARSHIP PROGRAM

Type of Assistance: Grants averaging $9,947 per year.
Applicant Eligibility: Individuals.
Objective: To assure an adequate supply of physicians, dentists and other health professionals for the National Health Service Corps for service in health manpower shortage areas in the United States. Scholarships are to be used to support students who pursue full-time courses of study in health professions schools.
Contact: National Health Service Corps Scholarship Program, Parklawn Building, 5600 Fishers Lane, Room 7-16, Rockville, MD 20857, 800-638-0842. (In Maryland, 301-443-2320, call collect.)

13.293 STATE HEALTH PLANNING AND DEVELOPMENT AGENCIES

Type of Assistance: Grants ranging from $98,096 to $1,596,257.
Applicant Eligibility: State governments.

Objective: To provide support to the state health planning agencies conducting physical and mental health planning and development functions. Funds may be used by a state health planning and development agency in meeting the cost of its operation, including the administration of the state program and assisting the statewide health coordinating council in the performance of its functions.
Contact: Director, Bureau of Health Maintenance Organizations and Resources Development, Parklawn Building, 5600 Fishers Lane, Rockville, MD 20857, 301-443-1993.

13.294 HEALTH PLANNING—HEALTH SYSTEMS AGENCIES
Type of Assistance: Grants beginning at $100,000.
Applicant Eligibility: Nonprofit organizations, state and local governments.
Objective: To provide for effective health resources planning at the area level to meet problems in health care delivery systems, maldistribution of health care facilities and manpower, and increasing cost of health care.
Contact: Director, Bureau of Health Maintenance Organizations and Resources Development, Parklawn Building, 5600 Fishers Lane, Rockville, MD 20857, 301-443-1993.

13.297 NATIONAL RESEARCH SERVICE AWARDS
Type of Assistance: Grants.
Applicant Eligibility: Individuals.
Objective: To prepare qualified professional nurses to conduct nursing research, collaborate in interdisciplinary research, and function as faculty in schools of nursing at the graduate level. To provide up to five years of support in the aggregate for full-time predoctoral study, and three years for postdoctoral study.
Contact: Chief, Advanced Nurse Training Resources Branch, Division of Nursing, BHPR, HRSA, 5600 Fishers Lane, Room 5C-26, Rockville, MD 20857, 301-443-6333.

13.298 NURSE PRACTITIONER AND NURSE MIDWIFE EDUCATION AND TRAINEESHIPS
Type of Assistance: Grants ranging from $3,725 to $88,112; students may receive stipends up to $5,040 plus tuition and other expenses.
Applicant Eligibility: Nonprofit organizations, state and local governments.
Objective: To educate registered nurses who will be qualified to provide primary health care.
Contact: Division of Nursing, 5600 Fishers Lane, Room 5C-26, Rockville, MD 20857, 301-443-6333.

13.299 ADVANCED NURSE TRAINING PROGRAM
Type of Assistance: Grants ranging from $19,405 to $334,909.
Applicant Eligibility: Nonprofit organizations, state and local governments.

Objective: To prepare registered nurses at the master's and doctoral levels to teach in the various fields of nurse training and to serve in administrative or supervisory capacities, in nursing specialties and as nurse clinicians.
Contact: Division of Nursing, 5600 Fishers Lane, Room 5C-26, Rockville, MD 20857, 301-443-6333.

13.306 LABORATORY ANIMAL SCIENCES AND PRIMATE RESEARCH

Type of Assistance: Grants ranging from $5,385 to $4,276,742.
Applicant Eligibility: Individuals, nonprofit organizations, state and local governments.
Objective: To provide animal resources with which the biomedical scientist can develop knowledge for prevention and control of disease in man through experimentation with animal models.
Contact: Animal Resources Branch, Division of Research Resources, National Institutes of Health, Building 31, Room 5B59, Bethesda, MD 20205, 301-496-5175.

13.333 CLINICAL RESEARCH

Type of Assistance: Grants ranging from $287,461 to $2,338,014.
Applicant Eligibility: Nonprofit organizations and local governments.
Objective: To create and sustain, on a stable basis, highly specialized institutional resources in which clinical investigators can observe and study human disease.
Contact: General Clinical Research Centers Program Branch, Division of Research Resources, National Institutes of Health, Building 31, Room 5B59, Bethesda, MD 20205, 301-496-6595.

13.337 BIOMEDICAL RESEARCH SUPPORT

Type of Assistance: Grants.
Applicant Eligibility: Nonprofit organizations and local governments.
Objective: To strengthen, balance and stabilize Public Health Service–supported biomedical and behavioral research; enable quick and effective response to emerging opportunities and unpredictable requirements; enhance creativity, encourage innovation and improve the quality of project grant proposals; develop and maintain physical and human research resources; and strengthen and/or expand health-related research in eligible institutions to improve the training of manpower for clinical professions or health-related research.
Contact: Biomedical Research Support Program, Division of Research Resources, National Institutes of Health, Building 31, Room 5B35, Bethesda, MD 20205, 301-496-6743.

13.339 HEALTH PROFESSIONS—CAPITATION GRANTS

Type of Assistance: Grants ranging from $54,040 to $460,018.
Applicant Eligibility: Nonprofit organizations and local governments.
Objective: To provide financial assistance to schools of medicine, osteopathy, dentistry, public health, veterinary medicine, optometry,

pharmacy and podiatry in return for addressing geographic specialty requirements for enrollment goals.

Contact: Grants Management Officer, Health Resources & Services Administration Center Building, 5600 Fishers Lane, Room 8C-22, Rockville, MD 20857, 301-443-6880.

13.342 HEALTH PROFESSIONS—STUDENT LOANS

Type of Assistance: Grants ranging from $200 to $8,000.

Applicant Eligibility: Nonprofit organizations, state and local governments.

Objective: To increase educational opportunities for students in need of financial assistance to pursue a course of study in specified health professions by providing long-term low-interest loans.

Contact: Division of Student Assistance, Health Resources & Services Administration, Parklawn Building, Room 8-44, 5600 Fishers Lane, Rockville, MD 20857, 301-443-1173.

13.358 PROFESSIONAL NURSE TRAINEESHIPS

Type of Assistance: Grants ranging from $8,799 to $609,502; students may receive stipends up to $5,040 plus tuition and other expenses.

Applicant Eligibility: Nonprofit organizations, state and local governments.

Objective: To prepare registered nurses as administrators, supervisors, teachers, nursing specialists and nurse practitioners for positions in hospitals and related institutions, in public health agencies, in schools of nursing and in other roles requiring advanced training.

Contact: Division of Nursing, BHM, HRA, PHS/DHHS, 5600 Fishers Lane, Room 5C-26, Rockville, MD 20857, 301-443-6333.

13.359 NURSE TRAINING IMPROVEMENT— SPECIAL PROJECTS

Type of Assistance: Grants ranging from $7,142 to $233,064.

Applicant Eligibility: Nonprofit organizations, state and local governments.

Objective: To help schools of nursing and other institutions improve the quality and availability of nursing education through projects for specified purposes, such as opportunities for individuals from disadvantaged backgrounds.

Contact: Division of Nursing, Health Resources & Services Administration, 5600 Fishers Lane, Room 5C-26, Rockville, MD 20857, 301-443-6193.

13.361 NURSING RESEARCH PROJECT GRANTS

Type of Assistance: Grants ranging from $11,878 to $394,649.

Applicant Eligibility: Individuals, nonprofit organizations, state and local governments.

Objective: To support basic and applied research activities in nursing education, practice and administration.

Contact: Division of Nursing, Health Resources Administration, Department of Health & Human Services, 5600 Fishers Lane, Room 5C-26, Rockville, MD 20857, 301-443-6315.

13.364 NURSING STUDENT LOANS
Type of Assistance: Grants ranging from $500 to $2,500.
Applicant Eligibility: Nonprofit organizations and local governments.
Objective: To assist students in need of financial assistance to pursue a course of study in professional nursing education by providing long-term, low-interest loans.
Contact: Division of Student Assistance, Health Resources & Services Administration, Parklawn Building, Room 8-44, 5600 Fishers Lane, Rockville, MD 20857, 301-443-1173.

13.371 BIOTECHNOLOGY RESEARCH
Type of Assistance: Grants ranging from $7,500 to $1,824,703.
Applicant Eligibility: Nonprofit organizations and local governments.
Objective: To assist academic and other nonprofit institutions in developing and sustaining sophisticated technological capabilities, such as computer centers, biological structure resources and biomedical engineering resources which are vital to modern biomedical research.
Contact: Biotechnology Resources Branch, Division of Research Resources, National Institutes of Health, Building 31, Room 5B-41, Bethesda, MD 20205, 301-496-5411.

13.375 MINORITY BIOMEDICAL RESEARCH SUPPORT
Type of Assistance: Grants ranging from $100,000 to $1 million per year for 3 to 4 years.
Applicant Eligibility: Nonprofit organizations, state and local governments.
Objective: To increase the numbers of ethnic minority faculty, students and investigators engaged in biomedical research, and to broaden the opportunities for participation in biomedical research of ethnic minority faculty, students and investigators by providing support for biomedical research programs at eligible institutions.
Contact: Minority Biomedical Support Program Branch, Division of Research Resources, National Institutes of Health, Building 31, Room 5B-35, Bethesda, MD 20205, 301-496-6743.

13.379 GRANTS FOR GRADUATE TRAINING
IN FAMILY MEDICINE
Type of Assistance: Grants ranging from $3,942 to $324,000.
Applicant Eligibility: Nonprofit organizations, state and local governments.
Objective: To increase the number of physicians practicing family medicine. Funds are used to cover the cost of developing and operating approved (or provisionally approved) residency training programs, and to provide financial assistance to participants in approved residency programs in the field of family medicine.

Contact: Director, Division of Medicine, Health Resources & Services Administration, Parklawn Building, Room 4C-25, 5600 Fishers Lane, Rockville, MD 20857, 301-443-6910.

13.381 HEALTH PROFESSIONS— FINANCIAL DISTRESS GRANTS

Type of Assistance: Grants ranging from $442,000 to $5,500,000.

Applicant Eligibility: Nonprofit organizations, state and local governments.

Objective: To assist schools of medicine, osteopathy, dentistry, optometry, pharmacy, podiatry, public health and veterinary medicine which are in serious financial distress to meet costs of operation or have special financial needs to meet accreditation requirements or to carry out appropriate operational, managerial and financial reforms.

Contact: Bureau of Health Professions, Health Resources & Services Administration, 5600 Fishers Lane, Room 8C-22, Rockville, MD 20857, 301-443-6880.

13.389 RESEARCH CENTERS IN MINORITY INSTITUTIONS

Type of Assistance: Project grants up to $1 million per year for five years.

Applicant Eligibility: Individuals, nonprofit organizations, state and local government.

Objective: To expand research in health sciences by assisting minority institutions offering doctoral degrees in health sciences and to promote biomedical and/or behavioral research at such institutions.

Contact: Program Director, RCMI, Division of Research Services, National Institutes of Health, Bethesda, MD 20205, 301-496-6023.

13.390 ACADEMIC RESEARCH ENHANCEMENT AWARD

Type of Assistance: Project grants up to $50,000.

Applicant Eligibility: Nonprofit organizations, state and local governments.

Objective: To develop the research environment of educational institutions that are not major participants in NIH programs.

Contact: Extramural Programs Management Office, National Institutes of Health, Bethesda, MD 20205, 301-496-2241.

13.392 CANCER—CONSTRUCTION

Type of Assistance: Grants ranging from $200,000 to $500,000.

Applicant Eligibility: Nonprofit organizations, state and local governments.

Objective: To provide new cancer research facilities and expand and upgrade existing ones to meet laboratory safety and animal care standards, in order to achieve a geographic distribution of cancer research facilities and centers.

Contact: Research Facilities Branch, National Cancer Institute, 8300 Colesville Road, Silver Spring, MD 20910, 301-427-8804.

13.393 CANCER CAUSE AND PREVENTION RESEARCH

Type of Assistance: Grants ranging from $2,000 to $3,516,430.

Applicant Eligibility: Individuals, nonprofit organizations, state and local governments.

Objective: Cause and prevention research is concerned with identification of those factors which cause cancer in man, and with the development of mechanisms for preventing cancer in man.

Contact: Division of Cancer Etiology, National Cancer Institute, Bethesda, MD 20205, 301-496-6618.

13.394 CANCER DETECTION AND DIAGNOSIS RESEARCH

Type of Assistance: Grants ranging from $8,500 to $643,227.

Applicant Eligibility: Nonprofit organizations, state and local governments.

Objective: To identify cancer in patients early enough and precisely enough so that the latest methods of treatment can be applied toward control of the disease.

Contact: Extramural Research Program, Division of Cancer Research Resources and Centers, National Cancer Institute, Bethesda, MD 20205, 301-496-7028.

13.395 CANCER TREATMENT RESEARCH

Type of Assistance: Grants ranging from $3,000 to $3,102,005.

Applicant Eligibility: Individuals, nonprofit organizations, state and local governments.

Objective: To develop the means to cure as many cancer patients as possible and to control the disease in those patients who are not cured.

Contact: Chief, Division of Cancer Treatment, National Cancer Institute, Bethesda, MD 20205, 301-496-6404.

13.396 CANCER BIOLOGY RESEARCH

Type of Assistance: Grants ranging from $2,000 to $1,700,000.

Applicant Eligibility: Individuals, nonprofit organizations, state and local governments.

Objective: To provide fundamental information on the cause and nature of cancer in man, with the expectation that this will result in better methods of prevention, detection and diagnosis, and treatment of neoplastic diseases.

Contact: Chief, Extramural Research Program, Division of Cancer Biology & Diagnosis, National Cancer Institute, Bethesda, MD 20205, 301-496-7028.

13.397 CANCER CENTERS SUPPORT

Type of Assistance: Grants ranging from $250,000 to $6,500,000.

Applicant Eligibility: Nonprofit organizations, state and local governments.

Objective: To provide core funds to assist in the development and maintenance of multidisciplinary cancer centers for laboratory and clinical research, as well as training in and demonstration of the latest diagnostic and treatment techniques.

Contact: Director, Centers and Community Oncology Program, Division of Cancer Prevention and Control, National Cancer Institute, 8300 Colesville Road, Silver Spring, MD 20910, 301-427-8636.

13.398 CANCER RESEARCH MANPOWER
Type of Assistance: Grants ranging from $5,000 to $420,000.
Applicant Eligibility: Nonprofit organizations, state and local governments.
Objective: To make available support for nonprofit institutions interested in providing biomedical training opportunities for individuals pursuing careers in basic and clinical research which support important areas of the National Cancer Program
Contact: Chief, Center Training Branch, Division of Cancer Prevention and Control, National Cancer Institute, Blair 727, Bethesda, MD 20205, 301-427-8898.

13.399 CANCER CONTROL
Type of Assistance: Grants ranging from $18,000 to $2 million.
Applicant Eligibility: Nonprofit organizations, state and local governments.
Objective: To establish and support demonstration, education and other programs for the detection, diagnosis, prevention and treatment of cancer and for rehabilitation and counseling related to cancer.
Contact: Deputy Director, Division of Cancer Prevention and Control, National Cancer Institute, 5333 Westbard Avenue, Bethesda, MD 20205, 301-496-6616.

OFFICE OF HUMAN DEVELOPMENT SERVICES

13.600 ADMINISTRATION FOR CHILDREN, YOUTH AND FAMILIES—HEAD START
Type of Assistance: Grants ranging from $75,000 to $23 million.
Applicant Eligibility: Nonprofit organizations, state and local governments.
Objective: To provide comprehensive health, educational, nutritional, social and other services primarily to economically disadvantaged preschool children and their families, and to involve parents in activities with their children so that the children will attain overall social competence.
Contact: Administration for Children, Youth and Families—Head Start, Office of Human Development Services, DHHS, PO Box 1182, Washington, DC 20013, 202-755-7782.

13.608 ADMINISTRATION FOR CHILDREN, YOUTH AND FAMILIES—CHILD WELFARE RESEARCH AND DEMONSTRATION
Type of Assistance: Grants ranging from $50,000 to $500,000.
Applicant Eligibility: Nonprofit organizations, state and local governments.

Objective: To provide financial support for research and demonstration projects in the area of child and family development and welfare.
Contact: Grants Coordinator, Research and Evaluation Division, Administration for Children, Youth and Families, Office of Human Development Services, DHHS, PO Box 1182, Washington, DC 20013, 202-755-7758.

13.612 NATIVE AMERICAN PROGRAMS—FINANCIAL ASSISTANCE GRANTS

Type of Assistance: Grants ranging from $15,000 to $400,000.
Applicant Eligibility: Nonprofit organizations, state and local governments.
Objective: To promote the economic and social self-sufficiency of American Indians, Native Hawaiians and Alaskan Natives.
Contact: Administration for Native Americans, Room 5300 N, DHHS, 330 Independence Avenue, SW, Washington, DC 20201, 202-245-7714.

13.623 ADMINISTRATION FOR CHILDREN, YOUTH AND FAMILIES—RUNAWAY YOUTH

Type of Assistance: Grants ranging from $25,000 to $75,000.
Applicant Eligibility: Nonprofit organizations, state and local governments.
Objective: To develop local facilities to address the immediate needs of runaway youth.
Contact: Associate Commissioner, Family and Youth Services Bureau, Administration for Children, Youth and Families, Office of Human Development Services, DHHS, Washington, DC, 20201, 202-472-4426.

13.630 ADMINISTRATION FOR DEVELOPMENTAL DISABILITIES—BASIC SUPPORT AND ADVOCACY GRANTS

Type of Assistance: Grants ranging from $300,000 to $3,895,087.
Applicant Eligibility: State governments.
Objective: To assist states in the provision of comprehensive services to ensure that developmentally disabled persons receive services necessary to enable them to achieve their maximum potential to ensure the protection of their legal and human rights.
Contact: Commissioner, Administration on Developmental Disabilities, Office of Human Development Services, Office of the Secretary, DHHS, Washington, DC 20201, 202-245-2890.

13.631 ADMINISTRATION FOR DEVELOPMENTAL DISABILITIES—SPECIAL PROJECTS

Type of Assistance: Grants ranging from $50,000 to $200,000.
Applicant Eligibility: Nonprofit organizations, state and local governments.
Objective: To provide support for projects to improve the quality of service to the developmentally disabled, public awareness and informational programs, demonstration of new or improved service deliv-

ery, training or coordination of available community resources, and technical assistance.

Contact: Division of Program Development and Demonstration, Administration on Developmental Disabilities, Office of Human Development Services, DHHS, Washington, DC 20201, 202-245-1961.

13.632 ADMINISTRATION ON DEVELOPMENTAL DISABILITIES—UNIVERSITY-AFFILIATED FACILITIES

Type of Assistance: Grants ranging from $150,000 to $348,211.

Applicant Eligibility: Nonprofit organizations, state and local governments.

Objective: To assist with the cost of administration and operation of facilities for interdisciplinary training of personnel concerned with developmental disabilities, the demonstration of the provision of exemplary services for the developmentally disabled, and the demonstration of findings related to the provision of those services.

Contact: Division of Program Development and Demonstrations, Administration on Developmental Disabilities, Office of Human Development Services, DHHS, Washington, DC 20201, 202-245-1961.

13.633 SPECIAL PROGRAMS FOR THE AGING—GRANTS FOR SUPPORTIVE SERVICES & SENIOR CENTERS

Type of Assistance: Grants ranging from $157,592 to $24,347,688.

Applicant Eligibility: State governments.

Objective: To provide assistance to state and area agencies for the statewide planning of programs for older persons and for area planning and provision of social services, including multipurpose senior centers.

Contact: Associate Commissioner, Office of State and Tribal Programs, Administration on Aging, Office of Human Development Services, DHHS, Washington, DC 20201, 202-245-0011.

13.635 SPECIAL PROGRAMS FOR THE AGING— NUTRITION SERVICES

Type of Assistance: Grants ranging from $42,541 to $30,760,649.

Applicant Eligibility: State governments.

Objective: To provide older Americans with low-cost, nutritious meals, appropriate nutrition education and other appropriate nutrition services. Meals may be served in a congregate setting or delivered to the home.

Contact: Associate Commissioner, Office of State and Tribal Programs, Administration on Aging, Office of Human Development Services, DHHS, Washington, DC 20201, 202-245-0011.

13.645 CHILD WELFARE SERVICES—STATE GRANTS

Type of Assistance: Grants ranging from $112,530 to $4,420,291.

Applicant Eligibility: State governments.

Objective: To establish, extend and strengthen preventive or protective services provided by state and local public welfare programs to enable children to remain in their own homes or to provide alternate permanent homes for them.

Contact: Children's Bureau, Administration for Children, Youth and Families, Office of Human Development Services, DHHS, PO Box 1182, Washington, DC 20013, 202-755-7418.

13.646 WORK INCENTIVE PROGRAM
Type of Assistance: Grants.
Applicant Eligibility: State governments.
Objective: To move men, women and out-of-school youth aged 16 or older from dependency on Aid to Families with Dependent Children grants to economic independence through permanent, productive employment by providing appropriate employment training, job placement and other related services, supplemented by child care and other social services when needed to enable a person to participate or secure employment.
Contact: Executive Director, National Coordination Committee, Work Incentive Program, Washington, DC 20213, 202-376-6890.

13.647 SOCIAL SERVICES RESEARCH AND DEMONSTRATION
Type of Assistance: Grants ranging from $100,000 to $250,000.
Applicant Eligibility: Nonprofit organizations, state and local governments.
Objective: To discover, test, demonstrate and promote new social service concepts concerning dependent and vulnerable populations such as the poor, the aging, children and youth, Native Americans and the handicapped.
Contact: Director, Division of Research and Demonstrations, Office of Program Development, DHHS, H. Humphrey Building, Room 732-E, 200 Independence Avenue, SW, Washington, DC 20201, 202-245-6233.

13.648 CHILD WELFARE SERVICES TRAINING GRANTS
Type of Assistance: Grants averaging $50,000.
Applicant Eligibility: Nonprofit organizations and local governments.
Objective: To develop and maintain an adequate supply of qualified and trained personnel for the field of services to children and their families, and to improve educational programs and resources for preparing personnel for this field.
Contact: Children's Bureau, DHHS, PO Box 1182, Washington, DC 20013, 202-755-7820.

13.652 ADMINISTRATION FOR CHILDREN, YOUTH AND FAMILIES—ADOPTION OPPORTUNITIES
Type of Assistance: Grants ranging from $50,000 to $500,000.
Applicant Eligibility: Nonprofit organizations, state and local governments.
Objective: To provide financial support for demonstration projects to improve adoption practices. To gather information on adoptions and to provide training and technical assistance to provide improved adoption services.

Contact: Director, Program Support Division, Children's Bureau, Administration for Children, Youth and Families, DHHS, PO Box 1182, Washington, DC 20013, 202-755-7820.

13.655   SPECIAL PROGRAMS FOR THE AGING— GRANTS TO INDIAN TRIBES
Type of Assistance: Grants ranging from $42,849 to $100,000.
Applicant Eligibility: Native Americans.
Objective: To promote the delivery of services to older Indians.
Contact: Associate Commissioner, Office of State and Tribal Programs, Administration on Aging, Office of Human Development Services, DHHS, Washington, DC 20201, 202-245-0011.

13.658   FOSTER CARE
Type of Assistance: Grants ranging from $20,000 to $161,318,000.
Applicant Eligibility: U.S. states and territories.
Objective: To provide federal financial participation in assistance on behalf of eligible children needing care away from their families (in foster care) who are in the placement and care of the state agency administering the program and to provide Federal Financial Participation (FFP) in the cost of proper and efficient administrative and training costs.
Contact: Associate Commissioner, Children's Bureau, PO Box 1182, Washington, DC 20013, 202-755-7418.

13.659   ADOPTION ASSISTANCE
Type of Assistance: Grants.
Applicant Eligibility: U.S. states and territories.
Objective: To provide Federal Financial Participation (FFP) to states in the maintenance costs for children with special needs who are adopted.
Contact: Childrens' Bureau, PO Box 1182, Washington, DC 20013, 202-755-7418.

13.661   NATIVE AMERICAN PROGRAMS— RESEARCH, DEMONSTRATION AND EVALUATION
Type of Assistance: Grants ranging from $10,000 to $180,000.
Applicant Eligibility: Native Americans and private or public nonprofit organizations.
Objective: To promote the goal of social and economic self-sufficiency for American Indians, Native Hawaiians and Alaskan Natives.
Contact: Administration for Native Americans, DHHS, 330 Independence Avenue, SW, Room 5300, Washington, DC 20201, 202-245-7714.

13.662   NATIVE AMERICAN PROGRAMS— TRAINING AND TECHNICAL ASSISTANCE
Type of Assistance: Grants ranging from $7,400 to $15,000.
Applicant Eligibility: Native Americans.
Objective: To promote the goal of economic and social self-sufficiency for American Indians, Native Hawaiians and Alaskan Natives.

Contact: Administration for Native Americans, DHHS, 330 Independence Avenue, SW, Room 5300 North, Washington, DC 20201, 202-245-7714.

13.665 COMMUNITY SERVICES BLOCK GRANT

Type of Assistance: Grants ranging from $123,225 to $29,346,400.
Applicant Eligibility: U.S. states and territories and the governing bodies of Indian tribes.
Objective: To provide a range of services and activities having a measurable and potential major impact on causes of poverty in the community or those areas of the community where poverty is a particularly acute problem.
Contact: Office of State and Project Assistance, Office of Community Services, 1200 19th Street, NW, Room 500A, Washington, DC 20506, 202-653-5675.

13.667 SOCIAL SERVICES BLOCK GRANT

Type of Assistance: Grants ranging from $93,966 to $289,368,191.
Applicant Eligibility: U.S. states and territories.
Objective: To enable each state as far as practicable to furnish a variety of social services best suited to the needs of the individuals residing in the state in the most efficient and effective method possible by using federal block grant funds to provide services directed toward one of the five goals specified in the law.
Contact: Office of Policy and Legislation, Office of Human Development Services, 200 Independence Avenue, SW, Washington, DC 20201, 202-245-7027.

13.668 SPECIAL PROGRAMS FOR THE AGING— TRAINING, RESEARCH AND DISCRETIONARY PROJECTS AND PROGRAMS

Type of Assistance: Grants ranging from $1,100 to $487,500.
Applicant Eligibility: Public or private nonprofit agencies or organizations.
Objective: To provide adequately trained personnel in the field of aging, improve knowledge of the problems and needs of the elderly, and demonstrate better ways of improving the quality of life for the elderly.
Contact: Office of Program Development, Administration on Aging, DHHS, Washington, DC 20201, 202-245-0441.

13.669 ADMINISTRATION FOR CHILDREN YOUTH AND FAMILIES—CHILD ABUSE AND NEGLECT STATE GRANTS

Type of Assistance: Grants.
Applicant Eligibility: States.
Objective: To assist states to improve and increase activities for the prevention and treatment of child abuse.

Contact: Director, National Center on Child Abuse and Neglect, Children's Bureau, PO Box 1182, Washington, DC 20013, 202-245-2856.

13.670 ADMINISTRATION FOR CHILDREN, YOUTH AND FAMILIES—CHILD ABUSE AND NEGLECT DISCRETIONARY ACTIVITIES

Type of Assistance: Grants ranging from $30,000 to $300,000.
Applicant Eligibility: State and local governments and nonprofit organizations.
Objective: To improve activities for the prevention, identification and treatment of child abuse and neglect through research and demonstration of service improvement.
Contact: Director, National Center on Child Abuse and Neglect, Children's Bureau, PO Box 1182, Washington, DC 20013, 202-245-2056.

OFFICE OF THE SECRETARY

13.676 SURPLUS PROPERTY UTILIZATION

Type of Assistance: Sale, exchange or donation of property and goods.
Applicant Eligibility: States, public health institutions.
Objective: To convey or lease all available surplus Federal real properties which are needed and usable by eligible organizations and institutions to carry out health programs.
Contact: Director, Division of Health Facilities Planning, DHHS, 5600 Fishers Lane, Rockville, MD 20857, 301-443-2265.

13.679 CHILD SUPPORT ENFORCEMENT

Type of Assistance: Grants ranging from $176,872 to $83,629,147.
Applicant Eligibility: State governments.
Objective: To enforce the support obligations owed by absent parents to their children, locate absent parents, establish paternity and obtain child support.
Contact: Deputy Director, Office of Child Support Enforcement, DHHS, 6110 Executive Boulevard, Rockville, MD 20852, 301-443-4442.

HEALTH CARE FINANCING ADMINISTRATION

13.714 MEDICAL ASSISTANCE PROGRAM

Type of Assistance: Grants ranging from $14,096,000 to $3,761,887,000.
Applicant Eligibility: State and local governments.
Objective: To provide financial assistance to states for payments of medical assistance on behalf of cash assistance recipients and, in certain states, on behalf of other medically needy, who, except for income and resources, would be eligible for cash assistance.
Contact: Director, Bureau of Program Operations, Health Care Financing Administration, DHHS, Meadows East Building, Room 300, 6300 Security Boulevard, Baltimore, MD 21207, 301-594-9000.

13.766   HEALTH FINANCING RESEARCH, DEMONSTRATIONS AND EXPERIMENTS

Type of Assistance: Grants ranging from $25,000 to $1 million.

Applicant Eligibility: Nonprofit organizations, state and local governments.

Objective: To discover, test, demonstrate and promote utilization of health care financing concepts that will provide service to beneficiary population while at the same time providing incentives for efficient use of services and resources by provider and beneficiaries.

Contact: Director, Office of Research and Demonstrations, DHHS, 6325 Security Boulevard, Baltimore, MD 21207, 301-597-3195.

13.773   MEDICARE—HOSPITAL INSURANCE

Type of Assistance: Direct payments to cover most inpatient hospital services and posthospital extended care services.

Applicant Eligibility: Individuals.

Objective: To provide hospital insurance protection for covered services to any person 65 or above and to certain disabled persons.

Contact: Director, Bureau of Program Operations, Meadows East Building, Room 300, Baltimore, MD 21235, 301-594-9000.

13.774   MEDICARE—SUPPLEMENTARY MEDICAL INSURANCE

Type of Assistance: Direct payments to cover charges of physicians and other suppliers of medical services.

Applicant Eligibility: Individuals.

Objective: To provide medical insurance protection for covered services to persons 65 or over and certain disabled persons who elect this coverage.

Contact: Director, Bureau of Program Operations, Meadows East Building, Room 300, Baltimore, MD 21235, 301-594-9000.

13.775   STATE MEDICAID FRAUD CONTROL UNITS

Type of Assistance: Grants averaging $900,000 per year.

Applicant Eligibility: Entities of the state governments.

Objective: To control fraud in the states' Medicaid Program.

Contact: Director, State Fraud Branch, Office of the Secretary, DHHS, North Building, Room 5246, 300 Independence Avenue, SW, Washington, DC 20201, 202-472-3163.

13.777   STATE HEALTH CARE PROVIDERS SURVEY CERTIFICATION

Type of Assistance: Grants ranging from $9,560 to $5,499,666.

Applicant Eligibility: Designated state health agencies.

Objective: To provide financial assistance to any state which is able and willing to determine through its state health agency or other appropriate state agency that providers of health care surveys are in compliance with regulatory health and safety standards and conditions of participation in Medicare and Medicaid programs.

Contact: Office of Standards and Certification, Health Standards and Quality Bureau, Health Care Financing Administration, Meadows East Building, 6325 Security Boulevard, Baltimore, MD 21207, 301-594-5547.

SOCIAL SECURITY ADMINISTRATION

13.802   SOCIAL SECURITY—DISABILITY INSURANCE
Type of Assistance: Direct payments up to $1,364 monthly.
Applicant Eligibility: Individuals.
Objective: To replace part of the earnings lost because of a physical or mental impairment severe enough to prevent a person from working.
Contact: Office of Public Inquiries, Social Security Administration, Annex, 6401 Security Boulevard, Room 4100, Baltimore, MD 21235, 301-594-5970.

13.803   SOCIAL SECURITY—RETIREMENT INSURANCE
Type of Assistance: Direct payments up to $1,255 monthly.
Applicant Eligibility: Individuals.
Objective: To replace part of the earnings lost because of retirement.
Contact: Office of Public Inquiries, Social Security Administration, Annex, 6401 Security Boulevard, Room 4100, Baltimore, MD 21235, 301-594-5970.

13.804   SOCIAL SECURITY—SPECIAL BENEFITS FOR PERSONS AGE 72 AND OVER
Type of Assistance: Direct payments up to $134.40 monthly.
Applicant Eligibility: Individuals.
Objective: To assure some regular income to certain persons age 72 and over who had little or no opportunity to earn Social Security protection during their working years.
Contact: Office of Public Inquiries, Social Security Administration, Annex, 6401 Security Boulevard, Room 4100, Baltimore, MD 21235, 310-594-5970.

13.805   SOCIAL SECURITY—SURVIVORS INSURANCE
Type of Assistance: Direct payments.
Applicant Eligibility: Individuals.
Objective: To replace part of earnings lost to dependents because of worker's death.
Contact: Office of Public Inquiries, Social Security Administration, Annex, 6401 Security Boulevard, Room 4100, Baltimore, MD 21235, 301-594-5940.

13.806   SPECIAL BENEFITS FOR DISABLED COAL MINERS ("BLACK LUNG")
Type of Assistance: Direct payments up to $656 monthly.
Applicant Eligibility: Individuals.

Objective: To pay benefits to coal miners who have become disabled due to pneumoconiosis (black lung disease or other chronic lung disease) and their dependents or survivors.
Contact: Office of Public Inquiries, Social Security Administration, Annex, 6401 Security Boulevard, Room 4100, Baltimore, MD 21235, 301-594-5970.

13.807 SUPPLEMENTAL SECURITY INCOME
Type of Assistance: Direct payments averaging $191 per month.
Applicant Eligibility: Individuals.
Objective: To provide supplemental income to persons age 65 and over and to persons blind or disabled whose income and resources are below specified levels.
Contact: Office of Public Inquiries, Social Security Administration, Annex, 6401 Security Boulevard, Room 4100, Baltimore, MD 21235, 301-594-5970.

13.808 ASSISTANCE PAYMENTS—
MAINTENANCE ASSISTANCE (STATE AID)
Type of Assistance: Grants ranging from $2,360,361 to $1,586,346,359.
Applicant Eligibility: Local governments.
Objective: To set general standards for state administration; to provide the federal financial share to states for aid to families with dependent children, emergency assistance to families with children, assistance to repatriated U.S. nationals, and aid to the aged, blind, permanently and totally disabled; in Guam, Puerto Rico and the Virgin Islands and the administration of these welfare programs and monitoring of their performance.
Contact: Office of Family Assistance, Social Security Administration, DHHS, TransPoint Building, Room B442, 2100 Second St. SW, Washington, DC 20201, 202-245-2736.

13.811 CHILD SUPPORT ENFORCEMENT
INTERSTATE GRANTS
Type of Assistance: Project grants.
Applicant Eligibility: States.
Objective: To promote effective methods of enforcing support obligations in cases where children or their absent parents do not reside in the state where such cases are filed.
Contact: Program Analyst, Planning and Evaluation Branch, Office of Child Support Enforcement, 6110 Executive Boulevard, Rockville, MD 20852, 301-443-2980.

13.812 ASSISTANCE PAYMENTS—RESEARCH
Type of Assistance: Grants ranging from $55,000 to $350,000.
Applicant Eligibility: Nonprofit organizations, state and local governments.
Objective: To promote utilization of new concepts which will increase

cost-effectiveness, reduce welfare dependency, provide services and improve aid to families with dependent children program.
Contact: Director, Office of Research and Statistics, Social Security Administration, 2100 Second Street, SW, Washington, DC 20201, 202-245-3284.

13.814 REFUGEE ASSISTANCE— STATE-ADMINISTERED PROGRAMS
Type of Assistance: Direct payments.
Applicant Eligibility: State governments.
Objective: To help refugees resettle throughout the country, by funding, through state and local public assistance agencies, maintenance and medical assistance and social services for needy refugees; and to provide grants for training, services and related projects. Refugees in the US may be assisted regardless of national origin.
Contact: Director, Office of Refugee Resettlement, DHHS, 1332 Switzer Building, 330 C Street, SW, Washington, DC 20201, 202-245-0418.

13.815 REFUGEE ASSISTANCE— VOLUNTARY AGENCY PROGRAMS
Type of Assistance: Grants ranging from $36,000 to $1,069,700.
Applicant Eligibility: National voluntary resettlement agencies.
Objective: To assist refugees to become self-supporting and independent members of American society by providing grant funds to voluntary resettlement agencies currently resettling these refugees in the United States.
Contact: Director, Office of Refugee Resettlement, DHHS, 1332 Switzer Building, 330 C Street, SW, Washington, DC 20201, 202-245-0418.

13.818 LOW-INCOME HOME ENERGY ASSISTANCE PROGRAM
Type of Assistance: Grants averaging $200.
Applicant Eligibility: State governments.
Objective: To make funds available to states to provide eligible low-income individuals money to offset their rising costs of home energy consumption.
Contact: Office of Family Assistance, Social Security Administration, DHHS, TransPoint Building, Room B428, 2100 Second Street, SW, Washington, DC 20024, 202-245-2030.

PUBLIC HEALTH SERVICE—2

13.820 SCHOLARSHIPS FOR FIRST-YEAR STUDENTS OF EXCEPTIONAL FINANCIAL NEED
Type of Assistance: Grants averaging $15,958 a year.
Applicant Eligibility: Public or nonprofit private schools of medicine, dentistry, osteopathy, podiatry or veterinary medicine.

Objective: To make funds available to authorized health professions schools to award scholarships to full-time first-year health professions students of exceptional financial need.
Contact: Division of Student Assistance, DHHS, Parklawn Building, Room 8-44, 5600 Fishers Lane, Rockville, MD 20857, 301-443-1173.

13.821 PHYSIOLOGY AND BIOMEDICAL ENGINEERING
Type of Assistance: Grants ranging from $18,468 to $864,994.
Applicant Eligibility: Individuals, nonprofit organizations, state and local governments.
Objective: To support the basic research that applies concepts from mathematics, physics and engineering to biological systems, uses engineering principles in the development of computers for patient monitoring or is related to physiology, anesthesiology, trauma and burn studies, and related areas.
Contact: Director, Biophysics and Physiological Sciences, National Institute of General Medical Sciences, National Institutes of Health, Bethesda, MD 20205, 301-496-7891.

13.822 HEALTH CAREERS OPPORTUNITY PROGRAM
Type of Assistance: Grants ranging from $10,868 to $594,010.
Applicant Eligibility: Nonprofit organizations, state and local governments.
Objective: To identify, recruit and select individuals from disadvantaged backgrounds for education and training in a health profession; to facilitate their entry into such a school; to provide counseling or other needed services to assist such individuals to successfully complete their education; to provide preliminary education designed to assist them to successfully complete their course of education; and to publicize existing sources of financial aid.
Contact: Grants Management Office, BHM, HRA, DHHS, 5600 Fishers Lane, Rockville, MD 20857, 301-443-6857.

13.824 AREA HEALTH EDUCATION CENTERS
Type of Assistance: Grants ranging from $45,468 to $6,646,250.
Applicant Eligibility: Accredited public or nonprofit schools of medicine or osteopathy.
Objective: To improve the distributions, supply, quality, utilization and efficiency of health personnel in the health service delivery system and for the purpose of increasing the regionalization of educational responsibilities for health professional schools.
Contact: Division of Medicine, Bureau of Health Professions, DHHS, Parklawn Building, 5600 Fishers Lane, Rockville, MD 20857, 301-443-6190.

13.837 HEART AND VASCULAR DISEASES RESEARCH
Type of Assistance: Grants ranging from $9,399 to $4,187,070.
Applicant Eligibility: Individuals, nonprofit organizations, local governments and eligible small businesses.

Objective: To foster research, prevention, education and control activities related to heart and vascular diseases, and to develop young science investigators in these areas.
Contact: Director, Division of Heart and Vascular Diseases, National Heart, Lung, and Blood Institute, Bethesda, MD 20205, 301-496-2553.

13.838 LUNG DISEASES RESEARCH
Type of Assistance: Grants ranging from $6,400 to $1,472,724.
Applicant Eligibility: Individuals, nonprofit organizations, local governments, eligible small businesses.
Objective: To use available knowledge and technology to solve specific disease problems of the lungs; to promote further studies on the structure and function of the lung; and to achieve improvement in prevention and treatment of lung diseases.
Contact: Director, Division of Lung Diseases, National Heart, Lung, and Blood Institute, Bethesda, MD 20205, 301-496-7208.

13.839 BLOOD DISEASES AND RESOURCES RESEARCH
Type of Assistance: Grants ranging from $4,503 to $2,164,116.
Applicant Eligibility: Individuals, nonprofit organizations, local governments and eligible small businesses.
Objective: To further the development of blood resources and coordinate national and regional activities of blood centers; to promote research on blood diseases including sickle cell disease; and to develop new scientists for such research.
Contact: Director, Division of Blood Diseases, National Heart, Lung, and Blood Institute, Bethesda, MD 20205, 301-496-4868.

13.845 DENTAL RESEARCH INSTITUTES
Type of Assistance: Grants ranging from $1 million to $2 million.
Applicant Eligibility: Nonprofit organizations, state and local governments.
Objective: To conduct multidisciplinary oral health research that utilizes the biological, social, physical and clinical sciences in the university setting.
Contact: Extramural Programs, National Institute of Dental Research, National Institutes of Health, Bethesda, MD 20205, 301-496-6324.

13.846 ARTHRITIS, MUSCULOSKELETAL AND SKIN DISEASES RESEARCH
Type of Assistance: Grants ranging from $17,361 to $1,371,221.
Applicant Eligibility: Individuals, nonprofit organizations, state and local governments, eligible small businesses.
Objective: To support basic laboratory research and clinical investigations and to provide postdoctoral biomedical research training for individuals interested in careers in health sciences and fields related to these programs.
Contact: Director, Division of Arthritis, National Institute of Arthritis, National Institutes of Health, Bethesda, MD 20205, 301-496-4353.

13.847 DIABETES, ENDOCRINOLOGY AND METABOLISM RESEARCH
Type of Assistance: Grants ranging from $6,700 to $1,986,000.
Applicant Eligibility: Individuals, nonprofit organizations, state and local governments and eligible small businesses.
Objective: To support basic laboratory research and clinical investigations and to provide postdoctoral biomedical research training for individuals interested in careers in health sciences and fields related to these programs.
Contact: Director, Division of Diabetes, Building 31, Room 9416, National Institutes of Health, Bethesda, MD 20205, 301-496-7348.

13.848 DIGESTIVE DISEASES AND NUTRITION RESEARCH
Type of Assistance: Grants ranging from $10,500 to $1,464,000.
Applicant Eligibility: Individuals, nonprofit organizations, local governments and eligible small businesses.
Objective: To support basic laboratory research and clinical investigations and to provide postdoctoral biomedical research training for individuals interested in careers in health sciences and fields related to these programs.
Contact: Division of Extramural Program Activities, National Institute of Arthritis, Metabolism and Digestive Diseases, National Institutes of Health, Westwood Building, Room 655, Bethesda, MD 20205, 301-496-7793.

13.849 KIDNEY DISEASES, UROLOGY AND HEMATOLOGY RESEARCH
Type of Assistance: Grants ranging from $10,800 to $1,564,000.
Applicant Eligibility: Individuals, nonprofit organizations, local governments and eligible small businesses.
Objective: To support basic laboratory research and clinical investigations and to provide postdoctoral biomedical research training for individuals interested in careers in health sciences and fields related to these programs.
Contact: Division of Extramural Program Activities, National Institute of Arthritis, National Institutes of Health, Westwood Building, Room 655, Bethesda, MD 20205, 301-496-7793

13.853 CLINICAL RESEARCH
Type of Assistance: Grants.
Applicant Eligibility: Individuals, nonprofit organizations, state and local governments.
Objective: Directed toward the solution of problems directly relevant to patients with neurological disorders or disorders of human communication such as deafness, speech and language.
Contact: Extramural Activities Program, NINCDS, National Institutes of Health, Bethesda, MD 20205, 301-496-9248.

13.854 NEUROLOGICAL BASIS RESEARCH
Type of Assistance: Grants.
Applicant Eligibility: Any public or private institution.
Objective: The program includes 1) neurological and communicative science basic research; 2) research on pathological conditions of the nervous system and hearing; 3) research on neurological and communicative disorders; and 4) research training in the basic communicative sciences and basic neurological sciences.
Contact: Extramural Activities Program, National Institutes of Health, Federal Building, Room 1016, Bethesda, MD 20205, 301-496-9248.

13.855 IMMUNOLOGY, ALLERGIC AND IMMUNOLOGIC DISEASES RESEARCH
Type of Assistance: Grants ranging from $1,000 to $622,983.
Applicant Eligibility: Individuals, nonprofit organizations, state and local governments.
Objective: To assist public and private nonprofit institutions and individuals to establish, expand and improve biomedical research and research training in allergic and immunologic diseases and related areas; and to assist public, private and commercial institutions to conduct developmental research, to produce and test research materials and to provide research services as required by the agency for research programs in allergic and immunologic diseases.
Contact: Grants Management Branch, National Institute of Allergy and Infectious Diseases, National Institutes of Health, Bethesda, MD 20205, 301-496-7075.

13.856 MICROBIOLOGY AND INFECTIOUS DISEASES RESEARCH
Type of Assistance: Grants ranging from $1,000 to $466,414.
Applicant Eligibility: Individuals, nonprofit organizations, state and local governments.
Objective: To assist public and private nonprofit institutions and individuals to establish, expand and improve biomedical research and research training in infectious diseases and related areas; and to assist public, private and commercial institutions to conduct developmental research, produce and test research materials and provide research services as required by the agency for research programs in infectious diseases.
Contact: Grants Management Branch, National Institute of Allergy and Infectious Diseases, National Institutes of Health, Bethesda, MD 20205, 301-496-7075.

13.859 PHARMACOLOGICAL SCIENCES
Type of Assistance: Grants ranging from $17,040 to $718,506.
Applicant Eligibility: Nonprofit organizations, state and local governments and eligible small businesses.
Objective: To improve medical therapy through acquisition of in-

creased knowledge of the mechanisms of drug action and of ways to increase efficacy and safety and diminish toxicity.
Contact: Program Director, Pharmacological Sciences, National Institute of General Medical Sciences, National Institutes of Health, Bethesda, MD 20205, 301-496-7707.

13.862 GENETICS RESEARCH
Type of Assistance: Grants ranging from $17,000 to $1,129,618.
Applicant Eligibility: Individuals, nonprofit organizations, state and local governments, eligible small businesses.
Objective: To support basic research ultimately aimed at the prevention, therapy and control of genetic diseases in man, including those multifactorial illnesses with a strong hereditary component.
Contact: Program Director, Genetics, National Institute of General Medical Sciences, National Institutes of Health, Bethesda, MD 20205, 301-496-7087

13.863 CELLULAR AND MOLECULAR BASIS OF DISEASE RESEARCH
Type of Assistance: Grants ranging from $17,040 to $814,042.
Applicant Eligibility: Individuals, nonprofit organizations, state and local governments, eligible small businesses.
Objective: To support research on the structure and function of living cells and their component parts, with the expectation that a greater understanding of these aspects will contribute to ultimate control of all forms and manifestations of human disease.
Contact: Program Director, Cellular and Molecular Basis of Disease, National Institute of General Medical Sciences, National Institutes of Health, Bethesda, MD 20205, 301-496-7021.

13.864 POPULATION RESEARCH
Type of Assistance: Grants ranging from $3,000 to $777,279.
Applicant Eligibility: Individuals, nonprofit organizations, state and local governments, eligible small businesses.
Objective: To seek solutions to the fundamental problems of the reproductive processes; to develop and evaluate safe and more effective and convenient contraceptives; and to understand how population dynamics affects the health and well-being of individuals and society.
Contact: Office of Grants and Contracts, National Institute of Child Health and Human Development, National Institutes of Health, Bethesda, MD 20205, 301-496-5001.

13.865 RESEARCH FOR MOTHERS AND CHILDREN
Type of Assistance: Grants from $3,000 to $763,755.
Applicant Eligibility: Individuals, nonprofit organizations, state and local governments, eligible small businesses.
Objective: To improve the health and well-being of mothers, children

and families as the key to assuring a healthy adult population. Research in this field studies the health problems of the period of life from conception through adolescence and centers on the major problems of pregnancy and infancy, developmental biology and nutrition, human learning and behavior, and mental retardation and developmental disabilities.
Contact: Office of Grants and Contracts, National Institute of Child Health and Human Development, National Institutes of Health, Bethesda, MD 20205, 301-496-5001.

13.866 AGING RESEARCH
Type of Assistance: Grants ranging from $11,003 to $1,146,293.
Applicant Eligibility: Individuals, nonprofit organizations, state and local governments and eligible small businesses.
Objective: To be responsible for biomedical, social and behavioral research and research training directed toward greater understanding of the aging process and the needs and problems of the elderly. The primary goal is to improve the health and well-being of the elderly through the development and application of new knowledge.
Contact: National Institute on Aging, National Institutes of Health, Bethesda, MD 20205, 301-496-4996.

13.867 RETINAL AND CHOROIDAL DISEASES RESEARCH
Type of Assistance: Grants ranging from $19,040 to $870,000.
Applicant Eligibility: Individuals, nonprofit organizations, state and local governments, eligible small businesses.
Objective: To support research and training to study how the retina responds to light and converts it into electrical signals that travel to the brain resulting in sight; to advance understanding of how the retina is damaged by diseases; to develop methods of prevention, early detection and treatment of retinal diseases; and to develop animal models of various retinal diseases to facilitate laboratory and clinical research.
Contact: Associate Director for Extramural and Collaborative Programs, National Eye Institute, National Institutes of Health, Bethesda, MD 20205, 301-496-4903.

13.868 CORNEAL DISEASES RESEARCH
Type of Assistance: Grants ranging from $19,000 to $870,000.
Applicant Eligibility: Individuals, nonprofit organizations, state and local governments, eligible small businesses.
Objective: To reduce the impact of this leading cause of visual disability through improved methods of treatment, prevention and diagnosis; to develop and test drugs and improve corneal surgery and develop means for delivery of nutrients and medication to the cornea; and to provide base research on the structure and function of the cornea.

Contact: Director for Extramural and Collaborative Programs, National Eye Institute, National Institutes of Health, Bethesda, MD 20205, 301-496-4903.

13.869   CATARACT RESEARCH
Type of Assistance: Grants ranging from $19,000 to $870,000.
Applicant Eligibility: Individuals, nonprofit organizations, state and local governments, eligible small businesses.
Objective: To support research and training to identify the causes of cataract disorders and develop methods for its prevention and improved treatment.
Contact: Director for Extramural and Collaborative Programs, National Eye Institute, National Institutes of Health, Bethesda, MD 20205, 301-496-4903.

13.870   GLAUCOMA RESEARCH
Type of Assistance: Grants ranging from $19,000 to $870,000.
Applicant Eligibility: Individuals, nonprofit organizations, state and local governments, eligible small businesses.
Objective: To support research and training to determine the cause of glaucoma, develop techniques for prevention and detection of the disease and improve methods of treatment.
Contact: Director for Extramural and Collaborative Programs, National Eye Institute, National Institutes of Health, Bethesda, MD 20205, 301-496-4903.

13.871   STRABISMUS, AMBLYOPIA
AND VISUAL PROCESSING
Type of Assistance: Grants ranging from $19,000 to $870,000.
Applicant Eligibility: Individuals, nonprofit organizations, state and local governments, eligible small businesses.
Objective: To support laboratory and clinical investigations of the optic nerve and the development and function of those activities of the brain and the eye muscles which make vision possible. Support is also provided for the development of rehabilitation techniques and vision substitution devices.
Contact: Director for Extramural and Collaborative Programs, National Eye Institute, National Institutes of Health, Bethesda, MD 20205, 301-496-4903.

13.879   MEDICAL LIBRARY ASSISTANCE
Type of Assistance: Grants ranging from $4,000 to $200,000.
Applicant Eligibility: Nonprofit organizations, state and local governments.
Objective: To improve health information services by providing funds to train professional personnel, strengthen library resources, support biomedical publications and conduct research in ways of improving information transfer.

Contact: Extramural Programs, National Library of Medicine, Bethesda, MD 20209, 301-496-6131.

13.880 MINORITY ACCESS TO RESEARCH CAREERS
Type of Assistance: Grants ranging from $9,292 to $279,538.
Applicant Eligibility: Individuals, nonprofit organizations, state and local governments.
Objective: To assist minority institutions to train larger numbers of scientists and teachers in health-related fields; and to increase the number of minority students who can compete successfully for entry into graduate programs which lead to the Ph.D. degree in biomedical science fields.
Contact: Program Director, MARC Program, National Institute of General Medical Sciences, National Institutes of Health, Bethesda, MD 20205, 301-496-7941.

13.884 GRANTS FOR RESIDENCY TRAINING IN GENERAL INTERNAL MEDICINE AND/OR GENERAL PEDIATRICS
Type of Assistance: Grants ranging from $14,580 to $474,122.
Applicant Eligibility: Nonprofit organizations, state and local governments.
Objective: Grants are made to promote the graduate education of physicians who plan to enter the practice of general internal medicine or general pediatrics.
Contact: Director, Division of Medicine, DHHS, Parklawn Building, Room 4C-25, 5600 Fishers Lane, Rockville, MD 20857, 301-443-6190.

13.886 GRANTS FOR PHYSICIAN ASSISTANT TRAINING PROGRAM
Type of Assistance: Grants ranging from $57,564 to $242,549.
Applicant Eligibility: Nonprofit organizations, state and local governments.
Objective: To enable public or nonprofit private health or educational entities to meet the cost of projects; to plan, develop and operate or maintain programs for the training of physician assistants.
Contact: Director, Division of Medicine, DHHS, Parklawn Building, Room 4C-25, 5600 Fishers Lane, Rockville, MD 20857, 301-443-6190.

13.891 ALCOHOL RESEARCH CENTER GRANTS
Type of Assistance: Grants ranging from $479,000 to $900,000.
Applicant Eligibility: Nonprofit organizations, state and local governments.
Objective: To provide long-term support for multidisciplinary research efforts into the problems of alcohol use and alcoholism by coordinating the activities of investigators from biomedical, behavioral and social science disciplines.
Contact: Division of Extramural Research, National Institute on Alcohol Abuse and Alcoholism, ADAMHA, DHHS, 5600 Fishers Lane, Rockville, MD 20857, 301-443-2530.

13.894 RESOURCE AND MANPOWER DEVELOPMENT

Type of Assistance: Grants ranging from $165,000 to $2,448,000.

Applicant Eligibility: Nonprofit organizations, state and local governments.

Objective: To provide long-term support for broadly based multidisciplinary research and training in environmental health problems in Environmental Health Sciences Centers (EHS Centers), and Marine and Freshwater Biomedical Centers (MFB Centers). Overall, these centers are to serve as national focal points and resources for research and manpower development in health problems related to air, water and food pollution; occupational and industrial neighborhood health and safety; heavy metal toxicity; agricultural chemicals hazards; the relationships of the environment to cancer, birth defects, behavioral anomalies, respiratory and cardiovascular diseases and diseases of other specific organs; basic aspects of toxicity mechanisms, body defense mechanisms and the influence of age, nutrition and other factors in chemically induced injury and disease; and to increase the pool of trained research manpower in the environmental health sciences through support of individual and institutional National Research Service Awards. (NRSA).

Contact: Director for Extramural Programs, National Institute of Environmental Health Sciences, PO Box 12233, Research Triangle Park, NC 27709, 919-541-7634.

13.895 GRANTS FOR FACULTY DEVELOPMENT IN FAMILY MEDICINE

Type of Assistance: Grants ranging from $38,907 to $231,259.

Applicant Eligibility: Nonprofit organizations, state and local governments.

Objective: To increase the supply of physician faculty available to teach in family medicine programs and to enhance the pedagogical skills of faculty currently teaching in family medicine.

Contact: Director, Division of Medicine, DHHS, Parklawn Building, Room 4C-25, 5600 Fishers Lane, Rockville, MD 20857, 301-443-6190.

13.896 GRANTS FOR PREDOCTORAL TRAINING IN FAMILY MEDICINE

Type of Assistance: Grants ranging from $32,524 to $206,839.

Applicant Eligibility: Nonprofit organizations, state and local governments.

Objective: To assist schools of medicine and osteopathy in meeting the costs of projects to plan, develop and operate (or participate in) professional predoctoral training programs in the field of family medicine.

Contact: Director, Division of Medicine, DHHS, Parklawn Building, Room 4C-25, 5600 Fishers Lane, Rockville, MD 20857, 301-443-6190.

**13.897   RESIDENCY TRAINING IN THE
GENERAL PRACTICE OF DENTISTRY**
Type of Assistance: Grants ranging from $14,580 to $184,464.
Applicant Eligibility: Nonprofit organizations, state and local governments.
Objective: To plan, develop and operate an approved residency program in the general practice of dentistry.
Contact: Dental Health Branch, Division of Associated & Dental Health Professions, DHHS, Parklawn Building, 5600 Fishers Lane, Rockville, MD 20857, 301-443-6837.

PUBLIC HEALTH SERVICE—3

13.900   GRANTS FOR FACULTY DEVELOPMENT
Type of Assistance: Grants.
Applicant Eligibility: Public or private nonprofit organizations.
Objective: To promote faculty skills in physicians who are teaching or planning to teach in general internal medicine or general pediatrics programs with emphasis on primary care.
Contact: Director, Division of Medicine, 5600 Fishers Lane, Room 4C-25, Rockville, MD 20857, 301-443-6190.

**13.962   HEALTH ADMINISTRATION GRADUATE
TRAINEESHIPS**
Type of Assistance: Grants ranging from $3,539 to $44,147.
Applicant Eligibility: Nonprofit organizations and local governments.
Objective: To support eligible students enrolled in accredited graduate degree programs in health administration, hospital administration or health policy analysis and planning.
Contact: Grants Management Officer, Bureau of Health Professions, HRSA, 5600 Fishers Lane, Room 8C-22, Rockville, MD 20857, 301-443-6880.

**13.963   GRADUATE PROGRAMS IN HEALTH
ADMINISTRATION**
Type of Assistance: Grants averaging $49,172.
Applicant Eligibility: Nonprofit organizations and local governments.
Objective: To support accredited graduate educational programs in health administration, hospital administration and health planning.
Contact: Grants Management Office, Bureau of Health Professions, HRSA, Room 8C-22, Rockville, MD 20857, 301-443-6880.

**13.964   TRAINEESHIPS FOR STUDENTS IN SCHOOLS OF
PUBLIC HEALTH AND OTHER GRADUATE PUBLIC
HEALTH PROGRAMS**
Type of Assistance: Grants ranging from $31,025 to $234,465.
Applicant Eligibility: Nonprofit organizations, state and local governments.

Objective: To support traineeships for students in graduate educational programs in schools of public health or other public or nonprofit educational entities.
Contact: Grants Management Officer, Bureau of Health Professions, HRSA, 5600 Fishers Lane, Room 8C-22, Rockville, MD 20857, 301-443-6880.

13.965 COAL MINERS' RESPIRATORY IMPAIRMENT TREATMENT CLINICS AND SERVICES (BLACK LUNG CLINICS)

Type of Assistance: Grants ranging from $30,000 to $150,000.
Applicant Eligibility: Nonprofit organizations, state and local governments.
Objective: To develop high-quality-oriented, integrated systems of care where there are significant numbers of active and inactive miners; to emphasize patient and family-member education to maximize the patient's ability for self-care; and to expand the local capacity to perform examination of miners seeking eligibility for black lung benefits.
Contact: Director, Regional Commissions Health Programs, Health Services Administration, Bureau of Community Health Services, DHHS, Parklawn Building, Room 7A-55, 5600 Fishers Lane, Rockville, MD 20857, 301-443-2270.

13.969 HEALTH PROFESSIONS SPECIAL EDUCATIONAL INITIATIVES

Type of Assistance: Grants.
Applicant Eligibility: Nonprofit organizations and local governments.
Objective: To assist health profession schools, allied health and nurse training institutions or other public or nonprofit entities in the development and implementation of new course materials in applied nutrition, environmental health, geriatrics and humanistic health care.
Contact: HRSA, Public Health Service, DHHS, 5600 Fishers Lane, Rockville, MD 20857, 301-443-6887.

13.970 HEALTH PROFESSIONS RECRUITMENT PROGRAM FOR INDIANS

Type of Assistance: Grants ranging from $42,170 to $269,000.
Applicant Eligibility: Native Americans, public or private nonprofit health or educational entities.
Objective: To identify Indians with a potential for education or training in the health professions and encouraging and assisting them to enroll in health or allied health profession schools.
Contact: Contracts and Grants Management Branch, Indian Health Service, Health Services Administration, PHS, DHHS, 5600 Fishers Lane, Room 6A-29, Rockville, MD 20857, 301-443-5204.

13.971 HEALTH PROFESSIONS PREPARATORY SCHOLARSHIP PROGRAM FOR INDIANS

Type of Assistance: Grants ranging from $5,000 to $14,000.
Applicant Eligibility: Native Americans.

Objective: To make scholarship grants to Indians for the purpose of completing compensatory preprofessional education to enable the recipient to qualify for enrollment or re-enrollment in a health profession school.
Contact: Contracts and Grants Management Branch, Indian Health Service, Health Services Administration, PHS, DHHS, 5600 Fishers Lane, Rockville, MD 20857, 301-443-5204.

13.972 HEALTH PROFESSIONS SCHOLARSHIP PROGRAM FOR INDIANS

Type of Assistance: Grants ranging from $7,474 to $25,000.
Applicant Eligibility: Native Americans.
Objective: To make scholarship grants to Indians and others for the purposes of completing health profession education. Upon completion, grantees are required to fulfill an obligated service payback requirement.
Contact: Contracts and Grants Management Branch, Indian Health Service, Health Services Administration, PHS, DHHS, 5600 Fishers Lane, Rockville, MD 20857, 301-443-5204.

13.973 SPECIAL LOANS FOR NATIONAL HEALTH SERVICE CORPS MEMBERS TO ENTER PRIVATE PRACTICE

Type of Assistance: Direct loans of $12,500 for one year.
Applicant Eligibility: Individuals.
Objective: To assist National Health Service Corps scholarship recipients in the establishment of their own private practice in a health manpower shortage area.
Contact: National Health Resources and Service Corps, DHHS, Parklawn Building, Room 6-40, 5600 Fishers Lane, Rockville, MD 20857, 301-443-2900.

13.974 FAMILY PLANNING SERVICES DELIVERY IMPROVEMENT RESEARCH GRANTS

Type of Assistance: Grants ranging from $40,000 to $250,000.
Applicant Eligibility: Local governments.
Objective: To provide techniques for service delivery improvement through demonstration projects, operational research or technology development and technical assistance.
Contact: Office of Population Affairs, DHHS, HHS North Building, Room 1351, 330 Independence Avenue, SW, Washington, DC, 202-245-0151.

13.977 PREVENTIVE HEALTH SERVICE— VENEREAL DISEASE CONTROL GRANTS

Type of Assistance: Grants ranging from $26,000 to $3,050,400.
Applicant Eligibility: Nonprofit organizations and state governments.
Objective: The purpose of the venereal disease control program is to reduce morbidity and mortality by preventing cases and complications of these diseases. Project grants emphasize the development and im-

plementation of national uniform control programs which focus on intervention activities to reduce the incidence of these diseases.
Contact: Director, Centers for Disease Control, PHS, DHHS, 1600 Clifton Road, NE, Atlanta, GA 30333, 404-329-3291.

13.978 PREVENTIVE HEALTH SERVICE—VENEREAL DISEASE RESEARCH, DEMONSTRATION AND PUBLIC INFORMATION AND EDUCATION GRANTS
Type of Assistance: Grants ranging from $24,000 to $208,000.
Applicant Eligibility: Nonprofit organizations, state and local governments.
Objective: The purpose of the venereal disease research, demonstrations and public information and education grants is to provide assistance to programs designed for the conduct of research, demonstrations and public information and education for the prevention and control of venereal disease.
Contact: Grants Management Office, Center for Disease Control, PHS, DHHS, 1600 Clifton Road, NE, Atlanta, GA 30333, 404-262-6575

13.982 MENTAL HEALTH DISASTER ASSISTANCE AND EMERGENCY MENTAL HEALTH
Type of Assistance: Grants ranging from $80,000 to $158,000.
Applicant Eligibility: Nonprofit organizations, state and local governments.
Objective: Provision of supplemental emergency mental health counseling to individuals affected by major disasters, including the training of volunteers to provide such counseling.
Contact: Disaster Assistance and Emergency Mental Health Section, National Institute of Mental Health, 5600 Fishers Lane, Rockville, MD 20857, 301-443-1910.

13.984 GRANTS FOR ESTABLISHMENT OF DEPARTMENTS OF FAMILY MEDICINE
Type of Assistance: Grants ranging from $37,800 to $259,886.
Applicant Eligibility: Nonprofit organizations, state and local governments.
Objective: To assist in establishing and/or maintaining family medicine academic administrative units that are comparable in status, faculty and curriculum to those of other clinical units at the applying school.
Contact: Director, Division of Medicine, PHS, DHHS, Parklawn Building, Room 4C-25, 5600 Fishers Lane, Rockville, MD 20857, 301-443-6190.

13.985 EYE RESEARCH–FACILITY CONSTRUCTION
Type of Assistance: Grants ranging from $100,000 to $700,000.
Applicant Eligibility: Nonprofit organizations.
Objective: To support projects in new construction, alteration or renovation of existing facilities, and acquisition of specialized laboratory instrumentation.

Contact: Director, Extramural and Collaborative Programs, National Eye Institute, National Institutes of Health, Bethesda, MD 20205, 301-496-4903.

13.987 HEALTH PROGRAMS FOR REFUGEES
Type of Assistance: Grants ranging from $10,000 to $1,869,795.
Applicant Eligibility: State and local health agencies.
Objective: To assist states and localities in meeting the public health needs of their refugee population and in providing general health assessments of refugees when necessary.
Contact: Director, Center for Disease Control, PHS, DHHS, Atlanta, GA 30333, 404-329-3291.

13.988 COOPERATIVE AGREEMENTS FOR STATE-BASED DIABETES CONTROL CENTERS
Type of Assistance: Grants ranging from $55,000 to $338,000.
Applicant Eligibility: Official state health agencies.
Objective: To improve the quality of life and effectiveness of health services for diabetics.
Contact: Director, Centers for Disease Control, PHS, DHHS, Atlanta, GA 30333, 404-329-3291.

13.989 SENIOR INTERNATIONAL AWARDS PROGRAM
Type of Assistance: Grants ranging from $12,000 to $37,100.
Applicant Eligibility: Individuals.
Objective: To promote the exchange of ideas and information about the latest advances in the biomedical and behavioral sciences between U.S. biomedical scientists and those of other nations of the world.
Contact: International Awards Branch, Fogarty International Center, Bethesda, MD 20205, 301-496-6688.

13.990 NATIONAL HEALTH PROMOTION
Type of Assistance: Grants ranging from $30,000 to $75,000.
Applicant Eligibility: Public or private nonprofit organizations.
Objective: To educate the public about environmental, occupational, societal and behavioral factors that affect health in order that individuals may make informed decisions about health-related behavior.
Contact: Program Management Program, Office of Disease Prevention and Health Promotion, 330 C Street, Room 2132, SW, Washington, DC 20201, 202-472-5370.

13.991 PREVENTIVE HEALTH SERVICES
Type of Assistance: Grants ranging from $37,790 to $6,540,843.
Applicant Eligibility: State governments and tribal organizations.
Objective: To provide states with resources for comprehensive preventive medical services including emergency medical services, health incentive activities, hypertension programs, rodent control, fluoridation programs, health education and risk reduction programs, home health services and services for rape victims.

Contact: Director, Field Activities, Centers for Disease Control, Atlanta, GA 30333, 404-329-3850.

13.992 ALCOHOL AND DRUG ABUSE AND MENTAL HEALTH SERVICES BLOCK GRANT

Type of Assistance: Grants ranging from $9,000 to $44 million.
Applicant Eligibility: US states, Indian tribal organizations.
Objective: To support projects for the development of more effective prevention, treatment and rehabilitation programs and activities to deal with alcohol and drug abuse; and to support community mental health centers for chronically mentally ill individuals, severely mentally disturbed children and adolescents.
Contact: Office of the Administrator, ADAMHA, PHS, 5600 Fishers Lane, Rockville, MD 20857, 301-443-4564.

13.993 PRIMARY CARE BLOCK GRANT

Type of Assistance: Grants.
Applicant Eligibility: US states and Indian tribal governments.
Objective: To support and strengthen states' capacity to organize and deliver primary health services through Community Health Centers in medically underserved areas.
Contact: Bureau of Health Care Delivery and Assistance, Health Resources and Services Administration, Parklawn Building, Room 7-05, 5600 Fishers Lane, Rockville, MD 20857, 301-443-2380.

13.994 MATERNAL AND CHILD HEALTH SERVICES BLOCK GRANT

Type of Assistance: Grants.
Applicant Eligibility: State health agencies.
Objective: To enable states to maintain and strengthen their leadership in planning, promoting, coordinating and evaluating health care for mothers and children and in providing health services for mothers and children who do not have access to adequate health care.
Contact: Division of Maternal and Child Health, Health Resources and Services Administration, DHHS, Parklawn Building, Room 6-05, 5600 Fishers Lane, Rockville, MD 20857, 301-443-2170.

13.995 ADOLESCENT FAMILY LIFE DEMONSTRATION PROJECTS

Type of Assistance: Grants ranging from $40,000 to $408,000.
Applicant Eligibility: State and local governments; nonprofit public or private organizations.
Objective: To promote positive, family-centered approaches to the problem of adolescent premarital sexual relations, including adolescent pregnancies; to promote adoption as an alternative; and to establish comprehensive approaches to the delivery of care services.
Contact: Office of Adolescent Pregnancy Programs, DHHS, HHS North Building, Room 1351, 330 Independence Avenue, SW, Washington, DC 20201, 202-245-0146.

US DEPARTMENT OF HOUSING AND URBAN DEVELOPMENT

HOUSING—FEDERAL HOUSING COMMISSIONER

14.103 INTEREST REDUCTION PAYMENTS— RENTAL AND COOPERATIVE HOUSING FOR LOWER-INCOME FAMILIES

Type of Assistance: Direct payments and guaranteed/insured loans.
Applicant Eligibility: Nonprofit organizations.
Objective: To provide good quality rental and cooperative housing for persons of low- and moderate-income by providing interest reduction payments in order to lower their housing costs.
Contact: Director, Office of Multifamily Housing Management, HUD, Washington, DC 20410, 202-426-3968.

14.108 REHABILITATION MORTGAGE INSURANCE

Type of Assistance: Guaranteed/insured loans.
Applicant Eligibility: Individuals.
Objective: To help families repair or improve, purchase and improve, or refinance and improve existing residential structures more than one year old.
Contact: Director, Single Family Development Division, Office of Single Family Housing, HUD, Washington, DC 20410, 202-755-6720.

14.110 MANUFACTURED (MOBILE) HOME INSURANCE— FINANCING PURCHASE OF MOBILE HOMES AS PRINCIPAL RESIDENCES OF BORROWERS

Type of Assistance: Guaranteed/insured loans up to $40,500.
Applicant Eligibility: Individuals.
Objective: To make possible reasonable financing of mobile home purchases.
Contact: Director, Title I Insurance Division, Office of Single Family Housing, HUD, Washington, DC 20410, 202-755-6880.

14.112 MORTGAGE INSURANCE— CONSTRUCTION OR SUBSTANTIAL REHABILITATION OF CONDOMINIUM PROJECTS

Type of Assistance: Guaranteed/insured loans up to $36,000.
Applicant Eligibility: Individuals.
Objective: To enable sponsors to develop condominium projects in which individual units will be sold to home buyers.

Contact: Insurance Division, Office of Multifamily Housing Development, HUD, Washington, DC 20410, 202-755-6223.

14.115 MORTGAGE INSURANCE—DEVELOPMENT OF SALES-TYPE COOPERATIVE PROJECTS
Type of Assistance: Guaranteed/insured loans.
Applicant Eligibility: Nonprofit organizations and eligible mortgagors.
Objective: To make it possible for nonprofit cooperative ownership housing corporations or trusts to sponsor the development of new housing that will be sold to individual cooperative members.
Contact: Director, Insurance Division, Office of Multifamily Housing Development, HUD, Washington, DC 20410, 202-755-6223.

14.116 MORTGAGE INSURANCE GROUP PRACTICE FACILITIES
Type of Assistance: Guaranteed/insured loans.
Applicant Eligibility: Nonprofit organizations.
Objective: To help develop group health practice facilities and to insure lenders against loss on mortgage loans. These loans may be used to finance the construction or rehabilitation of facilities, including major movable equipment, for the provision of preventive, diagnostic and treatment services by a medical, dental, optometric, osteopathic or podiatric group.
Contact: Insurance Division, Office of Multifamily Housing Development, HUD, Washington, DC 20410, 202-755-6223.

14.117 MORTGAGE INSURANCE—HOMES
Type of Assistance: Guaranteed/insured loans averaging $39,356.
Applicant Eligibility: Individuals.
Objective: To help families undertake home ownership, and to insure lenders against loss on mortgage loans. These loans may be used to finance the purchase of proposed, under-construction, or existing one- to four-family housing, as well as to refinance debts on existing housing.
Contact: Director, Single Family Development Division, Office of Single Family Housing, HUD, Washington, DC 20410, 202-755-6720

14.119 MORTGAGE INSURANCE— HOMES FOR DISASTER VICTIMS
Type of Assistance: Guaranteed/insured loans.
Applicant Eligibility: Individuals.
Objective: To help victims of a major disaster undertake home ownership on a sound basis, and to insure lenders against loss on mortgage loans. These loans may be used to finance the purchase of proposed, under-construction, or existing single-family housing for the occupant-mortgagee who is a victim of a major disaster.
Contact: Director, Single Family Development Division, Office of Single Family Housing, HUD, Washington, DC 20410, 202-755-6720.

14.120 MORTGAGE INSURANCE—HOMES FOR LOW- AND MODERATE-INCOME FAMILIES

Type of Assistance: Guaranteed/insured loans up to $42,000.

Applicant Eligibility: Individuals.

Objective: To make home ownership more readily available to families displaced by urban renewal or other government actions as well as other low-income and moderate-income families, and to insure lenders against loss on mortgage loans. These loans may be used to finance the purchase of proposed or existing low-cost one- to four-family housing or the rehabilitation of such housing.

Contact: Director, Single Family Development Division, Office of Single Family Housing, HUD, Washington, DC 20410, 202-755-6720.

14.121 MORTGAGE INSURANCE— HOMES IN OUTLYING AREAS

Type of Assistance: Guaranteed/insured.

Applicant Eligibility: Individuals.

Objective: To help families purchase homes in outlying areas, and to insure lenders against loss on mortgage loans. These loans may be used to finance the purchase of proposed, under-construction, or existing one-family non-farm housing, or new farm housing on five or more acres adjacent to a highway.

Contact: Director, Single Family Development Division, Office of Single Family Housing, HUD, Washington, DC 20410, 202-755-6720.

14.122 MORTGAGE INSURANCE— HOMES IN URBAN RENEWAL AREAS

Type of Assistance: Guaranteed/insured loans.

Applicant Eligibility: Individuals.

Objective: To help families purchase or rehabilitate homes in urban renewal areas, and to insure lenders against loss on mortgage loans. These loans may be used to finance acquisition or rehabilitation of one- to eleven-family housing in approved urban renewal or code enforcement areas.

Contact: Director, Single Family Development Division, Office of Single Family Housing, HUD, Washington, DC 20410, 202-755-6720.

14.123 MORTGAGE INSURANCE— HOUSING IN OLDER, DECLINING AREAS

Type of Assistance: Guaranteed/insured loans averaging $9,400.

Applicant Eligibility: Individuals.

Objective: To help families purchase or rehabilitate housing in older, declining urban areas, and to insure lenders against loss on mortgage loans. These loans may be used to finance the purchase, repair, rehabilitation, and construction of housing in older, declining urban areas where conditions are such that certain normal eligibility requirements for mortgage insurance under a particular program cannot be met. The property must be an acceptable risk, giving consideration to the need for providing adequate housing for low- and moderate-income families.

Contact: Director, Single Family Development Division, Office of Single Family Housing, HUD, Washington, DC 20410, 202-755-6500.

14.124 MORTGAGE INSURANCE— INVESTOR-SPONSORED COOPERATIVE HOUSING

Type of Assistance: Guaranteed/insured loans up to $36,000.
Applicant Eligibility: Individuals.
Objective: To provide good quality multifamily housing to be sold to nonprofit cooperatives, ownership housing corporations or trusts and to insure lenders against loss on mortgage loans. Insured mortgages may be used to finance the construction or rehabilitation of detached, semidetached, row, walk-up or elevator-type structures with five or more units.
Contact: Insurance Division, Office of Multifamily Housing Development, HUD, Washington, DC 20410, 202-755-6223.

14.125 MORTGAGE INSURANCE— LAND DEVELOPMENT AND NEW COMMUNITIES

Type of Assistance: Guaranteed/insured loans (dollar amount not available).
Applicant Eligibility: Individuals.
Objective: To assist the development of large subdivisions or new communities on a sound economic basis, and to insure lenders against loss on mortgage loans. These loans may be used to assist in financing the purchase of land and the development of building sites for subdivisions or new communities including water and sewer systems, streets and lighting and other installations needed for residential communities.
Contact: Director, Single Family Development Division, Office of Single Family Housing, HUD, Washington, DC 20410, 202-755-6720.

14.126 MORTGAGE INSURANCE— MANAGEMENT-TYPE COOPERATIVE PROJECTS

Type of Assistance: Guaranteed/insured loans up to $36,000.
Applicant Eligibility: Nonprofit organizations.
Objective: To make it possible for nonprofit cooperative ownership housing corporations or trusts to acquire housing projects to be operated as management-type cooperatives, and to insure lenders against loss on mortgage loans. Insured mortgages may be used to finance construction, acquisition of existing, or rehabilitation of detached, semidetached, row, walk-up or elevator-type housing consisting of five or more units.
Contact: Insurance Division, Office of Insured Multifamily Housing Development, HUD, Washington, DC 20410, 202-755-6223.

14.127 MORTGAGE INSURANCE—MOBILE HOME PARKS

Type of Assistance: Guaranteed/insured loans up to $9,000 per mobile home space.
Applicant Eligibility: Individuals.
Objective: To make possible the financing of construction or rehabil-

itation of mobile home parks, and to insure lenders against loss on mortgage loans. Insured mortgages may be used to finance the construction or rehabilitation of mobile home parks consisting of five or more spaces.

Contact: Insurance Division, Multifamily Development Division, Office of Multifamily Housing Development, HUD, Washington, DC 20410, 202-755-6223.

14.128 MORTGAGE INSURANCE—HOSPITALS

Type of Assistance: Guaranteed/insured loans (dollar amount not available).

Applicant Eligibility: Nonprofit organizations.

Objective: To make possible the financing of hospitals, and to insure lenders against loss on mortgage loans. The loans may be used to finance the construction or rehabilitation of private nonprofit and proprietary hospitals including major movable equipment.

Contact: Insurance Division, Office of Multifamily Housing Development, HUD, Washington, DC 20410, 202-755-6223.

14.129 MORTGAGE INSURANCE—NURSING HOMES AND INTERMEDIATE CARE FACILITIES

Type of Assistance: Guaranteed/insured loans (dollar amount not available).

Applicant Eligibility: Individuals and nonprofit organizations.

Objective: To make possible financing for construction or rehabilitation of nursing homes and intermediate care facilities, to provide loan insurance to install fire safety equipment, and to insure lenders against loss on mortgage loans. Insured mortgages may be used to finance construction or renovation of facilities to accommodate 20 or more patients requiring skilled nursing care and related medical services, or those while not in need of nursing home care are in need of minimum but continuous care provided by licensed or trained personnel.

Contact: Insurance Division, Office of Multifamily Housing Development, HUD, Washington, DC 20410, 202-755-6223.

14.130 MORTGAGE INSURANCE— PURCHASE BY HOMEOWNERS OF FEE-SIMPLE TITLE FROM LESSORS

Type of Assistance: Guaranteed/insured loans up to $10,000 per family unit.

Applicant Eligibility: Individuals.

Objective: To help homeowners obtain fee-simple title to the property that they hold under long-term leases and on which their homes are located, and to insure lenders against loss on mortgage loans. These loans may be used to finance the purchase from lessors by homeowners of fee-simple title to property that is held under long-term leases and on which their homes are located.

Contact: Director, Single Family Development Division, Office of Single Family Housing, HUD, Washington, DC 20410, 202-755-6720.

14.132 MORTGAGE INSURANCE—
PURCHASE OF SALES-TYPE COOPERATIVE
HOUSING UNITS

Type of Assistance: Guaranteed/insured loans up to $67,500.

Applicant Eligibility: Nonprofit organizations.

Objective: To make available good quality new housing for purchase by individual members of a housing cooperative, and to insure lenders against loss on mortgage loans. Insured mortgages may be used to finance purchase by a cooperative member of single family detached, semidetached, or row housing constructed under the sponsorship of a nonprofit cooperative with five or more units.

Contact: Insurance Division, Office of Insured Multifamily Development, HUD, Washington, DC 20410, 202-755-6720.

14.133 MORTGAGE INSURANCE—
PURCHASE OF UNITS IN CONDOMINIUMS

Type of Assistance: Guaranteed/insured loans up to $67,500.

Applicant Eligibility: Individuals.

Objective: To enable families to purchase units in condominium projects and to insure lenders against loss on mortgage loans. These loans may be used to finance the acquisition of individual units in proposed or existing condominium projects containing four or more units.

Contact: Director, Single Family Development Division, Office of Single Family Housing, HUD, Washington, DC 20410, 202-755-6720.

14.134 MORTGAGE INSURANCE—RENTAL HOUSING

Type of Assistance: Guaranteed/insured loans up to $36,000.

Applicant Eligibility: Eligible mortgagors.

Objective: To provide good quality rental housing, and to insure lenders against loss on mortgage loans. Insured mortgages may be used to finance the construction or rehabilitation of rental detached, semidetached, row, walk-up or elevator-type structures with five or more units.

Contact: Director, Insurance Division, Multifamily Development Division, Office of Multifamily Housing Development, HUD, Washington, DC 20410, 202-755-6223.

14.135 MORTGAGE INSURANCE—RENTAL HOUSING FOR
MODERATE-INCOME FAMILIES

Type of Assistance: Guaranteed/insured loans up to $37,870.

Applicant Eligibility: Nonprofit organizations.

Objective: To provide good quality rental housing within the price range of low- and moderate-income families, and to insure lenders against loss on mortgage loans. Insured mortgages may be used to finance construction or rehabilitation of detached, semidetached, row, walk-up or elevator-type rental housing containing five or more units.

Contact: Director, Insurance Division, Multifamily Development Division, Office of Multifamily Housing Development, HUD, Washington, DC 20410, 202-755-6223.

14.137 MORTGAGE INSURANCE—RENTAL AND COOPERATIVE HOUSING FOR LOW- AND MODERATE-INCOME FAMILIES, MARKET INTEREST RATE

Type of Assistance: Guaranteed/insured loans up to $38,840.

Applicant Eligibility: Individuals and nonprofit organizations.

Objective: To provide good quality rental or cooperative housing within the price range of low- and moderate-income families.

Contact: Director, Multifamily Development Division, Office of Multifamily Housing Development, HUD, Washington, DC 20410, 202-755-6223.

14.138 MORTGAGE INSURANCE— RENTAL HOUSING FOR THE ELDERLY

Type of Assistance: Guaranteed/insured loans up to $34,846.

Applicant Eligibility: Individuals and nonprofit corporations.

Objective: To provide good quality rental housing for the elderly, and to insure lenders against loss on mortgages. Insured mortgages may be used to finance construction or rehabilitation of detached, semidetached, walk-up or elevator-type rental housing designed for occupancy by elderly or handicapped individuals and consisting of eight or more units.

Contact: Director, Insurance Division, Multifamily Development Division, Office of Multifamily Housing Development, HUD, Washington, DC 20410, 202-755-6223.

14.139 MORTGAGE INSURANCE—RENTAL HOUSING IN URBAN RENEWAL AREAS

Type of Assistance: Guaranteed/insured loans up to $36,000.

Applicant Eligibility: Eligible mortgagors.

Objective: To provide good quality rental housing in urban renewal areas and to insure lenders against loss on mortgage loans. Insured mortgages may be used to finance proposed construction or rehabilitation of detached, semidetached, row, walk-up or elevator-type rental housing, or finance purchase of properties which have been rehabilitated by a local public agency.

Contact: Director, Insurance Division, Multifamily Development Division, Office of Multifamily Housing Development, HUD, Washington, DC 20410, 202-755-6223.

14.140 MORTGAGE INSURANCE—SPECIAL CREDIT RISKS

Type of Assistance: Guaranteed/insured loans up to $18,000.

Applicant Eligibility: Individuals.

Objective: To make home ownership possible for low- and moderate-income families who cannot meet normal HUD requirements, and to insure lenders against loss on mortgage loans. These loans may be used to finance the purchase of new, existing or substantially rehabilitated single family homes.

Contact: Director, Single Family Development Division, Office of Single Family Housing, HUD, Washington, DC 20410, 202-755-6720.

14.141 NONPROFIT SPONSOR ASSISTANCE PROGRAM
Type of Assistance: Direct loans (dollar amount not available).
Applicant Eligibility: Nonprofit organizations.
Objective: To assist and stimulate prospective private nonprofit sponsors to develop sound housing projects for the elderly or handicapped, and to make interest-free loans to nonprofit sponsors to cover 80 percent of preconstruction expenses for planning housing projects for the elderly or handicapped.
Contact: Director, Elderly, Office of Elderly and Assisted Housing, Office of Multifamily Housing Development, HUD, Washington, DC 20410, 202-426-8730.

14.142 PROPERTY IMPROVEMENT LOAN INSURANCE FOR IMPROVING ALL EXISTING STRUCTURES AND BUILDING OF NEW NONRESIDENTIAL STRUCTURES
Type of Assistance: Guaranteed/insured loans up to $43,750.
Applicant Eligibility: Individuals.
Objective: To facilitate the financing of improvements to homes and other existing structures and the erection of new nonresidential structures, and to insure lenders against losses on loans. Insured loans may be used to finance alterations, repairs and improvements for existing structures, and the erection of new nonresidential structures which substantially protect or improve the basic livability or utility of the properties.
Contact: Director, Title I, Insurance Division, Office of Single Family Housing, HUD, Washington, DC 20410, 202-755-6880.

14.149 RENT SUPPLEMENTS—RENTAL HOUSING FOR LOWER-INCOME FAMILIES
Type of Assistance: Direct payments (dollar amount not available).
Applicant Eligibility: Individuals and nonprofit organizations.
Objective: To make good quality rental housing available to low-income families at a cost they can afford, and to make payments to owners of approved multifamily rental housing projects to supplement the partial rental payments of eligible tenants.
Contact: Director, Office of Multifamily Housing Management, Housing, HUD, Washington, DC 20410, 202-755-5654.

14.151 SUPPLEMENTAL LOAN INSURANCE— MULTIFAMILY RENTAL HOUSING
Type of Assistance: Guaranteed/insured loans (dollar amount not available).
Applicant Eligibility: Individuals.
Objective: To finance additions and improvements to any multifamily project, group practice facility, hospital or nursing home insured or held by HUD. Major movable equipment for nursing homes or group

practice facilities or hospitals may be covered by a mortgage under this program.
Contact: Director, Multifamily Development Division, Insurance Division, Office of Multifamily Housing Development, Housing, HUD, Washington, DC 20410, 202-755-6223.

14.152 MORTGAGE INSURANCE—EXPERIMENTAL HOMES

Type of Assistance: Guaranteed/insured loans averaging $35,000.
Applicant Eligibility: Individuals.
Objective: To help finance, by providing mortgage insurance, the development of homes that incorporate new or untried construction concepts designed to reduce housing costs, raise living standards and improve neighborhood design.
Contact: Assistant Secretary for Policy Development and Research, HUD, 451 Seventh Street, SW, Washington, DC 20410, 202-755-5544.

14.155 MORTGAGE INSURANCE FOR THE PURCHASE OR REFINANCING OF EXISTING MULTIFAMILY HOUSING PROJECTS

Type of Assistance: Guaranteed/insured loans up to $6,500 per unit.
Applicant Eligibility: Individuals.
Objective: To provide mortgage insurance for the purchase or refinancing of existing multifamily housing projects whether conventionally financed or subject to federally insured mortgages at the time of application for mortgage insurance.
Contact: Director, Office of Multifamily Housing Development, Multifamily Housing Development Division, Housing, HUD, Washington, DC 20410, 202-755-6223.

14.156 LOWER-INCOME HOUSING ASSISTANCE PROGRAM (SECTION 8)

Type of Assistance: Direct payments (dollar amount not available).
Applicant Eligibility: Individuals, nonprofit organizations, state and local governments.
Objective: To aid lower-income families in obtaining decent, safe and sanitary housing in private accommodations and to promote economically mixed existing, newly constructed and substantially and moderately rehabilitated housing. Payments are used to make up the difference between the maximum approved rent due to the owner for the dwelling unit which is reasonable in relation to comparable market units and the occupant family's required contribution toward rent. Assisted families are required to contribute not less than 15 or more than 25 percent of their adjusted family income toward rent.
Contact: Office of Elderly and Assisted Housing, HUD, Washington, DC 20410, 202-755-6887.

14.157 HOUSING FOR THE ELDERLY OR HANDICAPPED

Type of Assistance: Direct loans averaging $2,216,718.
Applicant Eligibility: Nonprofit organizations.

Objective: To provide for rental or cooperative housing and related facilities (such as central dining) for the elderly or handicapped. Loans may be used to finance the construction or rehabilitation of rental or cooperative detached, semidetached, row, walk-up or elevator-type structures.
Contact: Director, Office of Elderly and Assisted Housing, HUD, Washington, DC 20410, 202-426-8730.

14.159   SECTION 245 GRADUATED PAYMENT MORTGAGE PROGRAM

Type of Assistance: Guaranteed/insured loans.
Applicant Eligibility: Individuals.
Objective: To facilitate early home ownership for households that expect their incomes to rise. Program allows homeowners to make smaller monthly payments initially and to increase their size gradually over time.
Contact: Director, Single Family Development Division, Office of Single Family Housing, HUD, Washington, DC 20410, 202-755-6720.

14.161   SINGLE FAMILY HOME MORTGAGE CO-INSURANCE

Type of Assistance: Guaranteed/insured loans.
Applicant Eligibility: Individuals.
Objective: To help families undertake home ownership. Loans may be used to finance the purchase of proposed, under-construction or existing one- to four-family housing, as well as to refinance debts on existing housing.
Contact: Director, Single Family Development Division, Office of Single Family Housing, HUD, Washington, DC 20410, 202-755-6720.

14.162   MORTGAGE INSURANCE—COMBINATION AND MOBILE HOME LOT LOANS

Type of Assistance: Guaranteed/insured loans up to $54,000.
Applicant Eligibility: Individuals.
Objective: To make possible reasonable financing of mobile home purchase and the lot to place it on.
Contact: Director, Title I Insurance Division, Office of Single Family Housing, HUD, Washington, DC 20410, 202-755-6880.

14.163   MORTGAGE INSURANCE— COOPERATIVE FINANCING

Type of Assistance: Guaranteed/insured loans.
Applicant Eligibility: Individuals.
Objective: To provide insured financing for the purchase of shares of stock in a cooperative project. Ownership of the shares carries the right to occupy a unit located within the cooperative project.
Contact: Director, Single Family Development Division, Office of Single Family Housing, HUD, Washington, DC 20410, 202-755-6720.

14.164 OPERATING ASSISTANCE FOR TROUBLED MULTIFAMILY HOUSING PROJECTS

Type of Assistance: Grants and direct payments averaging $331,000.
Applicant Eligibility: Individuals.
Objective: To provide assistance to restore or maintain the financial soundness, assist in the management, and maintain the low- to moderate-income character of certain projects assisted or approved for assistance under the National Housing Act or under the Housing and Urban Development Act of 1965.
Contact: Chief, Program Support Branch, Office of Multifamily Housing Management and Occupancy, HUD, Washington, DC 20410, 202-755-5654.

14.165 MORTGAGE INSURANCE— HOMES IN MILITARY IMPACTED AREAS

Type of Assistance: Guaranteed/insured loans.
Applicant Eligibility: Individuals.
Objective: To help families undertake home ownership in military impacted areas.
Contact: Director, Single Family Development Division, Office of Single Family Housing, HUD, Washington, DC 20410, 202-755-6720.

14.166 MORTGAGE INSURANCE—HOMES FOR MEMBERS OF THE ARMED SERVICES

Type of Assistance: Guaranteed/insured loans up to $67,500.
Applicant Eligibility: Military personnel.
Objective: To help members of the armed services on active duty to purchase a home.
Contact: Single Family Development Division, Office of Single Family Housing, HUD, Washington, DC 20410, 202-755-6720.

14.167 MORTGAGE INSURANCE— TWO-YEAR OPERATING LOSS LOANS

Type of Assistance: Guaranteed/insured loans averaging $206,800.
Applicant Eligibility: Individuals.
Objective: To insure a separate loan covering operating losses incurred during the first two years following the date of completion of a multifamily project.
Contact: Office of Multifamily Housing Development, Housing, Room 6128, HUD, Washington, DC 20410, 202-755-6223.

14.169 HOUSING COUNSELING ASSISTANCE PROGRAM

Type of Assistance: Grants ranging from $5,000 to $50,000.
Applicant Eligibility: State and local governments, nonprofit organizations.
Objective: To counsel homeowners, home buyers and tenants under HUD–assisted, –owned and –insured housing programs in order to assure successful home ownership and rentership, and thereby prevent and reduce delinquencies, defaults and foreclosures.

Contact: Office of Single Family Housing, HUD, 451 Seventh Street, SW, Washington, DC 20410, 202-755-7330.

14.170 CONGREGATE HOUSING SERVICES PROGRAM
Type of Assistance: Grants.
Applicant Eligibility: Public housing projects.
Objective: To prevent premature or unnecessary institutionalization of the elderly, elderly-handicapped, nonelderly-handicapped, and temporarily disabled; to provide a variety of innovative approaches that will improve the delivery of meals and nonmedical supportive services while utilizing existing service programs; and to fill gaps in existing service systems and ensure availability of funding for meals and appropriate services needed to maintain independent living.
Contact: Office of Elderly and Assisted Housing, HUD, Washington, DC 20410, 202-755-5866.

14.172 MORTGAGE INSURANCE—
GROWING EQUITY MORTGAGES
Type of Assistance: Guaranteed/insured loans.
Applicant Eligibility: Individuals.
Objective: To provide a rapid principal reduction and shorter mortgage term by increasing payments over a ten-year period, thereby expanding housing opportunities to the home-buying public.
Contact: Single Family Development Division, Office of Single Family Housing, HUD, Washington, DC 20410, 202-755-6720.

14.173 CO-INSURANCE FOR PRIVATE LENDERS
Type of Assistance: Guaranteed/insured loans.
Applicant Eligibility: Public or private mortgagors.
Objective: To provide mortgage insurance for the purchase or refinancing of existing multifamily housing projects. HUD authorizes approved lenders for co-insurance mortgage loans.
Contact: Office of Multifamily Housing Development, HUD, Washington, DC 20410, 202-426-7113.

COMMUNITY PLANNING AND DEVELOPMENT

14.175 ADJUSTABLE RATE MORTGAGES
Type of Assistance: Guaranteed/insured loans.
Applicant Eligibility: Individuals.
Objective: To provide mortgage insurance for an adjustable rate mortgage that offers lenders more assurance of long-term profitability than a fixed rate mortgage, while offering consumer protection features.
Contact: Director, Single Family Development Division, HUD, Washington, DC 20410, 202-755-6720.

14.218 COMMUNITY DEVELOPMENT BLOCK GRANTS/ENTITLEMENT GRANTS

Type of Assistance: Grants (dollar amount not available).
Applicant Eligibility: State and local governments.
Objective: To develop viable urban communities, including decent housing and a suitable living environment, and expand economic opportunities, principally for persons of low and moderate income.
Contact: Entitlement Cities Division, Office of Block Grant Assistance, HUD, 451 Seventh Street, SW, Washington, DC 20410, 202-755-9267.

14.219 COMMUNITY DEVELOPMENT BLOCK GRANTS/SMALL CITIES PROGRAM

Type of Assistance: Grants ranging from $24,000 to $800,000.
Applicant Eligibility: State and local governments.
Objective: To assist communities in providing decent housing and a suitable living environment and expanded economic opportunities, principally for persons of low and moderate income.
Contact: State & Small Cities Division, HUD, 451 Seventh Street, SW, Washington, DC 20410, 202-755-6587.

14.220 SECTION 312 REHABILITATION LOANS

Type of Assistance: Direct loans up to $27,000 per dwelling unit.
Applicant Eligibility: Individuals.
Objective: To promote the revitalization of neighborhoods by providing funds for rehabilitation of residential, commercial and other non-residential properties.
Contact: Community Planning and Development, Office of Urban Rehabilitation, HUD, 451 Seventh Street, SW, Washington, DC 20410, 202-755-6336 or -5685.

14.221 URBAN DEVELOPMENT ACTION GRANTS

Type of Assistance: Grants averaging $2,200,000.
Applicant Eligibility: State and local governments.
Objective: To assist severely distressed cities and urban counties in alleviating physical and economic deterioration through economic development, neighborhood revitalization, job creation and strengthening of the tax base, and to assist cities and urban counties containing severely distressed pockets of poverty.
Contact: Office of Urban Development Action Grants, Community Planning and Development, HUD, 451 Seventh Street, SW, Washington, DC 20410, 202-755-6290.

14.222 URBAN HOMESTEADING

Type of Assistance: Sale, exchange or donation of property.
Applicant Eligibility: State and local governments.
Objective: To provide home ownership to individuals and families and to revitalize neighborhoods, and to provide one- to four-unit properties to units of general local government, states or their designated public

agencies, for use in an Urban Homesteading program. Homestead properties received from HUD must be conditionally conveyed without substantial consideration.
Contact: Director, Urban Homesteading Division, Office of Urban Rehabilitation and Community Reinvestment, HUD, 451 Seventh Street, SW, Washington, DC 20410, 202-755-5324.

14.223 INDIAN COMMUNITY DEVELOPMENT BLOCK GRANT PROGRAM
Type of Assistance: Grants.
Applicant Eligibility: Indian tribes or nations.
Objective: To provide assistance to Indian tribes and Alaskan natives in the development of viable Indian communities and to provide community development assistance to American Samoa, Guam, the Northern Mariana Islands and the Virgin Islands.
Contact: Office of Program Policy Development, Community Development and Planning, HUD, 451 Seventh Street, SW, Washington, DC 20410, 202-755-6090.

14.228 COMMUNITY DEVELOPMENT BLOCK GRANTS/STATE'S PROGRAM
Type of Assistance: Grants.
Applicant Eligibility: State governments.
Objective: The development of viable urban communities by providing decent housing, a suitable living environment and expanding economic opportunities, principally for persons of low and moderate income.
Contact: State and Small Cities Division, Office of Block Grant Assistance, Community Planning, HUD, 51 Seventh Street, SW, Washington, DC 20410.

14.401 FAIR HOUSING ASSISTANCE PROGRAM
Type of Assistance: Grants up to $250,000.
Applicant Eligibility: State and local governments.
Objective: To provide to those agencies to whom HUD must refer Title VIII complaints both the incentives and resources required to develop an effective work force to handle complaints and provide technical assistance and training to ensure that HUD-referred complaints are properly and efficiently handled.
Contact: Assistant Secretary for Fair Housing and Equal Opportunity, HUD, 451 Seventh Street, SW, Washington, DC 20410, 202-426-3500.

14.403 COMMUNITY HOUSING RESOURCE BOARD (CHRB) PROGRAM
Type of Assistance: Grants up to $25,000.
Applicant Eligibility: CHRB.
Objective: To provide funding to Community Housing Resource Boards that have the responsibility of providing implementation assistance to housing industry groups.
Contact: HUD, Office of Fair Housing and Equal Opportunity, Washington, DC 20410, 202-755-5992.

OFFICE OF POLICY DEVELOPMENT AND RESEARCH

14.506 GENERAL RESEARCH AND TECHNOLOGY ACTIVITY

Type of Assistance: Grants ranging from $150 to $500,000.

Applicant Eligibility: Nonprofit organizations, state and local governments.

Objective: To carry out applied research and demonstration projects of high priority and preselected by the Department to serve the needs of housing and community development groups and to improve the operations of the Department's programs.

Contact: Assistant Secretary for Policy Development and Research, HUD, 451 Seventh Street, SW, Washington, DC 20410, 202-755-6996.

14.509 MORTGAGE INSURANCE— EXPERIMENTAL RENTAL HOUSING

Type of Assistance: Guaranteed/insured loans averaging $2,314,814.

Applicant Eligibility: Individuals.

Objective: To provide mortgage insurance to help finance the development of multifamily housing that incorporates new or untried construction concepts designed to reduce housing costs, raise living standards, and improve neighborhood design.

Contact: Secretary for Policy Development and Research, Department of Housing and Urban Development, 451 Seventh Street, SW, Washington, DC 20410, 202-755-5544.

US DEPARTMENT OF THE INTERIOR

BUREAU OF INDIAN AFFAIRS

15.103 INDIAN SOCIAL SERVICES— CHILD WELFARE ASSISTANCE

Type of Assistance: Direct payments ranging from $100 to $1,000 per child per month.
Applicant Eligibility: Native Americans.
Objective: To provide foster home care and appropriate institutional care for dependent, neglected and handicapped Indian children residing on or near a reservation, including those children living in jurisdictions under the Bureau of Indian Affairs in Alaska and Oklahoma, when these services are not available from state or local public agencies.
Contact: Division of Social Services, Office of Indian Services, Bureau of Indian Affairs, 18th and C Streets, NW, Washington, DC 20245, 202-343-6434.

15.108 INDIAN EMPLOYMENT ASSISTANCE

Type of Assistance: Grants ranging from $800 to $5,500.
Applicant Eligibility: Native Americans.
Objective: To provide vocational training and employment opportunities for Indians.
Contact: Office of Indian Services, Division of Job Placement and Training, Bureau of Indian Affairs, Room 1350, 18th and C Streets, NW, Washington, DC 20245, 202-343-3668.

15.113 INDIAN SOCIAL SERVICES—GENERAL ASSISTANCE

Type of Assistance: Direct payments depending on need.
Applicant Eligibility: Native Americans.
Objective: To provide assistance for living needs to needy Indians on or near reservations, including those Indians living in jurisdictions under the Bureau of Indian Affairs in Alaska and Oklahoma, when such assistance is not available from state or local public agencies.
Contact: Division of Social Services, Office of Indian Services, Bureau of Indian Affairs, 18th and C Streets, NW, Washington, DC 20245, 202-343-6434.

15.114 INDIAN EDUCATION— HIGHER EDUCATION GRANT PROGRAM

Type of Assistance: Grants ranging from $200 to $7,000.
Applicant Eligibility: Native Americans.
Objective: To encourage Indian students to continue their education and training beyond high school.

Contact: Office of Indian Education Programs, Bureau of Indian Affairs, 1951 Constitution Avenue, NW, Washington, DC 20245, 202-343-4871.

15.123 INDIAN LOANS—CLAIMS ASSISTANCE
Type of Assistance: Direct loans ranging from $500 to $250,000.
Applicant Eligibility: Native Americans.
Objective: To enable Indian tribes or identifiable groups of Indians without available funds to obtain expert assistance in the preparation and processing of claims pending before the US Court of Claims.
Contact: Director, Office of Indian Services, Bureau of Indian Affairs, 18th and C Streets, NW, Room 4600, Washington, DC 20245, 202-343-3657.

15.124 INDIAN LOANS—ECONOMIC DEVELOPMENT (INDIAN CREDIT PROGRAM)
Type of Assistance: Direct loans and guaranteed/insured loans ranging from $100 to $1 million.
Applicant Eligibility: Native Americans.
Objective: To provide assistance to Indians, Alaskan Natives, tribes and Indian organizations to obtain financing from private and governmental sources which serve other citizens. When otherwise unavailable, financial assistance through the Bureau of Indian Affairs is provided to eligible applicants for any purpose that will promote the economic development of a federal Indian reservation.
Contact: Office of Indian Services, Bureau of Indian Affairs, 18th and C Streets, NW, Room 4600, Washington, DC 20245, 202-343-3657.

15.130 INDIAN EDUCATION—ASSISTANCE TO SCHOOLS
Type of Assistance: Direct payments.
Applicant Eligibility: Native Americans.
Objective: To assure adequate educational opportunities for Indian children attending public schools and tribally operated previously private schools.
Contact: Branch of Supplemental Support Services, Office of Indian Education Programs, Bureau of Indian Affairs, 18th and C Streets, NW, Washington, DC 20245, 202-343-6364.

15.141 INDIAN HOUSING ASSISTANCE
Type of Assistance: Grants up to $45,000.
Applicant Eligibility: American Indians.
Objective: To eliminate substantially substandard Indian housing.
Contact: Division of Housing Assistance, Office of Indian Services, Bureau of Indian Affairs, 18th and C Streets, NW, Washington, DC 20245, 202-343-4876.

15.142 SELF-DETERMINATION GRANTS— INDIAN TRIBAL GOVERNMENTS
Type of Assistance: Grants (dollar amount not available).
Applicant Eligibility: Native Americans.

Objective: To improve tribal governing capabilities; to prepare tribes for contracting of Bureau programs; to enable tribes to provide direction to the Bureau, and to have input to other federal programs intended to serve Indian people.
Contact: Division of Self-Determination Services, Office of Indian Services, Bureau of Indian Affairs, 1951 Constitution Avenue, NW, Washington, DC 20240, 202-343-4796.

15.143 TRAINING AND TECHNICAL ASSISTANCE— INDIAN TRIBAL GOVERNMENTS

Type of Assistance: Grants (dollar amount not available).
Applicant Eligibility: Native Americans.
Objective: To help Indian tribes exercise self-determination; to provide training and technical assistance options; to help develop skills needed to utilize options; to enhance capability to contract for Bureau and other federal programs; to strengthen tribal government; to encourage personnel use options; and to improve capabilities to direct Bureau and other federal programs.
Contact: Division of Self-Determination Services, Office of Indian Services, Bureau of Indian Affairs, 1951 Constitution Avenue, NW, Washington, DC 20240, 202-343-4796.

15.144 INDIAN CHILD WELFARE ACT—TITLE II GRANTS

Type of Assistance: Grants from $25,000 upward.
Applicant Eligibility: Local governments.
Objective: To promote the stability and security of Indian tribes and families by the establishment of minimum federal standards for the removal of Indian children from their families and the placement of such children in foster or adoptive homes; and to provide assistance to Indian tribes in the operation of child and family service programs.
Contact: Division of Social Services, Office of Indian Services, Bureau of Indian Affairs, 1951 Constitution Avenue, NW, Washington, DC 20245, 202-343-6434.

BUREAU OF LAND MANAGEMENT

15.214 NON-SALE DISPOSALS OF MINERAL MATERIAL

Type of Assistance: Sale, exchange or donation of property and goods.
Applicant Eligibility: Federal nonprofit institutions or state agencies.
Objective: To permit free use of certain mineral material from federally owned lands under the jurisdiction of the Bureau by governmental units and nonprofit organizations.
Contact: Division of Mining Law and Saleable Minerals, Bureau of Land Management, Department of the Interior, Washington, DC 20240, 202-343-8537.

**15.219 WILDLIFE HABITAT
MANAGEMENT TECHNICAL ASSISTANCE**
Type of Assistance: Grants.
Applicant Eligibility: State wildlife or fish agencies.
Objective: To plan, develop, maintain and coordinate programs for the conservation and rehabilitation of wildlife, fish and game on lands administered by the Bureau of Land Management.
Contact: Division of Wildlife (240), Bureau of Land Management, Department of the Interior, 18th and C Streets, NW, Washington, DC 20240, 202-343-4843.

OFFICE OF SURFACE MINING
RECLAMATION AND ENFORCEMENT

**15.250 REGULATION OF SURFACE COAL MINING
AND SURFACE EFFECTS OF UNDERGROUND
COAL MINING**
Type of Assistance: Grants and direct payments ranging from $15,000 to $4,498,263.
Applicant Eligibility: State governments.
Objective: To protect society and the environment from the adverse effects of surface coal mining operations consistent with assuring the coal supply essential to the nation's energy requirements.
Contact: Office of Surface Mining Reclamation and Enforcement, Department of the Interior, 1951 Constitution Avenue, NW, Washington, DC 20245, 202-343-5351.

15.252 ABANDONED MINE LAND RECLAMATION PROGRAM
Type of Assistance: Grants ranging from $33,439 to $31,172,148.
Applicant Eligibility: State and local governments.
Objective: To protect the public and correct the environmental damage caused by coal- and noncoal-mining practices that occurred before August 3, 1977.
Contact: Office of Surface Mining, Division of Abandoned Mined Lands, Department of the Interior, 1951 Constitution Avenue, NW, Washington, DC 20245, 202-343-7921.

BUREAU OF MINES

**15.308 GRANTS FOR MINING AND MINERAL RESOURCES
AND RESEARCH INSTITUTES**
Type of Assistance: Grants averaging $1 million.
Applicant Eligibility: Public colleges.
Objective: To support research and training in mining and mineral resources; to improve the advanced training of mineral scientists and

engineers; to support research centers of generic expertise in mineral technology.

Contact: Office of Mineral Institutes, Bureau of Mines, 2401 E Street, NW, Washington, DC 20241, 202-634-1328.

BUREAU OF RECLAMATION

15.501   IRRIGATION DISTRIBUTION SYSTEM LOANS

Type of Assistance: Direct loans.

Applicant Eligibility: State governments.

Objective: To provide fully reimbursable federal loans to organized irrigation districts with lands included within congressionally authorized reclamation projects to plan, design and construct irrigation and municipal and industrial water distribution or drainage systems in lieu of federal construction.

Contact: Bureau of Reclamation, Department of the Interior, Washington, DC 20240, 202-343-5501.

15.502   IRRIGATION SYSTEMS REHABILITATION
AND BETTERMENT

Type of Assistance: Direct loans averaging $2 million.

Applicant Eligibility: State governments.

Objective: To rehabilitate and improve irrigation facilities on projects governed by reclamation law.

Contact: Bureau of Reclamation, Department of the Interior, Washington, DC 20240, 202-343-5471.

15.503   SMALL RECLAMATION PROJECTS

Type of Assistance: Grants and direct loans ranging from $700,000 to $18 million.

Applicant Eligibility: State governments.

Objective: To provide fully reimbursable federal loans and possible grants to public nonfederal organizations for rehabilitation and betterment or construction of water resource development projects located in the 17 westernmost contiguous states and Hawaii.

Contact: Bureau of Reclamation, Department of the Interior, Washington, DC 20240, 202-343-5501.

US FISH AND WILDLIFE SERVICE

15.600   ANADROMOUS FISH CONSERVATION

Type of Assistance: Grants ranging from $6,000 to $632,800.

Applicant Eligibility: Individuals, nonprofit organizations, state and local governments.

Objective: To conserve, develop and enhance the anadromous fish resources of the nation and the fish of the Great Lakes and Lake Champlain that ascend streams to spawn.

Contact: Fish and Wildlife Service, Department of the Interior, Washington, DC 20240, 202-632-8748.

15.603   FARM FISH POND MANAGEMENT (FARM POND STOCKING)

Type of Assistance: Sale, exchange or donation of property and goods.
Applicant Eligibility: Individuals.
Objective: To serve as an impetus to farm pond construction and water conservation, to supply high-protein food, and to supply fish to stock new or reclaimed farm and ranch ponds.
Contact: Fish and Wildlife Service, Department of the Interior, Box 700, Kearneysville, WV 25430, 364-725-5316.

15.605   FISH RESTORATION

Type of Assistance: Grants ranging from $116,867 to $1,753,000.
Applicant Eligibility: State governments.
Objective: To support projects designed to restore and manage sport fish population for the preservation and improvement of sport fishing and related uses of these fisheries resources.
Contact: Fish and Wildlife Service, Department of the Interior, Washington, DC 20240, 703-235-1526.

15.611   WILDLIFE RESTORATION

Type of Assistance: Grants ranging from $108,183 to $3,245,500.
Applicant Eligibility: State governments.
Objective: To support projects to restore or manage wildlife populations and the provision of public use of these resources; and to provide facilities and services for conducting a hunter safety program.
Contact: Fish and Wildlife Service, Department of the Interior, Washington, DC 20240, 703-235-1526.

15.612   ENDANGERED SPECIES CONSERVATION

Type of Assistance: Grants ranging from $1,000 to $150,000.
Applicant Eligibility: State governments.
Objective: To provide federal financial assistance to any state, through its respective state agency, which has entered into a cooperative agreement to assist in the development of programs for the conservation of endangered and threatened species.
Contact: Fish and Wildlife Service, Department of the Interior, Washington, DC 20240, 703-235-2760.

NATIONAL PARK SERVICE

15.900   DISPOSAL OF SURPLUS WILDLIFE

Type of Assistance: Sale, exchange or donation of property and goods.
Applicant Eligibility: Nonprofit organizations, state and local governments.
Objective: To obtain the maximum public benefit of animals surplus

to agency needs by providing animals for restocking of wildlife ranges, zoo display animals, scientific specimens and meat.

Contact: Chief Biological Resources Division, National Park Service, Department of the Interior, 18th and C Streets, NW, Washington, DC 20240, 202-343-8125.

15.904 HISTORIC PRESERVATION GRANTS-IN-AID

Type of Assistance: Grants ranging from $46,000 to $760,000.

Applicant Eligibility: State governments.

Objective: To expand and maintain the National Register of Historic Places—the nation's listing of districts, sites, buildings, structures and objects significant in American history, architecture, archaeology and culture at the national, state and local levels; to provide matching survey and planning grants-in-aid to assist in the identification, evaluation and protection of historic properties; to provide matching acquisition and development grants-in-aid, through the states, to public and private parties for preservation for public benefit of National Register–listed properties; to provide matching grants-in-aid to the National Trust for Historic Preservation to assist in the accomplishment of its congressionally chartered responsibilities (63 Stat. 927) to preserve historic resources.

Contact: Associate Director, Cultural Resources, National Park Service, Department of the Interior, Washington, DC 20240, 202-343-7625.

15.916 OUTDOOR RECREATION— ACQUISITION, DEVELOPMENT AND PLANNING

Type of Assistance: Grants ranging from $150 to $5,450,000.

Applicant Eligibility: State governments.

Objective: To provide financial assistance to the states and their political subdivisions for the preparation of comprehensive statewide outdoor recreation plans and acquisition and development of outdoor recreation areas and facilities for the general public, to meet current and future needs.

Contact: Chief, Recreation Grants Division, National Park Service, Department of the Interior, PO Box 37127, Washington, DC 20013-7127, 202-343-3700.

15.919 URBAN PARK AND RECREATION RECOVERY PROGRAM

Type of Assistance: Grants ranging from $2,750 to $5,250,000.

Applicant Eligibility: Local governments.

Objective: Federal grants to economically hard-pressed communities specifically for the rehabilitation of critically needed recreation areas, facilities and development of improved recreation programs for a period of five years.

Contact: National Park Service, Recreation Grants Division, Department of the Interior, PO Box 37127, Washington, DC 20013-7127, 202-343-3700.

US DEPARTMENT OF JUSTICE

OFFICE OF JUVENILE JUSTICE AND DELINQUENCY PREVENTION

16.540   JUVENILE JUSTICE AND DELINQUENCY PREVENTION—ALLOCATION TO STATES
Type of Assistance: Grants ranging from $56,250 to $225,000.
Applicant Eligibility: State governments.
Objective: To increase the capacity of state and local governments to conduct effective juvenile justice and delinquency prevention programs by providing matching grants to each state and territory; to develop guidelines for state plans that meet the requirements set forth in the Juvenile Justice and Delinquency Prevention Act of 1974 as amended, and to assist states in developing such plans.
Contact: Office of Juvenile Justice and Delinquency Prevention, Department of Justice, Washington, DC 20531, 202-724-5921.

16.541   JUVENILE JUSTICE AND DELINQUENCY PREVENTION—SPECIAL EMPHASIS AND TECHNICAL ASSISTANCE PROGRAMS
Type of Assistance: Grants (dollar amount not available).
Applicant Eligibility: Individuals, nonprofit organizations, state and local governments.
Objective: To develop and implement programs that support effective approaches to preventing and controlling juvenile delinquency through community-based alternatives to traditional forms of official justice system processing; to improve the capability of public and private agencies to provide delinquency prevention services to youth and their families; to develop new approaches to reducing school dropouts, unwarranted suspensions and expulsions; to support groups and organizations committed to the legal rights and welfare of youth; to provide technical assistance to federal, state and local governments, courts, public and private agencies, institutions and individuals, in the planning, establishment, operation or evaluation of juvenile delinquency programs; and to assist operating agencies having direct responsibilities for prevention and treatment of juvenile delinquency in meeting standards established through the Office of Juvenile Justice and Delinquency Prevention and the priorities for formula grant programs.
Contact: Office of Juvenile Justice and Delinquency Prevention, Department of Justice, Washington, DC 20531, 202-724-5930.

16.542 NATIONAL INSTITUTE FOR JUVENILE JUSTICE AND DELINQUENCY PREVENTION
Type of Assistance: Grants (dollar amount not available).
Applicant Eligibility: Individuals and nonprofit organizations.
Objective: To encourage, coordinate and conduct research and evaluation of juvenile justice and delinquency prevention activities; to provide a clearinghouse and information center for collecting, publishing and distributing information on juvenile delinquency; to conduct a national training program; and to establish standards for the administration of juvenile justice.
Contact: Office of Juvenile Justice and Delinquency Prevention, Deputy Administrator, Department of Justice, Washington, DC 20531, 202-724-7560.

BUREAU OF JUSTICE STATISTICS

16.550 CRIMINAL JUSTICE STATISTICS DEVELOPMENT
Type of Assistance: Grants ranging from $10,000 to $150,000.
Applicant Eligibility: State agencies.
Objective: To provide financial and technical assistance to states and local governments regarding the collection, analysis, utilization and dissemination of justice statistics.
Contact: Bureau of Justice Statistics, Department of Justice, Washington, DC 20531, 202-724-7770.

NATIONAL INSTITUTE OF JUSTICE

16.560 JUSTICE RESEARCH AND DEVELOPMENT PROJECT GRANTS
Type of Assistance: Project grants and dissemination of technical information.
Applicant Eligibility: State and local governments, private, profit and nonprofit organizations.
Objective: To encourage and support research and development to further understanding of the causes of crime and to improve the criminal justice system.
Contact: National Institute of Justice, Department of Justice, Washington, DC 20531, 202-724-2942.

16.561 NATIONAL INSTITUTE OF JUSTICE VISITING FELLOWSHIPS
Type of Assistance: Grants (dollar amount not available).
Applicant Eligibility: Individuals.
Objective: To provide opportunities for experienced criminal justice professionals to pursue promising new ideas for improved understanding of crime, delinquency and criminal justice administration by sponsoring research projects of their own creation and design.

Contact: National Institute of Justice, Department of Justice, Washington, DC 20531, 202-724-7684.

16.562 CRIMINAL JUSTICE RESEARCH AND DEVELOPMENT—GRADUATE RESEARCH FELLOWSHIPS

Type of Assistance: Grants up to $11,000 per year.
Applicant Eligibility: Accredited institutions of higher education offering a doctoral degree program.
Objective: To enhance the criminal justice system by providing support to doctoral students engaged in dissertation research and writing.
Contact: National Institute of Justice, Department of Justice, Washington, DC 20531, 202-724-7684.

OFFICE OF JUSTICE ASSISTANCE, RESEARCH & STATISTICS

16.571 PUBLIC SAFETY OFFICERS' DEATH BENEFITS PROGRAM

Type of Assistance: Direct payments.
Applicant Eligibility: Individuals.
Objective: To provide a $50,000 death benefit to the eligible survivors of state and local public safety officers whose death is the direct and proximate result of a personal injury sustained in the line of duty on or after September 29, 1976.
Contact: Director, Public Safety Officers' Benefits Program, Department of Justice, Washington, DC 20531, 202-724-7620.

16.573 CRIMINAL JUSTICE BLOCK GRANTS

Type of Assistance: Grants ranging from $250,000 to $4,200,000.
Applicant Eligibility: States.
Objective: To provide financial assistance to states and units of local government in carrying out criminal justice programs.
Contact: Office of Justice Programs, Bureau of Justice Assistance, Department of Justice, Washington, DC 20531, 202-272-6838.

16.574 CRIMINAL JUSTICE DISCRETIONARY GRANTS

Type of Assistance: Grants.
Applicant Eligibility: Public agencies and private nonprofit organizations.
Objective: To provide financial assistance for education and training to criminal justice personnel, technical assistance to states and local governments, projects that are national or multi-state in scope, and demonstration programs.
Contact: Office of Justice Programs, Bureau of Justice Assistance, Department of Justice, Washington, DC 20531, 202-272-6838.

16.575 CRIME VICTIM ASSISTANCE

Type of Assistance: Grants.
Applicant Eligibility: States.

Objective: To provide funds to be distributed among states to support crime victim assistance programs.
Contact: Program Manager, Office for Victims of Crime, Office of Justice Programs, Department of Justice, 633 Indiana Avenue, NW, Washington, DC 20531, 202-724-5947.

16.576 CRIME VICTIM COMPENSATION
Type of Assistance: Grants ranging from $584 to $635,000.
Applicant Eligibility: States.
Objective: To provide funds to be distributed among states to support crime victim compensation programs.
Contact: Office for Victims of Crime, Office of Justice Programs, Victims Resource Center, Department of Justice, Washington, DC 20531.

BUREAU OF PRISONS

16.601 CORRECTIONS—
TRAINING AND STAFF DEVELOPMENT
Type of Assistance: Dissemination of technical information and grants ranging from $1,500 to $300,000.
Applicant Eligibility: Individuals, nonprofit organizations, state and local governments.
Objective: To devise and conduct in various geographical locations, seminars, workshops and training programs for law enforcement officers, judges and judicial personnel, probation and parole personnel, correctional personnel, welfare workers and other personnel, including lay ex-offenders and paraprofessionals, connected with the treatment and rehabilitation of criminal and juvenile offenders; and to develop technical training teams to aid in the development of seminars, workshops and training programs with the state and local agencies that work with prisoners, parolees, probationers and other offenders.
Contact: National Institute of Corrections, Department of Justice, Room 200, 320 First Street, NW, Washington, DC 20534, 202-724-3106.

16.602 CORRECTIONS—RESEARCH AND EVALUATION AND POLICY FORMATION
Type of Assistance: Specialized services and grants ranging from $1,500 to $200,000.
Applicant Eligibility: Individuals, nonprofit organizatons, state and local governments.
Objective: To conduct, encourage and coordinate research relating to corrections, including the causes, prevention, diagnosis and treatment of criminal offenders; and to conduct evaluation programs that study the effectiveness of new approaches to improve the corrections system.
Contact: Chief, Correctional Services Division, National Institute of Corrections, Department of Justice, Room 200, 320 First Street, NW, Washington, DC 20534, 202-724-3106.

16.603   CORRECTIONS—TECHNICAL ASSISTANCE

Type of Assistance: Specialized services and grants ranging from $1,500 to $50,000.

Applicant Eligibility: Individuals, nonprofit organizations, state and local governments.

Objective: To encourage and assist federal, state and local government programs and services, and programs and services of other public and private agencies in their efforts to develop and implement improved corrections programs; and to serve in a consulting capacity to federal, state and local courts, departments and agencies in the development, maintenance and coordination of programs, facilities and services for training, treatment and rehabilitation of criminal and juvenile offenders.

Contact: Technical Assistance Coordinator, National Institute of Corrections, Department of Justice, 320 First Street, NW, Room 200, Washington, DC 20534, 202-724-3106.

US DEPARTMENT OF LABOR

EMPLOYMENT AND TRAINING ADMINISTRATION

17.207   EMPLOYMENT SERVICE
Type of Assistance: Specialized services and grants.
Applicant Eligibility: State employment security agencies.
Objective: To place persons in employment by providing a variety of placement-related services to job seekers and to employers seeking qualified individuals to fill job openings.
Contact: Director, United States Employment Service, Employment and Training Administration, Department of Labor, Washington, DC 20213, 202-376-6750.

17.225   UNEMPLOYMENT INSURANCE
Type of Assistance: Grants and direct payments ranging from $1,200,000 to $200 million.
Applicant Eligibility: State unemployment insurance agencies.
Objective: To administer programs of unemployment insurance for eligible workers through federal and state cooperation and to administer payment of worker adjustment assistance.
Contact: Administrator, Unemployment Insurance Service, Employment and Training Administration, Department of Labor, 601 D Street, NW, Washington, DC 20210, 202-376-6336.

17.235   SENIOR COMMUNITY SERVICE EMPLOYMENT PROGRAM
Type of Assistance: Grants (dollar amount not available).
Applicant Eligibility: Nonprofit organizations and state governments.
Objective: To provide, foster and promote useful part-time work opportunities up to 20 hours per week in community service activities for low-income persons who are 55 years old and older and who have poor employment prospects.
Contact: Chief, Division of Older Worker Programs, Employment and Training Administration, Department of Labor, 601 D Street, NW, Washington, DC 20213, 202-376-6232.

17.245   TRADE ADJUSTMENT ASSISTANCE—WORKERS
Type of Assistance: Specialized services and direct weekly payments.
Applicant Eligibility: Individuals.
Objective: To provide adjustment assistance to workers adversely affected by increase of imports of articles similar to or directly competitive with articles produced by such workers' firm.

Contact: Director, Office of Trade Adjustment Assistance, Employment & Training Administration, Department of Labor, 601 D Street, NW, Room 6438, Washington, DC 20213, 202-376-2646.

17.246 EMPLOYMENT AND TRAINING ASSISTANCE— DISLOCATED WORKERS
Type of Assistance: Grants.
Applicant Eligibility: States.
Objective: To assist dislocated workers in obtaining unsubsidized employment through training and related employment services using a decentralized system of state and local programs.
Contact: Employment and Training Administration, Department of Labor, 601 D Street, NW, Washington, DC 20213, 202-376-6093.

17.247 MIGRANT AND SEASONAL FARM WORKERS
Type of Assistance: Grants ranging from $100,000 to $5 million.
Applicant Eligibility: Nonprofit organizations, state and local governments.
Objective: To provide necessary employment, training and supportive services to help migrant and seasonal farm workers and their families find economically viable alternatives to seasonal agricultural labor, and to improve the lifestyle of seasonal agricultural workers who remain in the agricultural labor market.
Contact: Office of Special Targeted Programs, Employment and Training Administration, Department of Labor, 601 D Street, NW, Room 6122, Washington, DC 20213, 202-376-6225.

17.248 EMPLOYMENT AND TRAINING RESEARCH AND DEVELOPMENT PROJECTS
Type of Assistance: Grants ranging from $1,000 to $1 million.
Applicant Eligibility: Individuals, nonprofit organizations, state and local governments.
Objective: To support employment and training studies to develop policy and programs for achieving the fullest utilization of the nation's human resources; to improve and strengthen the functioning of the nation's employment and training system; to develop new approaches to facilitate employment of the difficult to employ; and to conduct research and development addressing the employment implications of long-term social and economic trends and forces.
Contact: Director, Office of Research and Development, Employment and Training Administration, Department of Labor, 601 D Street, NW, Washington, DC 20213, 202-376-7335.

17.251 EMPLOYMENT AND TRAINING— INDIANS AND NATIVE AMERICANS
Type of Assistance: Grants ranging from $50,000 to $7,500,000.
Applicant Eligibility: Native Americans.
Objective: To reduce the economic disadvantages among Indians and others of Native American descent and to advance the economic and

social development of such people in accordance with their goals and lifestyles.

Contact: Office of Indian and Native American Programs, Employment and Training Administration, Department of Labor, 601 D Street, NW, Washington, DC 20213, 202-376-6442.

EMPLOYMENT STANDARDS ADMINISTRATION

17.302 LONGSHOREMEN'S AND HARBOR WORKERS' COMPENSATION

Type of Assistance: Direct payments up to 66⅔ percent of average weekly wage.

Applicant Eligibility: Individuals.

Objective: To provide compensation for disability or death resulting from injury, including occupational disease, to longshoremen, harbor workers and certain other employees engaged in maritime employment on navigable waters of the United States and the adjoining pier and dock areas; employees engaged in activities on the Outer Continental Shelf; employees of nonappropriated fund instrumentalities; employees of private employers engaged in work outside the United States under contracts with the United States Government; and others as specified, including survivors of the above.

Contact: Office of Workers' Compensation Programs, Division of Longshoremen's and Harbor Workers' Compensation, Department of Labor, Washington, DC 20210, 202-523-8721.

17.307 COAL MINE WORKERS' COMPENSATION (BLACK LUNG)

Type of Assistance: Direct payments averaging $415.14 monthly.

Applicant Eligibility: Individuals.

Objective: To provide benefits to coal miners who have become totally disabled owing to coal workers' pneumoconiosis (CWP), and to widows and other surviving dependents of miners who have died of this disease or who were totally disabled from the disease at the time of death.

Contact: Division of Coal Mine Workers' Compensation, Office of Workers' Compensation Programs, Employment Standards Administration, Department of Labor, Washington, DC 20210, 202-523-6692.

OCCUPATIONAL SAFETY AND HEALTH ADMINISTRATION

17.500 OCCUPATIONAL SAFETY AND HEALTH

Type of Assistance: Dissemination of technical information, investigation of complaints, and grants (dollar amount not available).

Applicant Eligibility: Individuals, nonprofit organizations, state governments.

Objective: To assure safe and healthful working conditions.
Contact: Assistant Secretary, Occupational Safety and Health Administration, Department of Labor, 200 Constitution Avenue, NW, Washington, DC 20210, 202-523-9361.

MINE SAFETY AND HEALTH ADMINISTRATION

17.600 MINE HEALTH AND SAFETY GRANTS

Type of Assistance: Grants ranging from $7,875 to $659,400.
Applicant Eligibility: State governments.
Objective: To assist states in developing and enforcing effective mine health and safety laws and regulations, to improve state workmen's compensation and occupational disease laws and programs, and to promote federal-state coordination and cooperation in improving health and safety conditions.
Contact: State Grants Program Office, Mine Safety and Health Administration, Department of Labor, Ballston Towers Number 3, Arlington, VA 22203, 703-235-8264.

US DEPARTMENT OF STATE

OFFICE OF THE LEGAL ADVISER

19.200   CLAIMS AGAINST FOREIGN GOVERNMENTS
Type of Assistance: Specialized services.
Applicant Eligibility: Individuals.
Objective: To obtain settlements of all legally valid claims of nationals of the United States against foreign governments. A claim may result from any one of a number of situations in which a national of the United States may be injured by a foreign government in violation of international law. It can, for example, be based upon a taking of property without payment of prompt, adequate and effective compensation; other acts or omissions of governmental organs incompatible with international obligations; acts of individuals, insurgents and mobs under circumstances establishing a lack of due diligence on the part of government officials; etc.
Contact: Assistant Legal Adviser for International Claims, Office of the Legal Adviser, Department of State, Washington, DC 20520, 202-632-5040.

19.201   PROTECTION OF SHIPS FROM FOREIGN SEIZURE
Type of Assistance: Insurance unlimited.
Applicant Eligibility: Individuals.
Objective: To reimburse a financial loss to owners of vessels registered in the United States for fines paid to secure the release of vessels seized for operation in waters which are not recognized as territorial waters by the United States.
Contact: Assistant Legal Adviser for International Claims, Office of the Legal Adviser, Department of State, Washington, DC 20520, 202-632-5040.

19.203   CLAIMS AGAINST FOREIGN MISSIONS
Type of Assistance: Insurance.
Applicant Eligibility: Individuals.
Objective: To assure that all persons in the US who are damaged in motor vehicle, vessel or aircraft accidents, in which foreign mission personnel are at fault, will have an opportunity to recover compensation for damages.
Contact: Office of Foreign Missions, Department of State, Washington, DC 20520, 202-632-3416.

US DEPARTMENT OF TRANSPORTATION

UNITED STATES COAST GUARD

20.002 COAST GUARD COOPERATIVE MARINE SCIENCES PROGRAM

Type of Assistance: Use of property, facilities and equipment.

Applicant Eligibility: Federal, state and local government agencies, academic institutions, nonprofit institutions.

Objective: To provide optimum utilization of specialized Coast Guard facilities in any area where cooperative effort may enhance the national marine sciences effort.

Contact: Ice Operations Division, US Coast Guard Headquarters, Washington, DC 20593, 202-426-1881.

FEDERAL AVIATION ADMINISTRATION

20.106 AIRPORT IMPROVEMENT PROGRAM

Type of Assistance: Grants ranging from $25,000 to $12,900,000.

Applicant Eligibility: States.

Objective: To assist sponsors, owners or operators of public-use airports in the development of a nationwide system of airports adequate to meet the needs of civil aeronautics.

Contact: Grants-in-Aid Division, Federal Aviation Administration, Office of Airports Planning and Programming, 800 Independence Avenue, SW, Washington, DC 20591, 202-426-3831.

FEDERAL HIGHWAY ADMINISTRATION

20.205 HIGHWAY PLANNING AND CONSTRUCTION

Type of Assistance: Grants ranging from $9,812 to $910,953,000.

Applicant Eligibility: State governments.

Objective: To assist state highway agencies in constructing and rehabilitating the Interstate highway system and building or improving primary, secondary and urban systems roads and streets; to provide aid for their repair following disasters; to foster safe highway design; and to replace or rehabilitate unsafe bridges. Also provides for the improvement of some highways in Guam, the Virgin Islands; American Samoa and the Northern Mariana Islands.

Contact: Chief, Office of Engineering, Federal Highway Administrator, Federal Highway Administration, 400 Seventh Street, SW, Department of Transportation, Washington, DC 20590, 202-426-4853.

20.214   HIGHWAY BEAUTIFICATION— CONTROL OF OUTDOOR ADVERTISING AND CONTROL OF JUNKYARDS

Type of Assistance: Grants ranging from $2,300 to $143,700.
Applicant Eligibility: State highway agencies.
Objective: To beautify areas adjacent to Interstate and federal-aid primary highways.
Contact: Federal Highway Administrator, Federal Highway Administration, Department of Transportation, Washington, DC 20590, 202-426-0142.

FEDERAL RAILROAD ADMINISTRATION

20.303   GRANTS-IN-AID FOR RAILROAD SAFETY— STATE PARTICIPATION

Type of Assistance: Grants up to $32,000 per state inspector.
Applicant Eligibility: State governments.
Objective: To promote safety in all areas of railroad operations; to reduce railroad-related accidents; to reduce deaths and injuries to persons and damage to property caused by accidents involving any carrier of hazardous materials by providing for state participation in the enforcement and promotion of safety practices.
Contact: Associate Administrator for Safety, Federal Railroad Administration, 400 Seventh Street, SW, Washington, DC 20590, 202-426-0895.

20.308   LOCAL RAIL SERVICE ASSISTANCE

Type of Assistance: Grants ranging from $100,000 to $1,300,000.
Applicant Eligibility: State governments.
Objective: To maintain efficient local rail freight services. Grants may be used by states to assist in the continuation of local rail freight service on lines eligible to be abandoned by finding of the Interstate Commerce Commission pursuant to Section 803 of the Rail Revitalization and Regulatory Reform Act. Grants may also be used for rehabilitation and improvement on lines certified by the railroad as having carried three million gross ton miles per mile or less during the prior year, state rail planning, and substitute service projects.
Contact: Office of Freight Assistance Programs, Federal Railroad Administration, Room 5410, 400 Seventh Street, SW, Washington, DC 20590, 202-426-1677.

20.309   RAILROAD REHABILITATION AND IMPROVEMENT— GUARANTEE OF OBLIGATIONS

Type of Assistance: Guaranteed/insured loans ranging from $5 million to $75 million.

Applicant Eligibility: Individuals, nonprofit organizations, state and local governments.
Objective: To provide financial assistance for the acquisition or rehabilitation and improvement of railroad facilities or equipment. Equipment and facilities include locomotives, freight cars, track, roadbed and related structures, communication and power transmission systems, signals, yard and terminal facilities and shop or repair facilities.
Contact: Office of National Freight Assistance Programs, Federal Railroad Administration, 400 Seventh Street, SW, Washington, DC 20590, 202-472-9657.

20.310   RAILROAD REHABILITATION AND IMPROVEMENT—REDEEMABLE PREFERENCE SHARES

Type of Assistance: Direct loans ranging from $5 million to $100 million.
Applicant Eligibility: Individuals.
Objective: To provide railroads with financial assistance for the rehabilitation and improvement of equipment and facilities or such other purposes approved by the Secretary of Transportation.
Contact: Office of National Freight Assistance Programs, Room 5410, Federal Railroad Administration, 400 Seventh Street, SW, Washington, DC 20590, 202-472-5401.

URBAN MASS TRANSPORTATION ADMINISTRATION

20.500   URBAN MASS TRANSPORTATION CAPITAL IMPROVEMENT GRANTS

Type of Assistance: Grants ranging from $1,216 to $800 million.
Applicant Eligibility: Individuals, nonprofit organizations, state and local governments.
Objective: To assist in financing the acquisition, construction, reconstruction and improvement of facilities and equipment for use, by operation, lease or otherwise, in mass transportation service in urban areas, and in coordinating service with highway and other transportation in such areas.
Contact: Your regional office of the US Department of Transportation.

20.502   URBAN MASS TRANSPORTATION GRANTS FOR UNIVERSITY RESEARCH AND TRAINING

Type of Assistance: Grants up to $85,000.
Applicant Eligibility: Individuals, nonprofit organizations, state and local governments.
Objective: To sponsor research studies and training in the problem of transportation in urban areas.
Contact: Office of Technical Assistance, Urban Mass Transportation

Administration, Department of Transportation, 400 Seventh Street, SW, Washington, DC 20590, 202-426-0080.

20.503 URBAN MASS TRANSPORTATION MANAGERIAL TRAINING GRANTS

Type of Assistance: Grants ranging from $400 to $22,000.
Applicant Eligibility: Individuals.
Objective: To provide fellowships for training of managerial, technical and professional personnel employed in the urban mass transportation field.
Contact: Director, Office of Transportation Management, Urban Mass Transportation Administration, Department of Transportation, 400 Seventh Street, SW, Washington, DC 20590, 202-426-0080.

20.505 URBAN MASS TRANSPORTATION TECHNICAL STUDIES GRANTS

Type of Assistance: Grants ranging from $10,000 to $6,500,000.
Applicant Eligibility: State and local governments.
Objective: To assist in planning, engineering and designing of urban mass transportation projects and other technical studies in a program for a unified or officially coordinated urban transportation system.
Contact: Director, Office of Planning Assistance (UGM-20), Office of Grants Management, Urban Mass Transportation Administration, Department of Transportation, 400 Seventh Street, SW, Washington, DC 20590, 202-426-2360.

20.507 URBAN MASS TRANSPORTATION CAPITAL AND OPERATING ASSISTANCE FORMULA GRANTS

Type of Assistance: Grants (dollar amount not available).
Applicant Eligibility: Nonprofit organizations, state and local governments.
Objective: To assist in financing the acquisition, construction and improvement of facilities and equipment for use by operation or lease or otherwise in mass transportation service, and in the payment of operating expenses to improve or to continue such service by operation, lease, contract or otherwise.
Contact: Your regional office of the US Department of Transportation.

20.509 PUBLIC TRANSPORTATION FOR NONURBANIZED AREAS

Type of Assistance: Grants (dollar amount not available).
Applicant Eligibility: Nonprofit organizations, state and local governments.
Objective: To improve or continue public transportation service in rural and small urban areas by providing financial assistance for the acquisition, construction and improvement of facilities and equipment and the payment of operating expenses by operating contract, lease or otherwise.

Contact: Federal Highway Administration, Rural and Small Urban Areas Public Transportation Branch, Department of Transportation, 400 Seventh Street, SW, Washington, DC 20590, 202-426-0153.

NATIONAL HIGHWAY
TRAFFIC SAFETY ADMINISTRATION

20.600   STATE AND COMMUNITY HIGHWAY SAFETY
Type of Assistance: Grants ranging from $600,000 to $9,400,000.
Applicant Eligibility: State governments.
Objective: To provide a coordinated national highway safety program to reduce traffic accidents, deaths, injuries and property damage.
Contact: Chief, Program Operations Staff, Traffic Safety Programs, National Highway Traffic Safety Administration, Washington, DC 20590, 202-426-2131.

RESEARCH AND SPECIAL PROGRAMS
ADMINISTRATION

20.700   GAS PIPELINE SAFETY
Type of Assistance: Grants ranging from $10,520 to $430,108.
Applicant Eligibility: State agencies.
Objective: To develop and maintain state gas pipeline safety programs.
Contact: Department of Transportation, Materials Transportation Bureau, 400 Seventh Street, SW, Washington, DC, 20590, 202-426-3046.

MARITIME ADMINISTRATION

20.800   CONSTRUCTION-DIFFERENTIAL SUBSIDIES
Type of Assistance: Direct payments averaging $3,182,000.
Applicant Eligibility: Individuals.
Objective: To promote the development and maintenance of the US Merchant Marine by granting financial aid to equalize cost of construction of a new ship in a US shipyard with the cost of constructing the same ship in a foreign shipyard.
Contact: Assistant Administrator for Maritime Aids, Maritime Administration, Department of Transportation, 400 Seventh Street, Washington, DC 20590, 202-382-0364.

20.802   FEDERAL SHIP-FINANCING GUARANTEES
Type of Assistance: Guaranteed/insured loans ranging from $106,000 to $126,300,000.
Applicant Eligibility: Individuals.
Objective: To promote construction and reconstruction of ships in the foreign and domestic commerce of the United States by providing

government guarantees of obligations so as to make commercial credit more readily available.
Contact: Assistant Administrator for Maritime Aids, Maritime Administration, Department of Transportation, Washington, DC 20590, 202-382-0364.

20.803 MARITIME WAR RISK INSURANCE
Type of Assistance: Insurance (dollar amount not available).
Applicant Eligibility: Individuals.
Objective: To provide war risk insurance whenever it appears to the Secretary of Transportation that adequate insurance for waterborne commerce cannot be obtained on reasonable terms and conditions from authorized insurance companies in the United States.
Contact: Director, Office of Marine Insurance, Maritime Administration, Department of Transportation, Washington, DC 20590, 202-382-0369.

20.804 OPERATING-DIFFERENTIAL SUBSIDIES
Type of Assistance: Direct payments ranging from $5,434 to $13,300 per day.
Applicant Eligibility: Individuals.
Objective: To promote development and maintenance of the US Merchant Marine by granting financial aid to equalize cost of operating a US flagship with the cost of operating a competitive foreign flagship.
Contact: Associate Administrator for Maritime Aids, Maritime Administration, Department of Transportation, Washington, DC 20590, 202-382-0364.

20.806 STATE MARINE SCHOOLS
Type of Assistance: Grants of $1,200 per year to each student, plus $100,000 per year per school.
Applicant Eligibility: State governments.
Objective: To train Merchant Marine officers in state marine schools. Funds are used for the operation and maintenance of state marine schools; maintenance and repair of training vessels loaned by the federal government; and assistance to students in paying for uniforms, books and subsistence.
Contact: Director, Office of Maritime Labor and Training, Maritime Administration, Department of Commerce, Washington, DC 20590, 202-426-5755.

20.808 CAPITAL CONSTRUCTION FUND
Type of Assistance: Direct payments in the form of tax benefits.
Applicant Eligibility: Individuals.
Objective: To provide for replacement vessels, additional vessels or reconstructed vessels built and documented under the laws of the United States for operation in the United States foreign, Great Lakes or noncontiguous domestic trades.
Contact: Associate Administrator for Maritime Aids, Maritime

Administration, Department of Transportation, Washington, DC 20590, 202-382-0364.

20.811   RESEARCH AND DEVELOPMENT ASSISTANCE
Type of Assistance: Grants.
Applicant Eligibility: Marine firms, individuals, universities, state and local governments.
Objective: To improve the productivity of US shipbuilding, shipping, port and ancilliary industries.
Contact: Assistant for Program Development and Control, Department of Transportation, Washington, DC 20590, 202-382-0357.

20.812   CONSTRUCTION RESERVE FUND
Type of Assistance: Direct payments.
Applicant Eligibility: Individuals.
Objective: To promote the construction, reconstruction, reconditioning or acquisition of merchant vessels which are necessary for national defense and to the development of US commerce.
Contact: Administrator for Marine Aids, Maritime Administration, Department of Transportation, Washington, DC 20590, 202-382-0634.

US DEPARTMENT OF TREASURY

INTERNAL REVENUE SERVICE

21.006 TAX COUNSELING FOR THE ELDERLY
Type of Assistance: Direct payments ranging from $317 to $1,633,000.
Applicant Eligibility: Nonprofit organizations.
Objective: To authorize the Internal Revenue Service to enter into
agreement with private or public nonprofit agencies or organizations
to establish a network of trained volunteers to provide free income tax
information and return preparation assistance to elderly taxpayers.
Contact: Tax Counseling for the Elderly, Taxpayer Service Division,
D:R:T:I, Internal Revenue Service, 1111 Constitution Avenue, NW,
Washington, DC 20224, 202-566-4904.

OFFICE OF REVENUE SHARING

**21.300 STATE AND LOCAL GOVERNMENT FISCAL
ASSISTANCE—REVENUE SHARING**
Type of Assistance: Grants averaging $117,651.
Applicant Eligibility: State and local governments.
Objective: To provide financial assistance to state and local govern-
ments. Revenue sharing funds may be used by a recipient government
for any purpose which is a legal use of its own source revenues, pursuant
to authorization of the governing body following two public hearings
held specifically to permit the public to discuss possible uses of funds
and a proposed budget of revenue sharing funds.
Contact: Intergovernmental Relations Division, Office of Revenue
Sharing, Department of the Treasury, 2401 E Street, NW, Washington,
DC 20226, 202-634-5200.

APPALACHIAN REGIONAL COMMISSION

23.001 APPALACHIAN REGIONAL DEVELOPMENT
Type of Assistance: Grants.
Applicant Eligibility: Nonprofit organizations, state and local governments.
Objective: To stimulate substantial public investments in public facilities that will start the region on its way toward accelerated social and economic development; to help establish a set of institutions in Appalachia capable of permanently directing the long-term development of the region; and on a joint federal-state-local basis to develop comprehensive plans and programs to help accomplish the overall objectives of Appalachian development, including meeting the special demands created by the nation's energy needs and policies. This plan applies to designated counties in Alabama, Georgia, Kentucky, Maryland, Mississippi, New York, North Carolina, Ohio, Pennsylvania, South Carolina, Tennessee and Virginia, and all counties in West Virginia.
Contact: Executive Director, Appalachian Regional Commission, 1666 Connecticut Avenue, NW, Washington, DC 20235, 202-673-7874.

23.002 APPALACHIAN SUPPLEMENTS TO FEDERAL GRANTS-IN-AID (COMMUNITY DEVELOPMENT)
Type of Assistance: Grants ranging from $18,000 to $900,000.
Applicant Eligibility: Nonprofit organizations and state governments.
Objective: To meet the basic needs of local areas and assist in providing community development opportunities by funding such development facilities as water and sewer systems, sewage treatment plants, recreation centers, industrial sites and others. Grants may supplement other federal grants, or when sufficient federal funds are unavailable, funds may be provided entirely by this program.
Contact: Executive Director, Appalachian Regional Commission, 1666 Connecticut Avenue, NW, Washington, DC 20235, 202-673-7874.

23.003 APPALACHIAN DEVELOPMENT HIGHWAY SYSTEM
Type of Assistance: Grants (dollar amount not available).
Applicant Eligibility: State governments.
Objective: To provide a highway system which, in conjunction with other federally aided highways, will open up areas with development potential within the Appalachian region where commerce and communications have been inhibited by lack of adequate access.
Contact: Executive Director, Appalachian Regional Commission, 1666 Connecticut Avenue, NW, Washington, DC 20235, 202-673-7874.

23.004 APPALACHIAN HEALTH PROGRAMS

Type of Assistance: Grants ranging from $500 to $516,257.

Applicant Eligibility: Nonprofit organizations, state and local governments.

Objective: To make primary health care accessible, reduce infant mortality and recruit needed health manpower in designated "health-shortage" areas.

Contact: Executive Director, Appalachian Regional Commission, 1666 Connecticut Avenue, NW, Washington, DC 20235, 202-673-7874.

23.005 APPALACHIAN HOUSING PROJECT PLANNING LOAN, TECHNICAL ASSISTANCE GRANT AND SITE DEVELOPMENT AND OFF-SITE IMPROVEMENT GRANT

Type of Assistance: Grants ranging from $220,000 to $300,000.

Applicant Eligibility: Nonprofit organizations, state and local governments.

Objective: To stimulate the creation of jobs and private sector involvement through low- and moderate-income housing construction and rehabilitation, and to assist in developing site and off-site improvements for low- and moderate-income housing in the Appalachian region.

Contact: Executive Director, Appalachian Regional Commission, 1666 Connecticut Avenue, NW, Washington, DC 20235, 202-673-7874.

23.008 APPALACHIAN LOCAL ACCESS ROADS

Type of Assistance: Grants ranging from $5,601 to $8,214,860.

Applicant Eligibility: Nonprofit organizations, state and local governments.

Objective: To provide access to industrial, commercial, educational, recreational, residential and related transportation facilities which directly or indirectly relate to the improvement of the areas determined by the states to have significant development potential, and to meet the objectives stated under the program entitled Appalachian Regional Development.

Contact: Executive Director, Appalachian Regional Commission, 1666 Connecticut Avenue, NW, Washington, DC 20235, 202-673-7874.

23.009 APPALACHIAN LOCAL DEVELOPMENT DISTRICT ASSISTANCE

Type of Assistance: Grants ranging from $7,500 to $121,000.

Applicant Eligibility: Local governments.

Objective: To provide planning and development resources in multi-county areas; to help develop the technical competence essential to sound development assistance; and to meet the objectives stated under the program entitled Appalachian Regional Development.

Contact: Executive Director, Appalachian Regional Commission, 1666 Connecticut Avenue, NW, Washington, DC 20235, 202-673-7874.

23.010 APPALACHIAN MINE AREA RESTORATION

Type of Assistance: Grants.

Applicant Eligibility: Nonprofit organizations, state and local governments.

Objective: To further the economic development of the region by rehabilitating areas presently damaged by deleterious mining practices and by controlling or abating mine drainage pollution.

Contact: Executive Director, Appalachian Regional Commission, 1666 Connecticut Avenue, NW, Washington, DC 20235, 202-673-7874.

23.011 APPALACHIAN STATE RESEARCH, TECHNICAL ASSISTANCE AND DEMONSTRATION PROJECTS

Type of Assistance: Grants ranging from $2,500 to $80,000.

Applicant Eligibility: State and local governments.

Objective: To expand the knowledge of the region to the fullest extent possible by means of state-sponsored research, including investigations, studies, technical assistance and demonstration projects.

Contact: Executive Director, Appalachian Regional Commission, 1666 Connecticut Avenue, NW, Washington, DC 20235, 202-673-7874.

23.012 APPALACHIAN VOCATIONAL AND OTHER EDUCATION FACILITIES AND OPERATIONS

Type of Assistance: Grants ranging from $9,066 to $512,720.

Applicant Eligibility: Nonprofit organizations, state and local governments.

Objective: To provide the people of the region with the basic facilities, equipment and operating funds for training and education necessary to obtain employment at their best capability for available job opportunities.

Contact: Executive Director, Appalachian Regional Commission, 1666 Connecticut Avenue, NW, Washington, DC 20235, 202-673-7874.

23.013 APPALACHIAN CHILD DEVELOPMENT

Type of Assistance: Grants ranging from $24,763 to $1,433,461.

Applicant Eligibility: Nonprofit organizations, state and local governments.

Objective: To create a state and substate capability for planning child development programs and a program to provide child development services in underserved areas throughout the region and to test innovative projects and programs for replicability.

Contact: Executive Director, Appalachian Regional Commission, 1666 Connecticut Avenue, NW, Washington, DC 20235, 202-673-7874.

23.107 APPALACHIAN SPECIAL TRANSPORTATION-RELATED PLANNING, RESEARCH AND DEMONSTRATION PROGRAM

Type of Assistance: Grants ranging from $1,260 to $158,000.

Applicant Eligibility: Nonprofit organizations, state and local governments.

Objective: To encourage the preparation of action-oriented plans and programs that reinforce and enhance transportation (particularly highway) investments.
Contact: Executive Director, Appalachian Regional Commission, 1666 Connecticut Avenue, NW, Washington, DC 20235, 202-673-7874.

EQUAL EMPLOYMENT OPPORTUNITY COMMISSION

30.002   EMPLOYMENT DISCRIMINATION—STATE AND LOCAL ANTIDISCRIMINATION AGENCY CONTRACTS
Type of Assistance: Grants ranging from $35,000 to $1,299,900.
Applicant Eligibility: State and local governments.
Objective: To assist the Equal Employment Opportunity Commission in the enforcement of Title VII of the Civil Rights Act of 1964, as amended, by attempting settlement and investigating and resolving charges of employment discrimination based on race, color, religion, sex or national origin.
Contact: State and Local Division, Office of Field Services, Equal Employment Opportunity Commission, Room 4233, 2401 E Street, NW, Washington, DC 20506, 202-634-7056.

30.009   EMPLOYMENT DISCRIMINATION PROJECT CONTRACTS—INDIAN TRIBES
Type of Assistance: Grants (dollar amount not available).
Applicant Eligibility: Native American tribes.
Objective: To ensure the protection of employment rights of Indians working on reservations.
Contact: Office of Special Projects and Programs, Equal Employment Opportunity Commission, 2401 E Street, NW, Washington, DC 20506, 202-634-6806.

FEDERAL MEDIATION AND CONCILIATION SERVICE

34.002 LABOR-MANAGEMENT COOPERATION
Type of Assistance: Grants ranging from $20,140 to $150,000.
Applicant Eligibility: State and local governments, labor organizations.
Objective: To support the establishment or expansion of a joint labor-management committee at the plant, area and industrywide levels in order to improve labor-management relations, job security, economic development, and productivity.
Contact: Division of Labor Management Grant Programs, Federal Mediation and Conciliation Service, 2100 K Street, NW, Washington, DC 20427, 202-653-5320.

GENERAL SERVICES ADMINISTRATION

39.002   DISPOSAL OF FEDERAL SURPLUS REAL PROPERTY
Type of Assistance: Sale, exchange or donation of property and goods.
Applicant Eligibility: Individuals, nonprofit organizations, state and local governments.
Objective: To dispose of surplus real property. Surplus real property may be conveyed for public park or recreation use and public health or educational purposes at discounts up to 100 percent; public airport purposes; wildlife conservation; replacement housing; historic monument purposes without monetary consideration; and for general public purposes without restrictions at a price equal to the estimated fair market value of the property.
Contact: Office of Real Property, Federal Property Resource Service, General Services Administration, Washington, DC 20405, 202-535-7084.

39.003   DONATION OF FEDERAL SURPLUS PERSONAL PROPERTY
Type of Assistance: Sale, exchange or donation of property and goods.
Applicant Eligibility: Nonprofit organizations, state and local governments.
Objective: To transfer surplus property to the states for distribution to state and local public agencies for public purposes or to certain nonprofit educational and public activities; to public airports; and to educational activities of special interest to the armed services. Surplus items are used by state and local public agencies for carrying out or promoting one or more public purposes, for residents of a given political area, such as conservation, parks and recreation, education, public health, public safety and economic development; by certain nonprofit, tax-exempt educational or public health institutions or organizations; or by public airports for airport development, operation or maintenance.
Contact: Director, Donation Division, Office of Personal Property, Federal Property Resources Services, General Services Administration, Washington, DC 20406, 703-557-1234.

39.007   SALE OF FEDERAL SURPLUS PERSONAL PROPERTY
Type of Assistance: Sale, exchange or donation of property and goods.
Applicant Eligibility: Individuals, nonprofit organizations, state and local governments.
Objective: To sell property no longer needed by the government in an economical and efficient manner and obtain the maximum net return

from sales. General Services Administration conducts the sale of personal property for most of the civil agencies; the Department of Defense handles the sale of its own surplus property.

Contact: Director, Sales Division, Office of Property Management, Office of Federal Supply and Services, General Services Administration, Washington, DC 20405, 703-557-0814.

GOVERNMENT PRINTING OFFICE

**40.002 GOVERNMENT PUBLICATIONS—
         SALES AND DISTRIBUTION**

Type of Assistance: Sale, exchange or donation of property and goods.
Applicant Eligibility: All interested parties.
Objective: To make US Government publications available for purchase.
Contact: Superintendent of Documents, US Government Printing Office, Washington, DC 20402, 202-275-3347, 202-275-3345.

NATIONAL CREDIT UNION ADMINISTRATION

44.001 CREDIT UNION CHARTER, EXAMINATION, SUPERVISION AND INSURANCE

Type of Assistance: Specialized services and insurance (dollar amount not available).

Applicant Eligibility: Nonprofit associations of more than 300 members.

Objective: To offer to groups that have a common bond the opportunity to establish and operate their own credit unions.

Contact: Chairman, NCUA Board, National Credit Union Administration, Office of Examinations and Insurance, 1776 G Street, NW, Washington, DC 20456, 202-357-1000.

NATIONAL FOUNDATION ON THE ARTS AND THE HUMANITIES

NATIONAL ENDOWMENT FOR THE ARTS

45.001   PROMOTION OF THE ARTS—DESIGN ARTS

Type of Assistance: Grants and direct payments up to $20,000.

Applicant Eligibility: Individuals, nonprofit organizations, state and local governments.

Objective: To provide grants for projects including research, professional education and public awareness in architecture, landscape architecture and urban, interior, fashion, industrial and environmental design. The program attempts to encourage creativity and to make the public aware of the benefits of good design.

Contact: Director, Design Arts Program, National Endowment for the Arts, 1100 Pennsylvania Avenue, NW, Washington, DC 20506, 202-682-5437.

45.002   PROMOTION OF THE ARTS—DANCE

Type of Assistance: Grants and direct payments ranging from $3,000 to $350,000.

Applicant Eligibility: Individuals, nonprofit organizations, state and local governments.

Objective: To assist dancers, choreographers and dance organizations in making the highest-quality dance widely available.

Contact: Director, Dance Program, National Endowment for the Arts, 1100 Pennsylvania Avenue, NW, Washington, DC 20506, 202-682-5435.

45.003   PROMOTION OF THE ARTS—ARTISTS-IN-EDUCATION

Type of Assistance: Grants ranging from $5,000 to $231,000.

Applicant Eligibility: Nonprofit organizations, state and local governments.

Objective: To provide grants for special innovative projects in arts education; to enhance career development of artists and skills of teachers and administrators.

Contact: Director, Artists-in-Education Program, National Endowment for the Arts, 1100 Pennsylvania Avenue, NW, Washington, DC 20506, 202-682-5426.

45.004   PROMOTION OF THE ARTS—LITERATURE

Type of Assistance: Grants ranging from $8,000 to $20,000.

Applicant Eligibility: Individuals, nonprofit organizations, state and local governments.

Objective: To provide fellowships for creative writers: poets, novelists, short-story writers, essayists and translators of literary works.
Contact: Director, Literature Program, National Endowment for the Arts, 1100 Pennsylvania Avenue, NW, Washington, DC 20506, 202-682-5451.

45.005 PROMOTION OF THE ARTS—MUSIC

Type of Assistance: Grants and direct payments ranging from $1,500 to $15,000.
Applicant Eligibility: Individuals, nonprofit organizations, state and local governments.
Objective: To support excellence in music performance and creativity and to develop informed audiences for music throughout the country.
Contact: Director, Music Program, National Endowment for the Arts, 1100 Pennsylvania Avenue, NW, Washington, DC 20506, 202-682-5445.

45.006 PROMOTION OF THE ARTS— MEDIA ARTS: FILM/RADIO/TELEVISION

Type of Assistance: Grants ranging from $2,500 to $500,000.
Applicant Eligibility: Individuals, nonprofit organizations, state and local governments.
Objective: To provide grants in support of projects designed to assist individuals and groups in producing films, radio and video of high aesthetic quality, and to exhibit and disseminate media arts. The Endowment also assists the American Film Institute, which carries out a number of assistance programs for film.
Contact: Director, Media Arts Program, National Endowment for the Arts, 1100 Pennsylvania Avenue, NW, Washington, DC 20506, 202-682-5452.

45.007 PROMOTION OF THE ARTS—PUBLIC PARTNERSHIP

Type of Assistance: Grants ranging from $5,000 to $541,300.
Applicant Eligibility: State and local governments.
Objective: To assist state and regional public arts agencies in the development of programs for the encouragement of the arts and artists.
Contact: Directors, State Program, National Endowment for the Arts, 1100 Pennsylvania Avenue, NW, Washington, DC 20506, 202-682-5429.

45.008 PROMOTION OF THE ARTS—THEATER

Type of Assistance: Grants ranging from $5,000 to $325,000.
Applicant Eligibility: Nonprofit organizations, state and local governments.
Objective: To provide grants to aid professional theater companies and organizations.
Contact: Director, Theater Program, National Endowment for the Arts, 1100 Pennsylvania Avenue, NW, Washington, DC 20506, 202-682-5425.

45.009 PROMOTION OF THE ARTS—VISUAL ARTS

Type of Assistance: Grants ranging from $1,000 to $50,000.

Applicant Eligibility: Individuals, nonprofit organizations, state and local governments.

Objective: To provide grants to assist painters, sculptors, craftsmen, photographers and printmakers; to support institutions devoted to the development of the visual arts in America.

Contact: Director Visual Arts Program, National Endowment for the Arts, 1100 Pennsylvania Avenue, NW, Washington, DC 20506, 202-682-5448.

45.010 PROMOTION OF THE ARTS—EXPANSION ARTS

Type of Assistance: Grants ranging from $5,000 to $30,000.

Applicant Eligibility: Nonprofit organizations, state and local governments.

Objective: To provide grants to professionally directed, community-based arts organizations involved with urban, suburban and rural communities. Particular attention is given to those organizations whose major focus is to create, produce, exhibit and teach art that allows for direct community participation.

Contact: Director, Expansion Arts Program, National Endowment for the Arts, 1100 Pennsylvania Avenue, NW, Washington, DC 20506, 202-682-5443.

45.011 PROMOTION OF THE ARTS—INTER-ARTS

Type of Assistance: Grants ranging from $5,000 to $50,000.

Applicant Eligibility: Nonprofit organizations, state and local governments.

Objective: To provide grants for projects that involve two or more art forms and that have potential national or regional impact.

Contact: Director, Office of Inter-Arts, National Endowment for the Arts, 1100 Pennsylvania Avenue, NW, Washington, DC 20506, 202-682-5444.

45.012 PROMOTION OF THE ARTS—MUSEUMS

Type of Assistance: Grants up to $150,000.

Applicant Eligibility: Individuals, nonprofit organizations, state and local governments.

Objective: To provide grants in support of American museums' essential activities. Grants may be used for mounting special exhibitions, utilization of collections, visiting specialists, conservation, training museum professions, collection maintenance (climate control, security, storage), museum education, purchase of works by living American artists, and cataloguing.

Contact: Director, Museum Program, National Endowment for the Arts, 1100 Pennsylvania Avenue, NW, Washington, DC 20506, 202-682-5442.

45.013 PROMOTION OF THE ARTS—CHALLENGE GRANTS
Type of Assistance: Grants ranging from $100,000 to $1 million.
Applicant Eligibility: Nonprofit organizations, state and local governments.
Objective: To enable cultural organizations and institutions to increase the levels of continuing support and to increase the range of contributors to the programs of such organizations or institutions; to provide administrative and management improvements for cultural organizations and institutions, particularly in the field of long-range financial planning; to enable cultural organizations and institutions to increase audience participation and appreciation of programs sponsored by such organizations and institutions; to stimulate greater cooperation among cultural organizations and institutions especially designed to better serve the communities in which such organizations or institutions are located; and to foster greater citizen involvement in planning the cultural development of a community.
Contact: Challenge Grants Program, National Endowment for the Arts, 1100 Pennsylvania Avenue, NW, Washington, DC 20506, 202-682-5436.

45.014 PROMOTION OF THE ARTS—
OPERA & MUSICAL THEATER
Type of Assistance: Grants ranging from $3,000 to $300,000.
Applicant Eligibility: Nonprofit organizations, state and local governments.
Objective: To support excellence in the performance and creation of professional opera and musical theater throughout the nation.
Contact: Director, Opera/Musical Theatre Program, National Endowment for the Arts, 1100 Pennsylvania Avenue, NW, Washington, DC 20506, 202-682-5447.

45.015 PROMOTION OF THE ARTS—FOLK ARTS
Type of Assistance: Grants ranging from $1,000 to $50,000.
Applicant Eligibility: Nonprofit organizations, state and local governments, individuals.
Objective: To assist, foster and make publicly available the diverse traditional American folk arts.
Contact: Director, Folk Arts Program, National Endowment for the Arts, 1100 Pennsylvania Avenue, NW, Washington, DC 20506, 202-682-5449.

45.021 PROMOTION OF THE ARTS—
ARTS MANAGEMENT FELLOWSHIP PROGRAM
Type of Assistance: Grants up to $3,500 stipend plus round-trip travel.
Applicant Eligibility: Individuals.
Objective: To provide a limited number of 13-week fellowships for professionals and students in arts administration and related fields. The internship is located at Endowment headquarters in Washington, DC. The program is designed to acquaint the participants with the policies,

procedures and operations of the Endowment and to give them an overview of arts activities in this country.

Contact: Arts Management Fellowship Program, National Endowment Fellowship Program, National Endowment for the Arts, 1100 Pennsylvania Avenue, NW, Washington, DC 20506, 202-682-5786.

45.022 PROMOTION OF THE ARTS— ADVANCEMENT GRANTS

Type of Assistance: Grants ranging from $40,000 to $85,000.

Applicant Eligibility: Nonprofit organizations.

Objective: To assist arts organizations in strengthening their long-term institutional capacity and enhancing their artistic quality and diversity.

Contact: Advancement Grant Program, National Endowment for the Arts, 1100 Pennsylvania Avenue, NW, Washington, DC 20506, 202-682-5436.

NATIONAL ENDOWMENT FOR THE HUMANITIES

45.104 PROMOTION OF THE HUMANITIES— MEDIA HUMANITIES PROJECTS

Type of Assistance: Grants ranging from $4,000 to $750,000.

Applicant Eligibility: Nonprofit organizations, state and local governments.

Objective: To encourage and support radio and television production that advances public understanding and use of the humanities, including such fields as history, jurisprudence, literature, anthropology, philosophy and archaeology; that is of the highest professional caliber both in terms of scholarship in the humanities and in terms of technical production; and that is suitable for national or regional television broadcast and distribution, or for national, regional or local radio broadcast.

Contact: Media Humanities Projects, Division of General Programs, National Endowment for the Humanities, Room 420, Washington, DC 20506, 202-786-0278.

45.111 PROMOTION OF THE HUMANITIES— EXEMPLARY PROJECTS, NONTRADITIONAL PROGRAMS, AND TEACHING MATERIALS

Type of Assistance: Grants.

Applicant Eligibility: Individuals, nonprofit organizations, state and local governments.

Objective: To promote the development and testing of imaginative approaches to education in the humanities by supporting projects that can be completed within a specified period of time. Most projects are planned and implemented by small groups of faculty, last one or two years and are concerned with the design of model humanities programs intended for widespread use, the development of curriculum materials, and increased collaboration among educational and other cultural institutions. Projects also encourage excellence in teaching and promote serious attention to the central issues in the humanities by bringing groups of college faculty into residence at institutes for periods ranging from four to eight weeks or, in exceptional circumstances, longer for joint curriculum planning.

Contact: Assistant Director, Exemplary Projects, Nontraditional Programs, National Endowment for the Humanities, Room 302, Washington, DC 20506, 202-786-0384.

45.113 PROMOTION OF THE HUMANITIES— HUMANITIES PROJECTS FOR ADULTS

Type of Assistance: Grants ranging from $15,000 to $200,000.

Applicant Eligibility: Individuals, nonprofit organizations, state and local governments.

Objective: To encourage and support humanities projects that demonstrate new ways of relating the humanities to new audiences. Projects must draw upon resources and scholars in the fields of the humanities. Priorities include projects undertaken by national organizations which bring humanities programming to members and affiliates, and projects using previously untested techniques for involving the public in programs examining the cultural, philosophical and historical dimensions of contemporary society.

Contact: Humanities Projects for Adults, Division of General Programs, National Endowment for the Humanities, Room 426, Washington, DC 20506, 202-786-0271.

45.115 PROMOTION OF THE HUMANITIES— YOUNGER SCHOLARS

Type of Assistance: Grants ranging from $1,800 to $2,200.

Applicant Eligibility: Individuals, nonprofit organizations, state and local governments.

Objective: To support noncredit humanities projects during the summer initiated and conducted by young persons. Grants are awarded for research, education, film and community projects in one or more of the fields included in the humanities: history, philosophy, language, linguistics, literature, archaeology, jurisprudence, art history and criticism and the humanistic social sciences. (Youth grants are not awarded to anyone over the age of 30.)

Contact: Director, Office of Youth Programs, Room 426, National Endowment for the Humanities, Washington, DC 20506, 202-786-0273.

45.116 PROMOTION OF THE HUMANITIES— SUMMER SEMINARS FOR COLLEGE TEACHERS

Type of Assistance: Grants ranging from $50,000 to $75,000.

Applicant Eligibility: Individuals.

Objective: To provide opportunities for teachers at undergraduate private and state colleges and junior and community colleges to work during the summer in their areas of interest under the direction of distinguished scholars at institutions with first-rate libraries.

Contact: Program Officer for Summer Seminars for College Teachers, Division of Fellowships, National Endowment for the Humanities, Room 316, Washington, DC 20506, 202-786-0463.

45.121 PROMOTION OF THE HUMANITIES— SUMMER STIPENDS
Type of Assistance: Grants of $3,000.
Applicant Eligibility: Individuals.
Objective: To provide time for uninterrupted study and research to scholars, teachers, writers and other interpreters of the humanities who have produced or demonstrated promise of producing significant contributions to humanistic knowledge.
Contact: Program Officer for Summer Stipends, Division of Fellowships and Seminars, National Endowment for the Humanities, Room 316, Washington, DC 20506, 202-786-0466.

45.122 PROMOTION OF THE HUMANITIES— REGRANTS AT CENTERS FOR ADVANCED STUDY
Type of Assistance: Grants ranging from $40,000 to $123,000.
Applicant Eligibility: Individuals and nonprofit organizations.
Objective: To provide fellowships for study and research in the humanities to independent centers for advanced study in order to increase the opportunities for the uninterrupted and extended interchange of ideas which these centers make possible.
Contact: Division of Fellowships and Seminars, Fellowships at Centers for Advanced Study, Room 316, National Endowment for the Humanities, Washington, DC 20506, 202-786-0204.

45.124 PROMOTION OF THE HUMANITIES— REFERENCE MATERIALS ACCESS GRANTS
Type of Assistance: Grants ranging from $1,000 to $220,000.
Applicant Eligibility: Individuals, nonprofit organizations, state and local governments.
Objective: To fund, wholly or partially, projects that will improve and facilitate scholarly access to significant resources in order to contribute to greater knowledge and understanding of the humanities.
Contact: Director, Research Works Access, Division of Research Programs, National Endowment for the Humanities, Room 319, Washington, DC 20506, 202-786-0204.

45.125 PROMOTION OF THE HUMANITIES— HUMANITIES PROJECTS IN MUSEUMS AND HISTORICAL ORGANIZATIONS
Type of Assistance: Grants ranging from $15,000 to $500,000.
Applicant Eligibility: Individuals, state and local governments.
Objective: To assist museums and historical organizations in implementing effective and imaginative programs which convey and interpret knowledge of America's and other nations' cultural legacies to the general public.

Contact: Humanities Projects in Museums and Historical Organizations Division of Public Programs, Room 420, National Endowment for the Humanities, Washington, DC 20506, 202-786-0284.

45.127 PROMOTION OF THE HUMANITIES—INSTRUCTION IN ELEMENTARY AND SECONDARY SCHOOLS

Type of Assistance: Grants.

Applicant Eligibility: Individuals, nonprofit organizations, state and local governments.

Objective: To improve classroom teaching in history, foreign languages, English and other disciplines. To promote the development and testing of imaginative approaches to precollegiate education in the humanities by supporting demonstration projects that can be completed within a specified period of time. Most projects are planned and implemented by groups of school and/or university faculty, last one to two years and are concerned with the design of model courses or programs, teacher training institutes, or the development of curricular materials, including an emphasis on teacher training. Projects often involve increased collaboration between schools, higher education institutions and cultural institutions.

Contact: Humanities Instruction in Elementary and Secondary Schools, National Endowment for the Humanities, Room 302, Washington, DC 20506, 202-786-0377.

45.129 PROMOTION OF THE HUMANITIES— STATE PROGRAMS

Type of Assistance: Grants ranging from $201,000 to $349,000.

Applicant Eligibility: Nonprofit organizations and state governments.

Objective: To promote local humanities programming through renewable program grants to humanities councils within each of the states for the purpose of regranting funds to local organizations, institutions and groups.

Contact: Director, Division of State Programs, National Endowment for the Humanities, Room 411, Washington, DC 20506, 202-786-0254.

45.130 PROMOTION OF THE HUMANITIES— CHALLENGE GRANT PROGRAM

Type of Assistance: Grants ranging from $2,000 to $1,500,000.

Applicant Eligibility: Nonprofit organizations, state and local governments.

Objective: To provide financial assistance to institutions that store, research or disseminate the humanities; to broaden the base of financial support by "challenging" institutions to raise three private dollars for every federal grant dollar; to help secure financial stability in order to maintain existing services and resources.

Contact: Office of Challenge Grants, National Endowment for the Humanities, Room 429, Washington, DC 20506, 202-786-0361.

45.132 PROMOTION OF THE HUMANITIES— TEXT PUBLICATION SUBVENTION

Type of Assistance: Grants ranging from $2,000 to $10,000.
Applicant Eligibility: Individuals and nonprofit organizations.
Objective: To ensure through grants to publishing entities the dissemination of works of scholarly distinction that without support could not be published.
Contact: Assistant Director, Division of Research Programs for Research Materials, National Endowment for the Humanities, Room 319, Washington, DC 20506, 202-786-0207.

45.133 PROMOTION OF THE HUMANITIES— INTERPRETIVE RESEARCH/HUMANITIES, SCIENCE AND TECHNOLOGY

Type of Assistance: Grants ranging from $15,000 to $300,000.
Applicant Eligibility: Individuals, nonprofit organizations, state and local governments.
Objective: To support humanities research designed to deepen understanding of science and technology and their role in our culture.
Contact: Division of Research Programs, Basic Research, National Endowment for the Humanities, Room 319, Washington, DC 20506, 202-786-0207.

45.134 PROMOTION OF THE HUMANITIES— REGRANTS/RESEARCH CONFERENCES

Type of Assistance: Grants ranging from $5,200 to $10,000.
Applicant Eligibility: Individuals, nonprofit organizations, state and local governments.
Objective: To support conferences, symposia and workshops that enable scholars to discuss and advance the current state of research on a particular topic or to consider means of improving conditions for research.
Contact: Program Officer, Division of Research Programs, National Endowment for the Humanities, Room 319, Washington, DC 20506, 202-786-0207.

45.135 PROMOTION OF THE HUMANITIES— YOUTH PROJECTS FOR YOUTH

Type of Assistance: Grants.
Applicant Eligibility: Individuals, nonprofit organizations, state and local governments.
Objective: To support humanities projects that provide educational opportunities beyond those of in-school programs for large groups of young people under the direction of experienced professionals in the humanities and professionals in youth work. These may be sponsored by educational, cultural, scholarly, civic, media or youth organizations.
Contact: Division of General Programs, Humanities Projects for Youth/ Youth Projects, National Endowment for the Humanities, Room 426, Washington, DC 20506, 202-786-0271.

45.137 PROMOTION OF THE HUMANITIES—
HUMANITIES PROJECTS IN LIBRARIES

Type of Assistance: Grants ranging from $5,000 to $200,000.

Applicant Eligibility: Nonprofit organizations, state and local governments.

Objective: To encourage public interest in libraries' humanities resources and stimulate their use through thematic programs, exhibits, media, publications and other library activities.

Contact: Humanities Projects in Libraries, Division of General Programs, National Endowment for the Humanities, Room 420, Washington, DC 20506 202-786-0271.

45.140 PROMOTION OF THE HUMANITIES—
INTERPRETIVE RESEARCH/PROJECTS

Type of Assistance: Grants ranging from $5,000 to $300,000.

Applicant Eligibility: Individuals, nonprofit organizations, state and local governments.

Objective: To advance basic research that is interpretative in all fields of the humanities. Collaborative, interdisciplinary scholarship involving the efforts of several individuals at the professional, assistant and clerical levels is encouraged as well as the use of innovative methodologies. Foreign and domestic archaeology projects are supported in the program, as are research projects on the history and customs of American states, communities and regions.

Contact: Basic Research Program, Division of Research Programs, National Endowment for the Humanities, Room 319, Washington, DC 20506, 202-786-0207.

45.142 PROMOTION OF THE HUMANITIES—FELLOWSHIPS
FOR INDEPENDENT STUDY AND RESEARCH

Type of Assistance: Grants averaging $27,500.

Applicant Eligibility: Individuals.

Objective: To provide time for uninterrupted study and research to scholars, teachers and other interpreters of the humanities who can make significant contributions to thought and knowledge in the humanities. The fellowships free applicants from the day-to-day responsibilities of teaching and other work for extended periods of uninterrupted, full-time study and research so that fellows may enlarge their contributions and continue to develop their abilities as scholars and interpreters of the humanities.

Contact: Program Officer for Fellowships for Independent Study and Research, Division of Fellowships and Seminars, National Endowment for the Humanities, Room 316, Washington, DC 20502, 202-786-0466.

45.143 PROMOTION OF THE HUMANITIES—
FELLOWSHIPS FOR COLLEGE TEACHERS

Type of Assistance: Grants up to $27,500.

Applicant Eligibility: Individuals.

Objective: To provide opportunities for college teachers to pursue full-

time independent study and research that will enhance their abilities as teachers and interpreters of the humanities.
Contact: Division of Fellowships and Seminars, National Endowment for the Humanities, Room 316, Washington, DC 20506, 202-786-0466.

45.145 PROMOTION OF THE HUMANITIES— RESEARCH MATERIALS/TOOLS

Type of Assistance: Grants ranging from $2,500 to $150,000.
Applicant Eligibility: Individuals, nonprofit orgnizations, state and local governments.
Objective: To fund, wholly or partially, projects that create reference works and resources important for scholarly research as cultural documents.
Contact: Assistant Director, Division of Research Programs, Reference Works/Tools, National Endowment for the Humanities, Room 319, Washington, DC 20506, 202-786-0210.

45.146 PROMOTION OF THE HUMANITIES— TEXTS/EDITIONS

Type of Assistance: Grants ranging from $2,500 to $150,000.
Applicant Eligibility: Individuals, nonprofit organizations, state and local governments.
Objective: To fund, wholly or partially, projects that create editions of materials important for scholarly research in the humanities and as cultural documents.
Contact: Assistant Director, Division of Research Programs, Reference Works/Editions, National Endowment for the Humanities, Room 319, Washington, DC 20506, 202-786-0210.

45.147 PROMOTION OF THE HUMANITIES— TEXTS/TRANSLATIONS

Type of Assistance: Grants ranging from $2,500 to $300,000.
Applicant Eligibility: Individuals, nonprofit organizations, state and local governments.
Objective: To support the translation into English of texts and documents that will make an important contribution to research in the humanities and to greater public awareness of the traditions and achievements of other cultures.
Contact: Translations, Division of Research Programs, Reference Works/Translations, National Endowment for the Humanities, Room 319, Washington, DC 20506, 202-786-0210.

45.148 PROMOTION OF THE HUMANITIES— REGRANTS PROGRAM/INTERNATIONAL RESEARCH

Type of Assistance: Grants ranging from $50,000 to $500,000.
Applicant Eligibility: Nonprofit organizations, state and local governments.
Objective: To increase understanding of the traditions, culture and values of foreign countries as a base for the study of contemporary

international affairs, and to foster this nation's standing in international scholarship by providing support to American scholars to pursue research abroad in all fields of the humanities.
Contact: Research in Selected Areas/Intercultural Research, Room 319, National Endowment for the Humanities, Washington, DC 20506, 202-786-0204

45.149 PROMOTION OF THE HUMANITIES— OFFICE OF PRESERVATION
Type of Assistance: Grants ranging from $7,500 to $150,000.
Applicant Eligibility: Individuals and nonprofit organizations.
Objective: To fund projects that will promote the conservation and preservation of library and archival collections relative to the humanities in the United States.
Contact: Office of Preservation, National Endowment for the Humanities, Washington, DC 20506, 202-786-0570.

45.150 PROMOTION OF THE HUMANITIES—CENTRAL DISCIPLINES IN UNDERGRADUATE EDUCATION
Type of Assistance: Grants.
Applicant Eligibility: Educational institutions, state and local governments.
Objective: To assist colleges and universities in establishing or sustaining the disciplines of the humanities in a central role in undergraduate education.
Contact: Central Disciplines in Undergraduate Education, National Endowment for the Humanities, Room 302, Washington, DC 20506, 202-786-0380.

45.151 PROMOTION OF THE HUMANITIES—SUMMER SEMINARS FOR SECONDARY SCHOOL TEACHERS
Type of Assistance: Grants ranging from $34,000 to $70,000.
Applicant Eligibility: Teachers/scholars.
Objective: To provide opportunities for teachers in secondary schools to work during the summer under the direction of a master teacher and distinguished scholar at colleges and universities, studying seminal works in the humanities in a systematic and thorough way.
Contact: Summer Seminars for Secondary School Teachers, Division of Fellowships and Seminars, National Endowment for the Humanities, Room 316, Washington, DC 20506, 202-786-0463.

FEDERAL COUNCIL ON THE ARTS AND THE HUMANITIES

45.201 ARTS AND ARTIFACTS INDEMNITY
Type of Assistance: Insurance ranging from $500,000 to $50 million.
Applicant Eligibility: Individuals, nonprofit organizations, state and local governments.

Objective: To provide for indemnification against loss or damage for eligible art works, artifacts and objects when borrowed from abroad on exhibition in the US; and from the US for exhibition abroad when there is an exchange exhibition from a foreign country.
Contact: Indemnity Administrator, Museums Program, National Endowment for the Arts, Washington, DC 20506, 202-682-5442.

INSTITUTE OF MUSEUM SERVICES

45.301   INSTITUTE OF MUSEUM SERVICES
Type of Assistance: Grants ranging from $1,000 to $75,000.
Applicant Eligibility: Museums.
Objective: To support the efforts of museums to conserve the nation's historic, scientific and cultural heritage; to maintain and expand their educational role; and to ease the financial burden borne by museums as a result of their increasing use by the public.
Contact: Institute of Museum Services, 1100 Pennsylvania Avenue, NW, Room 609, Washington, DC 20202, 202-786-0539.

NATIONAL SCIENCE FOUNDATION

47.009   GRADUATE RESEARCH FELLOWSHIPS
Type of Assistance: Grants up to $11,000.
Applicant Eligibility: Individuals.
Objective: To provide tangible encouragement to highly talented graduate students for advanced study in the sciences and engineering.
Contact: Fellowships Section, National Science Foundation, 1800 G Street, NW, Washington, DC 20550, 202-357-7856.

47.041   ENGINEERING GRANTS
Type of Assistance: Grants ranging from $1,000 to $1 million.
Applicant Eligibility: Individuals, nonprofit organizations, state and local governments.
Objective: To strengthen the engineering research base of the US and enhance the links between research and applications in meeting national goals.
Contact: Programs and Resources Officer, Directorate for Engineering and Applied Science, National Science Foundation, Room 1110, 1800 G Street, NW, Washington, DC 20550, 202-357-9774.

47.049   MATHEMATICAL AND PHYSICAL SCIENCES
Type of Assistance: Grants ranging from $10,000 to $4,200,000.
Applicant Eligibility: Individuals, nonprofit organizations, public and private colleges and universities.
Objective: To promote the progress of science and thereby ensure the continued scientific strength of the nation; and to increase the store of scientific knowledge and enhance understanding of major problems confronting the nation. Most of the research supported is basic in character. The program includes support of research project grants in the following disciplines: physics, chemistry, mathematical sciences, materials research and computer research. Support is also provided for research workshops, symposia and conferences, and for the purchase of scientific equipment. In addition, awards are made to encourage innovative engineering research by scientists recently awarded their Ph.D. degrees.
Contact: Assistant Director, Mathematical and Physical Sciences, National Science Foundation, 1800 G Street, NW, Washington, DC 20550, 202-357-9742.

47.050 ASTRONOMICAL, ATMOSPHERIC, EARTH AND OCEAN SCIENCES

Type of Assistance: Grants ranging from $1,200 to $3 million.

Applicant Eligibility: Individuals, nonprofit organizations, state and local governments.

Objective: To strenghthen and enhance the national scientific enterprise through the expansion of fundamental knowledge and increased understanding of the earth's natural environment and of the universe. Activities include encouragement and support of basic research in the astronomical, atmospheric, earth and ocean sciences, and in the biological and physical disciplines in the Antarctic and Arctic. Major objectives include new knowledge of astronomy and atmospheric sciences over the entire spectrum of physical phenomena; a better understanding of the physical and chemical makeup of the earth and its geological history; increased insight into the world's oceans, their composition, structure, behavior and tectonics; and new knowledge of natural phenomena and processes in the Antarctic and Arctic regions.

Contact: National Science Foundation, 1800 G Street, NW, Washington, DC 20550, 202-357-9488.

47.051 BIOLOGICAL, BEHAVIORAL AND SOCIAL SCIENCES

Type of Assistance: Grants ranging from $700 to $1,574,000.

Applicant Eligibility: Individuals, nonprofit organizations, state and local governments, public and private colleges and universities.

Objective: To promote the progress of science and thereby ensure the continued scientific strength of the nation, and to increase the store of scientific knowledge and enhance understanding of major problems confronting the nation. Most of the research supported is basic in character. The program includes support of research project grants in the following disciplines: physiology, cellular and molecular biology, behavioral and neural sciences, environmental biology, and social and economic science. Support is also provided for research workshops, symposia and conferences, and for the purchase of scientific equipment. In addition, awards are made to improve the quality of doctoral dissertations in behavioral, social and environmental sciences.

Contact: Assistant Director, Biological, Behavioral and Social Sciences, National Science Foundation, 1800 G Street, NW, Washington, DC 20550, 202-357-9854.

47.053 SCIENTIFIC, TECHNOLOGICAL AND INTERNATIONAL AFFAIRS

Type of Assistance: Grants ranging from $1,000 to $800,000.

Applicant Eligibility: Individuals, nonprofit organizations, state and local governments, public and private colleges and universities.

Objective: To address a broad range of scientific and technological issues of concern to policy makers and research and development managers in the public and private sector. Programs are designed to monitor and analyze the nation's science and technology enterprise and to improve national and international exchange of scientific information.

Contact: Assistant Director, Directorate for Scientific, Technological and International Affairs, National Science Foundation, 1800 G Street, NW, Washington, DC 20550, 202-357-7631.

47.065 ADVANCED SCIENTIFIC COMPUTING RESOURCES
Type of Assistance: Grants ranging from $20,000 to $13 million.
Applicant Eligibility: Public and private colleges and universities, small businesses.
Objective: To increase access, cooperation and sharing of advanced computing resources for the scientific and engineering research community.
Contact: Director, Office of Advanced Scientific Computing, National Science Foundation, 1800 G Street, NW, Washington, DC 20550, Room 504, 202-357-7558.

47.066 TEACHER ENHANCEMENT AND INFORMAL SCIENCE EDUCATION
Type of Assistance: Grants (dollar amount not available).
Applicant Eligibility: Public and private colleges and universities and nonprofit organizations.
Objective: To attract talented persons to precollege science and math careers and to keep good teachers employed by devising incentives and self-renewal opportunities.
Contact: Division of Teacher Enhancement and Informal Science Education, National Science Foundation, 1800 G Street, NW, Washington, DC 20550.

47.067 MATERIALS DEVELOPMENT AND RESEARCH
Type of Assistance: Grants (dollar amount not available).
Applicant Eligibility: Public and private colleges and universities.
Objective: To increase the quality of the nation's precollege educational system in math, science and technology.
Contact: Division of Precollege Education in Science and Engineering, National Science Foundation, 1800 G Street, NW, Washington, DC 20550, 202-357-7452.

47.068 STUDIES AND PROGRAM ASSESSMENT
Type of Assistance: Grants ranging from $9,000 to $450,000.
Applicant Eligibility: Public and private colleges and universities.
Objective: To improve science and engineering education in the US.
Contact: Office of Studies and Program Assessment, National Science Foundation, 1800 G Street, NW, Washington, DC 20550, 202-357-7425.

47.069 RESEARCH INITIATION AND IMPROVEMENT
Type of Assistance: Grants ranging from $5,000 to $250,000.
Applicant Eligibility: Minority, women and physically handicapped scientists and engineers.
Objective: To increase opportunities for women and minority and physically handicapped investigators to participate more fully in the

nation's scientific and engineering enterprise. Programs include: Minority Research Initiation, Research Improvement in Minority Institutions, Research Opportunities for Women, Visiting Professorships for Women, Research in Undergraduate Institutions, and Facilitation Awards for Handicapped Scientists and Engineers.

Contact: Division of Research Initiation and Improvement, National Science Foundation, 1800 G Street, NW, Washington, DC 20550, 202-357-7552, (TDD 357-7492).

RAILROAD RETIREMENT BOARD

57.001   SOCIAL INSURANCE FOR RAILROAD WORKERS
Type of Assistance: Direct payments up to $1,314 monthly.
Applicant Eligibility: Individuals.
Objective: To protect against loss of income for railroad workers and their families resulting from retirement, death, disability, unemployment or sickness of the wage earner.
Contact: Public Affairs, Railroad Retirement Board, 844 Rush Street, Chicago, IL 60611, 312-751-4777.

57.003   BENEFITS FOR CONRAIL EMPLOYEES
Type of Assistance: Direct payments.
Applicant Eligibility: ConRail employees.
Objective: To provide assistance to employees adversely affected by actions taken by ConRail under the Regional Rail Reorganization Act or the Northeast Rail Service Act.
Contact: Bureau of Unemployment and Sickness Insurance, Railroad Retirement Board, 844 Rush Street, Chicago, IL 60611, 312-751-4800.

59.003 LOANS FOR SMALL BUSINESSES

Type of Assistance: Direct loans and guaranteed/insured loans up to $350,000.

Applicant Eligibility: Individuals.

Objective: To provide loans to small businesses owned by low-income persons or located in areas of high unemployment.

Contact: Associate Administrator for Management Assistance, Small Business Administration, 1441 L Street, NW, Washington, DC 20416, 202-653-6881.

59.007 MANAGEMENT AND TECHNICAL ASSISTANCE FOR DISADVANTAGED BUSINESSES

Type of Assistance: Grants ranging from $15,000 to $306,250.

Applicant Eligibility: Individuals and nonprofit organizations.

Objective: To provide management and technical assistance through public or private organizations to existing or potential businessmen who are economically or socially disadvantaged; or who are located in areas of high concentration of unemployment; or who are participants in activities authorized by sections 7 (i) and 8a of the Small Business Act.

Contact: Assistant Administrator for Minority Small Business, Small Business Administration, 1441 L Street, Room 317, NW, Washington, DC 20416, 202-653-6407.

59.008 PHYSICAL DISASTER LOANS

Type of Assistance: Direct loans and guaranteed/insured loans up to $500,000.

Applicant Eligibility: Individuals.

Objective: To provide loans to restore, as nearly as possible, the living conditions of victims of physical-type disasters to predisaster condition.

Contact: Disaster Assistance Division, Small Business Administration, 1441 L Street, NW, Washington, DC 20416, 202-653-6879.

59.011 SMALL BUSINESS INVESTMENT COMPANIES

Type of Assistance: Direct loans and guaranteed/insured loans ranging from $50,000 to $35 million.

Applicant Eligibility: Individuals.

Objective: To make equity and venture capital available to the small business community with maximum use of private sector participation, and a minimum of government interference in the free market; to provide advisory services and counseling.

Contact: Director, Office of Investment, Small Business Administration, 1441 L Street, NW, Washington, DC 20416, 202-653-6584.

59.012   SMALL BUSINESS LOANS

Type of Assistance: Direct loans and guaranteed/insured loans ranging from $1,000 to $500,000.

Applicant Eligibility: Individuals.

Objective: To aid small businesses that are unable to obtain financing in the private credit marketplace, including agricultural enterprises. Funds may be used to construct, expand or convert facilities; to purchase building equipment or materials; or for working capital.

Contact: Director, Office of Business Loans, Small Business Administration, 1441 L Street, NW, Washington, DC 20416, 202-653-6570.

59.013   STATE AND LOCAL DEVELOPMENT
COMPANY LOANS

Type of Assistance: Guaranteed/insured loans up to $500,000.

Applicant Eligibility: Nonprofit organizations, state and local governments.

Objective: To make federal funds available to state and local development companies to provide long-term financing to small business concerns located in their areas. Both state and local development companies are corporations chartered for the purpose of promoting economic growth within specific areas.

Contact: Office of Economic Development, Small Business Administration, 1441 L Street, NW, Room 720, Washington, DC 20416, 202-653-6574.

59.016   BOND GUARANTEES FOR SURETY COMPANIES

Type of Assistance: Guaranteed/insured loans ranging from $2,000 to $1 million.

Applicant Eligibility: Individuals.

Objective: To encourage the commercial surety market to make surety bonds more available to small contractors unable for various reasons to obtain a bond without a guarantee.

Contact: Chief, Surety Bond Guarantee Branch, Small Business Administration, 4040 North Fairfax Drive, Arlington, VA 22203, 703-235-2907.

59.021   HANDICAPPED ASSISTANCE LOANS

Type of Assistance: Direct loans and guaranteed/insured loans ranging from $500 to $350,000.

Applicant Eligibility: Individuals.

Objective: To provide loans and loan guarantees for nonprofit sheltered workshops and other similar organizations to enable them to produce and provide marketable goods and services; and to assist in the establishment, acquisition or operation of a small business owned by handicapped individuals.

Contact: Director, Business Loans, Small Business Administration, 1441 L Street, NW, Washington, DC 20416, 202-653-6570.

59.030 SMALL BUSINESS ENERGY LOANS
Type of Assistance: Direct loans and guaranteed/insured loans (dollar amount not available).
Applicant Eligibility: Individuals.
Objective: To assist small business concerns to finance plant construction, expansion, conversion or start-up, and the acquisition of equipment facilities, machinery, supplies or materials to enable such concerns to manufacture, design, market, install or service specific energy measures.
Contact: Business Loans, Small Business Administration, 1441 L Street, NW, Washington, DC 20416, 202-653-6570.

59.031 SMALL BUSINESS POLLUTION CONTROL FINANCING GUARANTEE
Type of Assistance: Guaranteed/insured loans up to $5 million.
Applicant Eligibility: Individuals.
Objective: To help small businesses meet pollution control requirements and remain competitive.
Contact: Chief, Pollution Control Financing Branch, Office of Special Guarantees, Small Business Administration, 4040 North Fairfax Drive, Suite 500, Arlington, VA 22203, 703-235-2902.

59.032 OFFICE OF WOMEN'S BUSINESS OWNERSHIP
Type of Assistance: Grants ranging from $5,000 to $150,000.
Applicant Eligibility: State and local governments, organizations.
Objective: To develop effective business management skills of potentially successful women entrepreneurs in significant numbers, and to improve the business environment for women-owned businesses.
Contact: Director, Office of Special Training and Counseling, Office of Women's Business Ownership, Small Business Administration, 1441 L Street, NW, Washington, DC 20416, 202-653-8000.

59.036 CERTIFIED DEVELOPMENT COMPANY LOANS
Type of Assistance: Guaranteed/insured loans up to $500,000.
Applicant Eligibility: Incorporated companies.
Objective: To assist small business concerns by providing long-term financing through the sale of debentures of the Federal Financing Bank. Loans are for the acquisition of land and buildings, construction, expansion, renovation and modernization, and machinery and equipment.
Contact: Office of Economic Development, Small Business Administration, Room 720, 1441 L Street, NW, Washington, DC, 20416.

59.037 SMALL BUSINESS DEVELOPMENT CENTER
Type of Assistance: Grants ranging from $100,000 to $2,300,000.
Applicant Eligibility: State agencies, institutions of higher education.
Objective: To provide management counseling, training and technical assistance to the small business community through Small Business Development Centers (SBDCs).

Contact: Small Business Administration, Small Business Development Center, 1441 L Street, NW, Room 317, Washington, DC 20416.

59.038   VETERANS LOAN PROGRAM
Type of Assistance: Direct loans ranging from $1,000 to $350,000.
Applicant Eligibility: Eligible veterans.
Objective: To provide financial assistance to Vietnam-era and disabled veterans.
Contact: Director, Office of Business Loans, Small Business Administration, 1441 L Street, NW, Washington, DC, 20416, 202-653-6570.

SMITHSONIAN INSTITUTION

60.001 SMITHSONIAN INSTITUTION PROGRAMS IN BASIC RESEARCH IN COLLABORATION WITH SMITHSONIAN INSTITUTION STAFF
Type of Assistance: Grants up to $25,000 a year.
Applicant Eligibility: Individuals.
Objective: To make available to qualified investigators at various levels of educational accomplishment, the facilities, collections and professional staff of the Smithsonian.
Contact: Administrative Officer, Office of Fellowships and Grants, Smithsonian Institution, Room 3300, 955 L'Enfant Plaza, Washington, DC 20560, 202-287-3271.

60.007 MUSEUMS—ASSISTANCE AND ADVICE
Type of Assistance: Grants ranging from $1,000 to $40,000.
Applicant Eligibility: Individuals, nonprofit organizations, state and local governments.
Objective: To support the study of museum problems, to encourage training of museum personnel and to assist research in museum techniques, with emphasis on museum conservation.
Contact: Program Coordinator, National Museum Act, Arts and Industries Building, Room 3465, Smithsonian Institution, Washington, DC 20560, 202-357-2257.

60.013 SMITHSONIAN INSTITUTION TRAVELING EXHIBITION SERVICE
Type of Assistance: Use of property, facilities and equipment.
Applicant Eligibility: Individuals or groups.
Objective: To provide a public service by the circulation of exhibition on a wide range of subjects throughout the US and abroad. A broad range of exhibitions is available to museums of all sizes and character, art galleries and educational organizations and institutions. May be used for educational purposes only.
Contact: Associate Director for Administration, Smithsonian Institution Traveling Exhibition Service, Office of Museum Programs, Smithsonian Institution, Washington, DC 20560, 202-357-2800.

60.016 SMITHSONIAN SPECIAL FOREIGN CURRENCY GRANTS FOR MUSEUM PROGRAMS, SCIENTIFIC AND CULTURAL RESEARCH AND RELATED EDUCATIONAL ACTIVITIES
Type of Assistance: Grants and direct payments ranging from $3,000 to $50,000.

Applicant Eligibility: Individuals, nonprofit organizations, state and local governments.

Objective: To support the research activities of American institutions of higher learning through grants in countries where the US Treasury has determined that the United States holds currencies in excess of its needs. Grants in the form of a contract between the Smithsonian and the grantee American institution of higher learning are awarded for basic research in subjects of Smithsonian competence: anthropology, archaeology and related disciplines; systematic and environmental biology; astrophysics and earth sciences; and museum programs.

Contact: Program Manager, Smithsonian Foreign Currency Program, Office of Fellowships and Grants, Smithsonian Institution, Washington, DC 20560, 202-287-3321.

60.020 WOODROW WILSON INTERNATIONAL CENTER FOR SCHOLARS—FELLOWSHIPS AND GUEST SCHOLAR PROGRAMS

Type of Assistance: Grants (dollar amount not available).

Applicant Eligibility: Individuals.

Objective: The theme of the fellowship program is designed to accentuate aspects of Wilson's ideals and concerns for which he is perhaps best known—his search for international peace and his imaginative new approaches in meeting the pressing issues of his day—translated into current terms.

Contact: Assistant Director for Fellowships, Woodrow Wilson International Center for Scholars, Smithsonian Institution, Washington, DC 20560, 202-357-2841.

TENNESSEE VALLEY AUTHORITY

62.001   NATIONAL FERTILIZER DEVELOPMENT
Type of Assistance: Sale, exchange or donation of property and goods; use of property, facilities and equipment.
Applicant Eligibility: Land-grant colleges, fertilizer industry firms and farmers.
Objective: To develop improved, cheaper fertilizer products and processes and to improve US agriculture.
Contact: General Manager, Tennessee Valley Authority, Knoxville, TN 37902, 615-632-2101.

VETERANS ADMINISTRATION

DEPARTMENT OF MEDICINE AND SURGERY

64.005 GRANTS TO STATES FOR CONSTRUCTION OF STATE HOME FACILITIES

Type of Assistance: Grants ranging from $47,000 to $16,456,000.
Applicant Eligibility: State governments.
Objective: To assist states in the construction of state home facilities for furnishing domiciliary or nursing home care to veterans, and to expand, remodel or alter existing buildings for furnishing domiciliary, nursing home or hospital care to veterans in state veterans homes.
Contact: Assistant Chief Medical Director for Extended Care (182), Veterans Administration, Central Office, Washington, DC 20420, 202-389-3679.

64.014 VETERANS STATE DOMICILIARY CARE

Type of Assistance: Grants ranging from $3,947 to $1,490,580.
Applicant Eligibility: State governments.
Objective: To provide financial assistance to states furnishing domiciliary care to veterans in state veterans homes that meet the standards prescribed by the VA Administrator.
Contact: Assistant Chief Medical Director for Geriatrics Extended Care (182), Veterans Administration, Central Office, 810 Vermont Avenue, NW, Washington, DC 20420, 202-389-3679.

64.015 VETERANS STATE NURSING HOME CARE

Type of Assistance: Grants ranging from $49,283 to $2,835,260.
Applicant Eligibility: State governments.
Objective: To provide financial assistance to states furnishing nursing home care to veterans in the state veterans homes that meet the standards prescribed by the VA Administrator.
Contact: Assistant Chief Medical Director for Geriatrics Extended Care (182), Veterans Administration, Central Office, 810 Vermont Avenue, NW, Washington, DC 20420, 202-389-3670.

64.016 VETERANS STATE HOSPITAL CARE

Type of Assistance: Grants ranging from $41,817 to $1,478,806.
Applicant Eligibility: State governments.
Objective: To provide financial assistance to states furnishing hospital care to veterans in state veterans homes that meet the standards prescribed by the VA Administrator.
Contact: Assistant Chief Medical Director for Geriatrics Extended Care (182), Veterans Administration, State Home Program Coordinator, Washington, DC 20420, 202-389-3679.

64.023   HEALTH PROFESSIONAL SCHOLARSHIPS
Type of Assistance: Grants.
Applicant Eligibility: Individuals.
Objective: To assist in providing an adequate supply of professional nurses for the Veterans Administration and for the nation. Scholarships support students in nursing.
Contact: Veterans Administration Health Professional Scholarship Program (14N), Veterans Administration Central Office, 810 Vermont Avenue, NW, Washington, DC 20420, 202-389-3588, toll free 800-368-5896.

DEPARTMENT OF VETERANS BENEFITS

64.100   AUTOMOBILES AND ADAPTIVE EQUIPMENT FOR CERTAIN DISABLED VETERANS AND MEMBERS OF THE ARMED FORCES
Type of Assistance: Direct payments up to $5,000.
Applicant Eligibility: Individuals.
Objective: To provide financial assistance to certain disabled veterans toward the purchase price of an automobile or other conveyance, and additional assistance for adaptive equipment deemed necessary to ensure that the eligible person will be able to operate or make use of the automobile or other conveyance.
Contact: Veterans Administration, Central Office, 810 Vermont Avenue, NW, Washington, DC 20420, 202-389-2356.

64.101   BURIAL EXPENSES ALLOWANCE FOR VETERANS
Type of Assistance: Direct payments up to $1,100.
Applicant Eligibility: Individuals.
Objective: To provide a monetary allowance not to exceed $300 toward the funeral and burial expenses plus $150 for plot or interment expenses if not buried in a national cemetery. If death is service-connected, $1,100 or the amount authorized to be paid in the case of a federal employee whose death occurs as a result of an injury sustained in the performance of duty, is payable for funeral and burial expenses. In addition to the statutory burial allowance, the cost of transporting the remains from place of death to site of burial is paid by VA if death occurs in a VA facility.
Contact: Veterans Administration, Central Office, 810 Vermont Avenue, NW, Washington, DC 20420, 202-389-2356.

64.102   COMPENSATION FOR SERVICE-CONNECTED DEATHS FOR VETERANS' DEPENDENTS
Type of Assistance: Direct payments up to $121 monthly.
Applicant Eligibility: Individuals.
Objective: To compensate surviving widows, widowers, children and dependent parents for the death of any veteran who died before January 1, 1957, because of a service-connected disability.

Contact: Veterans Administration, Central Office, 810 Vermont Avenue, NW, Washington, DC 20420, 202-389-2356.

64.103 LIFE INSURANCE FOR VETERANS
Type of Assistance: Direct loans and insurance (dollar amount not available).
Applicant Eligibility: Individuals.
Objective: To provide life insurance protection for veterans of World War I, World War II, the Korean conflict and service-disabled veterans of the Vietnam conflict, and to provide mortgage protection life insurance under a group policy for those disabled veterans who are given a VA grant to secure specially adapted housing.
Contact: Veterans Administration Center, P.O. Box 8079, Philadelphia, PA 19101, 215-438-5225.

64.104 PENSION FOR NONSERVICE-CONNECTED DISABILITY FOR VETERANS
Type of Assistance: Direct payments up to $5,709 annually for a veteran, $7,478 for a veteran with one dependent, plus $968 for each additional dependent.
Applicant Eligibility: Individuals.
Objective: To assist wartime veterans in need whose nonservice-connected disabilities are permanent and total and prevent them from following a substantially gainful occupation.
Contact: Veterans Administration, Central Office, 810 Vermont Avenue, NW, Washington, DC 20420, 202-389-2356.

64.105 PENSION TO VETERANS' SURVIVING SPOUSES AND CHILDREN
Type of Assistance: Direct payments up to $3,825 annually, and $5,011 for a surviving spouse and one child plus $968 for each additional child.
Applicant Eligibility: Individuals.
Objective: To provide a partial means of support for needy widows or widowers, and children of deceased wartime veterans whose deaths were not due to service.
Contact: Veterans Administration, Central Office, 810 Vermont Avenue, NW, Washington, DC 20420, 202-389-2356.

64.106 SPECIALLY ADAPTED HOUSING FOR DISABLED VETERANS
Type of Assistance: Direct payments up to $35,000.
Applicant Eligibility: Individuals.
Objective: To assist certain totally disabled veterans in acquiring suitable housing units, with special fixtures and facilities made necessary by the nature of the veterans' disabilities.
Contact: Veterans Administration Center, PO Box 8079, Philadelphia, PA 19101, 215-438-5225.

64.109 VETERANS COMPENSATION FOR SERVICE-CONNECTED DISABILITY
Type of Assistance: Direct payments up to $3,697 a month.
Applicant Eligibility: Individuals.
Objective: To compensate veterans for disabilities due to military service according to the average impairment in earning capacity such disability would cause in civilian occupations.
Contact: Veterans Administration, Central Office, 810 Vermont Avenue, NW, Washington, DC 20420, 202-389-2356.

64.110 VETERANS DEPENDENCY AND INDEMNITY COMPENSATION FOR SERVICE-CONNECTED DEATH
Type of Assistance: Direct payments up to $1,305 monthly.
Applicant Eligibility: Individuals.
Objective: To compensate surviving widows or widowers, children and parents for the death of any veteran who died on or after January 1, 1957, because of a service-connected disability.
Contact: Veterans Administration, Central Office, 810 Vermont Avenue, NW, Washington, DC 20420, 202-389-2356.

64.111 VETERANS EDUCATIONAL ASSISTANCE (GI BILL)
Type of Assistance: Direct payments up to $376-plus monthly.
Applicant Eligibility: Individuals.
Objective: To make service in the Armed Forces more attractive by extending benefits of a higher education to qualified young persons who might not otherwise be able to afford such an education; and to restore lost educational opportunities to those whose education was interrupted by active duty after January 31, 1955, and before January 1, 1977.
Contact: Veterans Administration, Central Office, 810 Vermont Avenue, NW, Washington, DC 20420, 202-389-2356.

64.114 VETERANS HOUSING— GUARANTEED AND INSURED LOANS
Type of Assistance: Guaranteed insured loans ranging from $39,000 to $78,600.
Applicant Eligibility: Individuals.
Objective: To assist veterans, certain service personnel and certain unmarried widows or widowers of veterans in obtaining credit for the purchase, construction or improvement of homes on more liberal terms than are generally available to nonveterans.
Contact: Veterans Administration, Central Office, 810 Vermont Avenue, NW, Washington, DC 20420, 202-389-2356.

64.116 VOCATIONAL REHABILITATION FOR DISABLED VETERANS
Type of Assistance: Direct payments and direct loans up to $310-plus monthly.

Applicant Eligibility: Individuals.
Objective: To train veterans for the purpose of restoring employability to the extent consistent with the degree of a service-connected disability.
Contact: Veterans Administration, Central Office, 810 Vermont Avenue, NW, Washington, DC 20420, 202-389-2356.

64.117 DEPENDENTS EDUCATIONAL ASSISTANCE

Type of Assistance: Direct payments up to $376 monthly.
Applicant Eligibility: Individuals.
Objective: To provide partial support to those seeking to advance their education who are qualifying spouses, surviving spouses or children of deceased or disabled veterans, or of service personnel who have been listed for a total of more than 90 days as missing in action or as prisoners of war.
Contact: Veterans Administration, Central Office, 810 Vermont Avenue, NW, Washington, DC 20420, 202-389-2356.

64.118 VETERANS HOUSING—
DIRECT LOANS FOR DISABLED VETERANS

Type of Assistance: Direct loans up to $33,000.
Applicant Eligibility: Individuals.
Objective: To provide certain severely disabled veterans with direct housing credit and to supplement grants authorized to assist the veterans in acquiring suitable housing units with special features or movable facilities made necessary by the nature of their disabilities.
Contact: Veterans Administration, Central Office, 810 Vermont Avenue, NW, Washington, DC 20420, 202-389-2356.

64.119 VETERANS HOUSING—
MANUFACTURED HOME LOANS

Type of Assistance: Guaranteed/insured loans ranging from $16,490 to $27,450.
Applicant Eligibility: Individuals.
Objective: To assist veterans, service persons and certain unremarried widows or widowers of veterans in obtaining credit for the purchase of a mobile home on more liberal terms than are available to nonveterans.
Contact: Veterans Administration, Central Office, 810 Vermont Avenue, NW, Washington, DC 20420, 202-389-2356.

64.120 POST-VIETNAM ERA VETERANS EDUCATIONAL
ASSISTANCE

Type of Assistance: Direct payments up to $8,100.
Applicant Eligibility: Individuals.
Objective: To provide educational assistance to persons first entering the Armed Forces after December 31, 1976; to assist young persons in obtaining an education they might otherwise not be able to afford; and to promote and assist the all-volunteer military program of the

United States by attracting qualified persons to serve in the Armed Forces.

Contact: Veterans Administration, Central Office, 810 Vermont Avenue, NW, Washington, DC 20420, 202-389-2356.

64.122 VOCATIONAL REHABILITATION FOR SERVICE-DISABLED VETERANS RECEIVING UNEMPLOYABILITY VA COMPENSATION

Type of Assistance: Direct payments (dollar amount not available).
Applicant Eligibility: Individuals.
Objective: To enable eligible veterans to become employable and to obtain and maintain employment consistent with their abilities.
Contact: Veterans Administration, Central Office, Washington, DC 20420.

64.123 VOCATIONAL TRAINING FOR CERTAIN VETERANS RECEIVING VA PENSION

Type of Assistance: Direct payments (dollar amount not available).
Applicant Eligibility: Individuals.
Objective: To assist new pension recipients to resume and maintain gainful employment by providing vocational training and other services.
Contact: Veterans Administration, Central Office, Washington, DC 20402.

DEPARTMENT OF MEMORIAL AFFAIRS

64.203 STATE CEMETERY GRANTS

Type of Assistance: Grants from $60,000 to $1,600,000.
Applicant Eligibility: States.
Objective: To assist states in the establishment, expansion and improvement of veterans' cemeteries.
Contact: State Cemetery Grants (40G), Department of Memorial Affairs, Veterans Administration, 810 Vermont Avenue, NW, Washington, DC 20402, 202-389-2313.

ENVIRONMENTAL PROTECTION AGENCY

OFFICE OF AIR, NOISE AND RADIATION

66.001   AIR POLLUTION CONTROL PROGRAM SUPPORT
Type of Assistance: Grants ranging from $7,025 to $6,449,000.
Applicant Eligibility: State and local governments.
Objective: To assist state, municipal, intermunicipal and interstate agencies in planning, developing, establishing, improving, and maintaining adequate programs for prevention and control of air pollution or implementation of national primary and secondary air quality standards.
Contact: Control Programs Development Division, Office of Air Quality Planning and Standards, Office of Air, Noise and Radiation, Environmental Protection Agency, Research Triangle Park, NC 27711, 919-541-5526.

66.003   AIR POLLUTION CONTROL MANPOWER TRAINING
Type of Assistance: Grants ranging from $45,000 to $55,000.
Applicant Eligibility: Nonprofit organizations, state and local governments.
Objective: To develop career-oriented personnel qualified to work in pollution abatement and control. Grants are awarded for maintenance of environmental training programs; to increase the number of adequately trained pollution control and abatement personnel; and to upgrade the level of training among state and local environmental control personnel.
Contact: Control Programs Development Division, Office of Air Quality Planning and Standards, Office of Air, Noise and Radiation, Environmental Protection Agency, Research Triangle Park, NC 27711, 919-541-2401.

OFFICE OF WATER

66.418   CONSTRUCTION GRANTS FOR WASTEWATER TREATMENT WORKS
Type of Assistance: Grants ranging from $675 to $290,800,000.
Applicant Eligibility: State and local governments.
Objective: To assist and serve as an incentive in construction of municipal sewage treatment works which are required to meet state and federal water quality standards.
Contact: Director, Municipal Construction Division, WH-547, Office

of Water Program Operations, Environmental Protection Agency, Washington, DC 20460, 202-382-5859.

66.419   WATER POLLUTION CONTROL—STATE AND INTERSTATE PROGRAM SUPPORT

Type of Assistance: Grants ranging from $8,000 to $2,870,000.

Applicant Eligibility: State and local governments.

Objective: To assist state and interstate agencies in establishing and maintaining adequate measures for prevention and control of water pollution.

Contact: Director, Analysis and Evaluation Division, Office of Water Regulations and Standards, Environmental Protection Agency, Washington, DC 20460, 202-382-7160.

66.432   STATE PUBLIC WATER SYSTEM SUPERVISION

Type of Assistance: Grants ranging from $94,900 to $1,774,300.

Applicant Eligibility: State governments.

Objective: To foster development of state program plans and programs to assist in implementing and enforcing the Safe Drinking Water Act.

Contact: Office of Drinking Water, Environmental Protection Agency, Washington, DC 20460, 202-382-5529.

66.433   STATE UNDERGROUND WATER SOURCE PROTECTION

Type of Assistance: Grants from $36,400 to $597,300.

Applicant Eligibility: State governments.

Objective: To foster development and implementation of underground injection control programs under the Safe Drinking Water Act.

Contact: Ground Water Protection Branch, Office of Water, Environmental Protection Agency, 401 M Street, SW, Washington, DC 20460, 202-382-5530.

66.438   CONSTRUCTION MANAGEMENT ASSISTANCE

Type of Assistance: Grants ranging from $493,000 to $10,473,744.

Applicant Eligibility: State governments.

Objective: To assist and serve as an incentive in the process of delegating to the states a maximum amount of authority for conducting day-to-day matters related to the management of the construction grant program. An overriding goal is to eliminate unnecessary duplicative reviews and functions.

Contact: Chief, Delegation Management, Municipal Construction Division, WH-547, Office of Water Programs Operations, Environmental Protection Agency, Washington, DC 20460, 202-382-7359.

66.454   WATER QUALITY MANAGEMENT PLANNING

Type of Assistance: Grants ranging from $100,000 to $2,500,000.

Applicant Eligibility: State Water Quality Management Agencies.

Objective: To assist states in carrying out water quality management planning.

Contact: Director, Analysis and Evaluation Division, Office of Water

Regulation, Office of Water, Environmental Protection Agency, Washington, DC 20460, 202-382-7160.

66.455 CONSTRUCTION GRANTS FOR WASTE WATER TREATMENT WORKS FOR COMBINED SEWER OVERFLOWS

Type of Assistance: Project grants ranging from $254,000 to $15 million.

Applicant Eligibility: State and local governments.

Objective: To assist and serve as incentive in construction of municipal waste water treatment works for abatement of combined sewer overflow pollution in order to meet state and federal water quality standards for marine bays and estuaries.

Contact: Director, Municipal Facilities Division, Office of Water Program Operations, Environmental Protection Agency, Washington, DC 20460, 202-382-7260.

66.456 COMPREHENSIVE ESTUARINE MANAGEMENT

Type of Assistance: Project grants ranging from $5,000 to $765,000.

Applicant Eligibility: States, public or private nonprofit organizations.

Objective: To assist water pollution control agencies in developing programs to protect and restore coastal resources in priority estuaries.

Contact: Chief, Technical Support Division, Office of Marine and Estuarine Protection, WH-566 M, Washington, DC 20460, 202-755-2927.

OFFICE OF RESEARCH AND DEVELOPMENT

66.500 ENVIRONMENTAL PROTECTION— CONSOLIDATED RESEARCH

Type of Assistance: Grants ranging from $4,534 to $650,000.

Applicant Eligibility: Individuals, nonprofit organizations, state and local governments.

Objective: To support research to determine the environmental effects and hence the control requirements associated with energy; to identify, develop and demonstrate necessary pollution control techniques; and to evaluate the economic and social consequences of alternative strategies for pollution control of energy systems. Also, to support research to explore and develop strategies and mechanisms for those in the economic, social, governmental and environmental systems to use in environmental management.

Contact: Director, Research Grants Staff, RD-675, Environmental Protection Agency, Washington, DC 20460, 202-382-7473.

66.501 AIR POLLUTION CONTROL RESEARCH

Type of Assistance: Grants ranging from $11,000 to $226,031.

Applicant Eligibility: Individuals, nonprofit organizations, state and local governments.

Objective: To support and promote research and development projects relating to the causes, effects, extent, prevention and control of air pollution.

Contact: Director, Research Grants Staff, RD-675, Office of Research and Development, Environmental Protection Agency, Washington, DC 20460, 202-382-7473.

66.502 PESTICIDES CONTROL RESEARCH

Type of Assistance: Grants averaging $75,000.

Applicant Eligibility: Individuals, nonprofit organizations, state and local governments.

Objective: To support and promote the coordination of research projects relating to human and ecological effects from pesticides, pesticide degradation products and alternatives to pesticides.

Contact: Director, Research Grants Staff, RD-675, Office of Research and Development, Environmental Protection Agency, Washington, DC 20460, 202-382-7473.

66.504 SOLID WASTE DISPOSAL RESEARCH

Type of Assistance: Grants ranging from $32,392 to $400,000.

Applicant Eligibility: Individuals, nonprofit organizations, state and local governments.

Objective: To support and promote the coordination of research and development in the area of collection, storage, utilization, salvage or final disposal of solid waste.

Contact: Director, Research Grants Staff, RD-675, Office of Research and Development, Environmental Protection Agency, Washington, DC 20460, 202-382-7473.

66.505 WATER POLLUTION CONTROL—RESEARCH, DEVELOPMENT AND DEMONSTRATION

Type of Assistance: Grants ranging from $6,384 to $370,000.

Applicant Eligibility: Individuals, nonprofit organizations, state and local governments.

Objective: To support and promote the coordination and acceleration of research, development and demonstration projects relating to the causes, effects, extent, prevention, reduction and elimination of water pollution.

Contact: Director, Research Grants Staff, RD-675, Office of Research and Development, Environmental Protection Agency, Washington, DC 20460, 202-382-7473.

66.506 SAFE DRINKING WATER RESEARCH AND DEMONSTRATION

Type of Assistance: Grants ranging from $2,000 to $1 million.

Applicant Eligibility: Individuals, nonprofit organizations, state and local governments.

Objective: To conduct research relating to the causes, diagnosis, treatment, control and prevention of physical and mental diseases and other impairments resulting directly or indirectly from contaminants in water;

and to the provision of a dependably safe supply of drinking water; to develop and demonstrate any project that will show a new or improved method, approach or technology for providing a dependably safe supply of drinking water to the public or will investigate and demonstrate health implications involved in the reclamation, recycle and reuse of waste waters for drinking, and/or the preparation of safe and acceptable drinking water.

Contact: Office of Research Grants, RD-675, Environmental Protection Agency, Washington DC 20460, 202-382-7473.

66.507 TOXIC SUBSTANCES RESEARCH

Type of Assistance: Grants averaging $95,000.

Applicant Eligibility: Individuals, nonprofit organizations, state and local governments.

Objective: To support and promote the coordination of research projects relating to the effects, extent, prevention and control of toxic chemical substances or mixtures.

Contact: Director, Research Grants Staff, RD-675, Environmental Protection Agency, Washington, DC 20460, 202-382-7473.

OFFICE OF ADMINISTRATION

66.600 ENVIRONMENTAL PROTECTION CONSOLIDATED GRANTS—PROGRAM SUPPORT

Type of Assistance: Grants (dollar amount not available).

Applicant Eligibility: State governments.

Objective: To enable states to coordinate and manage environmental approaches to their pollution control activities. Consolidated grants are alternate grant delivery mechanisms. These mechanisms provide for consolidation, into one grant instrument, those grants awarded separately to states for management of environmental protection activities including but not limited to air pollution control, water pollution control and solid waste management.

Contact: Grants Administration Division, PM 216, Environmental Protection Agency, Washington, DC 20460, 202-382-5297.

66.603 LOAN GUARANTEES FOR CONSTRUCTION OF TREATMENT WORKS

Type of Assistance: Guaranteed/insured loans (dollar amount not available).

Applicant Eligibility: State and local governments.

Objective: To assist and serve as an incentive in construction of municipal sewage treatment works which are required to meet state and federal water quality standards; and ensure that inability to borrow necessary funds from other sources on reasonable terms does not prevent the construction of any waste water treatment works for which a grant has been or will be awarded.

Contact: Grants Administration Division, PM 216, Environmental Protection Agency, Washington, DC 20460, 202-382-5240.

OFFICE OF PESTICIDES AND TOXIC SUBSTANCES

66.700 PESTICIDES ENFORCEMENT PROGRAM
Type of Assistance: Grants ranging from $15,000 to $563,000.
Applicant Eligibility: State governments.
Objective: To assist states in developing and maintaining comprehensive pesticide enforcement programs; sponsoring cooperative surveillance, monitoring and analytical procedures; training applicators in proper pesticide practices; and encouraging regulatory activities within the states.
Contact: Director, Office of Compliance Monitoring, Office of Pesticides and Toxic Substances, EN-342, Environmental Protection Agency, Washington, DC 20460, 202-382-3807.

66.701 TOXIC SUBSTANCES COMPLIANCE MONITORING COOPERATIVE AGREEMENTS
Type of Assistance: Project grants ranging from $100,000 to $150,000.
Applicant Eligibility: States.
Objective: To assist states in developing and maintaining comprehensive toxic substance enforcement programs, and to sponsor cooperative surveillance and encourage regulatory activities within states.
Contact: Director, Office of Compliance Monitoring, Office of Pesticides and Toxic Substances, EN-342, EPA, Washington, DC 20460, 202-382-3807.

66.702 ASBESTOS HAZARDS ABATEMENT (SCHOOLS) ASSISTANCE
Type of Assistance: Project grants, direct loans (dollar amount not available).
Applicant Eligibility: Local governments.
Objective: To create a program of information distribution, technical and scientific assistance, and financial support to local education agencies.
Contact: EPA, TS-788A, 401 M Street, SW, Washington, DC 20460, 202-382-3949.

OFFICE OF SOLID WASTE AND EMERGENCY RESPONSE

66.801 HAZARDOUS WASTE MANAGEMENT FINANCIAL ASSISTANCE TO STATES
Type of Assistance: Grants ranging from $208,000 to $4,160,000.
Applicant Eligibility: State and local governments.
Objective: To assist state governments in the development and imple-

mentation of an authorized hazardous waste management program to control the generation, transportation, treatment, storage and disposal of hazardous wastes.
Contact: Grants Administration Division, PM-216, Environmental Protection Agency, Washington, DC 20460, 202-382-2210.

66.802 HAZARDOUS SUBSTANCE RESPONSE TRUST FUND
Type of Assistance: Grants ranging from $35,000 to $19,350,000.
Applicant Eligibility: States.
Objective: To undertake remedial planning and remedial implementation actions to clean up the hazardous waste sites that are found to pose the most imminent hazards to human health.
Contact: Hazardous Site-Control Division, Office of Emergency and Remedial Response, Environmental Protection Agency, Washington, DC 20460, 202-382-2443.

66.804 STATE UNDERGROUND STORAGE TANKS PROGRAM
Type of Assistance: Project grants (dollar amount not available).
Applicant Eligibility: States.
Objective: To assist states in development and implementation of their own underground storage tank programs to operate in lieu of the federal program.
Contact: Director, Underground Storage Tank Program, OSWER, State Programs Branch, Environmental Protection Agency, 401 M Street, SW, Washington, DC 20460, 202-382-2210.

NATIONAL GALLERY OF ART

68.001   NATIONAL GALLERY OF ART EXTENSION SERVICE
Type of Assistance: Use of property, facilities and equipment.
Applicant Eligibility: Schools, colleges, libraries, clubs, museums, community organizations and individuals.
Objective: To provide educational material including slide programs, videocassettes and motion pictures free of charge except for transportation costs to schools, colleges and libraries across the nation.
Contact: Department of Extension Programs, National Gallery of Art, Washington, DC 20565, 202-737-4215.

OVERSEAS PRIVATE INVESTMENT CORPORATION

70.002 FOREIGN INVESTMENT GUARANTEES
Type of Assistance: Guaranteed/insured loans $1,750,000 to $50 million.
Applicant Eligibility: Individuals.
Objective: To guarantee loans and other investments made by eligible U.S. investors in developing friendly countries and areas.
Contact: Information Officer, Overseas Private Investment Corporation, Washington, DC 20527, 202-653-2800.

70.003 FOREIGN INVESTMENT INSURANCE
Type of Assistance: Insurance ranging from $4,000 to $100 million.
Applicant Eligibility: Individuals.
Objective: To insure investments of eligible US investors in developing friendly countries and areas, against the risks of inconvertibility, expropriation, and war, revolution and insurrection.
Contact: Information Officer, Overseas Private Investment Corporation, Washington, DC 20527, 202-653-2800.

70.004 PRE-INVESTMENT ASSISTANCE
Type of Assistance: Direct payments ranging from $1,000 to $100,000.
Applicant Eligibility: Individuals.
Objective: To initiate and support through financial participation the identification, assessment, survey and promotion of private investment opportunities.
Contact: Information Officer, Overseas Private Investment Corporation, Washington, DC 20527, 202-653-2800.

70.005 DIRECT INVESTMENT LOANS
Type of Assistance: Direct loans ranging from $100,000 to $4 million.
Applicant Eligibility: Individuals.
Objective: To make loans for projects in developing countries sponsored by or significantly involving US small businesses or cooperatives.
Contact: Information Officer, Overseas Private Investment Corporation, Washington, DC 20527, 202-653-2800.

ACTION

72.001 THE FOSTER GRANDPARENT PROGRAM
Type of Assistance: Grants ranging from $2,000 to $1,321,444.
Applicant Eligibility: Nonprofit organizations, state and local governments.
Objective: To provide part-time volunteer service opportunities for low-income persons 60 years of age and over and to render supportive person-to-person services in health, education, welfare and related settings in children having special or exceptional needs, through development of community-oriented, cost-shared projects.
Contact: Chief, Foster Grandparent Program, ACTION, 806 Connecticut Avenue, NW, Washington, DC 20525, 202-634-9349.

72.002 RETIRED SENIOR VOLUNTEER PROGRAM
Type of Assistance: Grants ranging from $10,000 to $450,000.
Applicant Eligibility: Nonprofit organizations, state and local governments.
Objective: To establish a recognized role in the community and a meaningful life in retirement by developing a wide variety of community volunteer service opportunities for persons 60 years of age or over through development of community-oriented, cost-shared projects.
Contact: Chief, Retired Senior Volunteer Program, ACTION, 806 Connecticut Avenue, NW, Washington, DC 20525, 202-634-9353.

72.005 SERVICE-LEARNING PROGRAMS
Type of Assistance: Grants averaging $20,000.
Applicant Eligibility: State or local governments, private nonprofit organizations.
Objective: To assist secondary and postsecondary educators and nonprofit organization educators to begin new and improve existing local student service-learning programs which provide services to the poverty community.
Contact: ACTION, 806 Connecticut Avenue, NW, Washington, DC 20525, 202-634-9410.

72.008 THE SENIOR COMPANION PROGRAM
Type of Assistance: Grants ranging from $2,000 to $335,000.
Applicant Eligibility: State and local governments.
Objective: To provide volunteer opportunities for low-income older people that enhance their ability to remain active and provide critically needed community services; to play a critical role in providing long-term care by assisting adults, primarily older persons with mental, emotional and physical impairments, to achieve and maintain their

fullest potential to be healthy and to manage their lives independently through development of community-oriented, cost-shared projects.
Contact: Chief, Senior Companion Program, ACTION, 806 Connecticut Avenue, NW, Washington, DC 20524, 202-634-9351.

72.010 MINI-GRANT PROGRAM
Type of Assistance: Grants ranging from $500 to $15,000.
Applicant Eligibility: State and local governments.
Objective: To provide money to local, public and private nonprofit organizations for the purpose of mobilizing relatively large numbers of part-time, uncompensated volunteers to work on human, social and environmental needs, particularly those related to poverty.
Contact: National Mini-Grant Program Manager, Office of Volunteer Liaison, Room M-207, ACTION, 806 Connecticut Avenue, NW, Washington, DC 20525, 202-254-8079.

72.011 STATE OFFICE OF VOLUNTARY CITIZEN PARTICIPATION
Type of Assistance: Grants up to $100,000.
Applicant Eligibility: State governments.
Objective: To provide grants to states to establish and/or strengthen offices of volunteer services to improve opportunities for volunteer efforts concerned with human, social and environmental needs, particularly those related to poverty.
Contact: Director, Office of Voluntary Citizen Participation, ACTION, Suite M-207, 806 Connecticut Avenue, NW, Washington, DC 20525, 800-424-8867.

72.012 VOLUNTEER DEMONSTRATION PROGRAM
Type of Assistance: Grants ranging from $8,575 to $193,248.
Applicant Eligibility: Nonprofit organizations, state and local governments.
Objective: To strengthen and supplement efforts to meet a broad range of human, social and environmental needs, particularly those related to poverty, by encouraging and enabling persons from all walks of life and from all age groups to perform constructive volunteer service; to test or demonstrate new or improved volunteer delivery systems or methods; to encourage wider volunteer participation, particularly on a short-term basis; and to identify segments of the poverty community that could benefit from volunteer efforts.
Contact: Policy Development Division, Office of Policy and Planning, ACTION, 806 Connecticut Avenue, NW, Washington, DC 20525, 202-634-9308.

72.013 TECHNICAL ASSISTANCE PROGRAM
Type of Assistance: Grants ranging from $5,000 to $30,000.
Applicant Eligibility: State and local governments, and nonprofit organizations.
Objective: To increase the capability of small voluntary organizations

to respond to the training, technical assistance and management needs of volunteers and organizations undertaking voluntary efforts; to stimulate capacity-building of grass roots organizations with volunteer components; and to develop and exchange materials and information related to volunteering.

Contact: National Program Manager, Office of Volunteer Liaison, ACTION, Room 207, 806 Connecticut Avenue, NW, Washington, DC 20525, 800-424-8867. (In Washington, DC, 202-254-8079.)

NUCLEAR REGULATORY COMMISSION

77.003 ENHANCE TECHNOLOGY TRANSFER AND DISSEMINATION OF NUCLEAR ENERGY PROCESS AND SAFETY INFORMATION

Type of Assistance: Grants ranging from $5,000 to $15,000.

Applicant Eligibility: Public and private nonprofit organizations, state and local governments.

Objective: To stimulate research to provide a technological base for the safety assessment of system and subsystem technologies used in nuclear power applications; to increase public understanding of nuclear safety; to enlarge the fund of theoretical and practical knowledge and technical information; and to enhance the protection of the public health and safety.

Contact: Office of Administration, Division of Contracts, Office of Nuclear Regulatory Research, Nuclear Regulatory Commission, Washington, DC 20555, 301-492-4294.

US DEPARTMENT OF ENERGY

81.004 UNIVERSITY-LABORATORY COOPERATIVE PROGRAM

Type of Assistance: Grants; use of property, facilities and equipment.
Applicant Eligibility: Individuals and faculties at institutions of higher education.
Objective: To provide college and university science and engineering faculty and students with energy-related training and experience in areas of energy research at DOE facilities.
Contact: Director, University and Industry Division, Office of Energy Research, Department of Energy, Washington, DC 20585, 202-252-6833.

81.011 UNIVERSITY REACTOR SHARING AND FUEL ASSISTANCE

Type of Assistance: Sale, exchange or donation of property; grants ranging from $1,200 to $40,800.
Applicant Eligibility: Private and public institutions of higher education.
Objective: To support the fabrication and use of nuclear fuel for university research and training reactors in order to help ensure the continued conduct of nuclear research, development and training activities by educational institutions.
Contact: Division of University and Industry Programs, Office of Energy Research, Department of Energy, Washington, DC 20585, 202-252-6833.

81.022 USED ENERGY-RELATED LABORATORY EQUIPMENT GRANTS

Type of Assistance: Sale, exchange or donation of property and goods.
Applicant Eligibility: Nonprofit educational institutions of higher learning and technical institutions or museums.
Objective: To assist US institutions of higher education in the equipment of their energy and energy-related science engineering laboratories for energy-related instructional purposes.
Contact: University and Industry Programs Division, Office of Field Operations Management, Department of Energy, Washington, DC 20585, 202-252-6833.

81.036 ENERGY-RELATED INVENTIONS

Type of Assistance: Use of property, facilities and equipment, and grants averaging $70,000.
Applicant Eligibility: Individuals and nonprofit organizations.
Objective: To encourage innovation in developing nonnuclear energy technology by providing assistance to individual inventors and small

business research and development companies in the development of promising energy-related inventions.
Contact: NBS Office of Energy-Related Inventions, National Bureau of Standards, Washington, DC 20234, 301-921-3694.

81.041 STATE ENERGY CONSERVATION
Type of Assistance: Grants ranging from $101,700 to $1,502,200.
Applicant Eligibility: State governments.
Objective: To promote the conservation of energy and reduce the rate of growth of energy demand by authorizing DOE to establish procedures and guidelines for the development and implementation of specific state energy conservation programs and to provide federal financial and technical assistance to states in support of such programs.
Contact: Chief, State Programs Branch, Department of Energy, CE-24, Forrestal Building, 1000 Independence Avenue, SW, Washington, DC 20585, 202-252-8295.

81.042 WEATHERIZATION ASSISTANCE FOR LOW-INCOME PERSONS
Type of Assistance: Grants averaging $3,600,000.
Applicant Eligibility: State and local governments.
Objective: To insulate the dwellings of low-income persons, particularly the elderly and handicapped, in order to conserve needed energy and to aid those persons least able to afford higher utility costs.
Contact: Weatherization Assistance Program, CE-25, Conservation and Energy, Department of Energy, Forrestal Building, 1000 Independence Avenue, SW, Washington, DC 20585, 202-252-2204.

81.049 BASIC ENERGY SCIENCES, HIGH ENERGY/ NUCLEAR PHYSICS, MAGNETIC FUSION ENERGY, HEALTH & ENVIRONMENTAL RESEARCH, PROGRAM ANALYSIS AND FIELD OPERATIONS MANAGEMENT
Type of Assistance: Grants ranging from $10,000 to $2 million.
Applicant Eligibility: Individuals.
Objective: To provide financial support for fundamental research in the basic sciences and advanced technological concepts and assessments in fields related to energy.
Contact: Office of Energy Research, Department of Energy, MailStop G-256, Washington, DC 20545, 301-353-4946.

81.050 ENERGY EXTENSION SERVICE
Type of Assistance: Grants averaging $168,421.
Applicant Eligibility: State governments.
Objective: To encourage individuals and small establishments to reduce energy consumption and convert to alternative energy sources; and to assist in building a credible, nonduplicative, state-planned and -operated energy outreach program responsive to local needs.
Contact: State Programs Branch, Department of Energy, CE-24, For-

restal Building, 1000 Independence Avenue, SW, Washington, DC 20585, 202-252-8295.

81.052 ENERGY CONSERVATION FOR INSTITUTIONAL BUILDINGS

Type of Assistance: Grants ranging from $150,000 to $1 million.
Applicant Eligibility: Nonprofit organizations, state and local governments.
Objective: To provide grants to states and to public and private nonprofit schools, hospitals, units of local government, and public care institutions to identify and implement energy conservation maintenance and operating procedures, and, for schools and hospitals only, to acquire energy conservation measures to reduce consumption.
Contact: Institutional Buildings Conservation Programs, CE, Room 26, 5G070, Department of Energy, Washington, DC 20585, 202-252-2198.

81.056 COAL LOAN GUARANTEES

Type of Assistance: Guaranteed/insured loans up to $30 million.
Applicant Eligibility: Individuals.
Objective: To encourage and assist small and medium-sized coal producers to increase production of underground low-sulfur coal and to enhance competition in the coal industry.
Contact: Project Manager, Office of Coal Loan Guarantee Programs, Department of Energy, Room C-156, Germantown, MD 20545, 301-353-4348.

81.057 UNIVERSITY COAL RESEARCH

Type of Assistance: Grants up to $175,000, from three to five years.
Applicant Eligibility: Nonprofit organizations, state and local governments.
Objective: To improve scientific and technical understanding of the fundamental processes involved in the conversion and utilization of coal; to furnish technical support for the ongoing and developing coal conversion process; to produce clean fuels in an environmentally acceptable manner; and to develop new approaches to the design of future coal conversion and utilization technologies.
Contact: Office of Technical Coordination, Fossil Energy, Department of Energy, Washington, DC 20545, 301-353-2786.

81.063 OFFICE OF MINORITY ECONOMIC IMPACT LOANS

Type of Assistance: Loans ranging from $1,000 to $25,000.
Applicant Eligibility: Minority business enterprises.
Objective: To provide direct loans to minority business enterprises to assist them in defraying bid and proposal costs they would incur in participating in Department of energy research, development, demonstration and contact activities.
Contact: Office of Minority Economic Impact, MI-3.2, Department

of Energy, Room 5B-110, Forrestal Building, 1000 Independence Avenue, SW, Washington, DC 20585, 202-252-8383.

81.065   NUCLEAR WASTE DISPOSAL SITING
Type of Assistance: Grants and direct payments ranging from $200,000 to $1 million.
Applicant Eligibility: Individuals, profit and nonprofit organizations, state and local governments.
Objective: To provide for the development of repositories for the disposal of high-level radioactive waste and spent nuclear fuel.
Contact: Office of Civilian Radioactive Nuclear Waste Management, 202-252-1116.

81.076   INDIAN ENERGY RESOURCES
Type of Assistance: Direct payments ranging from $1,000 to $200,000.
Applicant Eligibility: Indian tribal governments.
Objective: To encourage the development of Indian-owned energy resources through funded projects.
Contact: Indian Affairs, Intergovernmental Affairs, CP-60, Department of Energy, Washington, DC 20585, 202-252-5661.

81.077   UNIVERSITY RESEARCH INSTRUMENTATION
Type of Assistance: Project grants averaging $250,000.
Applicant Eligibility: Institutions of higher education.
Objective: To assist colleges and universities in conducting long-range research in areas of interest to DOE.
Contact: Division of University and Industry Programs, Office of Energy Research, Department of Energy, Washington, DC 20585, 202-252-8910.

81.078   INDUSTRIAL ENERGY CONSERVATION
Type of Assistance: Project grants ranging from $10,000 to $250,000.
Applicant Eligibility: Private nonprofit, profit organizations and businesses.
Objective: To perform research and development of high risk and assist in the transfer of energy efficient technologies and practices.
Contact: Office of Industrial Programs, CE-12, Department of Energy, Washington, DC 20585, 202-252-2093.

81.079   BIOMASS ENERGY TECHNOLOGY
Type of Assistance: Project grants averaging $605,000.
Applicant Eligibility: State, local government, profit and nonprofit organizations.
Objective: To conduct long-term research to provide the generic technology base for both feedstock production and conversion technologies.
Contact: Biomass Energy Technology Division, Department of Energy, Washington, DC 20585, 202-252-6746.

81.080   ENERGY POLICY, PLANNING AND DEVELOPMENT
Type of Assistance: Project grants ranging from $20,000 to $200,000.

Applicant Eligibility: Institutions of higher education, nonprofit institutions.
Objective: To provide financing for gathering experts together for seminars and conferences to discuss energy policies and the writing of reports.
Contact: Division of Budget and Administration, Policy, Safety, and Environment PE-3, 7E-090 Forrestal Building, 1000 Independence Avenue, SW, Washington, DC 20585, 202-252-2431.

81.081 ENERGY TASK FORCE FOR THE URBAN CONSORTIUM
Type of Assistance: Project grants ranging from $25,000 to $80,000.
Applicant Eligibility: Sponsored organizations.
Objective: To develop and implement cost-effective energy management techniques and technologies among the nation's municipal governments.
Contact: Branch Chief, Community Research and Development, Office of Conservation and Renewable Energy, 1000 Independence Avenue, SW, Room 6H-068, Mailstop CE-116, Washington, DC 20585, 202-252-9389.

81.083 MINORITY EDUCATIONAL INSTITUTION RESEARCH TRAVEL FUND
Type of Assistance: Direct payments ranging from $200 to $800.
Applicant Eligibility: Minority postsecondary educational institutions.
Objective: To provide travel funds to faculty and graduate students of designated minority postsecondary institutions to encourage energy-related research.
Contact: Office of Minority Economic Impact, MI-2.2, Department of Energy, Forrestal Building, Room 5B-110, Washington, DC 20585, 202-252-8383.

81.084 MINORITY HONORS VOCATIONAL TRAINING
Type of Assistance: Project grants ranging from $15,000 to $70,000.
Applicant Eligibility: Minority individuals.
Objective: To provide scholarship funding to needy minority honor students pursuing vocational training in energy-related technologies.
Contact: Office of Minority Economic Impact, MI-3, Department of Energy, Forrestal Building, Room 5B-110, Washington, DC 20585, 202-252-8383.

81.086 CONSERVATION RESEARCH AND DEVELOPMENT
Type of Assistance: Project grants ranging from $50,000 to $500,000.
Applicant Eligibility: Profit, nonprofit organizations, state and local governments.
Objective: To conduct long-term research to develop and transfer energy conservation technologies to the scientific and industrial communities and to government.

Contact: Office of Deputy Assistant Secretary for Conservation, Department of Energy, Washington, DC 20585, 202-252-9232.

81.087 RENEWABLE ENERGY RESEARCH AND DEVELOPMENT

Type of Assistance: Project grants ranging from $300,000 to $679,500.
Applicant Eligibility: Profit, nonprofit organizations, state and local governments.
Objective: To conduct research in the following energy technologies: solar buildings, photovoltaics, solar thermal, biomass, alcohol fuels, urban waste, wind, ocean, geothermal and hydropower.
Contact: Renewable Energy-Research and Technology Integration, Department of Energy, Washington, DC 20585, 202-252-9282.

81.088 INTERNATIONAL AFFAIRS AND ENERGY EMERGENCIES

Type of Assistance: Project grants and direct payments ranging from $10,000 to $200,000.
Applicant Eligibility: All interested persons.
Objective: To develop energy emergency contingency planning programs; to promote international energy research and development agreements.
Contact: Management Services Staff, International Affairs and Energy Emergencies, 7C-034, Forrestal Building, 1000 Independence Avenue, SW, Washington, DC 20585, 202-252-2994.

81.090 STATE HEATING OIL GRANTS

Type of Assistance: Project grants ranging from $6,000 to $20,500.
Applicant Eligibility: State governments.
Objective: To improve State No. 2 Heating Oil Data Collection Programs to respond to congressional and consumer inquiries regarding No. 2 heating oil.
Contact: Room 26-036, Energy Information Administration, EI-52, 1000 Independence Avenue, SW, Washington, DC 20585, 202-252-6612.

81.091 SOCIOECONOMIC AND DEMOGRAPHIC RESEARCH, DATA AND OTHER INFORMATION

Type of Assistance: Project grants ranging from $50,000 to $200,000.
Applicant Eligibility: Institutions of higher education and nonprofit organizations.
Objective: To provide financial support to determine minority energy consumption and usage patterns, and to evaluate the percentage of disposable income spent by minorities on energy compared to national usage patterns.
Contact: Department of Energy, Forrestal Building, Room 5B-110, Washington, DC 20585, 202-252-8383.

UNITED STATES INFORMATION AGENCY

82.00I   EDUCATIONAL EXCHANGE—GRADUATE STUDENTS (FULBRIGHT PROGRAM)
Type of Assistance: Grants ranging from $1,000 to $15,000.
Applicant Eligibility: Individuals.
Objective: To improve and strengthen the international relations of the United States by promoting better mutual understanding among the peoples of the world through educational exchanges.
Contact: Institute of International Education, 809 United Nations Plaza, New York, NY 10017, 212-883-8200.

82.002   EDUCATIONAL EXCHANGE—UNIVERSITY LECTURERS (PROFESSORS) AND RESEARCH SCHOLARS (FULBRIGHT-HAYS PROGRAM)
Type of Assistance: Grants ranging from $2,000 to $40,000.
Applicant Eligibility: Individuals.
Objective: To improve and strengthen the international relations of the United States by promoting better mutual understanding among the peoples of the world through educational exchanges.
Contact: Council for International Exchange of Scholars, 11 Dupont Circle, Suite 300, Washington, DC 20036, 202-833-4950.

FEDERAL EMERGENCY MANAGEMENT AGENCY

FEDERAL INSURANCE ADMINISTRATION

83.100   FLOOD INSURANCE
Type of Assistance: Insurance ranging from $1 to $100,000.
Applicant Eligibility: State and local governments.
Objective: To enable persons to purchase insurance against losses from physical damage to or loss of real or personal property caused by floods, mudslides or flood-caused erosion in the United States, and to promote wise flood plain management practices in the nation's flood-prone and mudslide-prone areas.
Contact: Administrator, Federal Insurance Administration, Federal Emergency Management Agency, Washington, DC 20472, 202-646-3443.

TRAINING AND FIRE PROGRAMS DIRECTORATE

83.400   EMERGENCY MANAGEMENT INSTITUTE-STUDENT EXPENSE PROGRAM
Type of Assistance: Direct payments averaging $258.00.
Applicant Eligibility: Individuals.
Objective: To assist in defraying the expenses of professional training for state and local emergency management defense personnel and training for instructors who conduct courses under contract.
Contact: Training and Education, Federal Emergency Management Agency, 16825 South Seton Avenue, Emmitsburg, MD 21727, 301-447-6771.

83.403   EMERGENCY MANAGEMENT INSTITUTE-FIELD TRAINING PROGRAM
Type of Assistance: Grants ranging from $53,000 to $250,000.
Applicant Eligibility: Individuals.
Objective: To provide regions with instructional capability for the training of Federal Emergency Management Agency support staffs, regional staffs of federal agencies, and elected state/local government staffs.
Contact: Emergency Management Institute, 16825 South Seton Avenue, Emmitsburg, MD 301-447-6771.

83.405 NATIONAL FIRE ACADEMY STUDENT STIPEND PROGRAM

Type of Assistance: Direct payments up to $277.
Applicant Eligibility: A student who is a member of a fire department and has been accepted to a course.
Objective: To provide stipends to students attending National Fire Academy Courses.
Contact: National Emergency Training Center, Office of Admissions and Registration, 16825 South Seton Avenue, Emmitsburg, MD 21727, 301-447-6771.

83.409 REIMBURSEMENT FOR FIREFIGHTING ON FEDERAL PROPERTY

Type of Assistance: Direct payments up to $500,000.
Applicant Eligibility: Fire departments.
Objective: To provide each fire service which engages in firefighting operations on federal property reimbursement for their direct expenses and direct losses incurred in firefighting.
Contact: Office of Management and Administration, Federal Emergency Management Agency, Washington, DC 20472, 202-646-2688.

STATE AND LOCAL PROGRAMS AND SUPPORT

83.503 EMERGENCY MANAGEMENT ASSISTANCE

Type of Assistance: Grants ranging from $29,900 to $4,608,200.
Applicant Eligibility: State governments.
Objective: To develop effective civil defense organizations in the states and their political subdivisions in order to plan for and coordinate emergency activities in the event of attack or natural disaster.
Contact: Emergency Management Programs Office, State and Local Programs and Support Directorate, Federal Emergency Management Agency, 1725 I Street, NW, Washington, DC 20472, 202-646-3516.

83.504 OTHER STATE AND LOCAL DIRECTION, CONTROL AND WARNING

Type of Assistance: Grants ranging from $1,000 to $236,000.
Applicant Eligibility: State and local governments.
Objective: To maintain the civil defense readiness of state and local governments by furnishing matching funds for annual recurring and maintenance costs for state and local civil defense direction, control, alerting and warning systems, and for emergency public information services and supplies required to conduct a viable civil defense program.
Contact: Chief, Communications and Control Branch, State and Local Programs and Support, Federal Emergency Management Agency, Washington, DC 20472, 202-646-3090.

83.505   STATE DISASTER PREPAREDNESS GRANTS
Type of Assistance: Grants ranging from $6,250 to $25,000.
Applicant Eligibility: State governments.
Objective: To assist states in developing and improving the state and
local plans, programs and capabilities for disaster preparedness and
prevention.
Contact: Emergency Management Programs Office, State and Local
Programs and Support, Federal Emergency Management Agency,
Washington, DC 20472, 202-656-3503.

83.506   EARTHQUAKE AND HURRICANE
PREPAREDNESS GRANTS
Type of Assistance: Grants ranging from $10,000 to $1 million.
Applicant Eligibility: State and local governments.
Objective: To prepare plans for all levels of government for prepar-
edness capabilities for severe earthquakes or hurricanes in certain high-
density, high-risk areas.
Contact: Earthquake and Natural Hazards Division, State and Local
Programs and Support, Federal Emergency Management Agency,
Washington, DC 20472, 202-646-2799.

83.508   RADIOLOGICAL SYSTEMS MAINTENANCE
Type of Assistance: Grants ranging from $42,500 to $405,000.
Applicant Eligibility: State and local governments.
Objective: To assist in developing a capability in every locality for the
detection and measurement of hazardous levels of radiation; to maintain all civil defense radiological instruments in a calibrated and op-
erationally ready condition; to assist in the development and maintenance
of radiological emergency plans.
Contact: Physical Scientist Administrator, Emergency Management
Programs Office, Federal Emergency Management Agency, Washington, DC 20472, 202-646-3080.

83.511   RADIOLOGICAL PROTECTION PROGRAM
Type of Assistance: Grants ranging from $15,000 to $50,000.
Applicant Eligibility: State and local governments.
Objective: To develop and implement a Radiological Defense (RADEF)
Program for the Radiological Hazards that are a potential threat to
the state and local jurisdictions.
Contact: Systems Development Division, Office of Emergency Man-
agement Programs, Washington, DC 20472, 202-646-3493.

83.512   STATE AND LOCAL EMERGENCY
OPERATING CENTERS
Type of Assistance: Grants (dollar amount not available).
Applicant Eligibility: States and political subdivisions.
Objective: To enhance effective, reliable and survivable direction and
control capabilities of state and local governments.
Contact: Communications and Control Branch, Emergency Manage-

ment Systems Support Division, Federal Emergency Management Agency, Washington, DC 20472, 202-646-3094.

83.513 STATE AND LOCAL WARNING AND COMMUNICATION SYSTEMS
Type of Assistance: Grants.
Applicant Eligibility: State and local governments.
Objective: To maintain the civil defense readiness of state and local governments by furnishing matching funds for the purchase of equipment and supporting materials for state and local direction and control, and alerting and warning systems.
Contact: Communications Management Officer, Federal Emergency Management Agency, Washington, DC 20472, 202-646-3095.

83.514 POPULATION PROTECTION PLANNING
Type of Assistance: Grants ranging from $20,000 to $730,000.
Applicant Eligibility: States.
Objective: To assist states and localities in the development of population protection plans to prepare for and respond to the full range of emergencies that a jurisdiction may face.
Contact: State and Local Programs and Support Directorate, Federal Emergency Management Agency, Washington, DC 20472, 202-646-3494.

83.515 EMERGENCY BROADCAST SYSTEM GUIDANCE AND ASSISTANCE
Type of Assistance: Grants ranging from $25,000 to $75,000.
Applicant Eligibility: Broadcast stations, state and local governments.
Objective: To enhance and develop an emergency broadcast capability to provide emergency information and direction to the public by national, state and local officials.
Contact: Emergency Management Officer, State and Local Programs and Support, Washington, DC 20472, 202-646-3083.

83.516 DISASTER ASSISTANCE
Type of Assistance: Grants ranging from $21 to $39,202,722.
Applicant Eligibility: Individuals, state and local governments.
Objective: To provide assistance to states, local governments, selected private nonprofit facilities, and individuals in alleviating suffering and hardship resulting from emergencies or major disasters declared by the President.
Contact: Office of Disaster Assistance Programs, Federal Emergency Management Agency, Washington, DC 20472, 202-646-3618.

83.518 EMERGENCY PUBLIC INFORMATION COMPETITIVE CHALLENGE GRANTS
Type of Assistance: Project grants ranging from $9,000 to $15,000.
Applicant Eligibility: State, local governments; public, private nonprofit organizations.

Objective: To stimulate the development of effective public information strategies at state and local levels.

Contact: Office of Public Affairs, Federal Emergency Management Agency, Washington, DC 20472.

83.519 HAZARD MITIGATION ASSISTANCE

Type of Assistance: Project grants ranging from $5,000 to $25,000.

Applicant Eligibility: State and local governments.

Objective: To assist states or local units of government in preparing a hazard mitigation plan which will contribute to reducing vulnerability to hazards within the project area.

Contact: Hazard Mitigation Branch, Disaster Assistance Programs, Federal Emergency Management Agency, 500 C Street, SW, Washington, DC 20472, 202-646-3681.

US DEPARTMENT OF EDUCATION

84.002 ADULT EDUCATION—STATE-ADMINISTERED PROGRAM
Type of Assistance: Grants ranging from $80,193 to $8,135,355.
Applicant Eligibility: State governments.
Objective: To expand educational opportunities for adults and to encourage the establishment of programs of adult education that will enable all adults to acquire basic skills necessary to function in society; to enable adults who so desire to continue their education to at least the level of completion of secondary school; and to make available the means to secure training that will enable adults to become more employable, productive and responsible citizens.
Contact: Division of Adult Education, Bureau of Occupational and Adult Education, Department of Education, Washington, DC 20202, 202-245-9793.

84.003 BILINGUAL EDUCATION
Type of Assistance: Grants ranging from $5,000 to $1,800,000 and direct payments.
Applicant Eligibility: Nonprofit organizations, state and local governments.
Objective: To develop and carry out elementary and secondary school programs, including activities at the preschool level, to meet the educational needs of children of limited proficiency in English; to demonstrate effective ways of providing such children instruction designed to enable them, while using their native language, to achieve competence in English; and to develop the human and material resources required for such programs.
Contact: Office of Bilingual Education, Department of Education, 400 Maryland Avenue, SW, Washington, DC 20202, 202-245-2609.

84.004 CIVIL RIGHTS TECHNICAL ASSISTANCE AND TRAINING
Type of Assistance: Grants ranging from $50,000 to $250,000.
Applicant Eligibility: Nonprofit organizations, state and local governments.
Objective: To provide direct and indirect technical assistance and training services to school districts to cope with educational problems occasioned by desegregation by race, sex and national origin.
Contact: Division of Educational Support, Bureau of Elementary and

Secondary Education, Department of Education, 400 Maryland Avenue, SW, Washington, DC 20202, 202-245-2181.

84.007 SUPPLEMENTAL EDUCATIONAL OPPORTUNITY GRANTS

Type of Assistance: Direct payments ranging from $200 to $90,386.
Applicant Eligibility: Higher education institutions.
Objective: To enable students with financial need to pursue higher education by providing grant assistance for educational expenses.
Contact: Division of Policy and Program Development, Student Financial Assistance Programs, Department of Education, 400 Maryland Avenue, SW, Washington, DC 20202, 202-245-9720.

84.009 PROGRAM FOR EDUCATION OF HANDICAPPED CHILDREN IN STATE-OPERATED OR -SUPPORTED SCHOOLS

Type of Assistance: Grants ranging from $222,000 to $24,476, 532.
Applicant Eligibility: State and local governments.
Objective: To extend and improve comprehensive educational programs for handicapped children enrolled in state-operated or state-supported schools.
Contact: Division of Assistance to States, Bureau of Education for the Handicapped, Department of Education, 400 Maryland Avenue, SW, Washington, DC 20202, 202-732-1014.

84.010 EDUCATIONALLY DEPRIVED CHILDREN— LOCAL EDUCATIONAL AGENCIES

Type of Assistance: Grants ranging from $623,586 to $280,628,132.
Applicant Eligibility: State governments.
Objective: To provide financial assistance to local educational agencies to meet the needs of educationally disadvantaged children in low-income areas, whether enrolled in public or in private elementary or secondary schools.
Contact: Compensatory Education Programs, Office of Elementary and Secondary Education, Department of Education, Seventh and D Streets, SW, ROB-3, Room 3616, Washington, DC 20202, 202-245-3081.

84.011 MIGRANT EDUCATION— BASIC STATE FORMULA GRANT PROGRAM

Type of Assistance: Grants (dollar amount not available).
Applicant Eligibility: State governments.
Objective: To expand and improve programs to meet the special educational needs of children of migratory agricultural workers or of migratory fishers.
Contact: Director, Division of Migrant Education, Office of Compensatory Educational Programs, Bureau of Elementary and Secondary Education, Department of Education, 400 Maryland Avenue, SW, ROB-3, Room 3616, Washington, DC 20202, 202-245-2722.

84.012 EDUCATIONALLY DEPRIVED CHILDREN— STATE ADMINISTRATION
Type of Assistance: Grants ranging from $50,000 to $3,388,524.
Applicant Eligibility: State governments.
Objective: To improve and expand educational programs for disadvantaged children through financial assistance to state education agencies.
Contact: Compensatory Education Programs, Office of Elementary and Secondary Education, Department of Education, Seventh and D Streets, SW, Washington, DC 20202, 202-245-3081.

84.013 NEGLECTED AND DELINQUENT CHILDREN
Type of Assistance: Grants ranging from $46,080 to $3,827,904.
Applicant Eligibility: State governments.
Objective: To expand and improve educational programs to meet the special needs of institutionalized children for whom the state has an educational responsibility.
Contact: Compensatory Education Programs, Office of Elementary and Secondary Education, Department of Education, Seventh and D Streets, SW, Washington, DC 20202, 202-245-3081.

84.014 FOLLOW THROUGH
Type of Assistance: Grants ranging from $63,000 to $660,000.
Applicant Eligibility: Nonprofit organizations, state and local governments.
Objective: To sustain and augment in primary grades the gains that children from low-income families make in Head Start and other quality preschool programs. Follow Through provides special programs of instruction as well as health, nutrition and other related services which will aid in the continued development of children to their full potential. Active participation of parents is stressed.
Contact: Compensatory Education Programs, Office of Elementary and Secondary Education, Department of Education, ROB-3, Room 3616 Seventh and D Streets, SW, Washington, DC 20202, 202-245-3081.

84.015 NATIONAL RESOURCE CENTERS AND FELLOWSHIPS PROGRAM FOR LANGUAGE & AREA OR LANGUAGE & INTERNATIONAL STUDIES
Type of Assistance: Grants ranging from $70,000 to $170,000, and fellowships at $7,500 per year.
Applicant Eligibility: Nonprofit organizations, state and local governments.
Objective: To promote instruction in those modern foreign languages and area and international studies critical to national needs by supporting the establishment and operation of such programs at colleges and universities; to meet the critical needs of American education for experts in foreign languages, area studies and world affairs by sup-

porting fellowships for advanced study at institutions for higher education.

Contact: Advanced Training and Research Branch, Center for International Education, Department of Education, ROB-3, Seventh and D Streets, SW, Washington, DC 20202, 202-245-9425.

84.016 UNDERGRADUATE INTERNATIONAL STUDIES AND FOREIGN LANGUAGE PROGRAMS

Type of Assistance: Grants ranging from $35,000 to $80,000.

Applicant Eligibility: Nonprofit organizations, state and local governments.

Objective: To strengthen the international and global focus in the curricula of institutions of higher education by establishing international and global studies programs at the graduate or undergraduate levels.

Contact: Division of International Services and Improvement, International Studies Branch, Department of Education, ROB-3, Seventh and D Streets, SW, Washington, DC 20202, 202-245-2794.

84.017 INTERNATIONAL RESEARCH AND STUDIES

Type of Assistance: Grants ranging from $6,000 to $100,000.

Applicant Eligibility: Individuals, nonprofit organizations, state and local governments, institutions of higher learning.

Objective: To improve foreign language and area studies training in the United States through support of research and studies, experimentation and development of specialized instructional materials.

Contact: Division of Advanced Training and Research, International Education Programs, Department of Education, ROB-3, Seventh and D Streets, SW, Washington, DC 20202, 202-245-9425.

84.018 SUMMER SEMINARS ABROAD— FULBRIGHT EXCHANGE

Type of Assistance: Grants (dollar amount not available).

Applicant Eligibility: Individuals.

Objective: To increase mutual understanding between the people of the United States and those of other countries by offering qualified American teachers opportunities to teach abroad in elementary and secondary schools, and in some instances in teacher training institutions, technical colleges, polytechnics or colleges of art. With the cooperation of American schools, teachers from other countries may teach for an academic year in the United States under the same program. There are also opportunities for American teachers to participate in short-term seminars abroad.

Contact: International Studies Branch, Center for International Education, Department of Education, ROB-3, Seventh and D Streets, SW, Washington, DC 20202, 202-245-2794.

84.019 FULBRIGHT-HAYS TRAINING GRANTS— FACULTY RESEARCH ABROAD

Type of Assistance: Grants ranging from $7,158 to $52,107.

Applicant Eligibility: Institutions of higher education.

Objective: To help universities and colleges strengthen their programs of international studies through selected opportunities for research and study abroad in foreign language and area studies; to enable key faculty members to keep current in their specialties; to facilitate the updating of curricula; and to help improve teaching methods and materials.

Contact: Center for International Education, Department of Education, ROB-3, Room 3928, Seventh and D Streets, SW, Washington, DC 20202, 202-245-2761.

84.020 FULBRIGHT-HAYS TRAINING GRANTS— FOREIGN CURRICULUM CONSULTANTS

Type of Assistance: Grants ranging from $9,422 to $16,865.

Applicant Eligibility: Nonprofit organizations, state and local governments.

Objective: To benefit American education at all levels by helping institutions bring specialists from other countries to the United States to assist in planning and developing local curricula in foreign language and area studies.

Contact: Office of Assistant Secretary for Postsecondary Education, ROB-3, Seventh and D Streets, SW, Washington, DC 20202, 202-245-2794.

84.021 FULBRIGHT-HAYS TRAINING GRANTS— GROUP PROJECTS ABROAD

Type of Assistance: Grants ranging from $13,120 to $281,000.

Applicant Eligibility: Nonprofit organizations, state and local governments.

Objective: To help educational institutions improve their programs in foreign language and area studies.

Contact: Office of Assistant Secretary for Postsecondary Education, Department of Education, ROB-3, Seventh and D Streets, SW, Washington, DC 20202, 202-245-2794.

84.022 FULBRIGHT-HAYS TRAINING GRANTS— DOCTORAL DISSERTATION RESEARCH ABROAD

Type of Assistance: Grants ranging from $1,800 to $33,000.

Applicant Eligibility: Institutions of higher education.

Objective: To provide opportunities for advanced graduate students to engage in full-time dissertation research abroad in modern foreign language and area studies. The program is designed to develop research knowledge and capability in world areas not widely included in American curricula.

Contact: Center for International Education, Department of Education, Room 3928, Mail Stop 3308, ROB-3, Seventh and D Streets, SW, Washington, DC 20202, 202-245-9425.

84.023 HANDICAPPED—INNOVATION AND DEVELOPMENT

Type of Assistance: Grants ranging from $4,000 to $500,000.

Applicant Eligibility: Nonprofit organizations, state and local governments.

Objective: To improve the education of handicapped children through research and development projects, and demonstrations of model programs.

Contact: Chief, Research Project Section, Division of Educational Services, Bureau of Education for the Handicapped, Department of Education, 400 Maryland Avenue, SW, Washington, DC 20202, 202-732-1109.

84.024 HANDICAPPED EARLY CHILDHOOD EDUCATION

Type of Assistance: Grants ranging from $50,000 to $180,000.

Applicant Eligibility: Nonprofit organizations, state and local governments.

Objective: To support experimental demonstration, dissemination and state implementation of preschool and early childhood projects for handicapped children.

Contact: Office of Assistant Secretary for Special Education and Rehabilitative Services, Division of Innovation and Development, Department of Education, 400 Maryland Avenue, SW, Washington, DC 20202, 202-732-1177.

84.025 DEAF-BLIND CENTERS

Type of Assistance: Grants ranging from $1,078,726 to $2,388,854.

Applicant Eligibility: Nonprofit organizations, state and local governments.

Objective: To establish model single-state and multistate centers to provide all deaf-blind children with comprehensive diagnostic and evaluative services, programs for their education, adjustment and orientation, and effective consultative services for their parents, teachers, and others involved in their welfare.

Contact: Division of Innovation and Development, Special Education Service, Office of Assistant Secretary for Special Education and Rehabilitative Services, Department of Education, 400 Maryland Avenue, SW, Washington, DC 20202, 202-723-1161.

84.026 HANDICAPPED MEDIA SERVICES
AND CAPTIONED FILMS

Type of Assistance: Direct payments and grants ranging from $2,400 to $4,650,000.

Applicant Eligibility: Nonprofit organizations, state and local governments.

Objective: To maintain a free loan service of captioned films for the deaf and instructional media for the educational, cultural and vocational enrichment of the handicapped; provide for acquisition and distribution of media materials and equipment; offer contracts and grants for research into the use of media; and train teachers, parents and others in media utilization.

Contact: Division of Innovation and Development, Special Education and Rehabilitative Services, Department of Education, Washington, DC 20202, 202-732-1172.

84.027 HANDICAPPED STATE GRANTS

Type of Assistance: Grants ranging from $722,000 to $92,859,791.
Applicant Eligibility: State governments.
Objective: To provide grants to states to assist them in providing a free appropriate public education to all handicapped children.
Contact: Division of Assistance to States, Bureau of Education for the Handicapped, Department of Education, 400 Maryland Avenue, SW, Washington, DC 20202, 202-733-1025.

84.028 HANDICAPPED REGIONAL RESOURCE CENTERS

Type of Assistance: Grants ranging from $100,000 to $800,000.
Applicant Eligibility: Nonprofit organizations, state and local governments.
Objective: To establish regional resource centers that provide advice and technical services to educators for improving education of handicapped children.
Contact: Division of Assistance to States, Special Education and Rehabilitative Services, Department of Education, 400 Maryland Avenue, SW, Washington, DC 20202, 202-732-1052.

84.029 SPECIAL EDUCATION PERSONNEL DEVELOPMENT

Type of Assistance: Grants ranging from $8,000 to $180,000.
Applicant Eligibility: Nonprofit organizations, state and local governments.
Objective: To improve the quality and increase the numbers of teachers, supervisors, administrators, researchers, teacher educators and speech correctionists working with the handicapped, and specialized personnel such as specialists in physical education and recreation, paraprofessionals and vocational/career education volunteers (including parents and parent coalitions).
Contact: Director, Division of Personnel Preparation, Department of Education, Bureau of Education for the Handicapped, 400 Maryland Avenue, SW, Washington, DC 20202, 202-732-1068.

84.030 HANDICAPPED TEACHER RECRUITMENT AND INFORMATION

Type of Assistance: Grants ranging from $25,000 to $75,000.
Applicant Eligibility: Nonprofit organizations, state and local governments.
Objective: To disseminate information that can help parents, consumer organizations, professionals and others interested in special education in making decisions that affect the education and general well-being of handicapped children.
Contact: Division of Innovation and Development, Special Education and Rehabilitative Services, Department of Education, 400 Maryland Avenue, SW, Washington, DC 20202, 202-732-1167.

84.031 HIGHER EDUCATION—INSTITUTIONAL AID

Type of Assistance: Grants ranging from $25,000 to $800,000.
Applicant Eligibility: Nonprofit organizations, state and local governments.
Objective: To strengthen developing colleges to improve their management and fiscal operations and assist in the development of their academic, administrative and student services programs.
Contact: Institutional Aid Programs, Office of Postsecondary Education, Department of Education, 400 Maryland Avenue, SW, Washington, DC 20202, 202-245-2384.

84.032 HIGHER EDUCATION ACT INSURED LOANS (GUARANTEED STUDENT LOANS)

Type of Assistance: Guaranteed/insured loans up to $2,500 annually per student.
Applicant Eligibility: Individuals.
Objective: To authorize low-interest deferred loans for educational expenses available from eligible lenders such as banks, credit unions, savings and loan associations, pension funds, insurance companies and schools to vocational, undergraduate and graduate students enrolled at eligible institutions. The loans are insured by a state or private nonprofit agency.
Contact: Guaranteed Student Loan Branch, Division of Policy and Program Development, Student Financial Assistance Programs, Office of Assistant Secondary for Postsecondary Education, Department of Education, 400 Maryland Avenue, SW, Washington, DC 20202, 202-245-2475.

84.033 COLLEGE WORK-STUDY PROGRAM

Type of Assistance: Direct payments ranging from $200 to $7,469,597.
Applicant Eligibility: Nonprofit organizations and local governments.
Objective: To promote the part-time employment of students, particularly those with great financial need, who require assistance to pursue courses of study at institutions of higher education.
Contact: Division of Policy and Program Development, Student Financial Assistance Programs, Office of Assistant Secretary for Postsecondary Education, 400 Maryland Avenue, SW, Washington, DC 20202, 202-245-9720.

84.034 LIBRARY SERVICES

Type of Assistance: Grants (dollar amount not available).
Applicant Eligibility: State governments.
Objective: To assist in extending public library services to areas without service or with inadequate service; establishing and expanding state institutional library services; offering library service to the physically handicapped; establishing and expanding library services to the disadvantaged in urban and rural areas, and strengthening the metropolitan public libraries which serve as national or regional resource centers; providing programs and projects to serve areas with high con-

centrations of persons of limited English-speaking ability; and strengthening major urban resource libraries.
Contact: Division of Library Programs, Center for Libraries and Education Improvement, Department of Education, 400 Maryland Avenue, SW, Washington, DC 20202, 202-254-9664.

84.035   INTERLIBRARY COOPERATION
Type of Assistance: Grants (dollar amount not available).
Applicant Eligibility: State library administrative agencies.
Objective: To provide for the systematic and effective coordination of the resources of school, public, academic and special libraries, and special information centers, to improve service to their particular clienteles.
Contact: Division of Library Programs, Center for Libraries and Education Improvements, Department of Education, 400 Maryland Avenue, SW, Brown Building, Room 613, Washington, DC 20202, 202-254-9664.

84.036   LIBRARY CAREER TRAINING
Type of Assistance: Grants ranging from $8,000 to $60,000.
Applicant Eligibility: Nonprofit organizations, state and local governments.
Objective: To assist institutions of higher education and library organizations and agencies in training persons in the principles and practices of librarianship and information science.
Contact: Division of Library Programs, Center for Libraries and Education Improvements, Department of Education, 400 Maryland Avenue, SW, Washington, DC 20202, 202-254-5090.

84.037   NATIONAL DEFENSE DIRECT STUDENT LOAN CANCELLATIONS
Type of Assistance: Direct payments ranging from $1 to $248,342.
Applicant Eligibility: Nonprofit organizations, state and local governments.
Objective: To reimburse institutions for their share of National Defense Student Loan recipients who cancel their loans by becoming teachers or performing active military service in the US Armed Forces.
Contact: Campus and State Grant Branch, Division of Program Operations, Student Financial Assistance Programs, 400 Maryland Avenue, SW, Washington, DC 20202, 202-245-2320.

84.038   NATIONAL DEFENSE/DIRECT STUDENT LOANS
Type of Assistance: Direct payments ranging from $200 to $1,364,576.
Applicant Eligibility: Nonprofit organizations, state and local governments.
Objective: To establish loan funds at eligible higher education institutions to permit needy undergraduate and graduate students to complete their education.
Contact: Office of Assistant Secretary for Postsecondary Education,

Division of Policy and Program Development, Student Financial Assistance Programs, 400 Maryland Avenue, SW, Washington, DC 20202, 202-245-9720.

84.039 LIBRARY RESEARCH AND DEMONSTRATION

Type of Assistance: Grants.
Applicant Eligibility: Nonprofit organizations, state and local governments.
Objective: To award grants and contracts for research and/or demonstration projects in areas of specialized services intended to improve library and information science practices and principles.
Contact: Division of Library Programs, Department of Education, 400 Maryland Avenue, SW, Washington, DC 20202-1630, 202-245-5090.

84.040 SCHOOL ASSISTANCE IN FEDERALLY AFFECTED AREAS—CONSTRUCTION

Type of Assistance: Grants ranging from $20,000 to $83 million.
Applicant Eligibility: Nonprofit organizations, state and local governments
Objective: To provide assistance for the construction of urgently needed minimum school facilities in school districts that have had substantial increases in school enrollment as a result of new or increased federal activities, or where reconstruction of facilities is necessary because of natural disaster.
Contact: Division of Impact Aid, State and Local Educational Programs, Department of Education, 400 Maryland Avenue, SW, Washington, DC 20202-6272, 202-245-8427.

84.041 SCHOOL ASSISTANCE IN FEDERALLY AFFECTED AREAS—MAINTENANCE AND OPERATION

Type of Assistance: Grants ranging from $3,000 to over $12 million.
Applicant Eligibility: Local governments.
Objective: To provide financial assistance to local educational agencies when enrollments or availability of revenue are adversely affected by federal activities; where the tax base of a district is reduced through the federal acquisition of real property; or where there is a sudden and substantial increase in school attendance as the result of federal activities. Also to assist local agencies in the education of children residing on federal or Indian lands and children whose parents are employed on federal property in the Uniformed Services.
Contact: Director, Division of Impact Aid, State and Local Educational Programs, Office of Elementary and Secondary Education, Department of Education, 400 Maryland Avenue, SW, Washington, DC 20202, 202-245-8427.

84.042 SPECIAL SERVICES FOR DISADVANTAGED STUDENTS

Type of Assistance: Grants ranging from $26,830 to $249,739.
Applicant Eligibility: Institutions of higher education.

Objective: To assist students who may be educationally, economically or culturally deprived, or physically handicapped, or who have limited English-speaking ability and are enrolled or accepted for enrollment by institutions which are recipients of grants to complete their postsecondary education.
Contact: Director, Division of Student Services, Office of Postsecondary Education, Department of Education, 400 Maryland Avenue, SW, Washington, DC 20202, 202-245-2165.

84.044   TALENT SEARCH

Type of Assistance: Grants ranging from $62,627 to $1,254,417.
Applicant Eligibility: Nonprofit organizations and local governments.
Objective: To identify youths of financial or cultural need with exceptional potential for postsecondary educational training; to assist them through financial aid in obtaining admissions to postsecondary schools; and to decrease the rate of secondary and postsecondary school dropouts and increase the number of secondary and postsecondary school dropouts who reenter educational programs.
Contact: Director, Division of Student Services, Education Outreach Branch, Office of Postsecondary Education, Department of Education, 400 Maryland Avenue, SW, Washington, DC 20202, 202-245-2165.

84.047   UPWARD BOUND

Type of Assistance: Grants ranging from $76,055 to $411,033.
Applicant Eligibility: Nonprofit organizations, state and local governments.
Objective: To generate the skill and motivation necessary for success in education beyond high school among young people from low-income families who have academic potential but who may lack adequate secondary school preparation. The goal of the program is to increase the academic performance and motivational levels of eligible enrollees so that such persons may complete secondary school and successfully pursue postsecondary educational programs.
Contact: Director, Division of Student Services, Education Outreach Branch, Office of Postsecondary Education, Department of Education, 400 Maryland Avenue, SW, Washington, DC 20202, 202-245-2165.

84.048   VOCATIONAL EDUCATION— BASIC GRANTS TO STATES

Type of Assistance: Grants ranging from $129,371 to $59,771,858.
Applicant Eligibility: State governments.
Objective: To assist states in improving planning for, and in conducting, vocational programs on the local level for persons who are handicapped or disadvantaged, who have single parents or not proficient in English and desire and need education and training for employment.
Contact: Director, Division of Vocational Education Services, Office of Assistant Secretary for Vocational and Adult Education, Department of Education, 400 Maryland Avenue, SW, Washington, DC 20202, 202-245-2165.

84.049 VOCATIONAL EDUCATION— CONSUMER AND HOMEMAKER EDUCATION

Type of Assistance: Grants ranging from $6,008 to $2,775,907.
Applicant Eligibility: State governments.
Objective: To assist states in conducting programs in consumer and homemaking education. Emphasis is placed on programs located in economically depressed areas or areas with high rates of unemployment.
Contact: Director, Division of Vocational Education Services, Office of Assistant Secretary for Vocational and Adult Education, Department of Education, 400 Maryland Avenue, SW, Washington, DC 20202, 202-472-3440.

84.051 NATIONAL VOCATIONAL EDUCATION RESEARCH

Type of Assistance: Grants ranging from $25,000 to $5,400,000.
Applicant Eligibility: Individuals, nonprofit organizations, state and local governments.
Objective: To provide support for a National Center for Research in Vocational Education, projects for research, curriculum development and demonstration in vocational education, and six curriculum coordination centers.
Contact: Division of Innovation and Development, Office of Assistant Secretary for Vocational and Adult Education, Department of Education, 400 Maryland Avenue, SW, Washington, DC 20202, 202-245-2278.

84.053 VOCATIONAL EDUCATION—STATE COUNCILS

Type of Assistance: Grants ranging from $116,350 to $208,772.
Applicant Eligibility: State governments.
Objective: To advise state boards for vocational education on the development and administration of state plans; evaluate vocational education programs, services and activities and publish and distribute the results; and prepare and submit through the state boards an annual evaluation report to the Governor, State Board, Secretaries of Education and Labor.
Contact: Director, Division of State Vocational Education, Office of Assistant Secretary for Vocational and Adult Education, Department of Education, 400 Maryland Avenue, SW, Washington, DC 20202, 202-472-3440.

84.055 HIGHER EDUCATION—COOPERATIVE EDUCATION

Type of Assistance: Grants ranging from $9,700 to $189,200.
Applicant Eligibility: Nonprofit organizations.
Objective: To provide federal support for cooperative education programs in institutions of higher education for the training of persons in the planning, establishment, administration and coordination of programs of cooperative education; for projects demonstrating or exploring the feasibility or value of innovative methods of cooperative education; and for research into methods of improving, developing or promoting

the use of cooperative education programs in institutions of higher education. Cooperative education programs are those in which periods of academic study alternate or parallel periods of public or private employment related to the student's academic program or professional goals.
Contact: Division of Higher Education Incentive Programs, Office of Assistant Secretary for Postsecondary Education, Department of Education, 400 Maryland Avenue, SW, Washington, DC 20202, 202-472-1357.

84.060 INDIAN EDUCATION—ENTITLEMENT GRANTS TO LOCAL EDUCATIONAL AGENCIES AND TRIBAL SCHOOLS
Type of Assistance: Grants ranging from $2,000 to $1,137,000.
Applicant Eligibility: Local governments.
Objective: To provide financial assistance to local educational agencies and tribally controlled schools to develop and implement elementary and secondary school programs designed to meet the special educational and culturally related academic needs of Indian children. More specifically to increase academic performance with special emphasis on basic skills; reduce dropout rates and improve attendance; and increase the relevance of academic offerings by the schools to the cultural heritage of Indian children.
Contact: Indian Education Programs, Office of Elementary and Secondary Education, Department of Education, 400 Maryland Avenue, SW, Washington, DC 20202, 202-732-1887.

84.061 INDIAN EDUCATION— SPECIAL PROGRAMS AND PROJECTS
Type of Assistance: Grants ranging from $31,978 to $500,000.
Applicant Eligibility: State and local governments.
Objective: To plan, develop and implement programs and projects for the improvement of educational opportunities for Indian children.
Contact: Indian Education Programs, Office of Elementary and Secondary Education, Department of Education, 400 Maryland Avenue, SW, Washington DC 20202, 202-732-1887.

84.062 INDIAN EDUCATION—ADULT INDIAN EDUCATION
Type of Assistance: Grants ranging from $24,822 to $261,648.
Applicant Eligibility: State and local governments.
Objective: To plan, develop and implement programs for Indian adults to decrease the rate of illiteracy, increase the mastery of basic skills, increase the number who earn high school equivalency diplomas, and encourage the development of programs relevant to the culture and heritage of Indian adults.
Contact: Indian Education Programs, Office of Elementary and Secondary Education, Department of Education, 400 Maryland Avenue, SW, Washington, DC 20202, 202-732-1887.

84.063   PELL GRANT PROGRAM

Type of Assistance: Direct payments ranging from $200 to $1,900.
Applicant Eligibility: Individuals.
Objective: To assist in making available the benefits of postsecondary education to qualified students.
Contact: Division of Policy and Program Development, Office of Student Financial Assistance, Department of Education, 400 Maryland Avenue, SW, Washington, DC 20202, 800-638-6700; in Maryland call 800-492-6602.

84.064   HIGHER EDUCATION—VETERANS' COST OF
INSTRUCTION PROGRAM

Type of Assistance: Direct payments ranging from $879 to $118,000.
Applicant Eligibility: Nonprofit organizations, state and local governments.
Objective: To encourage colleges and universities to serve the special needs of veterans, especially Vietnam-era and disadvantaged veterans.
Contact: Division of Higher Education Incentive Programs, Department of Education, 400 Maryland Avenue, SW, Washington, DC 20202, 202-245-3253.

84.066   EDUCATIONAL OPPORTUNITY CENTERS

Type of Assistance: Grants ranging from $124,800 to $467,999.
Applicant Eligibility: Nonprofit organizations, state and local governments.
Objective: To provide information on financial and academic assistance available for qualified adults who wish to attend college and to assist them in applying for admission.
Contact: Director, Division of Student Services, Education Outreach Branch, Office of Postsecondary Education, Department of Education, 400 Maryland Avenue, SW, Washington, DC 20202, 202-245-2165.

84.069   GRANTS TO STATES FOR
STATE STUDENT INCENTIVES

Type of Assistance: Grants ranging from $1,000 to $11,669,000.
Applicant Eligibility: State and local governments.
Objective: To make incentive grants to the states to develop and expand assistance to eligible students in attendance at institutions of postsecondary education.
Contact: Division of Policy and Program Development, Office of Student Financial Assistance, Department of Education, 400 Maryland Avenue, SW, Washington, DC 20202, 202-472-4265.

84.072   INDIAN EDUCATION—
GRANTS TO INDIAN- CONTROLLED SCHOOLS

Type of Assistance: Grants ranging from $79,335 to $289,200.
Applicant Eligibility: State and local governments.
Objective: To provide financial assistance to nonlocal educational agencies to develop and implement elementary and secondary school

programs designed to meet the special educational needs of Indian children. Nonlocal educational agencies are schools on or near a reservation which are governed by a nonprofit institution or organization of an Indian tribe.
Contact: Indian Education Programs, Department of Education, 400 Maryland Avenue, SW, Washington, DC 20202, 202-732-1887.

84.073 NATIONAL DIFFUSION PROGRAM
Type of Assistance: Grants ranging from $20,000 to $190,000.
Applicant Eligibility: Nonprofit organizations and local governments.
Objective: To promote and accelerate the systematic rapid dissemination, and adoption by public and nonpublic educational institutions nationwide, of educational practices, products and programs that were developed through federal, state and local government funds and whose effectiveness has been substantiated by the Joint Dissemination Review Panel of the Department of Education.
Contact: National Diffusion Network, Division of National Dissemination Programs, Department of Education, Room 613, Stop 1604-30, Brown Building, 1200 19th Street, NW, Washington, DC 20208, 202-653-7003.

84.077 BILINGUAL VOCATIONAL TRAINING
Type of Assistance: Grants and direct payments ranging from $100,000 to $350,000.
Applicant Eligibility: Nonprofit organizations, state and local governments.
Objective: To train individuals of limited English-speaking ability for gainful employment as semiskilled or skilled workers, technicians or subprofessionals in recognized, new and emerging occupations.
Contact: Office of Vocational and Adult Education, Department of Education, 400 Maryland Avenue, SW, ROB-3, Room 5028, Washington, DC 20202, 202-245-2614.

84.078 REGIONAL EDUCATION PROGRAMS FOR DEAF AND OTHER HANDICAPPED PERSONS
Type of Assistance: Grants ranging from $48,550 to $176,074.
Applicant Eligibility: Nonprofit organizations and local governments.
Objective: To develop and operate specially designed or modified programs of vocational, technical, postsecondary or adult education for deaf or other handicapped persons.
Contact: Division of Innovation and Development, Special Education Programs, Assistant Secretary for Special Education and Rehabilitation, Department of Education, 400 Maryland Avenue, SW, Washington, DC 20202, 202-732-1176.

84.083 WOMEN'S EDUCATIONAL EQUITY
Type of Assistance: Grants ranging from $6,000 to $600,000.
Applicant Eligibility: Nonprofit organizations, state and local governments.

Objective: To promote educational equity for women and girls at all levels of education, and to provide financial assistance to local educational institutions to meet the requirements of Title IX of the Education Amendments of 1972.
Contact: Director, Division of Educational Support, Office of Elementary and Secondary Education, Department of Education, 400 Maryland Avenue, SW, Washington, DC 20202, 202-245-7965.

84.086   INNOVATIVE PROGRAMS FOR SEVERELY HANDICAPPED CHILDREN
Type of Assistance: Grants ranging from $43,200 to $189,000.
Applicant Eligibility: Nonprofit organizations, state and local governments.
Objective: To improve and expand innovative educational and training services for severely handicapped children and youth, and improve the acceptance of such people by the general public, professionals and possible employers.
Contact: Division of Innovation and Development, Special Education Services, Office of Assistant Secretary for Special Education and Rehabilitation Services, Department of Education, 400 Maryland Avenue, SW, Room 4615, Washington, DC 20202, 202-732-1161.

84.087   INDIAN EDUCATION— FELLOWSHIPS FOR INDIAN STUDENTS
Type of Assistance: Grants ranging from $2,300 to $13,000.
Applicant Eligibility: Native Americans.
Objective: To provide support that enables American Indians to study for careers in medicine, law, engineering, natural resources, business administration, education and related fields.
Contact: Indian Education Programs, Office of Elementary and Secondary Education, Department of Education, 400 Maryland Avenue, SW, Washington, DC 20202, 202-732-1887.

84.091   STRENGTHENING RESEARCH LIBRARY RESOURCES
Type of Assistance: Grants ranging from $63,325 to $700,000.
Applicant Eligibility: Individuals, nonprofit organizations, local governments.
Objective: To promote high-quality research and education throughout the United States by providing financial assistance to help major research libraries maintain and strengthen their collections; and to assist major research libraries in making their holdings available to individual researchers and scholars outside their primary clientele and to other libraries whose users have need for research materials.
Contact: Division of Library Programs, Center for Libraries and Education Improvement, Department of Education, 400 Maryland Avenue, SW, Washington, DC 20202-1630, 202-254-5090.

84.094   GRADUATE AND PROFESSIONAL STUDY
Type of Assistance: Grants ranging from $4,500 to $75,000.
Applicant Eligibility: Individuals, nonprofit organizations, state and local governments.
Objective: To provide funds to institutions of higher education to strengthen and develop programs which would assist in providing graduate or professional education to persons with varied backgrounds and experiences including, but not limited to, members of minority groups that are underrepresented in colleges and universities and in academic and professional career fields. To provide fellowships to institutions to support full-time graduate and professional training of women and of members of minority groups, especially those who have been underrepresented in academic and other professional careers of importance to the national interest.
Contact: Division of Higher Education Incentive Programs, Office of Postsecondary Education, Department of Education, ROB-3, Seventh and D Streets, SW, Washington, DC 20202, 202-245-3253.

84.097   LAW SCHOOL CLINICAL EXPERIENCE PROGRAM
Type of Assistance: Grants ranging from $14,030 to $23,370.
Applicant Eligibility: Nonprofit organizations.
Objective: To establish and expand programs in law schools to provide clinical experience to students in the practice of law, develop new areas of clinical experience, increase the number of participating students; and develop and implement new teaching techniques.
Contact: Division of Higher Education Incentive Programs, Office of Postsecondary Education, Department of Education, Seventh and D Streets, SW, Washington, DC 20202, 202-245-3253.

84.099   BILINGUAL VOCATIONAL INSTRUCTOR TRAINING
Type of Assistance: Grants and direct payments ranging from $125,000 to $225,000.
Applicant Eligibility: Nonprofit organizations, state and local governments.
Objective: To provide training for instructors of bilingual vocational training programs.
Contact: Office of Vocational and Adult Education, Department of Education, 400 Maryland Avenue, SW, ROB-3, Room 5028, Washington, DC 20202, 202-245-2614.

84.100   BILINGUAL VOCATIONAL INSTRUCTIONAL
MATERIALS, METHODS AND TECHNIQUES
Type of Assistance: Grants and direct payments averaging $200,000.
Applicant Eligibility: Nonprofit organizations, state and local governments.
Objective: To develop bilingual instructional materials and encourage research programs and demonstration projects to meet the shortage of such instructional materials available for bilingual vocational training programs.

Contact: Office of Vocational and Adult Education, Department of Education, 400 Maryland Avenue, SW, Room 5028, Washington, DC 20202, 202-245-2614.

84.101 VOCATIONAL EDUCATION— INDIAN AND HAWAIIAN NATIVES

Type of Assistance: Grants ranging from $29,148 to $603,453.
Applicant Eligibility: Native Americans.
Objective: To make grants to Indian tribal organizations to plan, conduct, and administer programs or portions of programs that provide occupational training opportunities.
Contact: Division of Innovation and Development, Office of Assistant Secretary for Vocational and Adult Education, Department of Education, 400 Maryland Avenue, SW, Washington, DC 20202, 202-245-2774 and 202-245-2614.

84.103 TRAINING FOR SPECIAL PROGRAMS STAFF AND LEADERSHIP PERSONNEL

Type of Assistance: Grants averaging $95,967.
Applicant Eligibility: Nonprofit organizations, state and local governments.
Objective: To provide training for staff and leadership personnel associated with projects funded under the Special Programs for Students from Disadvantaged Backgrounds.
Contact: Division of Student Services, Office of Postsecondary Education, Department of Education, 400 Maryland Avenue, SW, Washington, DC 20202, 202-245-2165.

84.116 FUND FOR THE IMPROVEMENT OF POSTSECONDARY EDUCATION

Type of Assistance: Grants ranging from $5,000 to $150,000.
Applicant Eligibility: Nonprofit organizations, state and local governments.
Objective: To provide assistance for innovative programs which improve the access to and the quality of postsecondary education.
Contact: Fund for the Improvement of Postsecondary Education, Office of the Assistant Secretary for Postsecondary Education, Department of Education, Seventh and D Streets, SW, ROB-3, Room 3100, Washington, DC 20202, 202-245-8091.

84.117 EDUCATIONAL RESEARCH AND DEVELOPMENT

Type of Assistance: Grants ranging from $1,500 to $3,900,000.
Applicant Eligibility: Nonprofit organizations, state and local governments.
Objective: To support the conduct of educational research and development, dissemination, utilization and evaluation of the findings of educational research. Educational research includes basic and applied research, planning, surveys, assessments, investigations, experiments and demonstrations in the field of education.

Contact: Public Affairs Office, National Institute of Education, 1200 19th Street, NW, Washington, DC 20208, 202-254-5800.

84.120 MINORITY INSTITUTIONS SCIENCE IMPROVEMENT PROGRAM

Type of Assistance: Grants ranging from $15,000 to $500,000.

Applicant Eligibility: Colleges, universities, nonprofit organizations.

Objective: To assist institutions in the improvement of the quality of preparation of their students of minority work or careers in science. To increase the number of minority students graduating with majors in one of the sciences, mathematics or engineering. To improve access for minorities to careers in science and engineering through community outreach programs at eligible colleges and universities. To improve the capability of minority institutions for self-assessment, management and evaluation of their science programs and dissemination of their results.

Contact: Division of Higher Education Incentive Programs, Office of Postsecondary Education, Department of Education, Washington, DC 20202, 202-245-3253.

84.124 TERRITORIAL TEACHER TRAINING ASSISTANCE PROGRAM

Type of Assistance: Grants ranging from $95,000 to $420,000.

Applicant Eligibility: US territories.

Objective: To provide assistance for the training of teachers in schools in Guam, American Samoa, the Commonwealth of the Northern Mariana Islands, the Trust Territory of the Pacific Islands, and the Virgin Islands.

Contact: Director, Center for Libraries and Education Improvement, Department of Education, 400 Maryland Avenue, SW, Washington, DC 20202, 202-254-6572.

84.126 REHABILITATION SERVICES—BASIC SUPPORT

Type of Assistance: Grants ranging from $2,197,414 to $50,797,321.

Applicant Eligibility: State governments.

Objective: To provide vocational rehabilitation services to persons with mental and/or physical handicaps. Priority service is placed on needs of those persons with the most severe disabilities.

Contact: Office of Program Operations, Rehabilitation Services Administration, Office of Special Education and Rehabilitative Services, Department of Education, Washington, DC 20201, 202-732-1394.

84.128 REHABILITATION SERVICES—SPECIAL PROJECTS

Type of Assistance: Grants (dollar amount not available).

Applicant Eligibility: Nonprofit organizations, state and local governments.

Objective: To provide funds to state vocational rehabilitation agencies and public nonprofit organizations for projects and demonstrations which hold promise of expanding and otherwise improving services for the mentally and physically handicapped over and above those provided by the basic support programs administered by states.

Contact: Rehabilitative Services Administration, Office of Special Education and Rehabilitative Services, Department of Education, Washington, DC 20201, 202-732-1287.

84.129 REHABILITATION TRAINING
Type of Assistance: Grants ranging from $15,000 to $300,000.
Applicant Eligibility: Nonprofit organizations, state and local governments.
Objective: To support projects to increase the numbers of personnel trained in providing vocational rehabilitation services to handicapped individuals in areas targeted as having personnel shortages.
Contact: Rehabilitative Services Administration, Office of Special Education and Rehabilitative Services, Department of Education, Washington, DC 20201, 202-732-1325.

84.132 CENTERS FOR INDEPENDENT LIVING
Type of Assistance: Grants averaging $150,000 to $200,000.
Applicant Eligibility: Nonprofit organizations, state and local governments.
Objective: To provide independent living services to severely handicapped individuals in order for them to function more independently in family and community settings and secure and maintain appropriate employment.
Contact: Office of Developmental Programs, Rehabilitative Services Administration, OSERS, Department of Education, 400 Maryland Avenue, SW, Washington DC 20201, 202-732-1287.

84.133 NATIONAL INSTITUTE OF HANDICAPPED RESEARCH
Type of Assistance: Project grants ranging from $10,000 to $750,000.
Applicant Eligibility: Nonprofit organizations and local governments.
Objective: To support research and its utilization to improve the lives of people of all ages with physical and mental handicaps, especially the severely disabled, through identifying and eliminating causes and consequences of disability; maximizing the healthy physical and emotional status of handicapped persons and preventing or minimizing adverse personal, family, physical, mental, social, educational, vocational and economic effects of disability; and reducing or eliminating the barriers to service and assistance and to using their abilities in daily life.
Contact: Director, National Institute of Handicapped Research, Office of Special Education and Rehabilitative Services, Department of Education, Mail Stop 2305, 400 Maryland Avenue, SW, Washington, DC 20201, 202-732-1200.

84.136 LEGAL TRAINING FOR THE DISADVANTAGED
Type of Assistance: Grants up to $1,000.
Applicant Eligibility: Individuals from a low-income or economically disadvantaged background who will have graduated from college at the beginning of the summer may apply.

Objective: To provide educationally and economically disadvantaged students, many with marginal or less-than-traditional admissions credentials, an opportunity to attend an ABA–accredited law school by operating seven six-week institutes.
Contact: Division of Higher Education Incentive Programs, Higher Education Support Programs, Department of Education, Room 3022, Seventh and D Streets, SW, Washington, DC 20202, 202-245-3253.

84.141 MIGRANT EDUCATION—HIGH SCHOOL EQUIVALENCY PROGRAM

Type of Assistance: Grants (dollar amount not available).
Applicant Eligibility: Postsecondary schools.
Objective: To provide assistance to older migratory and seasonal farmworker children to attend college and/or attain a job or high school diploma.
Contact: Office of Migrant Education, Department of Education, 400 Maryland Avenue, SW, ROB-3, Room 3616, Washington, DC 20202, 202-245-2722.

84.142 HOUSING FOR EDUCATIONAL INSTITUTIONS

Type of Assistance: Loans ranging from $100,000 to $3,500,000.
Applicant Eligibility: Public and private colleges and universities.
Objective: To alleviate severe student and faculty housing shortages through construction, acquisition or rehabilitation to provide student and faculty housing and related dining facilities. To reduce fuel consumption or other operating costs of existing eligible housing and related dining facilities.
Contact: Division of Higher Education Incentive Programs, Office of Postsecondary Education, Department of Education, 400 Maryland Avenue, SW, Washington, DC 20202, 202-245-3253.

84.144 MIGRANT EDUCATION—INTERSTATE AND INTRASTATE COORDINATION PROGRAM

Type of Assistance: Grants (dollar amount not available).
Applicant Eligibility: State educational agencies.
Objective: To carry out activities, in consultation with the states, to improve the interstate and intrastate coordination among state and local educational agencies servicing migratory children and to operate a system for the transfer of migrant student records.
Contact: Office of Migrant Education, Compensatory Education Programs, Office of Elementary and Secondary Education, Department of Education, 400 Maryland Avenue, SW, Washington, DC 20202, 202-245-2722.

84.145 FEDERAL REAL PROPERTY ASSISTANCE PROGRAM

Type of Assistance: Sale, exchange or donation of property.
Applicant Eligibility: Organizations providing educational programs.
Objective: To sell or lease surplus Federal Real Property for educational purposes at fair market value. Granting public benefit allowance

for each month of successfully conducting its proposed publicly beneficial education programs.
Contact: Federal Real Property Assistance Program, Office of Management, Department of Education, 400 Maryland Avenue, SW, Washington, DC 20202, 202-245-0306.

84.146 TRANSITION PROGRAM FOR REFUGEE CHILDREN

Type of Assistance: Grants and direct payments averaging $150 per eligible child.
Applicant Eligibility: State educational agencies, nonprofit private organizations.
Objective: To provide federal assistance to state and local educational agencies to meet the special educational needs of eligible refugee children enrolled in elementary and secondary schools.
Contact: Office of Bilingual Education and Minority Languages Affairs, Department of Education, 400 Maryland Avenue, SW, Room 421, Reporters Building, Washington, DC 20201, 202-732-1842.

84.148 ALLEN J. ELLENDER FELLOWSHIP PROGRAM

Type of Assistance: Grants.
Applicant Eligibility: Nonpartisan, nonprofit educational foundation.
Objective: To provide in the name of Allen J. Ellender an opportunity for participation by students of limited economic means and by their teachers, in the week-long government studies program supported by the Close-Up Foundation. To increase understanding of the federal government among secondary school students and their teachers and communities.
Contact: Close-Up Foundation, 1235 Jefferson Davis Highway, Arlington, VA 22202, 703-892-5400.

84.149 MIGRANT EDUCATION—
COLLEGE ASSISTANCE MIGRANT PROGRAM

Type of Assistance: Grants.
Applicant Eligibility: Institutions of higher education.
Objective: To assist students who are engaged, or whose families are engaged, in migrant and other seasonal farmwork who are enrolled or are admitted for enrollment on a full-time basis in the first academic year at an institution of higher education.
Contact: Migrant Education Programs, Office of Elementary and Secondary Education, Department of Education, 400 Maryland Avenue, SW, Donohoe Building, Room 3616, Washington, DC 20201, 202-245-2722.

84.151 IMPROVING SCHOOL PROGRAMS—
STATE BLOCK GRANTS

Type of Assistance: Grants ranging from $2,229,304 to $42,084,402.
Applicant Eligibility: States and territories of the U.S.
Objective: To assist state and local education agencies in the improvement of elementary and secondary education, through consolidation

of 28 elementary and secondary programs into a single authorization. The goal is to reduce paperwork and assign responsibility for the design and implementation of programs to local educational agencies.
Contact: Division of Educational Support, State and Local Educational Programs, Office of Elementary and Secondary Education, Department of Education, 400 Maryland Avenue, SW, Room 2011, FOB-6 Donohoe Building, Washington, DC 20202, 202-245-7965.

84.153 BUSINESS AND INTERNATIONAL EDUCATION
Type of Assistance: Grants ranging from $3,250 to $110,000.
Applicant Eligibility: Institutions of higher learning.
Objective: To promote innovation and improvement in international education curricula and to serve the needs of the business community.
Contact: International Studies Branch, Division of International Services and Improvement, Department of Education, 400 Maryland Avenue, SW, ROB-3, Room 3916, Washington, DC 20202, 202-245-2794.

84.154 PUBLIC LIBRARY CONSTRUCTION
Type of Assistance: Grants.
Applicant Eligibility: State library extension agencies.
Objective: To assist with public library construction.
Contact: State and Public Library Services Branch, Division of Library Programs, Center for Education Improvement, Department of Education, Room 613, Brown Building, 400 Maryland Avenue, SW, Washington, DC 20202, 202-254-9664.

84.155 REMOVAL OF ARCHITECTURAL BARRIERS TO THE HANDICAPPED
Type of Assistance: Grants (dollar amount not available).
Applicant Eligibility: State educational agencies.
Objective: To provide financial assistance to state and local educational agencies for the removal of architectural barriers from existing buildings and equipment to aid the handicapped.
Contact: Special Education Programs, Office of the Assistant Secretary for Special Education and Rehabilitative Services, Department of Education, 400 Maryland Avenue, SW, Washington, DC 20202, 202-732-1025.

84.158 SECONDARY EDUCATION AND TRANSITIONAL SERVICES FOR HANDICAPPED YOUTH
Type of Assistance: Project grants ranging from $50,000 to $200,000.
Applicant Eligibility: Institutes of higher education, state and local governments.
Objective: To promote education, training and related services to the handicapped; to assist in the transition into postsecondary education; to improve and develop secondary special education programs.
Contact: Research Projects Branch, Division of Educational Services, Office of Special Education Programs, 400 Maryland Avenue, SW, Washington, DC 20202, 202-732-1064.

84.159 HANDICAPPED—SPECIAL STUDIES

Type of Assistance: Project grants ranging from $50,000 to $200,000.
Applicant Eligibility: State educational agencies.
Objective: To finance data collection for studies and evaluations; to measure the effectiveness of programs for handicapped children and youth; to provide support for the publication of an annual report to Congress.
Contact: Research Projects Branch, Chief, Division of Educational Services, Office of Special Education Programs, 400 Maryland Avenue, SW, Washington, DC 20202, 202-472-5040.

84.160 TRAINING INTERPRETERS FOR DEAF INDIVIDUALS

Type of Assistance: Project grants ranging from $70,000 to $125,000.
Applicant Eligibility: Public or nonprofit agencies, state and local governments.
Objective: To support projects and increase the numbers and improve the skills of manual and oral interpreters who provide services to deaf individuals.
Contact: Office of Special Education and Rehabilitative Services, Department of Education, Washington, DC 20202, 202-732-1357.

84.161 CLIENT ASSISTANCE FOR HANDICAPPED INDIVIDUALS

Type of Assistance: Grants ranging from $30,000 to $601,443.
Applicant Eligibility: States.
Objective: To provide clients with information about benefits available to them under the Rehabilitation Act; to assist clients in their relationships with service providers; to protect individual rights under the act.
Contact: Department of Education, Associate Commissioner for Program Operations, Rehabilitation Services Administration, Office of Special Education and Rehabilitative Services, Washington, DC 20202, 202-732-1396.

84.162 EMERGENCY IMMIGRANT EDUCATION ASSISTANCE

Type of Assistance: Grants (dollar amount not available).
Applicant Eligibility: States.
Objective: To assist states in providing educational services for immigrant children.
Contact: Office of Bilingual Education and Minority Languages Affairs, Department of Education, Reporters Building, 400 Maryland Avenue, SW, Room 421, Washington, DC 20202, 202-732-1842.

84.163 LIBRARY SERVICES FOR INDIAN TRIBES AND HAWAIIAN NATIVES

Type of Assistance: Project grants.
Applicant Eligibility: Recognized Indian tribes and Hawaiian natives.
Objective: To promote the extension of library services and programs to Indian people living on or near reservations.

Contact: Library Education, Research and Resources Branch, Division of Library Programs, Center for Libraries and Education Improvement, Office of Educational Research and Improvement, Department of Education, 400 Maryland Avenue, SW, Washington, DC 20202-1630, 202-245-5090.

84.164 STATE GRANTS FOR STRENGTHENING THE SKILLS OF TEACHERS AND INSTRUCTION IN MATHEMATICS, SCIENCE, FOREIGN LANGUAGES AND COMPUTER LEARNING

Type of Assistance: Grants averaging $1,713,633.
Applicant Eligibility: State educational agencies.
Objective: To improve the skills of teachers and the instruction materials in math, science, computer learning and foreign languages; to increase accessibility of instruction to students.
Contact: State and Local Educational Programs, Room 2011, FOB-6, 400 Maryland Avenue, SW, Washington, DC 20202, 202-245-7965.

84.165 MAGNET SCHOOLS ASSISTANCE

Type of Assistance: Project grants (dollar amount not available).
Applicant Eligibility: Local educational agencies.
Objective: To provide grants for use in magnet schools that are part of approved desegregation plans and that are designed to bring together students from different social, economic, racial and ethnic backgrounds. Funds may not be used for transportation, consultants or nonacademic activities.
Contact: State and Local Education Programs, Room 2011, FOB6, 400 Maryland Avenue, SW, Washington, DC 20202, 202-245-7965.

84.168 SECRETARY'S DISCRETIONARY PROGRAM FOR MATHEMATICS, SCIENCE, COMPUTER LEARNING AND CRITICAL FOREIGN LANGUAGES

Type of Assistance: Project grants ranging from $10,000 to $100,000.
Applicant Eligibility: State and local educational agencies, public nonprofit organizations including museums, libraries, math and engineering societies.
Objective: To provide support for projects that improve skills of teachers and instruction in math, science, computer learning and critical foreign languages; to increase the access of all students to such instruction.
Contact: Secretary's Discretionary Program, Office of the Secretary, Department of Education, Washington, DC 20202, 202-472-1762.

84.169 COMPREHENSIVE SERVICES FOR INDEPENDENT LIVING

Type of Assistance: Grants of $93,553.
Applicant Eligibility: State agencies.
Objective: To assist severely handicapped individuals in living and functioning independently in family settings or to maintain employment.

Contact: Office of the Assistant Secretary for Special Education and Rehabilitative Services, Department of Education, Office of Program Operations, Rehabilitation Services Administration, Washington, DC 20202, 202-732-1414.

84.170   NATIONAL GRADUATE FELLOWS
Type of Assistance: Project grants ranging from $2,000 to $27,000.
Applicant Eligibility: Individuals.
Objective: To provide fellowships to meritorious doctoral candidates to enable them to complete studies in the fields of art, humanities and social sciences.
Contact: Division of Higher Education Incentive Program, Education Department, Office of Postsecondary Education, Washington, DC 20202, 202-245-3253.

84.171   EXCELLENCE IN EDUCATION
Type of Assistance: Project grants ranging from $15,000 to $40,000.
Applicant Eligibility: Local educational agencies.
Objective: To provide assistance to individual public schools across the country in the carrying out of programs designed to achieve educational excellence.
Contact: The Excellence in Education Program, Office of the Secretary, Department of Education, Washington, DC 20202, 202-472-1762.

84.172   CONSTRUCTION, RECONSTRUCTION AND RENOVATION OF ACADEMIC FACILITIES
Type of Assistance: Project grants (dollar amount not available).
Applicant Eligibility: Accredited postsecondary institutions.
Objective: To provide assistance to postsecondary institutions in order to construct, reconstruct or renovate academic facilities.
Contact: Office of Postsecondary Education, Division of Higher Education Incentive Programs, Washington, DC 20202, 202-245-3253.

84.173   HANDICAPPED-PRESCHOOL INCENTIVE GRANTS
Type of Assistance: Grants ranging from $49,000 to $2,215,417.
Applicant Eligibility: State educational agencies.
Objective: To assist states in providing a free appropriate education to all preschool-age handicapped children.
Contact: Division of Assistance to States, Office of the Assistant Secretary for Special Education and Rehabilitative Services, Department of Education, 400 Maryland Avenue, SW, Washington, DC 20202, 202-732-1025.

HARRY S TRUMAN SCHOLARSHIP FOUNDATION

85.001   HARRY S TRUMAN SCHOLARSHIP PROGRAM
Type of Assistance: Direct payments ranging from $1,000 to $5,000 per year.
Applicant Eligibility: Individuals.
Objective: To honor the former President Harry S Truman through the operation of a perpetual educational scholarship program to develop increased opportunities for young Americans to prepare for and pursue careers in public service.
Contact: Executive Secretary, Harry S Truman Scholarship Program, 712 Jackson Place, NW, Washington, DC 20006, 202-395-4831.

PENSION BENEFIT GUARANTY CORPORATION

86.001   PENSION PLAN TERMINATION INSURANCE
Type of Assistance: Insurance.
Applicant Eligibility: Private businesses and organizations.
Objective: To encourage the continuation and maintenance of voluntary private pension plans for the benefit of their participants, to provide for the timely and uninterrupted payment of pension benefits to participants in and beneficiaries of covered plans, and to maintain premiums charged by the PBGC at the lowest level consistent with carrying out its obligations.
Contact: Pension Benefit Guaranty Corporation, 2020 K Street, NW, Washington, DC 20006, 202-254-4817.

89.003   NATIONAL ARCHIVES AND RECORDS ADMINISTRATION
Type of Assistance: Grants ranging from $5,000 to $90,000.
Applicant Eligibility: Nonprofit organizations, state and local governments.
Objective: To carry out the National Historical Documents Program, which will help preserve important historical documents.

INDEX

Academic facilities, *see* Educational equipment and facilities

Accident prevention:
  highway, 20.600
  mining, 17.600

Adolescence:
  sexual activity, 13.111, 133.995

Adoption:
  demonstration projects, 13.652
  handicapped children, 13.659

Aging and the aged:
  community service employment program, 17.235
  discretionary projects and programs, 13.668
  discrimination against, *see* Civil rights
  food and nonmedical support services in public projects, 14.170
  food distribution, 10.550
  foster grandparent volunteer program, 72.001
  housing—nonprofit sponsor assistance program, 14.141
  Indians, 13.655
  maintenance assistance for Guam, Puerto Rico, and Virgin Islands, 13.808
  medical education, 13.969
  medical research, 13.866
  nutrition, 10.550, 13.635
  personnel training, 13.668
  rental assistance, rural, 10.427
  rental housing financing, 14.157
  research grants, 13.668
  retired senior volunteer program, 72.002
  retirement insurance (Social Security), 13.803, 13.804
  senior centers, 13.633
  senior companions to adults with special needs, part-time volunteers, 72.008
  social services research and demonstration projects, 13.633, 13.647
  special benefits for persons age 72 and over (Social Security), 13.804
  tax counseling, 21.006
  weatherization assistance, 81.042

Agricultural commodities:
  commodity loans and purchases, 10.051
  crop insurance, 10.450
  direct food distribution, 10.550
  food distribution to Indians, 10.550, 10.567
  foreign market development and promotion, 10.600

Agricultural conservation:
  emergency aid, 10.054
  erosion control, 10.063, 10.900, 10.904
  Great Plains conservation, 10.900
  resource conservation and development loans, 10.414
  soil conservation and water development loans, 10.416
  water pollution, 10.063, 10.068
  wetlands protection, 10.062

Agricultural education:
  extension programs, 10.500
  graduate fellowship grants, 10.210
  higher education grants, 10.211

Agricultural labor, *see* Farm and migrant labor

Agricultural loans and loan insurance:
  aquaculture, 10.422
  commodity loans, 10.051
  emergency loans, 10.404
  family farms, 10.406, 10.407
  farm labor housing, 10.405
  farm operating expenses, 10.406
  farm ownership, 10.407
  housing sites, 10.411
  low-income housing, 10.410

Agricultural loans (*cont.*)
 rental housing, 10.415
 resource conservation and development, 10.414
 soil conservation and water development loans, 10.416
 storage facilities and equipment, 10.056
Agricultural marketing:
 commodity loans and purchases, 10.051
 cotton production, 10.052
 dairy indemnity payments, 10.053
 educational programs, 10.500
 exports, 10.156, 10.600
 Federal-State Marketing Improvement Program, 10.156
 grain production stabilization, 10.055
 information dissemination, 10.156
 natural disaster emergency loans, 10.404
 rice production stabilization, 10.065
 wheat production stabilization, 10.058
 wool and mohair production stabilization, 10.059
Agricultural research:
 animal health and disease, 10.207
 basic and applied research, 10.001
 biological stress on plants, 10.206
 competitive research grants, 10.206
 experiments under Hatch Act, 10.203
 fertilizer development, 62.001
 food animal productivity, 10.207
 forestry, 10.202, 10.652
 genetic, 10.206
 high-priority problems, 10.200
 land-grant colleges, 10.205, 10.209
 nitrogen fixation, 10.206
 nutrition, 10.206
 pesticides control research grants, 66.502
 photosynthesis, 10.206
 special research grants, 10.200
 Tuskegee Institute, 10.205, 10.209
Air pollution:
 consolidated state grants, 66.600
 manpower training grants, 66.003
 program development grants, 66.001

 research and development grants, 66.501
Alcohol abuse:
 applied, basic, and clinical research programs, 13.273
 block grants, 13.992
 minority researcher grants, 13.282
 National Research Service grants, 13.272
 research center grants, 13.891
 scientist development and research scientist grants, 13.271
 Small Business Innovation Research, 13.126
Aliens and refugees:
 emergency immigrant education assistance, 84.162
 mental health services, 13.128
 refugee assistance—voluntary agency programs, 13.815
 refugee health programs, 13.987
 Soviet refugees resettlement, 13.815
 transition program for refugee children in elementary and secondary schools, 84.146
Anthropology:
 Smithsonian special foreign currency grants, 60.016
Appalachian region:
 child development, 23.013
 demonstration projects, 23.011
 energy planning, 23.001
 highway system development, 23.003
 industrial development, 23.002
 local access roads, 23.008
 long-term development planning, 23.001
 planning and development resources in multicounty areas, 23.009
 primary health care, 23.004
 recreation, 23.002
 stimulating public investment in public facilities, 23.001
 technical assistance, 23.011
 transportation planning, research, and demonstration programs, 23.017
 vocational training, 23.012
 waste disposal systems, 23.002

Archaeology:
  basic research, 45.140
  Smithsonian special foreign currency grants, 60.016
  youth grants, 45.115
Architecture:
  grants and direct payments, 45.001
Art history:
  youth grants, 45.115
Arthritis research, *see* Medical research
Arts funding and promotion:
  advancement grants, 45.022
  architecture, 45.001
  art administration fellowships, 45.021
  Artists-in-Education Program, 45.003
  challenge grants, 45.013
  craftsmen, 45.009
  creative writing, 45.004
  dance, 45.002
  design arts, 45.001
  ethnic arts, 45.010
  film, 45.006
  folk arts, 45.015
  insurance for art works and artifacts from abroad, 45.201
  interior design, 45.001
  literature, 45.004
  media arts, 45.006
  music, 45.004
  musical theatre, 45.014
  National Endowment for the Arts internships, 45.021
  National Gallery of Art extension service, 68.001
  national graduate fellowships, 84.170
  opera, 45.014
  painters, 45.009
  photography, 45.009
  printmaking, 45.009
  public arts agencies grants, 45.007
  radio, 45.006
  rural communities, 45.010
  sculptors, 45.009
  suburban communities, 45.010
  television, 45.006
  theater, 45.008
  two or more art forms, 45.011
  urban and environmental design, 45.001

  urban communities, 45.010
  video, 45.006
  visual arts, 45.009
Astronomy:
  basic research, 47.050
  Smithsonian special foreign currency grants, 60.016
Atmospheric sciences:
  research, 47.050
Aviation:
  airport improvement program, 20.016
  federal surplus land conveyed for public airports, 39.002
  federal surplus personal property conveyed for public airports, 39.003

Banks and lending institutions:
  guaranteed student loans, 84.032
  National Defense Student loans, 84.038
  reimbursement of canceled National Defense Student loans, 84.037
Behavioral disorders:
  environmental health hazards, 13.113
Bilingual education:
  elementary and secondary schools, 84.003
  emergency immigrant education assistance, 84.162
  vocational instructional materials, methods, and techniques, 84.100
  vocational instructor training, 84.099
  vocational training, 84.077
Biology:
  basic research, 47.051
  biomedical engineering and research, 13.337, 13.371, 13.821
  cancer biology research, 13.396
  cellular, 47.051
  environmental, 47.051
  marine biology, 13.894
  microbiology and infectious diseases research, 13.856
  minority biomedical research support, 13.375, 13.389
  molecular, 47.501
  Smithsonian special foreign currency grants, 60.016

Birds, *see* Fish and wildlife
Birth control, *see* Family planning
Blindness and the blind:
  cataract research, 13.869
  corneal diseases research, 13.868
  deaf-blind children's centers, 84.025
  glaucoma research, 13.870
  retinal and choroidal diseases research, 13.867
  state aid for maintenance assistance, 13.808
  vision substitution devices, 13.871
  see also Handicapped
Business development:
  business and industrial loans, rural, 10.422
  Indian tribes, 10.422, 11.301, 15.124
Businesses, small, *see* Small businesses

Cancer:
  biology research, 13.396
  biometry and risk estimation, 13.115
  cause and prevention research, 13.393, 13.3999
  detection and diagnosis research, 13.394, 13.399
  environmental health hazards, 13.113, 13.894
  research facilities construction and expansion, 13.392
  research manpower grants, 13.398
  treatment research, 13.395, 13.399
Career guidance:
  cooperative extension service, 10.500
  Indians, 15.108
  see also Employment, employment services; Vocational training and rehabilitation
Charitable institutions:
  food assistance, 10.550
Chemicals, *see* Hazardous chemicals and wastes, Pesticides
Chemistry:
  basic research, 47.049
Child and family welfare:
  adoption demonstration projects, 13.652

adoption of children with special needs, 13.659
aid to families with dependent children, 13.808
child abuse and neglect, 13.669, 13.670
child support enforcement, 13.679, 13.811
demonstration project grants, 13.608
emergency assistance to families with children, 13.808
foster care, 13.658
Head Start, 13.600
Indian, 15.103, 15.144
locating absent parents, 13.679
research grants, 13.608, 13.812
runaway youth, 13.623
state grants for services, 13.645
survivors insurance (Social Security), 13.805
training grants, 13.648
Child development:
  Appalachian region, 23.013
  extension programs, 10.500
  foster grandparents, 72.001
  Head Start program, 13.600
Child health:
  block grants, 13.994
  emergency medical service, 13.127
  food distribution, general, 10.550
  food program, child care, 10.558
  food program, special supplemental, 10.557
  genetic disease testing, counseling, and information development, 13.110
  immunization grants, 13.268
  medical research, 13.865
  milk program, special, 10.556
  school breakfast program, 10.553
  school lunch program, 10.553
Civil defense:
  communications and control capabilities of state and local governments, 83.513
  emergency broadcast system guidance and assistance, 83.515
  personnel training, 83.400, 83.403
  population protection planning, 83.514
  radiological emergency preparedness, 83.508

radiological instruments calibra-
tion, 83.508
state and local civil defense readiness, 83.504
state and local emergency operating centers, 83.512
state civil defense management assistance, 83.503
see also Disaster preparation and
relief
Civil rights:
employment discrimination, 30.002
employment discrimination against
Indians, 30.009
technical assistance and training
for school districts, 84.004
Climatology:
intergovernmental climate-demon-
stration project, 11.428
Coal industry:
abandoned mine land reclamation
program, 15.250
abandoned mine program, rural,
10.910
Appalachian mine area restoration, 23.010
black lung clinics, 13.965
black lung disability benefits,
13.806, 17.307
coal conversion and utilization
technologies research, 81.057
coal loan guarantees for small and
medium-sized producers, 81.056
mine health and safety grants,
17.600
state grants for regulation of surface effects, 15.250
underground low-sulfur assistance,
81.056
see also Mining industries
Colleges and universities, *see* Education, higher
Commerce:
business and international education, 84.153
economic development loans,
11.301
foreign investment direct loans,
70.005
foreign investment insurance,
70.003
foreign investment loan guarantees, 70.002

foreign pre-investment assistance,
70.004
international trade adjustment assistance, 11.109
international trade promotion,
11.108
minority business development,
11.800
Communications:
emergency broadcast system guidance and assistance, 83.515
emergency public information
grants, 83.518
National Endowment for the Humanities grants, 45.104
National Endowment of the Arts
grants, 45.006
public telecommunications facilities grants, 11.550
rural Telephone Bank loans,
10.852
rural telephone loans and loan
guarantees, 10.851
state and local emergency warning
and communication systems,
83.513
see also Media arts, Radio, Television
Community development and planning:
adjustable rate mortgages,
14.175
American Samoa, 14.223
Appalachian region—local development district assistance,
23.009
Appalachian region—supplements
to federal grants-in-aid for,
23.002
block grants/entitlement grants,
14.218
block grants/small cities program,
14.219
block grants/state's program,
14.228
community facilities loans, rural,
10.423
community health centers, 13.129,
13.130, 13.224
Community Housing Resource
Board (CHRB) grants, 14.403
Guam, 14.223
Indian communities, 14.223

Community development and planning (*cont.*)
  neighborhood rehabilitation loans, 14.220
  new communities mortgage insurance, 14.125
  Northern Mariana Islands, 14.223
  public works grants, 11.300
  research on housing needs and community development, 14.506
  rural self-help housing technical assistance, 10.420
  rural water-based recreational facilities, 10.414
  Section 3 compliance complaints, 14.401
  urban development action grants, 14.221
  urban homesteading, 14.222
  Virgin Islands, 14.223
  see also Rural communities, Urban communities
Computer science:
  basic research, 47.049
  biomedical engineering, 13.821
  biotechnology research, 13.371
  teaching skills grants, 84.164, 84.168
Condominium housing:
  construction mortgages, 14.112
  substantial rehabilitation mortgages, 14.112
  unit purchase mortgages, 14.133
Construction, *see* Housing construction
Contraception:
  adolescent family life research grants, 13.111
  family planning services, 13.217
  product development, 13.864
Cooperative housing:
  elderly, 14.157
  handicapped, 14.157
  interest reduction payments, 14.103
  investor-sponsored—mortgage insurance, 14.124
  management-type—mortgage insurance, 14.126
  mortgage insurance for purchase of shares, 14.163
  sales-type—mortgage insurance, 14.115, 14.132

Cotton production:
  stabilization programs, 10.052
Craftsmen:
  National Endowment for the Arts grants, 45.009
Credit unions:
  establishment and operating assistance, 44.001
Crime victim:
  assistance and compensation programs, 16.575, 16.576
Criminal justice:
  block grants, 16.573
  corrections policy formation, 16.602
  corrections research and program evaluation, 16.602
  corrections seminars, workshops, and training programs, 16.601
  corrections training and staff development, 16.601
  discretionary grants, 16.574
  federal surplus personal property conveyed, 39.003
  graduate research fellowships, 16.562
  juvenile justice and delinquency, 16.540, 16.541, 16.542
  research and development project grants, 16.560
  statistics development, 16.550
  technical assistance, 16.603
  visiting fellowships, 16.561
Crop insurance, *see* Agricultural commodities
Cultural affairs, *see* Art history, Arts funding and promotion, Dance, Film, Humanities funding, Libraries, Museums, Music, Musical theatre, Opera, Painting, Photography, Printmaking, Radio, Television, Theater, Sculpture, Video, Visual Arts

Dairy industry:
  indemnification payments, 10.053
  pesticide residues, 10.053
Dance:
  grants and direct payments, 45.002
Deafness and the deaf:
  captioned films and instructional media, 84.026

centers for deaf-blind children,
84.025
clinical research, 13.853, 13.854
media research, 84.026
training interpreters, 84.160
Delinquency, *see* Juvenile justice
and delinquency
Dental education:
capitation grants, 13.339
general practice residency programs, 13.897
National Health Service scholarship program, 13.288
school financial distress grants,
13.381
Dental research:
research institutes development,
13.845
Design arts:
grants and direct payments, 45.001
Disabled:
adapted housing for disabled veterans, 64.106
adapted housing loans for disabled
veterans, 64.118
administration for developmental
disabilities—basic support and
advocacy grants, 13.630
administration for developmental
disabilities—special projects,
13.631
administration for developmental
disabilities—university-affiliated
facilities, 13.632
automobiles and adaptive equipment for veterans, 64.100
black lung disability compensation, 13.806, 17.307
disability insurance (Social Security), 13.802
disability insurance for longshoremen and harbor workers,
17.302
disability insurance for railroad
workers, 57.001
educational assistance for dependents of disabled veterans,
64.117
food and nonmedical support services in public housing, 14.170
maintenance assistance in Guam,
Puerto Rico, and Virgin Islands,
13.808

Medicare hospital insurance,
13.773
Medicare supplementary medical
insurance, 13.774
pensions for veterans' nonservice-
connected disabilities, 64.104
service-connected disability compensation, 64.109
state aid for maintenance assistance, 13.808
Supplemental Security Income
(Social Security), 13.807
veterans loan program, 59.038
veterans state domiciliary care,
64.014
veterans state hospital care,
64.016
veterans state nursing home care,
64.015
vocational training for disabled
veterans, 64.116
see also Handicapped; Veterans,
disabled
Disadvantaged, *see* Education for
the disadvantaged
Disaster preparation and relief:
assistance to states for disaster
prevention and preparedness,
83.505
civil defense assistance to states,
83.503
crop insurance, 10.450
dairy indemnity payments, 10.053
disaster assistance following Presi-
dential declaration, 83.516
earthquake preparedness grants,
83.506
emergency broadcast system guidance and assistance, 83.515
emergency conservation measures,
10.054
emergency loans, agricultural,
10.404
emergency public information
challenge grants, 83.518
farmlands rehabilitation, 10.054
FEMA support staff training,
83.403
flood insurance, 83.100
hazard mitigation assistance,
83.519
hurricane preparedness grants,
83.506

Disaster preparation and relief
(*cont.*)
mental health disaster assistance,
13.982
mortgage insurance for disaster
victims, 14.119
physical disaster loans, 59.008
population protection planning,
83.514
radiological emergency preparedness, 83.508
school facilities reconstruction,
84.040
small businesses, 59.008
state and local civil defense readiness, 83.504
state and local emergency management defense personnel
training, 83.400
state and local emergency operating centers, 83.513
state civil defense management assistance, 83.503
watershed management, 10.419,
10.652, 10.904
see also Fire prevention and control
Discrimination, *see* Civil rights, Employment discrimination
Drug abuse:
applied, basic, and clinical research grants, 13.279
block grants, 13.992
minority researcher grants,
13.282
National Research Service grants,
13.278
research scientist development and
research scientists award, 13.277
small business innovation research, 13.126
Drugs, *see* Food and drug research,
Pharmacology

Ecology, *see* Environmental health,
Environmental management
Economic development:
coastal energy impact program,
11.422
district operational assistance,
11.306
long-term economic deterioration
arrest and reversal, 11.307

minority business development,
11.800
public works and development facilities grants, 11.300
public works impact projects,
11.304
special economic and adjustment
assistance program, 11.307
state and local planning, 11.305,
11.307
support for planning organizations, 11.302
technical assistance, 11.303
Economics:
research grants, 47.501
Education, adult:
Indians, 84.062
regional programs for deaf and
other handicapped persons,
84.078
state-administered programs,
84.002
Education, early childhood:
bilingual, 84.003
Follow Through program,
84.104
handicapped early childhood assistance, 84.024
Head Start program, 13.600
Education, elementary and secondary:
bilingual, 84.003
dropout prevention, 84.044
educationally deprived children in
low-income areas, 84.010
educational opportunity centers,
84.066
emergency immigrant assistance,
84.162
excellence in education, 84.171
Follow Through program,
84.014
humanities curriculum development, 45.111
humanities instruction, 45.127
interlibrary cooperation, 84.035
magnet schools assistance, 84.165
materials development and research in math, science, and
technology, 47.067
migrant education—basic state
formula grant program, 84.011
migrant education—high school
equivalency program, 84.141

migrant education—interstate and intrastate coordination program, 84.144

National Gallery of Art extension service, 68.001

National Institute of Education research grants, 84.117

state block grants, 84.151

student service-learning programs, 72.005

transition program for refugee children, 84.146

Education, general:

cooperative education, 84.055

criminal justice discretionary grants, 16.574

federal lands sold or leased for public educational purposes, 84.145

National Diffusion Program, 84.073

venereal disease, 13.978

women's educational equity, 84.083

see also Student financial aid

Education, higher:

academic research enhancement award, 13.390

business and international education, 84.153

construction, reconstruction and renovation of academic facilities, 84.172

cooperative education programs support, 84.055

dropout prevention programs, 84.044

energy graduate traineeship program, 81.075

foreign languages instruction, 84.015, 84.016, 84.017

Fulbright graduate exchange students, 82.001

Fulbright-Hays visiting lecturers, 82.002

Fund for the Improvement of Post-secondary Education, 84.116

graduate and professional study program assistance, 84.094

graduate fellowship grants in food and agricultural sciences, 10.210

graduate research fellowships in science, 47.009

health science research in minority institutions, 13.389

housing construction, acquisition and rehabilitation for students and faculty, 84.142

humanities demonstration programs, 45.111

humanities fellowships at centers for advanced study, 45.122

humanities fellowships for college teachers, 45.143

humanities in undergraduate education, 45.150

international exchange programs, 82.001, 82.002

international studies, 84.015, 84.016, 84.017

materials development and research in precollege math, science and technology, 47.067

national graduate fellowships in arts, humanities and social sciences, 84.170

nontraditional humanities programs, 45.111

research initiation and improvement for minorities, women and the handicapped, 47.069

strengthening grants in food and agricultural sciences, 10.211

strengthening institutions under Higher Education Act of 1965, 84.031

studies and program assessment in science and engineering, 47.068

summer humanities seminars for college teachers, 45.116

summer humanities seminars for secondary school teachers, 45.151

teacher enhancement in precollege science and math, 47.066

see also Dental education, Legal education, Medical education, Nursing education, Teacher education

Educational equipment and facilities:

Appalachian region, 23.012

asbestos hazards abatement (schools) assistance, 66.702

Educational equipment and facilities (*cont.*)
  construction, reconstruction and renovation of academic facilities, 84.172
  construction assistance for school districts with enrollments substantially affected by federal activities, 84.040
  Defense Industrial Reserve equipment loans, 12.001
  energy conservation assistance, 81.052
  federal surplus personal property conveyed, 39.003
  federal surplus real property conveyed, 39.002
  maintenance and operations assistance for school districts with enrollments substantially affected by federal activities, 84.041
  reconstruction after natural disaster, 84.040
  removal of architectural barriers to the handicapped, 84.155
  schools and roads—grants to counties, 10.666
  schools and roads—grants to states, 10.665
  see also School meals
Education for the disadvantaged:
  Close Up Foundation government studies program, 84.148
  dropout prevention, 84.004
  education opportunity centers, 84.066
  emergency immigrant education assistance, 84.162
  Head Start program, 13.600
  institutionalized children, 84.103
  law school preparation, 84.136
  migrant college assistance program, 84.149
  migrant education—basic state formula grant program, 84.011
  migrant education—high school equivalency program, 84.141
  migrant education—interstate and intrastate coordination program, 84.144
  postsecondary preparation (Upward Bound program), 84.047

  postsecondary special services, 84.042
  staff and leadership personnel training, 84.103
  state administrative expenses, 84.012
  state grants for needs of children in low-income areas, 84.010
  state student incentives programs, 84.069
  transition program for refugee children, 84.146
  see also Minority education
Education for the handicapped:
  architectural barrier removal, 84.155
  captioned films and instructional media for the deaf, 84.026
  centers for deaf-blind children, 84.025
  demonstration projects, 84.023
  information dissemination, 84.030
  innovative programs for severely handicapped children, 84.086
  media research for the deaf, 84.026
  personnel training, 84.029
  postsecondary special services, 84.042
  preschool and school programs, 84.027
  preschool incentive grants, 84.173
  regional programs for deaf and other handicapped persons, 84.078
  regional resources center, 84.028
  research grants, 84.023
  research initiation and improvement in science and engineering, 47.069
  secondary education and transitional services for handicapped youth, 84.158
  state-operated or state-supported schools, 84.009
  teacher recruitment, 84.030
Emergency assistance, *see* Disaster preparation and relief
Employment, employment services:
  comprehensive services for independent living for handicapped, 84.169
  dislocated workers, 17.246

Indians, 15.108, 17.251
labor-management cooperation grants, 34.002
migrant and seasonal farm workers, 17.247
placement service grants, 17.207
research and development projects, 17.248
senior community service employment program, 17.235
workers adversely affected by imports, 17.245
see also Vocational training and rehabilitation
Employment discrimination:
Indians, 30.009
Title VII enforcement guards, 30.002
Energy:
alternative energy source conversions, 81.050
Appalachian regional development, 23.001
basic energy sciences research, 81.049
biomass energy technology, 81.079
coastal energy impact program—formula grants, 11.421
coastal energy impact program—planning grants, 11.422
conservation promotion, 81.041
energy conservation for institutional buildings, 81.052
energy conservation research and development, 81.086
energy policy, planning and development, 81.080
energy task force for urban consortium, 81.081
environmental effects, 66.500
extension service, 81.050
field operations management research, 81.049
fusion energy research, 81.049
gas pipeline safety, 20.700
heating oil grants, 81.090
Indian-owned energy resources development, 81.076
industrial energy conservation, 81.078
international affairs and energy emergencies, 81.088
invention promotion, 81.036
low-income home energy assistance program, 13.818
minority business loans to defray bid and proposal costs for DOE programs, 81.063
minority educational institution research travel fund, 81.083
minority vocational training in energy-related technologies, 81.084
nuclear energy public education, 77.003
nuclear energy safety research, 77.003
nuclear waste disposal siting, 81.065
renewable energy research and development, 81.087
rural electrification loans and loan guarantees, 10.850
small business energy loans, 59.030
socioeconomic and demographic research in minorities' energy consumption, 81.091
university-DOE laboratory cooperative program, 81.004
university reactor sharing and fuel assistance, 81.011
university research instrumentation, 81.007
used energy-related laboratory equipment grants, 81.022
weatherization assistance for low-income persons, 81.042
Engineering:
advanced scientific computing resources, 47.065
innovative postdoctoral research, 47.049
measurement and engineering research grants, 11.609
minority institutions science improvement programs, 84.120
national goals attainment, 47.041
physiology and biomedical engineering, 13.821
research grants, 47.041
research initiation and improvement for minorities, women and the handicapped, 47.069
studies and program assessment in education, 47.068
university-DOE laboratory cooperative program, 81.004

Environmental design:
grants and direct payments, 45.001
Environmental health:
applied toxicological research and
testing, 13.114
biomedical research, 13.112,
13.113, 13.894
biometry and risk estimation,
13.115
public education, 13.990
resource and manpower development, 13.894
special educational initiatives
grants, 13.969
Environmental management:
abandoned mine land reclamation
program, 15.252
abandoned mine program, rural,
10.910
Appalachian mine area restoration, 23.010
cooperative forestry assistance,
10.664
endangered species conservation,
15.612
erosion and sedimentation control,
10.063
estuarine management, comprehensive, 66.456
farm fish pond management,
15.603
Great Lakes fisheries conservation, 11.405
hazardous substance response trust
fund, 66.802
hazardous waste management financial assistance, 66.801
irrigation distribution system
loans, 15.501
irrigation systems rehabilitation
and betterment, 15.502
Lake Champlain fisheries conservation, 11.405
migratory waterfowl protection,
10.062
research grants on environmental
effects of energy systems,
66.500
resource conservation and development loans, 10.414
small business pollution control financing guarantee, 59.031
small reclamation projects, 15.503

sport fish restoration and management, 15.605
toxic substance enforcement programs, 66.701
underground storage tanks program, 66.804
watershed management, 10.419,
10.904
wetlands protection, 10.062
wildlife habitat management technical assistance, 15.219
wildlife restoration, 15.611
Equal employment, see Civil rights,
Employment discrimination
Exports:
expanding foreign agricultural
markets, 10.156, 10.600
Eye research:
amblyopia, 13.871
cataract disorders, 13.869
corneal disease, 13.868
facility construction, 13.985
glaucoma, 13.870
retinal and choroidal diseases,
13.867
strabismus, 13.871
vision substitution devices,
13.871
visual processing, 13.871
see also Blindness and the blind

Family planning:
adolescent family life demonstration projects, 13.995
adolescent family life research
grants, 13.111
family planning services grants,
13.217, 13.260
Farm and migrant labor:
housing loans and grants, 10.405
migrant education—basic state
formula grant program, 84.011
migrant education—high school
equivalency program, 84.141
migrant education—interstate and
intrastate coordination program,
84.144
migrant health centers, 13.246
rental assistance, 10.427
training and support services,
17.247
Farm home loans, see Housing construction

Fashion design:
grants and direct payments, 45.001
Federal lands and surplus property:
Defense Department obsolete
property donations, 12.700
Federal Real Property Assistance
Program for educational purposes, 84.145
General Services Administration
sale of surplus personal property, 39.007
migrant college assistance program, 84.149
mineral material sold, exchanged
or donated, 15.214
surplus real property conveyed,
39.002
surplus wildlife disposals, 15.900
Feed grain production:
stabilization programs, 10.053
Film:
National Endowment of the Arts
grants, 45.006
Fire prevention and control:
federal surplus personal property
conveyed, 39.003
forestry research grants, 10.652
National Fire Academy student
stipends, 83.405
reimbursement for firefighting on
federal property, 83.409
rural communities, 10.423
Fish and wildlife:
anadromous fish conservation, Interior Department, 15.600
anadromous fish conservation, National Fisheries Service, 11.405
business and industrial loans,
10.422
commercial fisheries research and
development, 11.407
cooperative forestry assistance,
10.664
endangered species conservation,
15.612
farm fish pond stocking, 15.603
federal surplus land conveyed for
wildlife conservation, 39.002
forestry research grants, 10.652
Great Lakes fisheries conservation, 11.405, 15.600
Lake Champlain fisheries conservation, 11.405, 15.600

migratory waterfowl protection,
10.062
plant materials donated, 10.905
shellfish sanitation, 13.103
sport fish restoration and management, 15.605
surplus wildlife disposals, 15.900
Water Bank Program, 10.062
watershed management, 10.419,
10.904
wildlife habitat management technical assistance, 15.219
wildlife restoration, 15.611
Fishing, commercial:
guaranty fund for seizure by foreign countries, 11.410
mortgage guarantees, 11.415
oil and gas spills contingency fund,
11.408
research and development grants,
11.407, 11.427
vessel and gear damage compensation fund, 11.409
Flood prevention and control:
farmlands rehabilitation, 10.054
flood insurance, 83.100
watershed management, 10.419,
10.652, 10.904
Folk arts:
National Endowment for the Arts
grants, 45.015
Food and drug research:
pharmacological sciences research,
13.859
Public Health Service research
grants, 13.103
see also Nutrition
Food assistance:
charitable institutions, 10.550
child care food programs, 10.558
child nutrition state administrative
expenses, 10.560
disabled in public housing projects, 14.170
elderly in public housing projects,
14.170
food stamps, 10.551
food stamps—state administrative
matching grants, 10.561
handicapped in public housing
projects, 14.170
Indians, 10.550, 10.567
infants, 10.557, 10.565

Food assistance (*cont.*)
  milk program for children, 10.556
  nutrition services for aged, 13.635
  pregnant, postpartum and breast-
    feeding women, 10.557, 10.565
  school breakfast program, 10.553
  school children, general, 10.550
  school lunch program, 10.555
  summer program for children,
    10.559
  WIC program, 10.557
  see also School meals
Foreign governments:
  claims against, 19.200
  compensation for vessel seizures
    by, 11.415, 19.200
Foreign investment:
  direct investment loans, 70.005
  insurance, 70.003
  loan guarantees, 70.002
Foreign missions:
  claims against, 19.203
Forestry:
  farmlands, 10.416
  research grants, 10.202, 10.652
  timber production, 10.064
  urban communities, 10.664
Foster care:
  federal financial participation
    (FFP), 13.658
  see also Child and family welfare

Geology:
  earthquake preparedness research
    grants, 83.506
  earth sciences and research grants,
    47.050
Gerontology, *see* Aging and the
  aged
Government publications:
  sales and distribution, 40.002
Grain production:
  stabilization programs, 10.055,
    10.067

Handicapped, elderly:
  food and nonmedical support ser-
    vices in public housing projects,
    14.170
Handicapped, general:
  administration for developmental
    disabilities—basic support and
    advocacy grants, 13.630

administration for developmental
  disabilities—special projects,
  13.631
administration for developmental
  disabilities—university-affiliated
  facilities, 13.632
architectural barrier removal, from
  educational institutions, 84.155
client assistance for individuals
  covered by Rehabilitation Act,
  84.161
comprehensive services for independent living, 84.169
food and nonmedical support services in public housing projects,
  14.170
housing—nonprofit sponsor assistance program, 14.141
independent living services, 84.132
library access, 84.034
National Institute of Handicapped
  Research grants, 84.133
rehabilitation services basic support, 84.126
rehabilitation services special projects, 84.128
rehabilitation teacher training,
  84.129
rental housing financing, 14.157
research initiation and improvement in science and engineering, 47.069
small business loans to sheltered
  workshops, 59.021
social services research and demonstration projects, 13.647
weatherization assistance, 81.042
see also Blindness and the blind,
  Deafness and the deaf, Disabled, Education for the handicapped, Vocational training and
  rehabilitation
Handicapped children:
  adoption assistance, 13.659
  deaf-blind centers, 84.025
  early childhood assistance, 84.024
  food program, child care, 10.558
  Indian, 15.103
  preschool and school programs,
    84.027
  preschool incentive grants, 84.173
  recreation, 84.029
  regional resource centers, 84.028

secondary education and transitional services, 84.158
special studies of, 84.159
see also Education for the handicapped
Hazardous chemicals and wastes:
applied toxicological research and testing, 13.114
asbestos hazards abatement (schools) assistance, 66.702
environmental health hazards, 13.113
hazardous solid waste management assistance to states, 66.801
hazardous substance response trust fund, 66.802
nuclear waste disposal siting, 81.065
pesticides control research grants, 66.502
pesticides enforcement program grants, 66.700
Radiological Defense Program, 83.511
radiological emergency preparedness, 83.508
railroad safety, 20.303
toxic substance enforcement programs, 66.701
toxic substances research, 66.507
underground storage tanks program, 66.804
Health facilities:
cancer centers support, 13.397
community health facilities, 13.129, 13.130, 13.224
eye research, 13.985
group practice mortgage insurance, 14.116
hemophilia diagnostic and treatment centers, 13.110
medical library assistance, 13.879
migrant health centers grants, 13.246
research facilities for heart, lung and blood diseases, 13.131
Health facilities construction:
cancer research facilities, 13.392
community health centers, 13.130, 13.224
energy conservation assistance, 81.052
eye research, 13.985

hospital mortgages, 14.128
intermediate care facility mortgages, 14.129
loans for rural communities, 10.423
nursing home mortgages, 14.129
research facilities for heart, lung and blood diseases, 13.131
supplemental loan insurance, 14.151
veterans state home facilities, 64.005
Health insurance:
community health centers grants, 13.224
health financing research, 13.766
health services research and development grants, 13.226
Medicaid fraud control grants, 13.775
Medicare and Medicaid compliance monitoring, 13.777
Medicare hospital insurance, 13.773
Medicare supplementary medical insurance, 13.774
Health professions, general:
capitation grants, 13.339
career and financial aid counseling, 13.822
education assistance loans, 13.108
Indian recruitment program, 13.970
National Health Service Corps scholarship program, 13.288
occupational medicine training grants, 13.263
physician assistant training program, 13.886
scholarships for first-year students of exceptional financial need, 13.820
special educational initiatives, 13.969
Health services, general:
Appalachian primary health care, 23.004
blood resources, 13.839
cash assistance for needy, 13.714
cost containment, 13.226, 13.294
diabetes control center, 13.988
efficiency, distribution and utilization of health personnel, 13.824

Health services, general (*cont.*)
  emergency medical service for
    children, 13.127
  Emergency Medical Services Sys-
    tems, 13.226
  Federal real property leased or
    conveyed, 13.676
  health and safety standards com-
    pliance monitoring, 13.777
  health financing research, 13.766
  health services research and devel-
    opment grants, 13.226
  health systems agencies grants,
    13.294
  maternal and child health services
    block grant, 13.994
  medically underserved areas,
    13.224, 13.258, 13.288, 13.973,
    13.992, 23.004
  migrant and seasonal farm work-
    ers, 13.246
  national health promotion,
    13.990
  National Health Service Corps,
    13.258, 13.973
  preventive health services, 13.991
  primary care block grants, 13.993
  primary care services, 13.130
  refugee health programs, 13.987
  research and development grants,
    13.226
  state health planning and develop-
    ment agencies grants, 13.293
  see also Medical research
Highways:
  Appalachian development highway
    system, 23.003
  junkyard control, 20.214
  outdoor advertising control,
    20.214
  planning and construction, 20.205
  safety, state programs, 20.600
Historic sites, documents and monu-
    ments:
  federal surplus land conveyed,
    39.002
  historic document preservation,
    89.003
  historic preservation grants-in-aid,
    15.904
  National Register listings, 15.904
  rehabilitation of historic proper-
    ties, 15.904

History:
  youth grants, 45.115
  see also Humanities funding
Home economics:
  extension programs, 10.500
  state grants for programs in eco-
    nomically depressed areas or in
    areas with high unemployment,
    84.049
Home improvement and rehabilita-
    tion:
  alternative energy source conver-
    sions, 81.050
  condominium reconstruction mort-
    gages, 14.112
  farm labor housing loans and
    grants, 10.405
  Indian housing assistance,
    15.141
  rural, low-income loans,
    10.410
  sewage disposal facilities, 10.410,
    10.417
  single-family mortgages, 14.108,
    14.142
  very-low-income rural home-
    owners, 10.417
  weatherization, 10.410, 10.417
  see also Public housing
Home ownership:
  experimental homes, mortgages
    for, 14.152
  fee-simple title from lessors, mort-
    gage for, 14.130
  graduated mortgage payments,
    14.159
  housing counseling assistance pro-
    gram, 14.169
  interest reduction payments,
    14.103
  low- and moderate-income fami-
    lies, mortgages for, 14.120
  mobile home mortgages, 14.110,
    14.162
  older, declining areas, mortgages
    for, 14.123
  outlying areas, mortgages for,
    14.121
  rural housing site loans, 10.411
  rural low-income housing loans,
    10.410
  rural self-help housing technical
    assistance, 10.420

single-family home mortgage coinsurance, 14.161
single-family home mortgages, 14.117, 14.140
special credit risk mortgages, 14.140
urban renewal areas, mortgages for, 14.122
veterans' mortgages, 64.114, 64.118, 64.119
see also Condominium housing, Cooperative housing, Indian housing, Rental housing, Rural housing
Hospitals, see Health facilities, Health facilities construction
Housing construction:
  Appalachian housing, 23.005
  community development block grants, 14.218, 14.219, 14.228
  experimental housing, 14.152, 14.509
  farm labor, 10.405
  housing for the elderly, 14.138, 14.157
  housing for the handicapped, 14.157
  housing in older, declining areas, 14.123
  mobile homes parks, 14.127
  multifamily rental housing supplemental loan insurance, 14.151
  rental housing in urban renewal areas, 14.139
  rural rental housing loans, 10.415
Housing discrimination, see Civil rights
Humanities funding:
  basic research, 45.140
  challenge grant program, 45.130
  exemplary projects, 45.111
  fellowships at centers for advanced studies, 45.122
  fellowships for college teachers, 45.143
  fellowships for independent study and research, 45.142
  foreign languages instruction, 84.015, 84.016, 84.017, 84.164, 84.168
  historical organizations, 45.125
  intercultural research program, 45.148
  international studies instruction, 84.015, 84.016, 84.017
  libraries, 45.137
  media grants, 45.104
  museums, 45.125
  national graduate fellowships, 84.170
  national humanistic concerns projects, 45.128
  nontraditional projects, 45.111
  promoting local humanities programming, 45.129
  publications dissemination, 45.132
  reference works, 45.145
  research conferences, 45.134
  research materials editions, 45.146
  research materials translations, 45.147
  research resources conservation and preservation, 45.149
  research resources organization and improvement, 45.124
  resources production, 45.145
  science values, 45.133
  Smithsonian Institution collaboration, 60.001
  state programs aid, 45.129
  summer seminars for college teachers, 45.116
  summer stipends, 45.121
  teaching materials, 45.111
  technology and the humanities, 45.133
  youth grants, 45.115
  youth programs, 45.135

Indian economic development:
  business and industrial loans, 10.422, 11.301, 15.124
  demonstration projects, 13.661
  energy resources development, 81.076
  financial assistance grants, 13.612
  loan assistance, 15.124
Indian education:
  adult education, 84.062
  dropout rate reduction efforts, 84.060
  elementary and secondary school assistance, 15.130, 84.041
  entitlement grants to local educational agencies and tribally controlled schools, 84.060

Indian education (*cont.*)
fellowships in medicine, law, engineering, natural resources, business administration, education, and related fields, 84.087
grants to Indian-controlled schools, 84.072
health professions preparatory scholarships, 13.971
health professions recruitment program, 13.970
health professions scholarships, 13.972
higher education grants, 15.114
high school equivalency diplomas, 84.062
library services for Indian tribes and Hawaiian natives, 84.163
special program planning and development, 84.061
vocational training program grants, 15.108, 17.251, 84.101
Indian health and social services:
aged, 13.655
alcohol and drug abuse block grants, 13.992
assistance in claims before Court of Claims, 15.123
child welfare assistance, 15.103
employment assistance, 15.108, 17.251
employment discrimination, 30.009
food distribution, 10.550, 10.567
general assistance, 15.113
health management development program, 13.228
health professions preparatory scholarships, 13.971
health professions recruitment program, 13.970
health professions scholarships, 13.972
housing assistance, 15.141
mental health services block grants, 13.992
research grants, 13.661
social services research and demonstration projects, 13.647
training and technical assistance, 13.662
Indian housing:
assistance grants, 15.141

Indian lands:
community development block grants, 14.223
mortgages, 10,421
recreational, 10.421
Indian tribal governments:
self-determination grants, 15.142
training and technical assistance, 15.143
Industrial design:
grants and direct payments, 45.001
Industrial development:
Appalachian region, 23.002
business and industrial loans, rural, 10.422
Industrial safety, *see* Occupational safety and health
Information science, *see* Library and information science
Insurance:
crop, 10.450
disability (Social Security), 13.802
disability, for longshoremen and harbor workers, 17.302
flood, 83.100
foreign investments, 70.003
life, for veterans, 64.103
maritime war risk, 20.803
pension plan termination insurance, 86.001
property subject to riot or civil disorder, 83.101
retirement (Social Security), 13.803, 13.804
unemployment, 17.225
see also Health insurance
Interior design:
grants and direct payments, 45.001
International trade:
guaranty fund for ship seizure by foreign countries, 11.410
trade adjustment assistance, 11.109
trade promotion, 11.108

Judiciary:
corrections seminars, workshops, and training programs, 16.601
Juvenile justice and delinquency:
clearing house and information center, 16.542
corrections training and staff development, 16.601

education of institutionalized children, 84.013
matching grants for prevention, 16.540
national training program, 16.542
program development, 16.540, 16.541
program evaluation, 16.542
runaway youth, 13.623
state guidelines development, 16.540
technical assistance, 16.603

Kidney disease research, 13.849

Languages, linguistics:
youth grants, 45.115
Law enforcement officers:
death benefit program, 16.571
Law enforcement training:
corrections seminars, workshops, and training programs, 16.601
juvenile justice and delinquency prevention, 16.540, 16.541, 16.542
Legal education:
clinical experience programs, 84.097
fellowships for Indians, 84.087
fellowships for underrepresented minorities, 84.094
law school preparation for the disadvantaged, 84.136
Libraries:
access to the handicapped, 84.034
humanities projects, 45.137
interlibrary cooperation, 84.035
medical library assistance, 13.879
National Gallery of Art extension service, 68.001
public library construction, 84.154
public library services, 84.034, 84.035
service in rural areas, 84.034
service in urban areas, 84.034
services for Indian tribes and Hawaiian natives, 84.163
state institutional library services, 84.034
strengthening research library resources, 84.091
Library and information science:
career training, 84.036

research and demonstration projects in specialized services, 84.039
Literature:
youth grants, 45.115

Marine conservation:
coastal zone management for estuarine sanctuaries, 11.420
coastal zone management program administration, 11.419
estuarine management, comprehensive, 66.456
Marine science:
biomedical research, 13.894
Coast Guard cooperative efforts, 20.002
marine pollution research, 11.426, 13.894
oceanography, 47.050
sea grant support, 11.417
shellfish sanitation, 13.103
Maritime industry:
capital construction fund, 20.808
construction reserve fund for national defense needs, 20.812
guaranty fund for seizure by foreign countries, 11.410
longshoremen's and harbor workers' disability compensation, 17.302
oil and gas spills contingency fund, 11.408
research and development assistance, 20.811
ship-financing guarantees, 20.802
state marine school grants, 20.806
subsidies for foreign construction competition, 20.800
subsidies for foreign operating competition, 20.804
vessel and gear damage compensation fund, 11.409
vessel obligation guarantees, 11.415
war risk insurance, 20.803
Mass transportation, urban:
capital assistance formula grants, 20.507
capital improvement grants, 20.500
managerial training grants, 20.503

Mass transportation, urban (*cont.*)
  operating assistance formula
    grants, 20.507
  technical studies grant, 20.505
  university research and training,
    20.502
Mathematics:
  basic research, 47.049
  minority institutions science im-
    provement program, 84.120
  precollege materials development
    and research, 47.067
  teacher enhancement in precollege
    math, 47.066
  teaching skills grants, 84.164,
    84.168
Measurement and engineering research grants, 11.609
Media arts:
  National Endowment for the Arts
    grants, 45.006
Medical education:
  academic research enhancement
    award, 13.390
  capitation grants, 13.339
  environmental health, 13.969
  faculty development grants,
    13.900
  family medicine departments es-
    tablished, 13.984
  family medicine faculty develop-
    ment, 13.895
  family medicine graduate training
    grants, 13.379
  family medicine predoctoral train-
    ing, 13.896
  fellowships for Indians, 84.087
  fellowships for underrepresented
    minorities, 84.094
  first-year students of exceptional
    financial need, 13.820
  geriatrics, 13.969
  health education assistance loans,
    13.108
  health sciences research in minor-
    ity institutions, 13.389
  humanistic health care, 13.969
  Indian recruitment program,
    13.970
  Indian scholarships, 13.972
  internal medicine residency train-
    ing, 13.884
  medical library assistance, 13.879

mental health clinical or service-
    related training grants. 13.244
National Health Service Corps
    scholarship program, 13.288
nurse anesthetist traineeships,
    13.124
nurse practitioner training pro-
    grams and traineeships, 13.298
nurse traineeships, professional,
    13.358
nurse training improvement
    grants, 13.359
nursing training program, ad-
    vanced, 13.299
nutrition, 13.969
pediatrics residency training,
    13.884
physician assistant training pro-
    gram, 13.886
preventive medicine residency
    program, 13.117
regionalizing responsibilities,
    13.824
research centers in minority insti-
    tutions, 13.389
school financial distress grants,
    13.381
see also Health professions, Nurs-
    ing education
Medical research:
  academic research enhancement
    award, 13.390
  aging, 13.866
  alcohol research, 13.271, 13.272,
    13.273, 13.891
  allergy, 13.855
  amblyopia, 13.871
  animal diseases transmissible to
    people, 10.207
  arthritis and musculoskeletal dis-
    eases, 13.846
  biological response to environ-
    mental health hazards, 13.113
  biologics, 13.103
  biomedical engineering, 13.821
  biomedical research support
    grants, 13.337
  biometry and risk estimation,
    13.115
  biotechnology research, 13.371
  blood diseases, 13.131, 13.839,
    13.849
  cancer biology, 13.396

cancer cause and prevention, 13.393, 13.399
cancer detection and diagnosis, 13.394, 13.399
cancer research manpower grants, 13.398
cancer treatment, 13.395, 13.399
cataract disorders, 13.869
cellular research, 13.863
child health, 13.865
clinical research grants, 13.333
corneal diseases, 13.868
deafness, 13.853, 13.854
diabetes, 13.847
diagnostic products, 13.103
digestive diseases, 13.848
drug abuse grants, 13.277, 13.278, 13.279
endocrinology and metabolism, 13.847
environmental health hazards, 13.112, 13.113, 13.894
eye research facility construction, 13.985
fetal health, 13.865
food and food additives, 13.103
genetic diseases, 13.110, 13.862
glaucoma, 13.870
heart and vascular diseases, 13.131, 13.837, 13.894
hemophilia, 13.110
immunology and immunologic diseases, 13.855
infectious diseases, 13.856
international exchange of ideas and information, 13.989
kidney diseases, 13.849
laboratory animal sciences and primate research, 13.306
maternal health, 13.865
medical devices, 13.103
medical library assistance, 13.879
mental health research scientist development and research scientist awards, 13.281
microbiology, 13.856
minority access, 13.282, 13.880
minority biomedical research support, 13.375
molecular research, 13.863
neurological disorders, 13.113, 13.853, 13.854
nutrition, 13.848, 13.865

occupational safety and health research grants, 13.262
pesticides use, 66.502
poisons, 13.103
population dynamics, 13.864
pregnancy, 13.865
radiation-emitting devices and materials, 13.103
research centers in minority institutions, 13.389
respiratory diseases, 13.131, 13.838, 13.894
retinal and choroidal diseases, 13.867
safe drinking water research, 66.506
skin diseases, 13.846
speech and language disorders, 13.853
strabismus, 13.871
tuberculosis control programs, 13.116
urology, 13.849
venereal disease, 13.978
visual processing, 13.871
see also Cancer, Neurological disorders
Medicare, Medicaid, see Health insurance
Mental health education:
clinical or service-related training grants, 13.244
Minority Access to Research Careers programs, 13.282
National Research Service awards for research training, 13.282
volunteer training for disaster assistance, 13.982
Mental health research:
biological response to environmental health hazards, 13.113
Minority Access to Research Careers programs, 13.282
National Institute of Handicapped Research grants, 84.133
National Institute of Mental Health research grants, 13.242, 13.281, 13.282
National Research Service awards, 13.282
research scientist development and research scientist awards, 13.281
small business innovation research, 13.126

Mental health services:
  block grants, 13.992
  planning and demonstration projects, 13.125
  refugee assistance, 13.128
  rehabilitation services basic support, 84.126
  rehabilitation services special projects, 84.128
Military personnel:
  mortgages, 14.166
Mining industries:
  abandoned mine land reclamation program, 15.252
  abandoned mine program, rural, 10.910
  Appalachian mine area restoration, 23.010
  black lung clinics, 13.965
  black lung disability benefits, 13.806, 17.307
  coal loan guarantees, 81.056
  coal research, 81.507
  health and safety grants, 17.600
  mining and mineral research, 15.308
  state grants for regulation of surface effects of coal mining, 15.250
  use of mineral materials from federal lands, 15.214
  see also Coal industry
Minority education:
  behavioral research, 13.389
  biomedical research, 13.389
  energy-related research travel fund, 81.083
  graduate and professional study fellowships, 84.094
  health science research, 13.389
  magnet schools assistance, 84.165
  medical research, 13.375, 13.389, 13.880
  mental health research training, 13.282
  Minority Access to Research Careers programs, 13.282, 13.880
  research centers in minority institutions, 13.389
  research initiation and improvement in science and engineering, 47.069

science improvement program, 84.120
socioeconomic and demographic research in energy consumption, 81.091
vocational training in energy-related technologies, 81.084
Minority enterprise:
  loans to defray bid and proposal costs for DOE programs, 81.063
  management and technical assistance, 11.800
Mortgages:
  adjustable rate, 14.175
  coinsurance for multifamily housing projects, 14.172
  coinsurance for single-family homes, 14.161
  condominium construction or rehabilitation, 14.112
  condominium unit purchases, 14.133
  cooperative housing, investor-sponsored, 14.124
  cooperative housing, management-type, 14.126
  cooperative housing, nonprofit, 14.115
  cooperative housing, sales-type, 14.132
  disabled veterans, 64.118
  experimental homes, 14.152
  experimental rental housing, 14.509
  farm labor housing, 10.405
  farm ownership, 10.407
  fee-simple title from lessors, 14.130
  fishing vessel obligation guarantees, 11.415
  graduated mortgage payments (Section 245), 14.159
  group health practice facilities, 14.116
  growing equity mortgages, 14.172
  health facility additions and improvements, 14.151
  hospitals, 14.128
  housing counseling assistance program, 14.169
  housing site loans, rural, 10.411
  Indian tribes and tribal corporations, 10.421, 10.422

intermediate care facilities, 14.129
land development, 14.125
low- and moderate-income families, 14.120
low-income housing loans, rural,
  10.410
military impacted areas, 14.165
military personnel, 14.166
mobile home lots, 14.162
mobile home parks, 14.127
mobile homes, 14.110, 14.162,
  64.119
multifamily housing projects—
  purchases and refinancing,
  14.155
new communities, 14.125
nonresidential structures, new,
  14.142
nursing homes, 14.129
older, declining areas, 14.123
outlying areas, 14.121
rehabilitation mortgage insurance,
  14.108, 14.142
rental housing for elderly, 14.138
rental housing for low- and moderate-income families, 14.135,
  14.137
rental housing in urban renewal
  areas, 14.139
single-family home mortgage coinsurance, 14.161
single-family homes, 14.117,
  14.140
special credit risks, 14.140
two-year operating loss loans,
  14.167
urban areas, 14.122
very-low-income housing repairs,
  rural, 10.417
veterans' housing, 64.114, 64.118,
  64.119
Museums:
  assistance and advice from Smith-
    sonian Institution, 60.007
  cataloguing, 45.012
  conservation, 45.012, 45.301
  Defense Department donated
    property, 12.700
  educational role, 45.301
  energy-related laboratory equip-
    ment grants, 81.022
  grants for increased use by public,
    45.301

humanities projects, 45.125
indemnification for lost or damaged artworks and artifacts from
  abroad or sent abroad, 45.201
National Gallery of Art extension
  service, 68.001
purchase of works by American
  artists, 45.012
renovation, 45.012
Smithsonian Institution traveling
  exhibition, 60.013
Smithsonian special foreign currency grants, 60.016
special exhibitions, 45.012
training museum professionals,
  45.012
visiting specialists, 45.012
Music:
  grants and direct payments, 45.005
Musical theatre:
  National Endowment for the Arts
    grants, 45.014

Narcotics, see Drug abuse
Neurological disorders:
  basic research, 13.854, 47.051
  clinical research, 13.853
  environmental health hazards,
    13.113
Nuclear energy and technology:
  fusion energy research, 81.049
  nuclear physics research, 81.049
  public education, 77.003
  Radiological Defense Program,
    83.511
  radiological emergency prepared-
    ness, 83.508
  safety research, 77.003
  university-DOE laboratory coop-
    erative program, 81.004
  university reactor sharing and fuel
    assistance, 81.011
  waste disposal siting, 81.065
Nursing education:
  advanced nursing training pro-
    gram, 13.299
  nurse anesthetist traineeships,
    13.124
  nursing research, 13.297
  occupational medicine training
    grants, 13.263
  professional nurse traineeships,
    13.358

Nursing education (*cont.*)
  student loans, 13.364
  training improvement grants,
    13.359
Nursing home care:
  energy conservation assistance,
    81.052
  state veterans' homes, 64.015
Nursing research:
  basic and applied research grants,
    13.361
  National Research Service awards,
    13.297
Nutrition:
  competitive research grants,
    10.206
  education and training program,
    10.564
  elderly, 10.550, 13.635
  extension programs, 10.500
  food stamps, 10.551
  food stamps, state administrative
    matching grants for, 10.561
  graduate fellowship grants, 10.210
  Head Start, 13.600
  higher education strengthening
    grants, 10.211
  Indians, 10.550, 10.567
  infants, supplemental food for,
    10.557, 10.565
  medical education, 13.969
  medical research, 13.848
  medical research—mothers and
    children, 13.865
  milk program for children,
    10.556
  pregnant, postpartum, and breast-
    feeding women, supplemental
    food for, 10.557, 10.565
  school breakfast program, 10.553
  school children, general, 10.550
  school lunch program, 10.555
  state administrative expenses for
    child nutrition, 10.560
  WIC program, 10.557
  see also School meals

Occupational safety and health:
  black lung clinics, 13.965
  black lung disability benefits,
    13.806, 17.307
  complaint investigation, 17.500
  longshoremen's and harbor work-
    ers disability compensation,
    17.302
  mine health and safety grants,
    17.600
  public education, 13.990
  research grants, 13.262
  resource and manpower develop-
    ment, 13.894
  technical information dissemina-
    tion, 17.500
  training grants, 13.263
Opera:
  National Endowment for the Arts
    grants, 45.014

Painting:
  National Endowment for the Arts
    grants, 45.009
Parent education:
  extension programs, 10.500
Pension plans:
  termination insurance, 86.001
Pesticides:
  alternatives exploration, 66.502
  degradation research, 66.502
  enforcement program grants,
    66.700
  medical research, 66.502
  milk contamination indemnifica-
    tion, 10.053
  toxic substance enforcement pro-
    gram, 66.701
  see also Environmental manage-
    ment
Pharmacology:
  drug hazards research, 13.103
  drug mechanism research, 13.859
  enhancing safety and efficacy of
    drugs, 13.859
Philosophy:
  youth grants, 45.115
Photography:
  National Endowment of the Arts
    grants, 45.009
Physical sciences:
  biomedical engineering, 13.821
Physics:
  basic research, 47.049
  high-energy physics research,
    81.049
  nuclear physics research, 81.049
  Smithsonian special foreign cur-
    rency grants, 60.016

Politics:
Woodrow Wilson International Center for Scholars fellowships, 60.020
Pollution, *see* Environmental management
Pregnancy:
adolescent family life demonstration projects, 13.995
adolescent family life research grants, 13.111
supplemental food program, 10.557
Printmaking:
National Endowment for the Arts grants, 45.009
Psychology:
basic research, 47.051
Public Health:
adolescent family life demonstration projects, 13.995
adolescent family life research grants, 13.111
childhood immunization grants, 13.268
community health care centers, 13.224
federal surplus personal property conveyed, 39.003
food and food additives research, 13.103
genetic disease testing, counseling, and information development, 13.110
health administration graduate programs, 13.964
health administration graduate traineeships, 13.962
health education assistance loans, 13.108
health services research and development grants, 13.226
Indian public health services, 13.228
migrant health centers grants, 13.246
pharmaceutical research, 13.103
poison control research, 13.103
public health graduate traineeships, 13.964
tuberculosis control programs, 13.116
venereal disease research and control, 13.977, 13.978

Public housing:
disabled support services, 14.170
elderly support services, 14.170
handicapped support services, 14.170

Radiation:
research on radiation-emitting devices and materials, 13.103
Radio:
emergency broadcast system guidance and assistance, 83.515
National Endowment for the Humanities grants, 45.104
National Endowment for the Arts grants, 45.006
Railroads:
Conrail employees' benefits, 57.003
death benefits, 57.001
disability insurance, 57.001
local rail freight service assistance, 20.308
railroad safety grants-in-aid, 20.303
rehabilitation and improvement of facilities and equipment, direct loans for, 20.310
rehabilitation and improvement of facilities and equipment, loan guarantees for, 20.309
state rail planning, 20.308
unemployment benefits, 57.001
Recreation:
Appalachian region, 23.002
coastal energy impact program, 11.421
community facilities loans, rural, 10.423
extension programs, 10.500
federal surplus land conveyed, 39.002
federal surplus personal property conveyed, 39.003
forests, 10.652
handicapped, 84.029
Indian lands, 10.421
state grants for outdoor recreation, 15.916
urban park and recreation recovery program, 15.919
water-based recreational facilities, rural, 10.414

Refugees, *see* Aliens and refugees
Rental housing:
  elderly, 14.157
  experimental—mortgage insur-
    ance, 14.509
  handicapped, 14.157
  interest and reduction payments,
    14.103
  mortgage insurance—elderly ten-
    ants, 14.138
  mortgage insurance—units for
    low- and moderate-income fami-
    lies, 14.135, 14.137
  mortgage insurance—urban re-
    newal areas, 14.139
  operating assistance for troubled
    multifamily housing projects,
    14.164
  rent supplements for low-income
    families, 14.149
  rural rental assistance payments,
    10.427
  rural rental housing loans, 10.415
  supplemental loan insurance for
    multifamily projects, 14.151
  two-year operating loss loans,
    14.167
  see also Public housing
Respiratory diseases:
  black lung clinics, 13.965
  black lung disability benefits,
    13.806, 17.307
  environmental health hazards,
    13.113
  tuberculosis control programs,
    13.116
Retirement:
  railroad workers, 57.001
  Social Security retirement benefits,
    13.803, 13.804
Revenue sharing, general, 21.300
Rice production:
  stabilization programs, 10.065
Rural communities:
  abandoned mine program,
    10.910
  arts promotion, 45.010
  business and industrial loans,
    10.422
  community facilities loans, 10.423
  community health centers, 13.224
  cooperative extension service,
    10.500

electrification loans and loan guar-
    antees, 10.850
  library services, 84.034
  public transportation, 20.509
  resource conservation and devel-
    opment, 10.901
  telephone bank loans, 10.852
  telephone loans and loan guaran-
    tees, 10.851
  water and waste disposal systems,
    10.418
  water-based recreational facilities,
    10.414
Rural housing:
  farm housing mortgages, 14.121
  farm labor housing, 10.405
  housing site loans, 10.411
  low-income housing loans, 10.410
  rental housing loans, 10.415
  self-help housing technical assis-
    tance, 10.420
  very-low-income housing repair
    loans and grants, 10.417

School meals:
  breakfast program, 10.553
  direct food distribution, 10.500,
    10.553
  lunch program, 10.555
  milk program, high school, 10.556
  state administrative expenses,
    10.560
Science education:
  precollege materials development
    and research, 47.067
  research initiation and improve-
    ment for minorities, women and
    the handicapped, 47.069
  studies and program assessment,
    47.068
  teacher enhancement, 47.066
  teaching skills grants, 84.164,
    84.168
Scientific research, general:
  advanced computing resources,
    47.065
  Arctic and Antarctic regions,
    47.050
  behavioral sciences, 47.051
  behavioral sciences at minority in-
    stitutions, 13.389
  coal conversion and utilization
    technologies, 81.057

conferences and symposia, 47.049,
47.051
earth sciences, 47.050
educational process, 84.117
equipment purchases, 47.049,
47.051
graduate research fellowships,
47.009
health sciences at minority institutions, 13.389
international exchange, 47.053
mining and mineral resources and
research institutes, 15.308
monitoring nation's science
and technology enterprise,
47.053
photosynthesis, 10.206
physiology, 47.051
research centers in minority institutions, 13.389
research initiation for minorities,
women and the handicapped,
47.069
social sciences, 47.051, 84.170
Sculpture:
National Endowment for the Arts
grants, 45.009
Sexual activity:
adolescence, 13.111, 13.995
Small businesses:
alcohol, drug and mental health
research grants, 13.126
bond guarantees for surety companies, 59.016
certified development company
loans, 59.036
loans for construction, expansion,
renovation and modernization,
59.036
loans for land and building acquisition, 59.036
loans for machinery and equipment, 59.036
loans to businesses in areas of
high unemployment, 59.003
loans to businesses owned by low-
income persons, 59.003
loans to make equity and venture
capital, 59.011
loans to meet energy needs,
59.030
loans to sheltered workshops,
59.021

loans to those without financing in
private credit marketplace,
59.012
management and technical assistance for disadvantaged businesses, 59.007
management and technical assistance through Small Business
Development Centers (SBDCs),
59.037
physical disaster loans, 59.008
pollution control financing guarantees, 59.031
state and local development company loans, 59.013
veterans loan program, 59.038
women's entrepreneurship training, 59.032
Smithsonian Institution programs:
museum assistance and advice,
60.007
research assistance, 60.001
special foreign currency grants,
60.016
traveling exhibition service, 60.013
Woodrow Wilson fellowships,
60.020
Social services and welfare, general:
client assistance for handicapped
individuals covered by Rehabilitation Act, 84.161
community services block grants,
13.665
crime victim programs, 16.575,
16.576
demonstration projects, 13.647
disability insurance (Social Security), 13.802
Foster Grandparent Program,
72.001
maintenance assistance, state aid
for, 13.808
Medicaid fraud control units,
13.775
medical assistance program,
13.714
Medicare hospital insurance,
13.773
Medicare supplementary medical
insurance, 13.774
mini-grants for volunteer programs, 72.010
research grants, 13.647, 13.812

Social services and welfare (*cont.*)
  retirement insurance (Social Security), 13.803
  senior community service employment program, 17.235
  social services block grants, 13.667
  special benefits for persons age 72 and over (Social Security), 13.802
  Supplemental Security Income (Social Security), 13.807
  survivor's insurance (Social Security), 13.805
  volunteer demonstration program grants, 72.012
Soil conservation:
  abandoned mine program, 10.910
  emergency aid, 10.054
  erosion control, 10.063, 10.900, 10.904
  Great Plains conservation, 10.900
  plant materials donated, 10.905
  resource conservation and development loans, 10.414
  soil and water loans, 10.416
Standards:
  research grants, 11.609
Student financial aid:
  college work-study programs, 84.033
  criminal justice graduate research fellowships, 16.562
  dependents of deceased or disabled veterans or of MIAs or POWs, 64.117
  family medicine graduate training grants, 13.379
  Fulbright exchange program, 82.001
  GI Bill, 64.111
  graduate fellowship grants in food and agricultural sciences, 10.210
  graduate fellowships in arts, humanities and social sciences, 84.170
  guaranteed student loans, 84.032
  Harry S Truman scholarships for public service career training, 85.001
  health professions capitation grants, 13.339
  health professions students of exceptional financial need in first year, 13.820

Indian health professions preparatory scholarships, 13.971
Indian health professions scholarships, 13.972
Indian higher education grants, 15.114
marine schools, state, 20.806
migrant college assistance program, 84.149
minority vocational training in energy-related technologies, 81.084
National Defense Student Loans, 84.038
National Fire Academy stipends, 83.405
National Health Service Corps scholarship program, 13.288
nurse anesthetist traineeships, 13.124
nursing student loans, 13.364
Pell grant program, 84.064
post-Vietnam era veterans educational assistance, 64.120
reimbursement of canceled National Defense Student Loans, 84.037
selected reserve educational assistance program, 12.609
state student incentives program, 84.069
supplemental educational opportunity grants, 84.007
talent search assistance for financially or culturally deprived students, 84.044
Veterans Administration nursing scholarships, 64.023

Tax counseling for the elderly, 21.006
Teacher education:
  bilingual education in elementary and secondary schools, 84.003
  bilingual vocational instructor training, 84.099
  civil rights training, 84.004
  consumer and homemaking education, 84.049
  energy-related training for college and university faculty, 81.004
  enhancement in precollege science and math, 47.066

Fulbright faculty research abroad, 84.019

Fulbright teacher international exchange program, 84.018

grants for strengthening skills in mathematics, science, foreign languages and computer learning, 84.164, 84.168

grants for teacher training in U.S. territories, 84.124

Higher Education Act assistance, 84.031

humanities curriculum in elementary and secondary schools, 45.127

humanities fellowships, 45.142, 45.143

humanities summer seminars for college teachers, 45.116

humanities workshops, 45.111

national defense student loan cancellations, 84.037

nursing education, 13.299

teacher recruitment for the handicapped, 84.030

vocational rehabilitation teacher training, 84.129

Telephone service:
 Rural Telephone Bank loans, 10.852
 rural telephone loans and loan guarantees, 10.851

Television:
 emergency broadcast system guidance and assistance, 83.515
 National Endowment for the Humanities grants, 45.104
 National Endowment for the Arts grants, 45.006

Theater:
 National Endowment for the Arts grants, 45.008

Timber production:
 cooperative forestry assistance, 10.664
 incentives program, 10.064
 research grants, 10.652

Transportation:
 airport improvement program, 20.106
 Appalachian region, 23.003, 23.008, 23.017

community facilities loans, rural, 10.423

Conrail employees' benefits, 57.003

economic development grants, 11.300

highway beautification, 20.214

highway educational grants, 20.216

highway planning and construction, 20.205

highway safety, state programs, 20.600

local rail freight service assistance, 20.308

mass transit capital assistance formula grants, 20.507

mass transit capital improvement grants, 20.500

mass transit managerial training grants, 20.503

mass transit operating assistance formula grants, 20.507

mass transit technical studies grants, 20.505

mass transit university research and training, 20.502

nonurban public transportation, 20.509

railroad safety, 20.303

rehabilitation of railroad facilities and equipment, 20.309, 20.310

schools and roads—grants to counties, 10.666

schools and roads—grants to states, 10.665

social insurance for railroad workers, 57.001

state rail planning, 20.308

see also Mass transportation, urban; Railroads

Unemployment:
 economic development planning, 11.302
 Indian vocational training and career counseling, 15.108
 public works impact projects, 11.304
 railroad workers, 57.001
 unemployment insurance, 17.225
 workers adversely affected by imports, 17.245

Work Incentive Program, 13.646

Urban communities:
  arts promotion, 45.010
  community development block
    grants/entitlement grants, 14.218
  community development block
    grants/small cities program,
    14.219
  community development block
    grants/state's program, 14.228
  forestry programs, 10.664
  library services, 84.034
  neighborhood rehabilitation loans
    (Section 312), 14.220
  park and recreation recovery pro-
    gram, 15.919
  urban development action grants,
    14.221
  urban homesteading, 14.222
  see also Mass transportation,
    urban
Urban design:
  grants and direct payments,
    45.001
Urban renewal areas:
  home mortgages, 14.122
  rental housing mortgages, 14.138

Veterans:
  loan program for Vietnam-era,
    59.038
Veterans, disabled:
  adaptive housing, 64.106
  adaptive housing loans, 64.118
  automobiles and adaptive equip-
    ment, 64.100
  compensation for service-
    connected disabilities, 64.109
  dependents' educational assis-
    tance, 64.117
  loan program, 59.038
  pensions for nonservice-connected
    disabilities, 64.104
  vocational training, 64.116, 64.122
Veterans' death benefits:
  burial expenses allowance, 64.101
  compensation for service-
    connected deaths before Janu-
    ary 1, 1957, 64.102
  compensation for service-
    connected deaths on or after
    January 1, 1957, 64.110
  dependents' educational assis-
    tance, 64.117

life insurance, 64.103
  pension to veterans' surviving
    spouses and children, 64.105
  state cemetery grants, 64.023
Veterans' education and training
    benefits:
  dependents educational assistance,
    64.117
  GI Bill, 64.111
  post-Vietnam era educational as-
    sistance, 64.120
  vocational rehabilitation for dis-
    abled, 64.116, 64.122
  vocational training for veterans
    receiving VA pension,
    64.123
Veterans' housing:
  adapted housing for disabled,
    64.106
  mobile homes, 64.119
  mortgages, 64.114, 64.118,
    64.119
  mortgages for disabled,
    64.118
Veterans' medical facilities and
    health services:
  construction of state home facili-
    ties, 64.005
  domiciliary care in state homes,
    64.014
  hospital care in state homes,
    64.016
  nursing care in state homes,
    64.015
Veterans' organizations:
  Defense Department donated
    property, 12.700
Veterinary education:
  capitation grants, 13.339
  school financial distress grants,
    13.381
Veterinary medicine:
  animal health and disease re-
    search, 10.207
  drug research, 13.103
  laboratory animal sciences and
    primate research, 13.306
Video:
  National Endowment for the Arts
    grants, 45.006
Visual arts:
  National Endowment for the Arts
    grants, 45.009

Vocational training and rehabilitation:
advising state boards, 84.053
Appalachian region, 23.012
basic grants to states, 84.048
bilingual education, 84.077
bilingual instructional materials, methods and techniques, 84.100
bilingual vocational instructor training, 84.099
client assistance for handicapped individuals covered by Rehabilitation Act, 84.161
consumer and homemaker education, 84.049
criminal justice discretionary grants, 16.574
curriculum coordination centers, 84.051
curriculum development, 84.051
demonstration programs, 84.051
disabled veterans, 64.116, 64.122
dislocated workers, 17.246
Indian tribes and organizations, 15.108, 17.251, 84.101
migrant and seasonal farm workers, 17.247
program evaluation, 84.053
programs for disadvantaged, 84.052
regional training for the deaf and other handicapped persons, 84.078
rehabilitation services for the handicapped, 84.128
research projects, 84.051
secondary education and transitional services for handicapped youth, 84.158
state grants for meeting federally mandated planning and evaluation requirements, 84.121
teacher training, 84.129
training in energy-related technologies for minorities, 81.084
training interpreters for deaf individuals, 84.160
VA pension veterans, 64.123
Volunteer programs:
demonstration program grants, 72.012
foster grandparents, 72.001
mini-grants, 72.010
Older American Volunteer Program, 72.002
Senior Companion Program, 72.008
technical assistance, 72.013

Waste disposal systems:
Appalachian region, 23.002
consolidated state grants, 66.600
construction loans, 66.603
hazardous solid waste management assistance to states, 66.801
public works grants, 11.300
rural communities. 10.418
rural housing site loans, 10.411
solid waste research and development, 66.504
underground storage tanks program, 66.804
very-low-income housing repair loans and grants, 10.417
wastewater treatment works construction grants, 66.418, 66.455
see also Environmental management
Water pollution:
abandoned mine program, 10.910
consolidated state grants, 66.600
construction management assistance grants, 66.438
estuarine management comprehensive, 66.456
farm and ranch programs, 10.063, 10.068
marine polution research, 11.426, 13.894
pesticides research, 66.502
research, development and demonstration grants, 66.505
Safe Drinking Water Act implementation grants, 66.432
safe drinking water research and demonstration grants, 66.506
state and interstate program grants, 66.419
underground injection control programs, 66.433
wastewater treatment works construction grants, 66.418, 66.455
water quality management planning, 66.454
see also Environmental management

Water resources:
  abandoned mine program,
    10.910
  anadromous fisheries conservation,
    11.405, 15.600
  business and industrial loans,
    10.422
  coastal energy impact program—
    formula grants, 11.421
  coastal zone management of es-
    tuarine sanctuaries, 11.420
  coastal zone management program
    administration, 11.419
  endangered species conservation,
    15.612
  estuarine management, compre-
    hensive, 66.456
  farm fish pond stocking, 15.603
  Great Lakes fisheries conserva-
    tion, 11.405, 15.600
  Great Plains conservation,
    10.900
  irrigation distribution system
    loans, 15.501
  irrigation systems rehabilitation
    and betterment, 15.502
  Lake Champlain fisheries conser-
    vation, 11.405, 15.600
  plant materials donated, 10.905
  resource conservation and devel-
    opment loans, 10.414
  rural water-based recreation,
    10.414
  sea grant support, 11.417
  sedimentation control, 10.063,
    10.904
  small reclamation projects, 15.503
  soil and water loans, 10.416
  sport fish restoration and manage-
    ment, 15.605
  watershed management, 10.419,
    10.652, 10.904
  water storage, 10.419
  wetlands protection, 10.062
Water systems and treatment:
  economic development grants,
    11.300
Wetlands protection:
  Water Bank Program, 10.062
Wheat production:
  stabilization programs, 10.058
Women:
  educational equity for, 84.083
  entrepreneurship training for,
    59.032
  graduate and professional study
    fellowships, 84.094
  research initiation and improve-
    ment in science and engineer-
    ing, 47.069
Wool and mohair production:
  stabilization programs, 10.059
Writers:
  fellowships, 45.004
  summer stipends, 45.121

Youth programs:
  extension programs, 10.500
  farm operating loans, 10.406
  foster care, 13.658
  Head Start, 13.600
  humanities grants, 45.115, 45.135
  juvenile delinquency prevention,
    16.540, 16.541, 16.542
  runaway youth, 13.623
  Work Incentive Program, 13.646

Zoos:
  surplus wildlife disposals, 15.900